THE UNDERSTANDING OF CAUSATION AND THE PRODUCTION OF ACTION

The Understanding of Causation and the Production of Action
From Infancy to Adulthood

Peter A. White
School of Psychology,
University of Wales College of Cardiff

LAWRENCE ERLBAUM ASSOCIATES, PUBLISHERS
Hove (UK)
Hillsdale (USA)

Lawrence Erlbaum Associates Ltd., Publishers
27 Palmeira Mansions
Church Road
Hove
East Sussex, BN3 2FA
UK

British Library Cataloguing in Publication Data

A catalogue record for this title is available from the British Library

ISBN 0-86377-341-9

Printed and bound in the United Kingdom by BPC Wheatons Ltd., Exeter

For Elizabeth

Contents

Acknowledgements

To be able to develop one's thoughts on the scale of a whole book is a tremendous privilege and a wonderfully satisfying experience. To be able to do so twice smacks of truly exceptional good fortune, and I am happy to express my profound indebtedness to the publishers who have given me these opportunities: David Stonestreet of Routledge for my first book, and Michael Forster of Lawrence Erlbaum Associates for this one. I can only hope that it will prove to be worth their while. My chief intellectual debts are, as before, to Rom Harré, Tom Shultz, Richard Taylor, and Mansur Lalljee: I wonder where I would be floundering now if I had not had the guidance their work provides. Several colleagues have also helped with advice, comments, and collaboration on some of the research discussed herein, and I would particularly like to mention John Pearce, Steve Payne, Lucy Johnston, Alan Milne, and Eleni Hatziyiannis. I am also most grateful to Eugene Subbotsky and Mani Das Gupta for their very generous and constructive comments on an earlier draft of the manuscript. Figure 5.3 is reproduced by kind permission of MIT Press. Figure 6.1 is reproduced by kind permission of Chester A. Insko.

Introduction

Our world is replete with happening. Cars collide; so do billiard balls. The wind blows. Machines malfunction. Plants grow. Prices rise; empires fall. People talk; form relationships; make choices; play games; fight; change from one day to the next. The words I use to describe these happenings make sense to you because you import into your reading of them a rich background of concepts, object knowledge, social knowledge, stereotypes, associations, instances, and other things. Our understanding of things that happen enters into every moment of our waking lives. We are constantly interpreting, reflectively or unreflectively, happenings around us, constantly using our understanding to interpret them.

It sometimes seems to me that the main concerns of psychology are too much with static things. The dominant topics in social cognition, for example, are categories and schemas, stereotypes, the self-concept, person memory, and judgement of likelihood (here I am drawing on the comprehensive survey by Fiske and Taylor, 1991). In vision, research on perception of objects far outweighs research on perception of events. The essential dynamism of the world, and of our interactions with the world, is neglected. Yet, because our every waking moment is filled with things happening, we are constantly perceiving, judging, interpreting, and constructing events and behaviour, their nature and causes, their place in the ordered dynamism of the world. It is hard to imagine anything more important to psychology than this.

The main goal of my own work is to develop a general and powerful theory. Theory has a hard time in my area. Some researchers and journal reviewers seem to regard anything theoretical as being philosophy and not relevant to what they do. In fact the essential core of science is the attempt to construct, test, refine, falsify, and reconstruct theories. There is nothing more essential to science than the explanation of diverse individual phenomena in terms of an integrated set of general principles, concepts, and propositions. A good theory has at least two features. (1) It is general: a theory that accounts for several kinds of phenomena is better than a theory that accounts for just a few of those kinds, *ceteris paribus*. (2) It is fundamental: a good theory explains surface phenomena by referring to underlying factors, conditions, or entities *because of which* the surface phenomena are as they are. Publication practices, at least in my area, positively discourage the development of scientifically valuable theories. Where a journal article reports an experiment or other empirical study, the amount of theoretical work that can be presented is limited not only by the space available to the writer but by the requirement to focus on what is directly relevant to the experiment. Theorising in a journal article is therefore inevitably narrow. The prevailing set of norms for journal publication are therefore partly responsible for the superficial nature of much work in my area.

When social psychology textbooks discuss what makes social psychology different from common sense, and thereby scientific, they generally concentrate on methods: the systematic methods of collection of information in social psychology, with experimental control, randomisation, and manipulation of independent variables, are singled out as enabling scientific progress to be made. Sound methods are important, no doubt. But there is no point in having the technique of Raphael if you only employ it in painting by numbers. In fact the current obsession with flawless methodology in some circles is reminiscent of the school of thought that equates art with flawless technique, and is wrong for equivalent reasons. We should aspire to goals that are worthy of our methodological competence. It is only by accepting theory, and dare I say metaphysics, as the equal partner and complement to method, that we can see what worthy goals there be.

In the light of this, one important reason for writing a book is that it gives one the opportunity to present a thorough and deeply considered piece of theoretical work. The ultimate goal is to unify and organise an extensive body of findings under a coherent, parsimonious, and above all fundamental theoretical account, one which hopefully exerts a guiding influence on future work, and is itself open to falsification. For work to be guided by theory and not by what makes a socially approved journal article would be a step towards making a scientific discipline worthy of respect.

Having laid emphasis on the importance of theory, I shall now introduce the theoretical work that guides and organises the content of this book.

At the end of my previous book, *Psychological Metaphysics*, I suggested that to give a complete account of some judgement (or inference or attribution) would require reference to six things:

1. Metaphysics. What is the foundation of the judgement in psychological metaphysics, the basic assumptions on which it depends, the basic concepts in terms of which it is constructed?
2. Function. What is it for, what does the judgement do for the person who makes it?
3. Development. How does the making of this sort of judgement originate and develop in the individual?
4. Culture. What is the contribution to judgement of culture, history, socialisation processes?
5. Process. How does it work, how is the judgement actually made, and are the same processes used for different instances of judgement?
6. Taxonomy. What kind of judgement is it? What are the natural kinds of judgement, and what makes them distinct as kinds?

In that book, as the title suggests, I concentrated on metaphysics, though without neglecting the other five things. In this book I concentrate on development, though again without neglecting the other five things. The central claim and organising principle of the book is that, by the end of the second year of life, the child has differentiated two core theories of how things happen. These theories are related by a common point of origin but distinct in most of their conceptual content. They give us two fundamental ways of understanding how things happen, which I am calling action and causation. Once established, the core theories of causation and action never change, but form a permanent metaphysical underpinning on which subsequent developments in the understanding of how things happen are erected. The story of development is therefore largely the story of how further concepts become attached to and integrated with the core theories. In this book, then, I combine a critical review of relevant psychological literature, and a brief account of some pertinent philosophy, with an exposition of the possible course of development of these two theories. This exposition is not intended to be definitive. There are immense gaps and areas of uncertainty, and questions remain about the interpretation of even the most innocent research finding. Nonetheless, the attempt to make a creative, coherent synthesis is vital if we are to avoid having a literature consisting of nothing more than isolated fragments of uncertain status and meaning.

The main purpose of *Psychological Metaphysics* was to elucidate the general organising principles of the psychological construction of reality, and specific metaphysical assumptions relating to action and causation. The main content of this book cannot be properly understood without at least a brief primer in psychological metaphysics, so I hope readers will excuse a short excursion into what may appear to be rather abstract realms. I recommend that readers, having reached the end of the book, return to this passage and read it again.

The key to the construction of reality in the mind is the notion of imaginary existential dependence. According to this principle, A is existentially dependent upon B if one cannot imagine A existing or occurring without B (strictly speaking, with B not being the case) in the world as it is or as it is held to be by the person doing the imagining. Many elements in the construction of the reality are independent of each other in terms of this principle, and there are also other principles of relation (such as class inclusion). But imaginary existential dependence is the fundamental organising principle; it is fundamental because it defines those elements in the construction of reality that are basic to it. Those are the elements on which everything else in the construction is dependent, but which are existentially dependent on nothing else themselves.

From this perspective, the starting point for a theory of the understanding of causation, or of action, must be to elucidate the metaphysical bases of that understanding. Causation and action are founded on a basic distinction between being and happening. Everything in the world is understood as either being or happening, and the original psychological criterion for distinguishing between being and happening is provided by the temporal integration function of iconic processing: happenings are those things that are detected as change in iconic processing (see White, 1993, and Chapter 2, for more on this). This definition changes during development, as people acquire a concept of happening or events which they apply to things that fall outside the iconic processing definition. All and only those things that are identified as happening are interpreted in terms of either causation or action, or both.

Consider causation first. There are many things that we understand as causal relations, including perception of collision sequences (the launching effect, described in Chapter 7), causal influences on people's behaviour, causal processes in nature and society (such as the fall of the Roman empire), action–outcome contingencies, and many others. These diverse things could be understood in many different ways. But they cannot be completely distinct from each other because we recognise them as being all of a kind, as having something in common by virtue of which they are of a kind; something that we recognise is not shared by other kinds of diachronic structure such as the relation between a flashing right indicator and a car then turning right. This something is a basic concept of the causal relation. A concept of what it is for something to cause something else is the only thing that can bind these diverse phenomena together as members of the same category, and distinguish them from all other things. Not only that, but it also serves to give the causal character to those phenomena, and in doing so to differentiate them from all perceptions, inferences, judgements, etc., that are not causal.

The best candidate for such a concept at the moment is the generative relations concept. This is the idea that causes actually produce or generate their effects. This is an ancient idea in philosophy which has been developed in several recent philosophical theories of causation (White, 1990), notably that of Harré and Madden (1975). There is strong evidence that children as young as two years use generative relations cues as guides to causal inference and prefer those cues to all others (Shultz, 1982b; Shultz, Fisher, Pratt, & Rulf, 1986), and that the generative relations notion is shared not only by young children but also by adults in both Western and non-Western societies (Shultz, 1982b).

The generative relations concept forms the core of my causal powers theory of causal understanding (White, 1989; 1992a; 1993). This theory is based to a considerable extent on the theory of powerful particulars (Harré & Madden, 1975). The central claim is that people have a basic concept of causation as the operation of causal powers of things actually producing or generating effects (often by acting on liabilities of other things) under suitable conditions that serve to release or activate those powers. For example, when people perceive a hammer smashing a plate, they interpret this as a generative relation in which the power of the hammer actually produces the effect of the plate smashing, under the condition of forcible contact between them. Such causal relations are usually understood as reflecting both the power of the cause and a liability of the object on the effect side: the power of the hammer was greater than the resistance of the plate.

Causal attribution is mainly a matter of seeking some object believed to possess the power to produce the effect in question, and checking if necessary that conditions were such that the power of that object could have done so. Causal attribution therefore depends to a considerable extent on acquired beliefs about the causal powers of things. These acquired beliefs gain their causal character from their metaphysical underpinning: that is, the basic repertoire of causal concepts just described constitutes the psychological metaphysics of causal understanding, together with the general metaphysical axioms described earlier.

The basic concept of action is considerably simpler. It is just that the actor performs or carries out his or her own actions, and that it is up to the actor what he or she does. This concept in turn is founded on an idea of the actor as an enduring substance. The psychological marker of action is just the experience of producing action (as opposed to the effects of actions on other things). Note that action is not required to be intentional, or to have an intention as its cause. I follow Taylor (1966) in maintaining that, while many actions may be performed in respect of intentions (whether prior intentions or intentions in action—Searle, 1983), the intention is not a *necessary* component of action. Moreover, the action is *never* caused by the intention: only the actor performs actions, and an intention constitutes, at most, part or whole of the actor's reason for acting. Many kinds of mental state may have functions in respect of action, for example providing motivation or relevant information which the actor may use in choosing how to behave. These things, however, are ancillary. The understanding people have of them in relation to action is dependent on the basic concept of action as described above: this concept is the metaphysical assumption about action on which all else related to action depends.

The importance of taking a developmental perspective on this is that the psychological metaphysics of action and causation are laid down early in life (or present from the start of it). The story of development is to a great extent a story of how additional, ancillary concepts and specific causal and action beliefs are acquired and attached to the psychological metaphysics of causation and action in an organised way. In looking at development we are looking at the building up of coherent and useful conceptual structures on foundations which date back to earliest times. In looking at infancy we are looking not merely at the earliest stage of understanding, but the stage at which the most basic elements of that understanding are established. Once established, the psychological metaphysics of causation and action never change. Everything else we learn and understand depends for its meaning on those basic concepts.

For most of this book I concentrate on what might be called the temporal map; placing understanding of action and causation at one point of time in relation to its state at other points of time. One could also aim to construct the equivalent of a spatial map, showing how understanding of causation and action at a given point of time is related to the understanding of other things at the same point of time. Obviously to do justice to this would take another book, but I can at least make a few general comments about the place of this topic in cognitive development, and direct readers to more comprehensive treatments elsewhere.

The traditional Piagetian view of cognitive development has, among others, three features worthy of note here. First, the cognitive system, while not a strict *tabula rasa*, constructs knowledge through the active selection and interpretation of information: at earliest times there is so little knowledge of the world that even the idea of the persistence of physical objects must be acquired. Second, development proceeds in co-ordinated stages: different domains of knowledge are developed to roughly the same kind and level of sophistication at any given time. Third, transitions from one major stage to another involve the radical transformation of pre-existing knowledge and ways of processing information, so that knowledge represented at one stage is at least locally incommensurate with knowledge represented at the next. All of these features have been contested recently.

First, several lines of research conspire to suggest a much more advanced construction of knowledge in early infancy than Piaget suspected. There is, for example, evidence for sophisticated understanding of physical objects before four months of age: infants seem to assume that physical objects are solid, rigid, and persistent in time despite complete visual occlusion (Baillargeon, 1987; Spelke, 1991). Infants also appear to experience the launching effect when perceiving simulated collisions between objects, in much the way that adults do (Leslie & Keeble, 1987, and see Chapter 2). There is an increasing tendency to favour nativist interpretations of this evidence: either infants are born with basic knowledge of physical objects, or they possess mechanisms that function in such a way as to construct that knowledge very early in development (Karmiloff-Smith, 1991; Spelke, 1991). The strength of the evidence, and the case for a nativist interpretation of it, have been contested by other authors (Fisher & Bidell, 1991), and the topic is currently one of high controversy.

In the case of causal perception, the nativist view has been put by Leslie and Keeble (1987), in their contention that the launching effect is mediated by a low level perceptual module which is unaffected by learning. An alternative possibility is that the infant is born with perceptual mechanisms which strongly facilitate the acquisition of the perceptual discriminations that constitute the evidence for the launching effect in infancy. Under my hypothesis (see Chapter 2), the key perceptual mechanism is the temporal integration function of iconic processing, which is operative from birth and directs the construction of knowledge in a coherent representation of events and change on short time-scales. Under the former interpretation some knowledge is innate; under the latter, only the mechanism for acquiring knowledge is innate. This debate has an obvious relevance to the topic of this book. To outline just two possibilities: (1) innate knowledge of causal relations, such as may be shown in the launching effect, could be the point of origin for all subsequent developments in the understanding of causation; (2) such knowledge is confined to fixed processing modules which neither affect nor are affected by subsequent learning, so that development of understanding of causation proceeds in a different and independent manner. The role played by the launching effect in development will be further considered in Chapter 2.

Second, different domains of knowledge now appear more independent from each other than in the Piagetian account. Children may possess remarkable conceptual sophistication in some areas compared to others, particularly if they have acquired expert knowledge of a domain (Chi, Hutchinson, & Robin, 1989; Keil, 1991). If cognitive development is to be viewed primarily as the acquisition of knowledge in many specific domains, then the idea of general constraints on or directors of development across domains appears less and less useful. The obvious implication of this would be that the development of understanding of causation and action could proceed in a manner partly or wholly independent of development in other domains of knowledge. There is evidence that children are able to master particular causal reasoning problems before they can solve formally equivalent logical reasoning problems (Bindra, Clarke, & Shultz, 1980), rather than at the same time or in the reverse order, as under the Piagetian account: this evidence supports the case for partial independence.

Despite the evidence for independence of domains, some tendencies appear quite general. For example, Gelman (1991) emphasised that, in the domain of number concepts, learners try first and foremost to fit data to their existing conceptual structures, even when the conceptual structures are inappropriate. The same tendency occurs in the interpretation of information relevant to hypotheses under test (Kuhn, 1989), an entirely different domain. It may be important to distinguish between the sophistication of content of knowledge and degree of conceptual differentiation within a domain on the one hand, and procedures, mechanisms, strategies, etc., for acquiring knowledge and differentiating concepts, on the other. While the former may show relatively high domain specificity, the latter is perhaps more likely to be general across domains. This issue too is controversial at present.

Third, the extent to which knowledge is profoundly transformed as development progresses has also been questioned. For example, Spelke (1991) has argued that basic knowledge of physical objects persists unaltered throughout life. She specified the basic principles as continuity of motion, solidity, rigidity, and no action at a distance, and in each case pointed to evidence that these continue to be unquestioned assumptions in adult thought. These she contrasted with knowledge of other object properties such as gravity and inertia, which appear to develop later and still to be imperfectly grasped by adults. She proposed (p.163) that: "all humans, including scientists, may seek primarily to extend their understanding by building on core conceptions that are universal and unquestioned".

This proposal has been contested by Carey (1991). Carey argued that Spelke's view was refuted by evidence that the child's concepts are incommensurable with the adult's in some respects. She cited supportive evidence from studies of the child's concept of weight, and the material/immaterial distinction. Although this evidence does support the contention that knowledge in some domains undergoes radical transformation during development, this is not sufficient to refute Spelke's claim entirely. Let me express the matter in the terms I use in this book. The fundamentals of understanding are things that function as metaphysical axioms. Later in this book I shall make some claims about the psychological metaphysics of the construction of action and causation, and it is also my claim that these axioms, once laid down early in life, remain constant throughout the lifespan, change occuring only at more superficial levels.

Now at first glance Carey's evidence of incommensurability appears to contradict this claim of developmental constancy. In fact, however, sharing metaphysical assumptions does not prevent concepts from being incommensurable. To take the example from the history of science that Carey used, the phlogiston and oxygen-burning theories are incommensurable, but they nonetheless share certain metaphysical assumptions, such as concrete material particularism (Harré & Madden, 1975). The example she takes from psychology, that of weight, has the same property. Evidence supports the claim that the child's and adult's concepts of weight are incommensurable, but they both share the metaphysical axioms of solidity, rigidity, and the unique occupation of space for physical objects.

So, lest anyone misunderstand what I claim in this book, I am happy that radical transformation of concepts may occur at any level above that of psychological metaphysics, and that at any such level the child's understanding and the adult's may be incommensurable. But neither of these things would refute the claim that psychological metaphysics, once established, remain constant throughout subsequent conceptual change. It is very difficult to think about the level of metaphysics, or to elucidate metaphysical assumptions so fundamental that they are taken for granted in our every thought about reality. But, to understand the conceptual systems of child and adult, this is what we must try to do. It is greatly to the credit of some researchers whose work is reviewed in this book that significant progress in this direction is now being made.

One further general issue must be considered at this point, which is whether infants can be said to have theories. To some extent this is a matter of definition. The term "theory" can be defined in different ways, and under some definitions infants have theories, and under other definitions they do not. Although some definitions can be proved wrong, it is not clear that any definition can be proved to be the sole correct definition. Let me begin with Wellman's (1988) account. A theory is a set of concepts, but not just any set of concepts. According to Wellman (1988, p.66) subscribers to a theory share three things: "a basic conception of what phenomena are encompassed by the theory [ontological distinctions]; a sense of how these phenomena and propositions about them are mutually interdependent [coherence]; and, consequently, what counts as a relevant and informative explanation of changes and relationships among the various phenomena [a causal–explanatory framework]". Wellman used this definition to defend the claim that young children have a theory of mind, and I shall be using it to defend the claim that the two basic theories of action and causation to be elucidated in Chapter 2 are also theories.

Other authors, however, have argued that this definition is incomplete. Hobson (1991) argued that, in order to have and apply a theory, one must know what it is to theorise: one must understand possibilities as possibilities, one must have a concept of a theory, and, in the case of theory of mind, of a person as having a theory-holding mind. Clearly infants do not have this kind of understanding, and under this definition infants do not possess theories. But this definition also is too restrictive. Knowing what it is to theorise is not necessary for having a theory, though it may be necessary for certain kinds of theory, or to enable the theory-holder to do certain sorts of things with their theory. If one follows Hobson's argument, then researchers studying theory of mind don't have theories either because, by Hobson's argument, they don't properly understand what a theory is. From this I infer that one *can* have a theory without properly understanding what it is to have a theory, and this conclusion leaves open the possibility that infants may have theories.

My claim in this book is only that infants have (at least) two theories under Wellman's (1988) definition of theory. It is possible that, under other definitions, infants do not have theories. Wellman's definition is a useful one, however, because it specifies things that really seem to be necessary to a theory, whereas the clause added by Hobson (1991) specifies an optional or contingent feature. I shall return to this issue at the end of Chapter 2.

It is psychological metaphysics that provides the organising, unifying framework for the manifest diversity of research findings. Following a brief account of some relevant philosophy, I shall present the story of development from this perspective, as best it can be understood at present.

CHAPTER ONE

Ideas About Causation and Action in Philosophy

There are close links between the study of action and causation in psychology and philosophy. Several psychological theories and hypotheses have been derived or developed from philosophical antecedents, and there is much that psychologists can learn from the ideas and analysis of issues to be found in philosophy. In this chapter I shall focus rather narrowly on the philosophical work that is most directly relevant to the psychological literature considered in this book. In the case of causation, a more wide-ranging survey of ideas can be found in White (1990), and in the philosophical literature Campbell (1976), Carr (1987), Farrington (1944; 1969), Toulmin and Goodfield (1961; 1962), Debus (1978), Bronowski (1951), Kuntz and Kuntz (1988), Dijksterhuis (1961), Santillana (1961), Baumer (1977), Collingwood (1945), Kant (1781/1929), and Emmet (1984) are especially pertinent, in addition to the works cited later in the chapter. An important theme in this literature is the place of ideas about causation within a world view, but space limitations preclude exploration of that theme here.

IDEAS ABOUT CAUSATION IN PHILOSOPHY

It is curious how similar two disciplines can sometimes seem when in reality they are on opposite sides of a great divide. Philosophers are concerned, roughly speaking, with what causation actually is or with the logical status of statements about causation (and this includes the idea that it may be just a construction of the human mind), whereas psychologists are not, or at least not directly. Psychology is concerned more with how people understand causation, how they perceive causal relations, make causal inferences and attributions, and so on. Although these two concerns may not be unrelated, there is no requirement for any psychological theory of causal processing to pay heed to the actual nature of causation, whatever that may be.

Perhaps more fundamentally, however, the methods of inquiry used in philosophy are essentially rational and use criteria such as logical coherence, imaginability, intelligibility, and freedom from ambiguity, whereas the methods used in psychology are essentially empirical and use criteria concerned with the status of evidence. Philosophy and psychology therefore engage in inquiries of different kinds, and the superficial resemblance of the questions asked in each should not be allowed to disguise their basic differences. One could no more design an experiment to test a philosophical notion than one could establish the truth or falsity of a psychological hypothesis by logic alone.

Nonetheless, philosophical ideas and theories have been taken as models for psychological hypotheses: psychologists have supposed, in effect, that people's understanding of causation might resemble that enshrined in some philosophical theory, and have designed empirical tests of this supposition. For example, Heider (1958) and Kelley (1967) supposed that people might make causal attributions by following the covariation principle, which they drew from Mill's (1843/1967) methodological principles of causal inference (specifically the Joint Method of Agreement and Difference, described later). It is therefore important to try to understand these psychological hypotheses by examining their philosophical roots. Philosophy can also, of course, serve as a source of further psychological hypotheses, and indeed of issues which have some psychological relevance. An obvious example is the question of the perception of actual causal relations, which some philosophers deem impossible (e.g. Hume, 1739/1978a), and others possible (e.g. Harré & Madden, 1975).

Regularity Theories

Regularity theories generally analyse causation in terms of empirical associations between events. The best known advocate of a regularity theory of causation is Hume (1739/1978a; 1740/1978b), although the notion of causation as constant conjunction between events goes back at least to Rome at the time of Cicero (Bunge, 1963). Hume's philosophical orientation was radical empiricism. In this, only the contents of experience (sense-impressions) can be known. Hume proposed an epistemological atomism in which the experienced world is a series of instantaneous, atomistic time slices, logically independent of one another. Thus, even the idea of a material object as persisting in time is a construction of the mind based on a series of time slices. This construction does not warrant the inference that the object will persist into the future: no inference about the future is justified under radical empiricism. The same degree of skepticism applies to inferences about relations between objects. "There is no object which implies the existence of any other if we consider these objects in themselves, and never look beyond the ideas which we form of them" (Hume, 1739/1978a, pp. 86–87). Hume treated causation, therefore, as a construction of the human mind, and sought to explain how the characteristics of that construction come about. He said nothing about causation outside of this construction, although he seemed to accept that there was such a thing and used causal terms in his own arguments (Ducasse, 1974b).

Hume argued that if there were only particular conjunctions (i.e. if there were no repetitions of the same type of conjunction), then one could never form the idea of cause and effect. The construction of causal relations therefore depends, in his account, on the tendency to relate different conjunctions by association on the basis of similarity. The idea of cause and effect is formed through experiences of repeated, or constant, conjunction of events. People have the idea that the causal relation involves power, necessity, and efficacy, but these are just ideas formed by the mind from the resemblance of repeated occurrences of the conjunction of two objects. The essence of the idea of necessity, for example, is a propensity of the mind to pass from one object to the idea of its usual attendant, a propensity derived from the experience of constant conjunction of the two. It is therefore important to note that, in Hume's theory, constant conjunction has nothing to do with the actual nature of causation, but only with how the idea of a causal relation is constructed in the mind.

Hume's main definition of cause, then, is: "an object precedent and contiguous to another, and where all the objects resembling the former are plac'd in like relation of precedency and contiguity to those objects, that resemble the latter" (1739/1978a, p.170). A second definition (1739/1978a, p.170) emphasises the fact that this is purely a mental construction: "A cause is an object precedent and contiguous to another, and so united with it, that the idea of one determines the mind to form the idea of the other, and the impression of the one to form a more lively idea of the other". Critical analysis of this can be found in Ducasse (1974b).

Two features of Hume's philosophy are worthy of emphasis. One is his assertion that *anything can be the cause of anything*. This is, indeed, the foundation of the empiricist account of causation: nothing can be ruled out as a cause of anything a priori, because there is no necessity in the causal relation; and, more relevant to psychology, nothing can be ruled out in advance of observations by preconceived ideas in the mind of the observer. Psychologists seeking to construct a Humean account of human causal judgement are inclined to overlook this essential feature of the Humean approach: a priori, the number of candidate causes of an effect is unlimited. The fact that people make selections, that is to say that they only consider a small number of the field of possible causes, means that they cannot be pure Humeans. They may still be attentive to constant conjunction, and constant conjunction may indeed lead to the emergence of a causal impression, but this is only part of Hume's prescription for causal analysis.

The other noteworthy feature is Hume's comment that his definition is *drawn from circumstances extrinsic to the cause*. That is to say, constant conjunction, precedency, and contiguity, are only signs or indicators of causation, whether valid or not: the conjunction of the three is not the cause, just a sign of the location of the cause. Hume's radical empiricism entailed that he was unable to say anything about the actual nature of causes. Instead, he confined himself to what is in effect a psychological theory of the construction of a causal impression, an associationist theory, and as such the true ancestor of such modern ideas as the associative comparator theory (Shanks & Dickinson, 1987).

Few philosophers now subscribe to Hume's regularity theory because it is overinclusive. Under Hume's main definition, for example, day would be the cause of night. Regularity and necessity theories of causation are still being developed, however. Under theories of these kinds it is contended that singular causal statements (i.e. statements about a causal relation on one occasion) are properly analysed in terms of the causal laws of which they are instances. That is, causal laws are basic and causal relations between events are logically supervenient on causal laws. The disagreement between regularity and necessity theories therefore concerns the form that causal laws should take. "Regularity exponents analyse laws as true, contingent, universal generalisations which are omnispatially and omnitemporally unrestricted in scope" (Beauchamp, 1974, p.36). Regularity theorists are therefore not necessarily radical empiricists.

Regularity theories can be identified as such by their denial of necessity in the causal relation and by their dependence on some kind of empirical association between events for defining the causal relation. One school of theories has analysed the causal relation in terms of conditionals. Mill (1843/1967), for example, argued that a cause is the whole set of necessary conditions jointly sufficient for the occurrence of an effect. Galileo held that an efficient cause is a necessary and sufficient condition for the appearance of something (Bunge, 1963). Other philosophers have argued that a cause is a sufficient condition for its effect. In the formulation offered by Sosa and Tooley (1993b, p.5), "C is a cause of E if and only if C and E are actual and

C is *ceteris paribus* sufficient for E" (italics in original). They ascribed this view to Mill and Popper, among others.

Statements about necessary conditions imply statements about sufficient conditions, and vice versa: if A is a sufficient condition for B, then B is a necessary condition for A. This shows that conditional relations are not relations of temporal priority. This is a problem for conditional analyses of causation because a cause is normally required to be prior to or contemporaneous with its effect: thus, sufficient condition formulations founder on what have been called the paradoxes of counterposition (Mulaik, 1986). In some accounts, therefore, a cause is a sufficient condition that is not later than its effect in time (Sosa, 1975).

A well-known modern example of a conditional theory of causation is that by Mackie (1965; 1974; 1975). Summaries of Mackie's ideas have already appeared in the psychological literature (Einhorn & Hogarth, 1986; Hastie, 1983; White, 1990). In Mackie's theory, a cause is an INUS condition. This can be explicated with the example of someone reporting that a fire was caused by a smouldering cigarette butt. In a case of this sort the smouldering butt is an ingredient of an implicit scenario that may include a careless smoker, a pile of flammable material near the discarded butt, and so on. This scenario is not a necessary condition for fire (fires may also occur under different scenarios) but, if adequately described, it is sufficient for the occurrence of a fire. The cigarette butt, by itself, is not sufficient for the occurrence of a fire (other conditions, such as the presence of oxygen, are also required), but it is a necessary condition for the fire under the scenario, because the scenario would not have led to a fire without the discarded butt. Thus, the smouldering butt is an **I**nsufficient but **N**ecessary part of a scenario that is **U**nnecessary but **S**ufficient for a fire to occur. This is an INUS condition, and this is Mackie's definition of a cause. Critical commentaries on this can be found in Sosa (1975).

A different type of modification to constant conjunction is the idea of analysing causation in probabilistic terms. The essential feature of such an approach is that causes make their effects more likely. This is usually expressed in terms of positive statistical relevance. This idea has been developed by Suppes (1970; 1984), among others. Suppes defined events as subsets of a fixed probability space, instantaneous, and with their times of occurrence included in the formal characterisation of the probability space. He then proposed (p.10) that "one event is the cause of another if the appearance of the first event is followed with a high probability by the appearance of the second, and there is no third event that we can use to factor out the probability relationship between the first and second events". Note the inclusion of temporal priority in this definition. This is still a regularity theory, but constant conjunction has been replaced by probable conjunction. The point of the final clause in the definition is to distinguish genuine from spurious causes. To express this in algebraic terms (from Suppes, 1984): an event C is a cause of an event E if and only if:

1. C occurs earlier than E
2. $P(C) > 0$
3. $P(E/C) > P(E)$

where $P(E)$ is the unconditional probability of E occurring and $P(E/C)$ is the probability of event E given event C.

Suppes (1970) dealt with statements about single occasions by saying that they imply probabilistic connections. For example, for the statement "I've been working all day and my feet are killing me", Suppes argued that the speaker means to imply a probabilistic relation such that the consequent does not happen every time the antecedent does, but when it does the antecedent is the cause of it: that is, the likelihood of the consequent is greater in the presence of the antecedent than in general. Suppes also reanalysed Mackie's INUS condition notion in terms of his probabilistic approach. This and other probabilistic theories of causation have been reviewed by Salmon (1984), Eells (1992), and Sosa and Tooley (1993a). Suppes' theory has also been critically assessed by Cheng and Novick (1992).

Mulaik (1986) has pointed out that conditional definitions of the causal relation take on the form of logical implication, though without the logical necessity usually associated with logical implication. Mulaik avoided defining causal relations in terms of logical relations by treating them instead as functional relations. A functional relation is (p.316): "a relation between two sets, a first set and a second set, such that to each element of the first set there corresponds one, and only one, element from the second set". Thus, where the first set is an independent variable and the second set is a dependent variable, functional relations associate with a given value of the independent variable a unique value of the dependent variable. An example would be variation of the pressure of a gas as a function of its temperature. The value of one variable varies as a function of the other, and this gives causal direction to the relation between the two variables. This approach maintains the modern tradition of regularity theories of analysing single causal relations in terms of causal laws, where a law describes the functional relation that holds between two variables. Mulaik argued that the functional relations formulation can be applied to probabilistic formulations such as that by Suppes (1970; 1984).

Mulaik's approach is essentially methodological, that is, it defines causation in terms of things that are not only observable but actually manipulable, and specifies the kinds of observations that justify the inference and description of a causal law. There is no concept of a cause or of causation other than a relation between two variables that is in principle observable. Furthermore, the criterion for assessing causality is not conformity of events to a definition, or to a methodological rule, but prediction: in principle, causal relations can be established by observations which confirm or disconfirm predictions. This approach is essentially pragmatic, designed for actual use in science.

Because of their focus on relations between events, regularity theories readily lend themselves to methodology: not necessarily to methodological principles that can actually be used, but to ideal methodological devices, that is to say devices from the use of which causal relations could validly be inferred if they could be used. Several such methodological principles have been proposed. Here are three of the principles proposed by Mill (1843/1967), cited here because of their use in psychology (Heider, 1958).

1. The method of agreement. "If two or more instances of the phenomenon under investigation have only one circumstance in common, the circumstance in which alone all the instances agree, is the cause (or effect) of the given phenomenon" (Mill, 1843/1967, p.255).

2. The method of difference. "If an instance in which the phenomenon under investigation occurs, and an instance in which it does not occur, have every circumstance in common save one, that occurring only in the former, the circumstance in which alone the two instances differ, is the effect, or the cause, or a necessary part of the cause of the phenomenon" (p.256).

3. The joint method of agreement and difference (also called the indirect method of difference). "If two or more instances in which the phenomenon occurs have only one circumstance in common, while two or more instances in which it does not occur have nothing in common save the absence of that circumstance; the circumstance in which alone the two sets of instances differ, is the effect, or cause, or a necessary part of the cause, of the phenomenon" (p.259).

A different type of methodological principle is the notion of a causal field, introduced by Anderson (1938) and elaborated by Mackie (1965; 1974). A causal field is a defined region within which an effect sometimes occurs and sometimes does not. Defining a causal field is a way of directing or limiting causal analysis: once a causal field has been defined, then causal analysis consists in a search for some difference between the times on which the effect occurred and times on which it did not. For example, in asking "what caused this man's skin cancer?", we may elect to set up a causal field that consists of the man's past history, and seek to answer the question by looking for a difference between the time when the skin cancer developed and the times when it did not. This has the important consequence that what one identifies as the cause may depend on how one defines the causal field. In this example, one may decide that the man's cancer was caused by exposure to radiation, on the grounds that he was exposed to radiation shortly before the skin cancer developed but not at any other time, when he did not develop skin cancer. Suppose, however, that one had asked, "Why did this man develop skin cancer, when other men who were exposed to radiation did not?". This question implies definition of a different causal field, and exposure to radiation cannot be identified as the cause because it does not differentiate the afflicted man from others in the causal field who were not similarly afflicted. The causal field is a general notion because there is no a priori constraint on how it should be defined, except so as to include both occurrence and non-occurrence of the effect: thus, Mill's method of difference and joint method of agreement and difference can be interpreted as setting up kinds of causal field, though the method of agreement cannot.

Hart and Honoré (1959; 1974) pointed out an important difference between causal explanations in common sense and in science. In science one usually seeks to explain types of occurrence that usually or normally happen, e.g. by postulating a causal law, but in common sense one generally seeks to explain a *particular* event that is a *departure* from what is usual or normal. From this, Hart and Honoré (1974, p.224) derived their notion of a cause as "essentially something which interferes with or intervenes in the course of events which would normally take place". Causal analysis is therefore founded on some notion of what the normal sequence of events would be under given circumstances. The interference can, but need not, be a human action. Usual or normal things can be conditions but not causes. This is a much more restrictive notion of cause than those implied in the methodological principles of Mill and Mackie: Definition of a causal field, and causal analysis within a causal field, is not affected at all by whether the effect to be explained is normal or not. This presumably means that some things that would be identified as causes by analysis within a causal field would not be identified as causes by the Hart and Honoré definition, because if the effect they cause is usual or normal one would just never look for an explanation of it, according to Hart and Honoré.

Causal analysis under the Hart and Honoré (1959; 1974) model requires some means of establishing what is normal and what is abnormal, as it is only proper to talk of causes in relation to abnormal occurrences. Gorovitz (1965; 1974) solved this problem by arguing that the words "normal" and "abnormal" should not be used, and that causes can be identified simply by referring to some particular standard for comparison. There is no philosophical prescription for selecting a standard for comparison: Gorovitz said only that selection will be guided by the aims of the broader enquiry within which causal analysis is taking place. For Gorovitz, then, causal analysis is "differentiating factor analysis". Causal analysis of any event can be given by identifying the factor that differentiates the state of affairs in which the event occurred from whatever standard for comparison is chosen. Thus, we can judge that the lighting of a match in a railroad smoking car is caused by its being struck against a box, because this is what differentiates that situation from all those wherein matches are not struck against boxes. Take a second example (Gorovitz, 1974, p.235), however: "A match, having been pulled from the assembly line in a match factory, is struck in a supposedly evacuated chamber, the purpose being to test the hardness of the match head. But the chamber has not been properly sealed, and the match lights". This time, it is the presence of oxygen that will be identified as the cause because that is the factor which differentiates the situation from all those in which matches are struck in vacuum chambers and do not light, this being the "most natural" standard of comparison.

Although regularity theories still exist in philosophy, they have recently come under strong attack (Bhaskar, 1975; Harré & Madden, 1975; Beauchamp, 1974; Strawson, 1992; Sosa & Tooley, 1993a). It would be a digression to explore these philosophical arguments too deeply here, but there is one point that is particularly relevant to the concerns of this book. It is a requirement of a valid regularity theory that regularity, however defined, be necessary and sufficient for valid inference of causal relation. For example, under Hume's (1739/1978) definition (mentioned earlier), repeated observation of the conjunction of objects A and B, such that A is contiguous and temporally prior to B, is necessary and sufficient for the valid inference that A causes B. This is a minimal requirement: if there were ever an instance in which A caused B but A did not meet the criteria specified in some regularity theory (violation of necessity), *or* an instance in which A met the criteria specified in the theory but did not cause B (violation of sufficiency), then the theory must be wrong.

Many philosophers have argued that regularity is not sufficient for inference of a causal generalisation or causal law: under Hume's definition, for example, day would be the cause of night, so clearly some regularities are not causal. Much of the impetus for the development of modern necessity theories of causation has arisen from the need to distinguish causal regularities from accidental regularities (Bunge, 1963; Harré & Madden, 1975; Bhaskar, 1975).

Bhaskar (1975) has argued that, not only is regularity not sufficient for a causal law, it is not necessary either. This is part of a complex philosophy of science which cannot be summarised here, but his main claim about regularity is that the real structures and natural mechanisms which form the theoretical content of causal laws transcend the observable facts, which Humean statements are not allowed to do. That is, our statements about causal laws tend to be independent of, and are often out of phase with, actual patterns of events. If Bhaskar is right, regularity is neither necessary nor sufficient for inference of causal relation, and this would be a damning indictment of regularity theories.

Counterfactual Dependence

A counterfactual statement such as "if the match had been struck at time t, it would have lit" clearly bears some relation to a causal law or a causal connection. Is it possible, then, that causal statements can be analysed in terms of counterfactual relations? The most pressing problem for this idea is that the concept of causation is usually regarded as more basic than the concept of counterfactual dependence. In this case, causation cannot be analysed in terms of counterfactuals; rather, the opposite is true. This apparently abstruse philosophical point is in fact pertinent to any attempt in psychology to model causal judgement in terms of counterfactuals. Such an attempt has been made by Lipe (1991; and see Chapter 6). Her model, and any like it, founders on the simple fact that it has things the wrong way round. Our understanding of causation is not founded on counterfactuals: Rather, our understanding of counterfactuals is founded on our understanding of causation. We could therefore in principle use a model of causal judgement as a basis for a psychological analysis of counterfactual reasoning, but we could not use a model of counterfactual reasoning as a basis for a psychological analysis of causal judgement. Lipe appears to have done the impossible, but only because causal concepts are implicitly imported into her model, in such a way that the analysis of counterfactual thinking depends on them. Indeed, the fact that the major part of her article is taken up with the use of covariation information as a substitute for counterfactual information betrays the logical weakness of her position.

All may not be lost, however, as there has been an attempt in philosophy to make a counterfactual analysis of causal statements (Lewis, 1993). His view has been concisely summarised by Sosa and Tooley (1993b, p.26): "His basic idea is to analyse causation in terms of a narrower notion of causal dependence, and then to analyse causal dependence in terms of counterfactual dependence. Thus, if we restrict attention to the case where C and E are actual events, to say that E is causally dependent upon C is, on Lewis's account, just to say that if C had not occurred, then E would not have occurred." A causal statement such as "C causes E" is then analysed in terms of causal dependence, such that there is an appropriate chain of causally dependent events linking E with C.

Several arguments have been propounded which effectively refute this analysis (see Sosa & Tooley, 1993a). One of particular relevance for present concerns was put forward by Kim (1993). If causal dependence can be analysed in terms of counterfactual dependence, then counterfactual dependence must be a sufficient condition for causal dependence. This requirement is not satisfied, however, because there are many other kinds of dependency relation that give rise to counterfactuals. Obviously if other dependency relations can also be analysed in terms of counterfactuals, then something basic is missing from the counterfactual analysis of causation. It is hard to see what this can be, other than a causal concept of some sort, and if this is the case then we return to the position from which the counterfactual analysis was intended to escape, that counterfactual statements are dependent upon causal laws, and not vice versa. At present, the prospects for a counterfactual analysis of causation look exceptionally dim (Sosa & Tooley, 1993a).

Singularist Theories

Regularity theories involve analysis at the level of causal laws rather than single occurrences. Many other theorists have argued that the proper level of analysis of causation is that of singular causal statements. Many of these have used a concept of the causal relation as generative or productive in nature, and I shall concentrate on one such theory. This is the theory of powerful particulars, developed by Harré and Madden (1975). The central concept in this theory is the "powerful particular". This is a thing (such as a physical object or a person) with a certain type of property, namely a power to produce certain sorts of effects. "Causation always involves a material particular which produces or generates something" (Harré & Madden, 1975, p.5). Harré and Madden rejected the traditional association of power in philosophy with animism and anthropomorphism, and argued that the causal powers of things are based on the "chemical, physical, or genetic natures of the entities involved" (p.5).

Although a causal power is a stable, persisting property of a thing, it only produces an effect under appropriate conditions, termed "releasing conditions". One of the examples used by Harré and Madden is the statement "acid solution can turn logwood solution red". According to Harré and Madden, this means that acid solution has the causal power to turn logwood solution red. This power, however, will only produce that effect when suitable conditions are met, for example when the two solutions are mixed together. Thus, words like *igniting*, *exploding*, *bending*, *breaking*, and *crushing* "are causal verbs expressing the powers that particulars have by virtue of their natures to make certain events occur under specific releasing conditions like scratching, alighting, falling, and submerging" (Madden & Humber, 1974, p.177). Every instance of causation involves both a causal power and a releasing condition. Releasing conditions include not only stimuli which activate a quiescent particular but also the absence or removal of a constraint, restriction, or interference. For example, the structure of a barn may be held up against the pull of gravity by a centre beam, so that if the centre beam is removed the operation of the power of gravity brings the structure down.

Harré and Madden (1975) also distinguished between *enabling conditions*, the satisfaction of which ensures that a thing or material is in a state of readiness, and *stimulus conditions* [releasing conditions] which bring about a response, on condition that a thing or material is in a state of readiness. Enabling conditions can be intrinsic or extrinsic. The satisfaction of intrinsic enabling conditions "ensures that a thing or material is of the right nature and in the right state for the exercise of a certain power" (p.88). For example, "the presence of an engine is an intrinsic enabling condition for a car to have the power to move and must be included in the specification of what it *is* to be a car. The presence of a driver is an extrinsic condition. A car does not cease to be properly a car when the driver steps out. The actions performed by the driver to set the car in motion are extrinsic stimuli [releasing conditions]" (p.88, italics in original).

Some of the dispositional properties of things are liabilities rather than powers. These differ from powers only in being capacities to undergo, rather than capacities to do. For example, in saying that copper is malleable, we are ascribing to it the liability to undergo certain sorts of change, such as changes of shape when hit with a hammer.

Under this theory, then, the causal connection is a generative relation in which the cause actually produces or generates an effect, and the generative mechanism is the operation of a causal power of some thing under a specific releasing condition. Harré and Madden (1975) argued that, under this account, causal relations can be directly perceived. The warrant for the perception of causation is on the same level as that for the perception of shape or motion. When we watch someone strike a match, for example, we perceive the causal connection between the striking of the match and its ignition, just as we perceive the shape of the match or its movement.

Singularist theories of other types have been proposed by several philosophers, including Bunge (1963), Taylor (1966), Shoemaker (1979; 1980), Ducasse (1965; 1969; 1974a), and Castaneda (1980) (see also White, 1990). Also under this general heading come several versions of manipulability theory (Reid, 1863a; 1863b; Collingwood, 1940; 1974; von Wright, 1974a; 1974b).

IDEAS ABOUT ACTION IN PHILOSOPHY

In this section I shall consider philosophical ideas about the nature of action and its origination. Not everything a human being does is an action in the sense treated under the philosophy of action. We move our eyeballs when in REM sleep, we digest our food, we fall over in a faint, we raise our arms, we start running. These are all things we do, but they are not all of the same kind. It is convenient to characterise actions as those things we do which are, in some sense, up to us. It is up to us whether we raise our arms or start running, and these therefore count as actions. It is not up to us whether we move our eyeballs when in REM sleep, whether or not we digest our food, whether or not we fall over when fainting; these things happen whether we wish them to or not. For this reason they do not count as actions. As a heuristic guide, something counts as an action if it makes sense to ask someone to refrain from it. Thus, it makes sense to ask someone not to raise their arm (unless we know that their doing so is a nervous tic over which they have no control), but it does not make sense to ask someone to stop digesting the food in their stomach.

The Intentional Theory of Action

There is a long history of attempts to identify and define a mental state as a cause of or antecedent to action, including states such as desires, trying, and volitions (Smith & Jones, 1986; Reid, 1872). The attempt that has been most influential in recent psychology is commonly known as the intentional theory of action. It seems obvious that intentions have something to do with action. After all, taking some of the examples listed earlier, I can raise my arm or start running intentionally, but the movement of my eyes when I am asleep is not intentional, and I do not digest the food in my stomach intentionally. This idea is not without problems: for example, playing a shot at tennis is an action, but some shots unintentionally go into the net. We can deal with this in principle by saying that such unintentional actions always have an intentional core: hitting the ball into the net involved something being done intentionally. We must also take care to distinguish different senses of the word "intention". For the purpose of analysing action, we do not mean prior intentions, because many actions have no prior intentions at all, and may indeed be contrary to prior intentions actually held by the actor. I may eat too much at my favourite restaurant despite the fact that I went there intending not to, and this in no way means that my eating too much was not an action, that it was not in some sense up to me how much I ate. When I make a bid at an auction I am certainly doing so on purpose, but I may not have intended to go quite so high in the bidding.

This being so, what is it to do something intentionally, or on purpose? Under the intentional theory of action, an action is intentional if there is a reason which makes the action comprehensible (Davidson, 1963; 1968; Smith & Jones, 1986). A reason for action is a very specific combination of things: "specifying the agent's reasons for acting is a question of mentioning a desire together with a belief to the effect that the action in question was the appropriate way of satisfying the desire" (Smith & Jones, 1986, p.130). (Exceptionally, no belief need be involved when all one desires is to perform the action itself.) To use an illustration which will reappear later in the book, Jane looked for her kitten under the piano because she wanted to find it and thought it was there. This appropriate combination of belief and desire constitutes the reason for Jane's action. An action is intentional, then, when the person acted because of an appropriate combination of desire and belief. The words "desire", "belief", and "because of" all need further comment.

"Desire" does not have its everyday meaning here. For example, one can intentionally visit the dentist without having the least desire to do so. A broader, and better, term is "pro-attitude", which Smith and Jones (1986) characterised as an attitude which inclines one towards a certain action. It can include desires, wantings, urgings, moral views, aesthetic principles, goals, and values, so long as these conform to the characterisation in terms of inclining the actor towards a certain action. It can include permanent character traits and passing fancies. Smith and Jones argued that most desires in the broad, pro-attitude sense are under our control, meaning that it is up to us whether we act on them or not, though there are exceptions, such as the desire for food.

The belief is specifically a belief that the desire can be attained or satisfied by the action. For example, the action of stepping into a shop doorway can be explained by the desire to avoid getting wet and the belief that the action of stepping into the shop doorway was a means of achieving that desire. Only that kind of belief will do. Other beliefs can also be referred to, but are not essential.

Finally, to give a causal account of the action, the belief and desire must be the ones *because* of which the action was carried out. For example, John might have wanted to get some fresh air, and believed that opening the window was a means of doing so, but he might still have carried out the action of opening the window for some other reason, e.g. to hail a friend across the street.

Note the appearance of the word "causal" in the previous paragraph. The intentional theory of action is a causal theory of action, in that relevant belief–desire combinations are construed as causes of action. Moreover, it is incorrect to interpret intentions as a kind of mental state or occurrence intervening between a belief–desire combination and action: to act intentionally is just to act as a direct result of particular beliefs and desires. It is beliefs and desires that are the mental causes of intentional actions. Under the intentional theory of action, then, giving reasons for action is a kind of causal explanation. Reasons explanations are a kind of causal explanation. It is important to note that this is a controversial aspect of the theory. Many philosophers have argued that reasons explanations and causal explanations are of fundamentally different kinds: Some versions of this argument are discussed shortly.

The presumed link between reasons and intentions means that reason explanations can only be given for what was intended about an action. For example, Oedipus intended to marry Jocasta but did not intend to marry his mother. This being so, it is appropriate to talk of Oedipus' reason for marrying Jocasta, but not of his reason for marrying his mother, because that was not something he intended to do. What is important about this example is that these are actually two alternative and valid ways of describing the same action. Thus, a reason can rationalise or explain a behaviour when it is described in one way and not when it is described in another way. It is therefore not proper to talk of a reason for action: one can only talk of a reason for action under a certain description of that action, and then only where the description is of the action as intended.

Taylor's Account of Action

I have juxtaposed Taylor's account to the intentional theory of action, because Taylor disagreed with most of the important claims of that theory; and Taylor's account is of some importance to the theoretical substance of this book (see particularly Chapter 2). Taylor did not reject the idea that there are such things as volitions, intentions, desires, and choices: What he rejected was the idea that they could be the *causes* of action (1966, p.77): "To speak wilfully or voluntarily or intentionally or deliberately is not first the will to speak, and then to find one's tongue and vocal apparatus carrying on from there, in response to what was thus inwardly initiated by the soul. To speak wilfully or intentionally is just to speak with a knowledge of what one is saying and why". In fact, people have sought such things as volitions and intentions as causes of action because they believe that only events can be causes, and therefore that there must be some kind of event that is the cause of action.

That is the approach that Taylor rejected. He revived the Aristotelian notion of a cause as an object that does something, and proposed that the object that does my actions is just I, myself (1974, p.55): "When I believe I have done something, I do believe that it was I who caused it to be done, I who made something happen, and not merely something within me, such as one of my own subjective states, which is not identical with myself". This is the most important thing about action, then, the reference to the agent: In talking about moving his finger to the right or to the left, "we cannot say merely that my finger moved, but rather, that *I* moved it" (1966, p.109, italics in original). And this is exclusive to acts. We can describe things that are not acts as if I were the cause of them, such as "I perspired"; but in such cases it is always possible to find acceptable paraphrases that do not suggest agent causation, such as "my hands perspired", or "perspiration developed on my hands". "Nothing can be represented as a simple act of mine unless I am the initiator or originator of it" (1966, p.112). "In saying that my acts are caused by myself, I mean *only* that I cause them or make them occur, and this is in fact inconsistent with saying that something else, to be referred to as my *self*, is the real cause of them" (1966, p.135). Taylor argued that this idea is compatible with deliberation and it being up to me what I do.

Simply saying that I initiate or originate my own actions may sound bland, but it is important to see the claim in the light of its metaphysical foundation: (1) a concept of a person "who is not merely a collection of things or events, but a substance and a self-moving being" (1974, p.55); and (2) a conception of causation according to which an agent—a substance and not an event—can be the cause of an event.

It is worth noting that the latter conception runs into trouble as it stands because it amounts to a denial of sufficiency in the causal relation: the mere existence of a substance is not sufficient for the occurrence of an event. Harré and Madden (1975) dealt with this by referring to conditions (in my terminology, "releasing conditions") under which powers operate to produce effects. Taylor preferred to deal with it by avoiding the word "causes", and opting for "initiates", "originates", or "performs".

Taylor (1966) paid special attention to purposeful behaviour. Only the actions of agents can be purposeful, though not all actions of agents are purposeful. Purposeful behaviour is behaviour that is directed towards some goal. More specifically, "An object can be regarded as behaving purposefully, then, only in case it *directs itself* towards some goal" (1966, p.226, italics in original). Objects can be directed towards goals by other things, as in a man throwing a stone at something, but they do not thereby become purposeful: They are used only for some purpose of the object that directs them.

Taylor's account already constitutes a powerful critique of causal theories of action, such as the intentional theory of action: Taylor also offered some specific arguments against the intentional theory of action. According to this theory purposeful behaviour is behaviour that is caused by a combination of desires and appropriate beliefs: that is, purposeful behaviour (or action) can be causally explained, and the causes are desires and beliefs. Taylor argued that this cannot be right as it stands because desires cause all sorts of things that one would not call purposeful actions. The desire for food causes salivation, but salivation is not a purposeful action, merely an automatic response. The point of this is that there is a difference in kind between salivation and purposeful action which is not captured by the idea that desires are the causes of action.

He also argued that, to be causes of action, desires must be of equivalent specificity to the actions they cause: that is, every action must have a desire as its cause. This is clearly impossible. For example, when I raise my arm, I do so in just this way, to just this height, at just this time, and so on, and to be the cause of that my desire must be exactly that specific. Moreover, in complex actions, such as a pianist playing a complex passage which requires a lot of things to be done in a short time, each individual thing that the pianist does must have its own desire, otherwise the notion of desire cannot explain why the pianist does this thing rather than that. Obviously it is absurd to suggest that the pianist is afflicted with such a torrent of desires.

Here is his summary statement (p.254): "An action has many effects—raising my hand to catch the speaker's attention, for example, also has the *effect* of attracting the attention of other persons, of elevating my ring, of disturbing the air nearby, and so on, but the *end* of my action is catching the speaker's attention rather than any of these other things. It is distinguished from them as an end, however, only in relation to my purpose. Similarly, in case this end is achieved, it has many causes—the conditions being such that my hand is visible to the speaker, the speaker's being so placed that he sees my hand, and so on. But these *causes* of his attention being attracted to me are not the *means* by which that end is achieved. The means, which is raising my hand, is distinguished from the other causes only in relation to some purpose of some agent—in the present case, in relation to my purpose or intention of achieving a certain effect" (italics in original).

Purposeful behaviour is self-originated, as is any action of an agent. In fact, Taylor (1966) claimed that the concept of purpose is as basic as he believed that of cause to be, and that neither can be reduced to the other. This has an important implication for explanation. Actions, he claimed, are explained in terms of their purposes (or aims or goals). "A purposeful explanation of an event or series of events is some statement that represents the events in question as the *means* to some *end* or goal" (1966, p.213, italics in original). Beliefs and desires are alluded to in explanations only as a way of elucidating the agent's purposes. Explanations of this kind are reasons explanations, that is, explanations which make reference to the agent's reasons for action. Since the concept of purpose is basic, and distinct from that of cause, and since self-originated behaviour is not causally necessitated, this means that reasons explanations are not a type of causal explanation. The two are fundamentally different kinds of explanation. Here, then, Taylor is in fundamental disagreement with the intentional theory of action.

Taylor did not advocate free will, and was explicitly agnostic on the question of free will versus determinism. He did argue that people act freely, but all he meant by that was that, when someone acts freely, it is the case that they could have acted other than they did.

Topics in the Philosophy of Action

The ideas sketched above were selected because of their relevance to the psychological work discussed in this book. It is important to bear in mind that they are only two among many contributions to the philosophy of action, and that other contributions may be very different in content and approach (see, for example, Harré & Secord, 1972; Searle, 1983; Ginet, 1990; Moya, 1990; Kenny, 1989). The purpose of this section is to attend to some themes and topics that are especially pertinent to psychology.

What is an Intention?

The term "intention" has been defined and used in many different ways by different philosophers. As a preliminary it must be distinguished from Intentionality. Intentionality in philosophy refers to the "aboutness" of mental states or events. Searle (1983, p.1) proposed that "Intentionality is that property of many mental states and events by which they are directed at or about or of objects and states of affairs in the world". (I am following Searle in using "Intentionality" with capital "I" for this sense.) Loosely, Intentionality refers to things like meaning and representation. It is important to distinguish Intentionality from intentions. "Intending to do something is just one form of Intentionality along with belief, hope, fear, desire, and lots of others" (Searle, 1983, p.3).

Shultz (1980, p.131) wrote: "I consider intention to refer to a mental state that guides and organises behaviour. It is essentially a determination to act in a certain way or to bring about a certain state of affairs". This characterisation, although useful, is both too inexact and too contentious. A similar, but more precise, definition, was drawn from Anscombe (1957) by Frye (1991, p.16): "An act is intentional if it is being done in relation to some future state of affairs and if what is being done is directed towards bringing about that state of affairs". Note that this definition does not identify a particular kind of mental state antecedent to action, contrary to Shultz. As Frye pointed out, however, this is really a definition of acts guided by *prior* intentions, and a prior intention may be held in mind for any amount of time before the action to which it refers is carried out. In the intentional theory of action, an action is intentional if it is comprehensible in terms of a reason, which is a combination of a desire (pro-attitude) and a belief that the action in question was an appropriate way to satisfy the desire. There is nothing to an intention other than a belief–desire combination. This definition, like Anscombe's, is functional but, like Anscombe's, it is perhaps best taken as defining action guided by prior intentions. To see what an intention can be other than a prior intention, consider Searle's (1983) analysis.

According to Searle (1983), an intention is an Intentional state with two features: a psychological mode (intending) and Intentional content (the thing intended). It carries conditions of satisfaction, which are the carrying out of the Intentional content. An intentional action, then, is the conditions of satisfaction of an intention. By "intentional action", though, Searle did not mean an action that is the carrying out of some *prior* intention. All actions are intentional, but only some actions have prior intentions. Many actions are just done spontaneously, without prior intentions, but these too are intentional actions. They are intentional actions because they involve what Searle called "intentions in action". An action has two components: an intention in action and the actual bodily movement. It is easiest to see what an intention in action is by contrasting it with the notion of a prior intention. Suppose I have a prior intention to raise my arm. It has this representative content: "I perform the action of raising my arm by way of carrying out this intention" (Searle, 1983, p.92). This representative content includes the whole action, both the actual movement and the intention in action. The Intentional content of the intention in action is (p.94): "My arm goes up as a result of this intention in action". There are two differences: the prior intention *represents* (1) the *whole action*, (2) (i.e. the intention in action and the movement) as the rest of its conditions of satisfaction, but the intention in action *presents* (does not represent) the *physical movement* (not the whole action) as the rest of its conditions of satisfaction. Also, the intention in action is more determinate than the prior intention because it specifies *exactly* how the arm goes up.

Note that the representative content of intentions includes phrases like "by way of carrying out this intention". This is an important component. Suppose I raise my arm. Now the content of the intention cannot be "that I perform the action of raising my arm" because I might, for example, forget about this intention and then raise my arm for some other reason. That is, under this content any action of raising one's arm counts as the conditions of satisfaction of the intention, and this will not do because some actions of raising one's arm are clearly not connected with this intention. We need a more stringent specification that serves to connect the one intention with just one particular action, and for this requirement the intentional content must be at least "that I perform the action of raising my arm by way of carrying out *this intention*" (Searle, 1983, p.85, italics in original). The phrase "carrying out" must mean that the intention plays a causal role in the action: It is therefore tied to the occurrence of the action.

This degree of specificity enables us to deal with some problematic cases. To give just one example, Oedipus intended to marry Jocasta but did not intend to marry his mother. Under Searle's account, the action of Oedipus in marrying Jocasta was intentional in that "marrying Jocasta" was part of the Intentional content of his intention in action; but it was also unintentional in that "marrying his mother" was not part of the Intentional content of his intention in action, even though it was an element of his action. The point is that the intention in action is required to have definite presentational content (and any prior intention is required to have representational content), and it is this requirement that enables us to identify what is intentional in some action, or whether some action (or an effect of some action) is intentional.

This is only one among many approaches to the definition of intentional action. To define intentional action, many philosophers analyse problem cases. Take an instance in which Jane shoots John. We would not want to say that Jane's shooting John was intentional if, in firing the gun, she missed him and the bullet accidentally struck the trigger of another loaded gun which fired and shot John. To deal with such cases Ginet (1990) brought in the notion of true and appropriately justified belief. For Jane's shooting John to be described as an intentional action, it must be the case that Jane believed that by firing the gun she would shoot John and that her belief was true and justified, for example in that she knew that her gun was loaded and pointing at John when she fired it. Such problem cases are important because they show that intentional action is not as simple as it may appear.

One final caveat for this section is that not all philosophers hold that an action has to be intentional. Taylor (1966; 1974), for example, maintained that what makes something an action is just the fact that the actor does it. Under this argument, the actual performance of action by an actor (and emphatically not by a mental state, whether it be an intention, a belief–desire combination, a volition, or anything else) is basic to action, and its being intentional is neither basic nor necessary. This, as we shall see, I take to be the key to the psychological concept of action.

Voluntary Actions, Deliberate Actions, and Responsibility

Not all intentional actions are voluntary. According to White (1968, p.6), "what I do, thinking I am obliged to do it, I do not voluntarily do, since I do it thinking I have to do it. What is done to me I do not voluntarily do, since I do not do it at all ... To do x voluntarily is to do x with the awareness that one has an alternative course open to one". Thus, we can divide intentional acts into obligatory acts and voluntary acts, as defined by White.

Unfortunately, this view is not shared by all authors. Smith and Jones (1986, p.255) offered an Aristotelian account of voluntary acts which is indistinguishable from their own account of intentional acts, and indeed they stated that the Greek word which they translated as "voluntary" could just as well be translated as "intentional". Evidently, "voluntary" as opposed to "obligatory" is not the same as "voluntary" as opposed to "involuntary". For the sake of terminological clarity, I shall reserve "voluntary" for the sense in which it is opposed to "obligatory".

Under this definition, there appear to be several classes of behaviour that do not count as voluntary. These include behaviour under coercion or obligation, where the action is intentional but not voluntary, muscle spasms, where the action is neither voluntary nor intentional, and behaviour where the actor lacks control over what he or she is doing because of lack of consciousness (Fitzgerald, 1968, who cites things done by a person asleep or because of a brain tumour or under effects of hypoglycaemia as examples). Under Fitzgerald's account, which is drawn from legal philosophy and practice, control is the central concept. He reported that the American Law Institute's Penal Code excludes as not voluntary "any bodily movements that otherwise are not products of the effort or determination of the actor, either conscious or habitual" (1968, p.132). He concluded (p.134) that "the common minimal requirement of the law seems to be that the accused should have had the ability to control his movements". The point for legal practice is that it makes no sense to try to deter people from committing involuntary acts, and that people are not at fault for what they cannot help doing.

The concept of responsibility, then, is confined in application to voluntary actions. We often hold the actions of small children and animals to be intentional, but despite this we do not hold them responsible for what they do. According to Aristotle we hold someone responsible for their actions when we believe that they have the capacity for reflective deliberation (not when they actually exercise that capacity but when we believe they could)—being capable of deliberative choice between alternative courses of action. This, evidently, matches White's definition of voluntary action. Thus, children and animals are not held responsible for their actions because, or when, they are thought not to have the capacity to reflect on their choice of action. There are various acknowledged classes of exception to this, such as acting under duress or in ignorance. This account enables us loosely to define deliberate action. If voluntary action is action carried out by someone when (we believe) they have the capacity for deliberation between alternative courses of action, then "deliberate action" can be reserved for those instances of voluntary behaviour in which the capacity for deliberation is actually exercised.

As with most terms, though, "responsibility" is ambiguous and can be used in different ways (see, e.g. Feinberg, 1968). Searle (1983, p.103) pointed out that intentions and responsibility are sometimes detached from each other: "We hold people responsible for many things they do not intend and we do not hold them responsible for many things they do intend. An example of the former type is the driver who recklessly runs over a child. He did not intend to run over the child but he is held responsible. And an example of the latter is the man who is forced at gunpoint to sign a contract. He intended to sign the contract but he is not held responsible".

Dispositions

In causal attribution, psychologists generally look at the extent to which people regard behaviour as due to some personality characteristic of the actor. This contrasts with the tendency of philosophers, shown in the foregoing, to focus on more transient mental states and events such as intentions, beliefs, and desires. Indeed, Urmson (1968) went so far as to say that if he asked "What caused Jones to do x?" and was told that Jones' character caused him to do it, he would feel surprised and cheated, and would in fact find such answers virtually unintelligible.

It seems that many psychologists think of personality characteristics as dispositions, or vice versa. The term "disposition" is used occasionally in philosophy, usually in treatments of the philosophy of mind or action. Philosophers do not precisely agree on what a disposition is. There are three broad approaches to the definition of mental states in philosophy, which may be called mentalistic or Cartesian, behaviourist, and functional.

Under the mentalistic approach, mental states are definable in terms of their intrinsic qualities as states. Thus, fear, for example, would be defined in terms of the intrinsic qualities of the experience of fear, those qualities which individuate fear as an experience and distinguish it from all other kinds of state.

The behaviourist approach is exemplified by Ryle (1949). Under this approach, a specific disposition is identified as a set of behaviours occurring under specifiable circumstances. A statement about a disposition is nothing other than a statement about how something would behave if certain circumstances were realised. For example, saying that something is brittle means just that if it were firmly struck it would shatter (etc.). We can use this definition to give an analysis of mental states such as belief: "Beliefs are to be identified ... with dispositions or tendencies to behave in certain appropriate ways depending on the circumstances. For example, your belief that it is about to rain is nothing other than a disposition on your part to bring in the washing (in appropriate circumstances, with no distractions) [etc.]" (Smith & Jones, 1986, p.142). This has the curious implication that a belief is not a state underlying behaviour. Having a disposition means just that certain conditional statements are true: It does not mean that dispositions are underlying mental states which make the conditional statements true.

Under functionalism, "mental states should be analysed in terms of their normal causal role, mediating between a specified input ... and a specified output" (Carruthers, 1986, p.112), rather than in terms of their intrinsic qualities as mental states. Under this approach, "disposition" can be defined as "a state of a person apt for producing certain ranges of behaviour" (Armstrong, 1970, p.75). For example:

Injury—Pain—Disposition to say "I am in pain"—Say "I am in pain"
Or: Frustration—Anger—Disposition to shout—Shout

Under this account, "the normal function of pain [for example] is to be the causal intermediary between a specified bodily cause and a specified sort of behavioural effect" (Carruthers, 1986, p.112). The function is not necessary, merely usual. In the case of dispositions, there is no particular kind of mental state that a disposition must be: Anything that can be said to function as an aptness for producing certain kinds of behaviour under certain circumstances qualifies as a disposition, whether it be a belief, a desire, a trait, an ability, a plan, or an intention. Functionalism appears to offer the most satisfactory account of dispositions at present, but Carruthers (1986) argued that not all expressions referring to mental states can be analysed in purely functional terms, and that there was a case for including intrinsic qualities with function in the analysis of mental states.

How Does Action Come About?
The causal attribution literature has no theory of the nature of action or of how it comes about. In fact, most writers content themselves with the theory-neutral term "behaviour". This lends a fatal ambiguity to all causal attribution research inasmuch as it ignores the fundamental distinction between action and behaviour that is not action. As we have seen, action can be loosely defined as things we do that are in some sense up to us. Thus, it is not up to us whether we digest our food or move our eyeballs when in REM sleep. This characterisation leaves a considerable twilight zone of actions that may or may not be up to us, such as habitual actions and actions which directly express emotions (Sutherland, 1959). There are therefore considerable practical, methodological problems to do with identifying actions, and with how people identify actions.

Lacking a theory of action, psychologists also naturally lack a theory of how action comes about. The following is a brief summary of various philosophical views.

1. Reid, Hobbes, Locke, et al.: It is caused by a volition or an act of will. Ginet (1990) attempted to redefine volition as not a cause of action but its initial part, the voluntary exertion of force.
2. The intentional theory of action: It is caused by an appropriate combination of beliefs and desires.
3. Taylor (1966; 1974): *I* do it, where I am an enduring substance endowed with powers.
4. Searle (1983): Through an intention in action, which has Intentional content and presents the physical movement as the

rest of its conditions of satisfaction. Note that the intention in action is the initial part of the action and not the cause of it, though it is what makes the bodily movement happen.

5. Harré and Secord (1972): It is produced by the operation of powers of the actor under the model of self-direction through the self-monitored following of rules and plans in accordance with the meaning ascribed to the situation.

How is Action Explained?

All philosophers agree that action is to be explained in terms of reasons. (This is not to say that it cannot also be explained in terms of causes that are not reasons.) They disagree, however, on whether reasons explanations are a type of causal explanation or not. Under the intentional theory of action they are, but according to Taylor (1966), Harré and Secord (1972), and Ginet (1990) they are not. Philosophers have claimed that various kinds of things can be referred to in reasons explanations, including belief/desire combinations (Davidson, 1963; 1968), purposes (Taylor, 1966; 1974), intentions, including prior intentions (Searle, 1983), the act of which an action is part (Harré & Secord, 1972; and see Chapter 5), and motives (Sutherland, 1959).

It should also be borne in mind that reasons explanations have different functions from cause explanations. Three functions of reasons explanations are listed by Toulmin (1970):

1. Reasons give justification for action (e.g. in response to a challenge).
2. Reasons signal intentions and purposes, explaining action as being done in order to bring about or achieve something else.
3. Reasons redescribe action. For example, "Why was John boasting?"; "because he was trying to impress Sue". In this sense, reasons render actions intelligible, whereas causes could be said to render them inevitable.

CHAPTER TWO

Origins and Early Development

The understanding of action and causation that we possess as adults is the product of a chain of development stretching back to the infant's earliest days. The most important links in this chain are the earliest ones insofar as they function as the axioms on which further development depends. The development of understanding is an interaction, in some ways a compromise, betweem genetic endowment and experience. For example, infants (and adults) are creatures of limited and specific cognitive capacities. They are directed in some ways more than others by specific areas of endowed competence, including such things as mechanisms of attention and iconic processing. These things must influence the kind of cognitive development that occurs, by limiting and guiding if not by constraining the acquisition of concepts and processes.

Perhaps even more important, infants' concepts are limited or constrained by their own mental activities and states. It is unlikely that infants can develop concepts of mental states that lie entirely outside their own experience. It is unlikely, for example, that infants could develop a concept of intention without having intentions themselves (Frye, 1991). This is not meant to imply that infants develop such concepts by reflecting on their experience, by utilising their awareness of their own mental states. An information-processing device or a neural network can acquire concepts, or at least develop states that function as if they were concepts, without anything like awareness being involved. So it may be for infants too. Concepts are just a kind of memorial structure, a kind of repository of experience. They may come about in many ways.

The difficulties of studying the ontogenesis of concepts in the infant are such that almost nothing can be stated with any certainty. Much of what has been written is admittedly speculative, as we shall see. Despite this, diverse ideas can be found, and this chapter reviews the claims of the main types of ideas to account for the origins of cause and action concepts.

PERCEPTION OF CAUSATION AND ACTION IN INFANCY

Research on the Launching Effect with Infants

Several studies of causal processing carried out on infants have taken as their model Michotte's (1963) research with adult subjects. Michotte presented visual stimuli involving what appeared to be two rectangles, A and B. A moved toward B at constant speed and came into contact with it, whereupon A remained at the point of contact and B moved off in the same direction at constant speed. Adult observers of this usually report that the movement of B is caused by the impact of A upon it, and that A pushes, kicks, or launches B. This is known in English as the "launching effect". Despite occasional reports that not all observers perceive the launching effect, several recent studies have established the phenomenon beyond reasonable doubt: this literature is discussed in Chapter 7.

Research on perception of the launching effect by infants began with two unpublished studies by Ball (1973) and Borton (1979), both yielding evidence suggestive of causal perception (see White, 1988). The most extensive and systematic series of studies is that carried out by Leslie. Leslie (1982) presented initial trials consisting of one of three films: (1) a standard launching effect sequence; (2) the same sequence except that A and B remained in contact for about 580 ms before B moved off; or (3) the same as (1) except that A stopped short of B and did not come into contact with it. He then measured dishabituation, in terms of duration of continuous gaze at the stimuli, to test films in which only one component of the movement in the initial films was presented: that is, either A's movement or B's but not both. Dishabituation was considerably greater for infants initially shown launching effect films than for infants shown either of the other initial films. Leslie's younger group ranged from 13 to 24 weeks old. There were no effects of or interactions with age.

The study shows that infants respond differently to launching effect trials than they do to trials in which either spatial contiguity or temporal contiguity is violated, just as adults do (Michotte, 1963). To what extent, however, do these findings show causal perception? One could argue that infants see launching effect trials simply as a single movement, whereas they see spatial and temporal discontiguity trials as two movements. Leslie (1982) pointed out that his findings contradicted this interpretation. His test films, as described above, included only a single movement of one of the rectangles. If his infants perceived the launching effect trials as a single movement, therefore, they should have dishabituated less to these single-movement test films than should infants shown trials involving two movements. In fact, the opposite happened. This supports the idea that causal perception was occurring among the infants he studied.

Later studies added weight to this interpretation. Leslie (1984a) found that infants perceive some kind of internal structure in the launching effect sequence: this was shown by the fact that they dishabituated to a simple reversal of the launching effect sequence (running the film backwards) but not to a reversal of a film of a single object moving. Leslie (1984a) asked what kind of internal structure the infants were perceiving. He set up two hypotheses:

1. "Hume would argue that infants will perceive two independent aspects of the event—the spatial contact and the temporal succession of the movements" (Leslie & Keeble, 1987, p.269).
2. Michotte "asserts that a causal relation will be registered directly" (Leslie & Keeble, 1987, p.269).

To distinguish these two hypotheses, Leslie (1984a) set up four films:

A. Direct launching (Michotte's standard launching effect sequence).
B. Delayed reaction (the standard sequence except that the two rectangles remained in contact for 500ms before the second one moved off).
C. Launching without collision (the standard sequence except that the two rectangles were 6cm apart when at their closest).
D. Delayed reaction without collision (the standard sequence with both delay and gap).

Adult observers only report perceiving the launching effect under A (Michotte, 1963), and under hypothesis 2 the same should hold for infants. Now Leslie pointed out that A and D contrast with each other in respect of both delay and gap, and so do B and C. So if infants simply encode these features of the sequence, as they should do under hypothesis 1, then they should show as much dishabituation to C after training with B as they do to D after training with A.

Leslie's results favoured hypothesis 2 over hypothesis 1. He also found, however, that each of the four films was discriminable from the others, and that there was nothing special about the direct launching sequence. His results suggested that the sequences are encoded on a single dimension, with A at one end, D at the other, and B and C somewhere in the middle. This is a dimension of spatiotemporal continuity. It is, therefore, uncertain from his results whether infants are discriminating on the basis of perception of causal relation or on the basis of judgement of spatiotemporal continuity.

Leslie and Keeble (1987) set out to distinguish these two possibilities. Their method was to measure dishabituation to reversals of the films. For film A, the launching effect sequence, this would mean reversal of both causal direction and spatiotemporal direction: for film B, delayed reaction, if this sequence is not perceived as causal then reversing the film means only reversing the spatiotemporal direction. In this case, if what is special about film A is perception of a causal relation, there should be more dishabituation to film A than to film B. Leslie and Keeble ran two studies and found this result in both of them. This differentiates spatiotemporal from causal features and shows responsiveness to causal features. Leslie and Keeble argued, moreover, that this differentiation could not be attributed either to better memory for A than for B or to infants' preference for looking at A over B.

Other findings conflict with this, however. Oakes and Cohen (1990), also using a dishabituation method, found evidence of causal perception in infants aged ten months, but not at six months of age, an apparent developmental trend. Oakes and Cohen argued that the results of Leslie (1984a) were confounded by differential preferences between types of stimuli, as measured by looking times on the first habituation trial. This does not apply, however, to the data reported by Leslie and Keeble (1987). It is therefore more likely that the discrepancy in results is due to differences in the stimuli. Leslie followed Michotte in using simple opaque rectangles, but Oakes and Cohen (1990) used more complex objects, a model plane and a model dinosaur, both on wheels. As they reported, research findings show that infants aged six months have problems integrating the parts of complex objects, tending to respond to parts rather than to wholes. This suggests that the younger infants studied by Oakes and Cohen may not have perceived a causal relation in launching effect trials not because they were incapable of doing so, but because their processing capacity was taken up with the problems of object perception. This would not trouble the infants in Leslie's studies because of the simplicity of the stimuli used. Alternatively, even if processing capacity is not exhausted, infants may not be able to perceive a causal relation between two objects until they succeed in perceiving the two objects as such. In either case, causal perception of this type may limited in scope at six months, occurring only for the simplest objects in the infant's environment. This would not be fatal, however, to the argument that this type of causal perception is basic to the development of causal concepts: it is the fact that it occurs at all at six months of age that matters.

Cohen and Oakes (1993) found that, even at 10 months, infants who had been habituated to a noncausal event (e.g. delayed launching) dishabituated to another noncausal event (e.g. launching without collision) as much as to a causal event. Cohen and Oakes (p.425) claimed that the infants were "not responding on the basis of causality but on the basis of the spatial and temporal differences among the events". It is certainly the case, however, that the infants were dishabituating to causal events after habituation with noncausal ones and vice versa: It is therefore possible that the infants were responding both to causality and to spatial and temporal features. It is just this ambiguity that the design used by Leslie and Keeble (1987) ruled out.

Leslie and Keeble (1987) proposed that the launching effect is mediated by a relatively low level visual mechanism, operating on information from lower level processes of motion perception. It is present from birth and not an outcome of learning. A perceptual mechanism of this sort is relatively impervious to other information, reasoning, and general knowledge, a claim supported by the results of studies by Schlottman and Shanks (1992—see Chapter 7). Such a mechanism is not completely isolated from further processing, however: The job of such a system is "to feed central learning systems with descriptions of the environment" (Leslie & Keeble, 1987, p.286). These descriptions form a basis, a set of assumptions in effect, on which further learning and conceptual development may take place. In this case, it is possible that the launching effect plays a fundamental role in the development of causal understanding; not only that, but higher order processes of causal attribution and inference are being applied to information which may already have been causally interpreted by lower level processes in visual perception.

This interpretation is not yet persuasive, for several reasons. First, Oakes and Cohen (1990) reported a developmental trend as described above, and if this finding is valid then it is hard to reconcile with the idea of a fixed visual module. Second, adult research to be reported in Chapter 7 has shown that object properties make a difference to perception of the launching effect, and this conflicts with the idea of a visual module driven only by motion properties. The third reason derives from Cohen and Oakes (1993, experiment 2). In this, infants were habituated to two sequences:

Object A—direct launching—object C
and Object B—delayed launching—object C

They were then tested with:

Object A—delayed launching—object C
and Object B—direct launching—object C

In this test the components of the sequences are all familiar but the sequences are novel. In both cases dishabituation occurred, suggesting that the infants had learned an association between object identity and type of launching. It is hard to reconcile the learning of such associations with a fixed visual module for causal perception, because object identity is not relevant to the module. Clearly, there is a need for replication and extension of studies in this area.

The Iconic Processing Hypothesis

This hypothesis, originally proposed in White (1988), draws on the notion of iconic processing. Iconic memory is a large capacity store prior to attentive processing in which visual information is held for brief amounts of time (Anderson, 1980; Kintsch, 1970). The amount of information held decays to the limited capacity of short-term memory, under near-ideal presentation conditions within about one second (Anderson, 1980; Sperling, 1960). Even under these conditions, however, most information has been lost after 300ms, and the traditional duration of the icon is 250ms (Haber, 1983b). Although originally conceived as a simple register of visual input, iconic memory is now looked on more as a device for perceiving dynamic change, inasmuch as the icon is usually continuously updated by new input (Haber, 1983a; 1983b). Iconic memory, therefore, is more than just a store of information: various forms of processing of information on the iconic time-scale may take place there. Iconic processing functions operate on material integrated over a span of not more than 250ms. Several authors have argued, with supporting evidence, that one function of iconic processing is temporal integration (Adelson, 1983; Bridgeman & Mayer, 1983; Klatzky, 1983; Mace & Turvey, 1983; Philips, 1983; Wilson, 1983). This involves the integration or relation of visual information input at different times but not more than about 250ms apart. This can subserve the detection of change and temporal continuity.

The key to the involvement of iconic processing in cognitive development is that it gives the original psychological definition of an event. An event is *"a sudden change in the amount or type of change in some property of a substance"* (White, 1993, p.47, italics in original), and the key term "sudden" is further defined as change within the time-span of iconic processing: that is, an event is a change of the sort described detected in the temporal integration function of iconic processing (White, 1993, pp.

47–48). Of course, the concept of an event changes during development, but this is where it starts. This observation is absolutely crucial to causal understanding (and to many other things) because causal relations involve events and cannot be comprehended without a concept of an event, or at least not without the psychological construction of events. Causal perception cannot occur unless there are things that we perceive as events (and, by corollary, other things that we perceive not as events).

In the stimuli used by Leslie (1982; 1984a) and Leslie and Keeble (1987) there are many events, only some of which are discriminated by infants as causal. There is a collision between two rectangles in which the moving rectangle stops and the one that was stationary moves. A solitary moving rectangle stops. A solitary stationary rectangle starts moving. A moving rectangle stops and a stationary one moves, despite no physical contact between them. These are all events, meaning that they are or would be detected as such by the temporal integration function of iconic processing. Only the first, however, is perceived causally. What distinguishes it from the others?

It cannot be that the infants are able to perceive actual causal connections because the causal connection perceived in this case is illusory: It is simply an animated film or, in Michotte's studies, a piece of equipment involving black lines painted onto a rotating disc. There is no actual causal relation to be perceived. The key to causal perception, I have argued (White, 1988; 1993), lies in the presence of a conflict between two sorts of cues to object identity. On one side are cues pertaining to object coherence, such as the perception of edges and boundedness, which indicate two objects in the launching effect sequence. On the other side are cues concerning motion, and here the continuity of motion cues is of a sort that would normally indicate just one object.

There is one critical finding bearing on this latter point. In his experiment 29, Michotte (1963) varied the time for which the two rectangles were in contact. Brief pauses did not affect the occurrence of the launching effect. But as contact time increased from about 100ms to about 150ms the launching effect was gradually replaced by perception of two unrelated movements. In experiment 30 Michotte showed subjects a single rectangle in uniform motion, except that it paused briefly in the middle of its movement. The duration of the pause was varied. Brief pauses were not perceived as such. The motion of the rectangle was perceived as discontinuous only when the pause duration was at least 84ms. Subjects perceived a halt on all trials when the pause was at least 168ms. This pattern is virtually identical to that of the change from the launching effect to perception of two unrelated movements in experiment 29. The perception of a causal relation (in experiment 29) was exactly correlated with the perception of continuity in motion of one object (experiment 30).

Only one difference exists between these two sets of stimuli. Michotte used one rectangle in experiment 30 and two, both clearly perceived as such by observers, in experiment 29. This observation demonstrates the role of the conflict between motion continuity cues and object coherence cues in the launching effect. In the launching effect infants (and adults) perceive two distinct objects, and the motion properties of one are transferred, or displaced, onto the other. This is the prototype of a causal relation. Infants are not designed to discriminate causal relations from other events: all we need suppose is that the temporal integration function of iconic processing is functioning in them, and that they use it to detect events, and are sensitive to cues to object unity. The rest follows from this. Nor need we suppose a sophisticated concept of causation: at this stage, no notion of power or efficacy or any such thing need be involved in their perception of the launching effect. It is just a transfer of motion properties from one object to another. This is what distinguishes the launching effect from all other stimuli to which infants in the studies by Leslie (1982; 1984a) and Leslie and Keeble (1987) were exposed.

Further supporting evidence is discussed in White (1993). In essence, under this hypothesis, when there is no conflict between object unity cues, no causal relation should be perceived; conversely, in cases where there is motion continuity but no conflict with other object unity cues, only one object and no causal relation should be perceived. The evidence supports both claims. It is important to note, finally, that the iconic processing hypothesis is compatible with evidence for learning of object–event associations (Cohen & Oakes, 1993), as iconic processing is not divorced from other perceptual and cognitive processes in the way that a fixed low-level visual module would be.

Perception and Action: Self-propelled Objects

Many of the events which an infant perceives, of course, are human actions, and many of these are actions by humans other than the infant perceiver. How do infants perceive such actions? Are they initially perceived just as mechanical interactions of the launching effect variety are perceived, or are there grounds for thinking that infants might distinguish actions from causal relations at the age of a few months?

One approach to this problem is to investigate whether infants discriminate human actions upon objects from other kinds of event. Leslie (1982) performed a relevant experiment. He used two films: one in which a hand entered the field, grasped a Russian doll, and lifted it out of the field, and one in which the same movements of the hand and the doll occurred, but they did not come into contact. Leslie habituated infants as young as three months to one of these and then showed them the other one.

Both orders of presentation were used, and significant dishabituation occurred in both cases. By contrast, comparing the contact film with a film in which the hand entered from the opposite side of the screen and grasped the doll led to no dishabituation.

Leslie (1984b) extended this line of work. His first study was a replication of the one already described, using infants with a mean age of 29 weeks. As Leslie pointed out, the results might just show that the infant is encoding spatial contiguity relations, rather than causal perception. If the former is the case, then it should make no difference what kind of thing picks up the doll. Accordingly, Leslie ran a second experiment in which the standard manual pick-up film was compared with a film in which a white oblong picked up the doll, and to a film in which a hand approached and contacted the doll but did not pick it up. There was also a film in which the oblong contacted the doll but did not pick it up. Each of these four kinds of contact film was compared with a version similar in all respects but involving non-contact: e.g. the white oblong pick-up film was compared with a film in which the same movements of oblong and doll occurred but without contact between them. Infants with a mean age of 28 weeks were habituated to a contact version and then tested with the corresponding non-contact version, or vice versa. The results showed that significant dishabituation occurred only for the manual pick-up film. This shows that infants are not just responding to spatial contiguity relations, but that there is something special about hands, at least as compared to oblongs. Leslie went on to show that this was not due just to the fact that the hand partially occluded the doll in picking it up.

It is not clear how this result should be interpreted. As Leslie (1984b, p.31) pointed out, "infants of this age have just begun to reach for and pick up objects themselves". It is therefore unlikely that the infants are generalising from their own experience of manual pick-up to other hands, although it is possible that infants are responding to the similarity between the manual pick-up and what they see when they pick things up themselves. One other possibility is that infants are perceiving hands (and not oblongs) as agents of change, or that they have some appreciation of the causal powers of hands, at least to the extent of understanding that manual manipulation requires contact. Leslie (1982; 1984b) did not commit himself to an interpretation of this kind, and more research would be necessary to assess it properly. For example, we know that infants do not see hands and oblongs in the same way as far as picking up dolls is concerned, but are there other objects which they do not discriminate from hands, or is there really something special about hands for the infant, in the case of object manipulation?

It is clear, however, that this is not the same kind of phenomenon as the launching effect findings reviewed above, because in this case the infant is discriminating types of object, not patterns of movement. It is hard to resist the notion that this represents some early understanding of what different kinds of objects can and cannot do. Also, if hands are special, this would surely facilitate the generalisation of cause or action concepts from one's own actions to the actions of other human beings. As we shall see, secondary circular reactions involving manual manipulation form a crucial element in the Piagetian account of the development of causal understanding, and if infants have already identified manual pick-up as a perceptual category then the stage is set for generalisation of concepts from their own hand movements to those of others. At present, however, this is mere conjecture.

It would be premature to conclude that infants at the age of six months are applying a concept of agency in perceptions of manual manipulation. There is a possibility, however, that infants could develop some sort of concept of agency from perception alone. A concept of agency is just the notion that a thing moves or behaves on its own, without the influence of external causation (Shultz, 1991). A concept of agency, therefore, could form the core of a concept of action.

The crucial factor, according to Premack (1990) and Shultz (1991), is the ability to distinguish between things that move by themselves and things that are moved by other things. Premack (1990, p.2) suggested that this ability is a hard-wired perception "based not on repeated experience but on appropriate stimulation". He suggested (p.3) that infants divide the world into two kinds of objects: those that are and those that are not self-propelled.

> Self-propelled objects are those objects that can both move and stop moving without assistance from another object; non self-propelled objects are those objects that cannot. Motion per se is not the critical parameter. The non self-propelled object can have as its initial state either rest or motion, but in either case it will retain this state unless acted upon by another object. Change is what is critical—from rest to motion (or vice versa), one speed to another, one direction to another—and the ability of an object to execute these transitions without assistance from another object.

Premack claimed that changes in the movement of self-propelled objects are what infants perceive as intentional. Premack used the term "intention" throughout his article, but "agency" would probably be more appropriate. A concept of intention is considerably more sophisticated than a concept of agency, in that it postulates a particular kind of internal or mental state that guides or controls behaviour (Shultz, 1991). One can have a concept of agency without having a concept of intention, but the converse is not possible. A conceptual distinction between self-propelled and non-self-propelled objects is in effect a concept of agency, but does not imply a concept of intention. In effect, then, Premack claimed that infants are born with a concept of agency which they apply to changes in the movement of self-propelled objects. It is a proposal about a rule for applying a concept.

Shultz (1991) put forward a more extensive proposal about rules. He distinguished two kinds of rule: synchronic rules, which categorise objects, and diachronic rules, which deal with how the environment changes over time. Synchronic rules form the basis for diachronic rules. The rule proposed by Premack is a synchronic rule. Shultz proposed two synchronic rules relating to agency:

1. Agent-move. "If an object moves and its movement has no external cause, then it is an agent" (p.82).
2. Patient-move. "If an object moves, its movement has an external cause, and it is not already known that this object is an agent, then it is a patient" (p.82).

These rules classify objects, not events. Once an object is identified as an agent, the identification sticks. Because of this, the rules are mutually exclusive: An object cannot be both an agent and a patient. The rules are similar to Premack's rule in being based on the distinction between movement that is externally caused and movement that is not, but different in focussing on the initiation of movement, not change. The diachronic rules express implications of the synchronic rules.

1. Move-patient. "If a person wants an object to move, and that object is known to be a patient, then the person should cause the object to move directly" (p.83).
2. Move-agent. "If a person wants an object to move, and that object is an agent, then the person should communicate to the object to move itself" (p.84).
3. Attribute-agent. "If an object moves and is an agent, then expect that there is no external cause of this movement" (p.85).
4. Attribute-patient. "If an object moves and that object is a patient, then assume that there is an external cause of this movement" (p.85).

Again, it is not clear how these rules, or the concept of agency on which they depend, are learned. The best evidence available suggests that they are acquired relatively late in infancy. Rule patient-move may have been acquired by 14 months, but not by 8 months (Poulin-Dubois & Shultz, 1988). Other evidence suggests that, even at 16 months, understanding of this rule remains imperfect (Golinkoff & Harding, 1980), though only one kind of object was used in this study (a chair). Rule move-patient may have been acquired by 10 months (Carlson, 1980), in which case the two synchronic rules must have been acquired by that age. Rule move-agent may be acquired around 17 months (Sexton, 1983).

An interesting feature of the rules proposed by Premack and Shultz is that they predict errors of classification by infants. For example, objects are often moved, or have their movement properties changed, by external causes that are not apparent. A rolling ball slows and stops because of friction; a balloon is blown hither and yon by the wind, which also causes candles to go out. Infants observing such events should classify rolling objects, balloons, and candles as agents, and interpret their behaviour as agency. Since the movement of agents is sometimes externally caused, the movement of objects that have been correctly classified as agents will be misinterpreted by use of the attribute-agent rule on such occasions. There is no evidence concerning whether infants make these errors or not.

In fact, it is not clear that the rules can be used for many objects. Clockwork toys move themselves, but also are moved. Infants move themselves, but are also moved (e.g. carried by adults). Are they agents or patients? It makes more sense for infants to have rules that classify events, not objects, so that infants attribute agency to things as and when they move without apparent external cause, but do not make any judgement that embodies an assumption about how the object will behave next. Problems due to the inconsistency with which things behave can be dealt with later in development. This may be the reason why the rules seem to emerge so late in infancy.

There is a fundamental problem with perceptual data as origins for concepts of agency and causation. When an object moves itself, or to be more precise moves (or changes) without apparent external cause, perceptual data do not reveal how this movement occurs. If we imagine a concept of agency as it would be created by perceptual data alone, it would be that objects just move by themselves. This idea seems nonsensically incomplete to an adult, but that is because we are so accustomed to thinking in terms of internal causes. Our concept of agency is remarkably specific. In the case of our own action, for example, it is not just "action happens", nor even "action happens and is internally caused"; it is, at its simplest, "I do (perform, carry out) my actions". I do not call upon some other kind of internal thing to do my actions for me: I do them myself, and this is basic to my understanding of action (Taylor, 1966). Of course, young infants may not have this concept, but we still have to ask how it can be acquired. How do infants come to see action as internally caused? How do they come to see it as done by "I", whatever that is? How do they learn, presumably later in development, that some agents (such as human beings) have an "I" that performs their actions, and that others (such as clockwork toys) do not? There is nothing in perceptual data alone that could answer these questions for us or give us our concept of action. Therefore it must come from some other source. No doubt perceptual data play a vital role in the development of the concept and of rules for its use, but for its origin we must look elsewhere.

There is a similar problem with the concept of causation. There is strong evidence that, by the age of two years, children understand the causal relation as generative in nature (Shultz, 1982b; Shultz, Fisher, Pratt, & Rulf, 1986). That is, they understand causes as actually producing or generating their effects by a transfer of energy or operation of a causal power. No amount of perceptual data could ever give children such an idea. The idea that would be given by the launching effect stimuli, for example, is one of transfer-of-properties: The movement properties of the cause rectangle are transferred to the effect rectangle. That is all that is perceived. Where do the ideas of power and generation come from? I shall return to this question later in the chapter.

Perception and Learning: The Empiricist Tradition

Premack (1990) took care to assert that the ability to distinguish self-propelled and non-self-propelled objects is not based on repeated experiences. Here he was alluding to a different tradition, according to which causal impressions are acquired by learning. In this empiricist tradition causal judgement is understood as a function of perceived or judged regularities of association, such as covariation between two occurrences or action-outcome contingencies. I shall be reviewing models of this kind in Chapter 6, as all of them have been directed at adult causal judgement. Insofar as they appeal to basic processes of learning, however, they should be applicable to infants as well, and should be able to account for the genesis of causal understanding.

The ancestor of recent empiricist models of causal judgement in psychology is Hume's (1739/1978a) radical empiricist account, described in Chapter 1. In this, causation is treated as a construction of the human mind, and a causal impression is said to arise out of repeated experiences of co-occurrence between two events that satisfy the additional requirements of contiguity and precedency. Psychological models have captured several varieties of regularity of association, including covariation or contingency, conditional relations, and probabilistic association (see Chapter 6). Some models (Shanks & Dickinson, 1987; Shanks, 1993) even account for the way in which a causal impression emerges during the course of experience, allowing for varying degrees of contingency between an effect and a possible cause, with or without other possible causes. The close resemblance between causal learning of this sort and learning phenomena in animal research has been remarked by several authors (Shanks & Dickinson, 1987; Shanks, 1993; Wasserman, 1990a).

The case for an empiricist account as a source of causal understanding depends largely on the claim that causal learning draws on basic processes of learning which operate in humans and other species, in principle at any stage of development. In fact, the empiricist account is fraught with problems. Many of these I have discussed elsewhere (White, 1989; 1992a; 1993; Chapter 6 below), so here I shall review just a few that are particularly relevant to the discussion about origins.

Watson (1984) has pointed out that causal learning in the infant is at least impaired if not precluded by several factors. Watson noted that instrumental learning in infants does not occur when the temporal delay between behaviour and reinforcement exceeds three seconds. The importance of this is revealed by data collected by Watson (1984), showing that contingencies in mother–infant interactions frequently involve temporal delays greater than three seconds, so that the probability that the infant will detect a relation between its behaviour and subsequent events is very low. In addition, the causal structure in the real world experienced by the infant is generally quite imperfect. Many of the infant's behaviours may have no (consistent) consequence (for example when the mother fails to respond to some behaviour as she usually does), and reinforcements, such as the mother's responses, are not always contingent on the infant's behaviour. Under natural conditions, therefore, Watson concluded that the infant would probably fail to perceive the existence of any causal relation. Watson (1984) attempted to save the day by proposing that the infant is naturally equipped to analyse contingencies between behaviour and consequent stimulus events. He suggested that the infant could mark and store events with both sensory qualities (e.g. intensity) and time of occurrence, and detect causal relations on the basis of similarities in sensory patterns. The general idea (p.156) is that "infants may use something analogous to conditional probability analysis in their perception of ... the causal efficacy of their behaviour". This places Watson's account in the same camp as the probabilistic contrast model (Cheng & Novick, 1990; 1992; and see Chapter 6), so it will be interesting to see whether research findings support Watson's ideas.

There are some action–outcome relations to which the problems identified by Watson do not apply. For example, Stern (1985, p.80) wrote:

Self events generally have contingent relations very different from events with another. When you suck your finger, your finger gets sucked—and not just generally sucked, but with a sensory synchrony between the tongue and palate sensations and the complementary sensations of the sucked finger. When your eyes close, the world goes dark. When your head turns and eyes move, the visual sights change. And so on. For virtually all self-initiated actions upon the self, there is a felt consequence. A constant schedule of reinforcement results.

Such events may provide the basis for an account of acquisition of causal understanding making reference to contingencies. However, event contingencies of the sort described by Stern are particularly bad candidates for generalisation to other objects, because the effects are private experiences that are not observable in others. Object manipulation (Leslie, 1984b) is a better candidate, but object manipulation does not commence until the stage of secondary circular reactions, which is too late for it to be the point of origin (see pp. 51–52).

There can be little doubt that action–outcome contingencies are important in the development of understanding; for example, you can't know if you have successfully realised an intention unless you compare what you got to what you wanted. But are such contingencies *basic* to the acquisition of concepts of causation and action? There are several reasons for thinking that they are not. One is the requirement of any empiricist theory that repeated occurrences are necessary for a causal impression to occur. Not only research on the launching effect (Leslie & Keeble, 1987) but also the work of Piaget (1954) shows that this is not correct and that single instances are sufficient for inference of causal relation under some circumstances. We shall see shortly how Piaget explained such immediate causal learning; at any rate, it shows that the excessive cognitive demands of the Humean approach, which involves storing and marking numerous instances in memory, are not necessary for causal learning.

Piaget (1954) had a further argument against the Humean approach. Suppose an infant perceives a causal relation entirely independent of his or her own actions; suppose, for example, that the infant observes an adult drumming his or her fingers on a tin box to make a sound. If the infant is a naïve regularity theorist, he or she should get the idea that the drumming of the fingers is the cause of the noise, from repeated observations of the association of the two in conjunction with temporal and spatial contiguity. The test for this is what happens when the adult ceases the activity; if the infant wants the effect to continue, how do they go about making it do so? If they have the idea that the drumming of the fingers is the cause, they should try to act on the cause, for example by giving the fingers a light push to get them to start again.

In fact nothing like that happened. Piaget reported several observations in which infants aged about seven months treated the cause, the fingers, as if its action depended on the infant's own action, for example by striking the hand or shaking it vigorously. In several more cases the infant did not try to act on the cause at all but merely put into operation magical procedures for bringing about effects, such as arching its back, as if these would make the effect happen again. This is contrary to what a regularity-based theory would predict; infants are not merely learning contingencies, but operating as if they had a simple, general theory under which what makes things happen is their own action. In the cases observed by Piaget, there was not the slightest empirical justification for such an idea.

Piaget's account depends heavily on observation and interpretation, often of an anecdotal character. But the general features of his interpretation are consistent with research on older children, to be reviewed later: there is a strong consensus that children are hypothesis-testers, who generate ideas from single instances rather than patterns of occurrences, and who are selective in their use of information to test their ideas, rather than neutral registers of information about regularities (Kuhn, 1989). Such a procedure is entirely contrary to the Humean approach because, at its extreme, judgement of covariation is determined by causal beliefs and hypotheses, rather than causal beliefs by judged covariation. Children are not Humeans; the most plausible extrapolation from this is that infants are not Humeans either.

The final and insurmountable obstacle for the learning theory approach is the point already made that the kind of perceptual data involved in Humean analysis simply do not yield causal ideas. The basic datum for Humean analysis is an instance of co-occurrence of two things. The only product of Humean analysis of multiple instances of a given sort is the idea of regular co-occurrence, or regular temporal succession, of the two things concerned. The data themselves do not generate any ideas other than that. If we ask where the idea of causal relation comes from, given a priori that there is an unlimited number of ideas that might be attached to the data, it is immediately clear that the empiricist tradition has no answer. Whatever role regularity information might have in the development of causal understanding, it is a subsidiary role, perhaps concerned with the acquisition of particular causal beliefs: it cannot explain how basic causal concepts originate.

ACTION AND CAUSATION: PIAGET ON EFFICACY AND PHENOMENALISM

Piaget proposed six main subdivisions of the sensorimotor period, during which the infant proceeds from a phenomenal world lacking any division between self and other, inner and outer space, objects, spatial relations, or abstract concepts with which to interpret experience, to one in which all of these things have been attained, at least at an elementary level. The development of causal understanding proceeds hand in hand with these general aspects of cognitive development.

Stages 1 and 2

The origins of causal understanding at these two stages lie with two kinds of experience that Piaget called efficacy and phenomenalism. Of these, efficacy is the more important. Efficacy is an experience that accompanies action, though it is not at all easy to define. Piaget (1954, p.228) wrote:

> Whether the nursling at the age of one or two months succeeds in sucking his thumb after having attempted to put it into his mouth or whether his eyes follow a moving object, he must experience, though in different degrees, the same impression: namely that, without his knowing how a certain action leads to a different result, in other words, that a certain complex of efforts, tension, expectation, desire, etc., is charged with efficacy.

The feeling of efficacy is located at the point of culmination of the action: the infant does not, however, know how a certain action leads to a certain result. Uzgiris (1984, p.132) commented that this places the source of causal understanding at "the juncture of effort and the resulting outcome". It is the word "juncture" that is important here, because there is no idea of cause and effect and relation between them; that is, no idea of two things related in a particular way; there is just the *one* thing, the experience of efficacy in the bringing about of things willed or desired.

The other half of the point of origin is phenomenalism, that is to say, the phenomenal contiguity of two events (Piaget & Inhelder, 1969). Phenomenal contiguity does not require spatial contiguity. Two events may go together in experience even though there is no spatial relation between them. This means that any two events may possess phenomenal contiguity for the infant: there are no limits on the possibilities, other than those imposed by the limited psychological functioning of the infant, and whatever structuring of experience may occur at this early stage. This in turn means that any two events may be candidates for causal relation; there is no restriction to things that are spatially contiguous, or to things that possess any specific quality or property. At these first two stages, there is only phenomenal contiguity: nothing more conceptually sophisticated is involved.

Stage 3

This is the stage of secondary circular reactions: infants are now able to co-ordinate prehension and vision, for example directing the movement of their hands while looking at them. According to Piaget (1954, p.233), the effect of this accomplishment for development of causal understanding is the dissociation of cause and effect, "the cause being identified with the effectual purpose and the effect with the phenomena perceived". Infants thus understand the efficacy of desire, effort, and purpose (p.234), "in short, the whole dynamism of conscious action".

There is, however, no notion of a causal mechanism other than the mere efficacy of action. Causal understanding is still dominated by phenomenal contiguity, and limited by a failure to appreciate spatial relations. Piaget observed that when infants at this stage achieve an interesting result, e.g. by pulling a string, they will tend to repeat the hand movement as if not appreciating the importance of contact with the string, as if the hand movement alone was sufficient to bring about the result. In fact, a gesture which an infant learns is efficacious in producing one thing is used as if it were efficacious in producing anything; the idea of a specific cause for a given effect has not yet been learned.

So at this stage the notion of efficacy still dominates the concept of the causal relation; cause and effect are dissociated with such things as intention, purpose, desire, and effort on the cause side and the outcome of action on the effect side, but there is no notion of limits on the efficacy of a particular cause, and phenomenal contiguity is enough. Any two things that possess phenomenal contiguity can be seen as causally related, given only the experience of efficacy as an accompaniment. Most important, infants' only idea of cause at this stage (seven months) is their own activity.

All of this must be qualified by one further observation, which is that causality by imitation occurs at this stage. As soon as infants have learned how to imitate, they use imitation as a way of bringing about the thing imitated. Piaget argued that this is not fundamentally different from the other causal understanding exhibited at this stage, in that the idea of the cause is still the infant's own activity. There is one difference, however, and that is that not just any activity will do; the thing about imitation is that the infant is using a specific activity to bring about a specific effect, and the match between the two matters. So it appears that, in this case at least, there is some appreciation of causal specificity.

Stage 4

This stage, occuring between nine and eleven months, is a transitional stage as far as causal development is concerned. The main development is an appreciation of spatial contiguity: efficacy comes to be understood as working only through physical contact with the thing acted upon. The first forms of this are drawing things to oneself and pushing them away.

There may also be some dim appreciation of other centres of causation. For example, when an infant pushes away a spoon bringing medicine to the mouth, Piaget (1954) argued that this is an attempt to prevent what the thing pushed away is going to do, and that this therefore shows understanding that the thing can do something—i.e. that it is an independent centre of action. Similarly, when an infant touches the mother's lips to make her start singing again, this shows not only a belief in the importance of physical contact for making something happen, but also an understanding of activity—singing, in this case—that is not their own activity.

According to Piaget there is still no true objectification of causation because infants have not yet achieved object permanence. But objectification, spatialisation, and the distinction between self and other, or inner and outer worlds, are beginning to emerge.

Stage 5

There are four main achievements at this stage, about 12 months. First, infants have now acquired the idea of object permanence, and with this goes a belief that objects can have lasting powers of their own. For example, "Jacqueline is before me and I blow into her hair. When she wants the game to continue she does not try to act through efficacious gestures nor even, as formerly, to push my arms or lips; she merely places herself in position, head tilted, sure that I will do the rest by myself" (Piaget, 1954, p.275). Piaget claimed (p.276) that "the child considers the person of another as an entirely autonomous source of actions".

Second, causal relations are fully spatialised. That is, infants have a full understanding of spatial relationships, such as one thing being on top of another. This enables the use of instruments such as sticks as intermediaries between the infant's own action and some other thing acted upon.

Third, infants understand the importance of specificity in the cause, that is that not just any action that feels efficacious will do to bring about some desired effect. This is important because it marks a transition from causation understood as the omnipotence of mere efficacy to causation understood as the operation of specific powers, each limited in scope.

Fourth, efficacy and phenomenalism become dissociated. Infants now distinguish between self and everything else, and no longer consider all things as caused by the efficacy of their own actions. Other things are independent centres of causal powers. Efficacy becomes confined to the realm of the infant's's own activity, and is understood as the direct power exerted by his or her own intentions or will on his or her body (Piaget, 1954, p.287). Phenomenalism becomes the basis for the understanding of physical causality. This dissociation reinforces the distinction between the outer world and the self.

Stage 6

Infants at stage 5 are limited in being able to perceive causes but not to "evoke them when only their effects are given" (Piaget, 1954, p.293). The accomplishment of stage 6, then, is the capability of representing causality: that is, infants can construct or imagine causes not seen, and can foresee effects by starting from a given cause. As Piaget stated (p.298), "representation is necessary to the concept of the universe as a lasting system of causal connections" and (p.308) "the construction of schemata of a causal kind is completely interconnected with that of space, of objects, and of temporal series". At this point infants leave the sensorimotor stage, and it is this capacity that underlies the rapid development of the concepts of intentionality and causation documented by research on young children (Shultz, 1980; 1982b).

Comments

The essence of Piaget's disagreement with the Humean tradition lies with the notion of circular reactions. Under the Humean scheme infants would be represented as basically passive, with ideas of causation merely arising out of repeated experiences of appropriate kinds, without any reasoning or process of understanding. Circular reactions, on the other hand, are directed, having a motive power which tends toward the reproduction of an interesting result. Piaget argued (1954, p.311) that "it is always, during the earliest stages, on the occasion of personal activity that causal connections are established", and his justification for this was that circular reactions show, indeed depend on, some appreciation of the connection between action and result. One cannot direct one's activity in such a way as to aim to reproduce an interesting result if one has no idea of any connection between action and result. The Piagetian infant is active, and discovers causality through action. The key features of secondary circular reactions are efficacy and phenomenal contiguity, and these form the basis for all subsequent development of causal understanding.

Understanding of infants' capacities has moved on since this account (Carey & Gelman, 1991). Piaget argued that infants do not achieve object permanence until late in the sensorimotor period, but research now suggests that infants may have object permanence as early as 3.5 months and probably by 4.5 months (Baillargeon, 1987). Thus, the cognitive foundation for a concept of causal powers as stable (and, indeed, for categorisation of objects as agents or patients) is laid much earlier than Piaget thought. He also argued that infants lack any appreciation of spatial relations until stage 4 of the sensorimotor period, around 10 months of age. The research by Leslie (1982; 1984a; 1984b; Leslie & Keeble, 1987) shows that infants have some appreciation of spatial relations around six months. For example in the manual pick-up films, infants discriminated contact from non-contact films (Leslie, 1982; 1984b). Infants discriminated contact from non-contact trials in the launching effect stimuli (Leslie, 1982; 1984a; Leslie & Keeble, 1987) at about the same age. These results suggest that the differentiation between concepts of action and causation may occur earlier than Piaget thought, or indeed that they have separate origins. There is evidence that imitation occurs as early as the first hour of life (Meltzoff & Moore, 1977; Meltzoff & Gopnik, 1989), although questions remain over both the replicability of these findings and whether the behaviours observed are really imitation or not (Flavell, Miller, & Miller, 1993). It remains unclear, however, how much use infants actually make of this capacity in cognitive development before reaching stage 3 of the sensorimotor period; in particular, whether it can be put to use in the specific role of causality by imitation, meaning the use of imitation deliberately to bring about a repetition of the event imitated.

Piaget also claimed that, in the earliest sensorimotor stages, infants have no differentiation between inner and outer worlds, or self and not-self, and no co-ordination of sensory modalities. These claims are rather unsatisfactorily grounded in the fact that there is no evidence to the contrary. The methodological problems of research on the conceptual and cognitive accomplishments of infants are so severe that we must beware of underestimating infantile capabilities, just as we must beware of inventing abilities and cognitive mechanisms that are more sophisticated than is strictly necessary to explain the infant's behavioural accomplishments.

A further problem is that Piaget lacked a theory of action, or, to be precise, a theory of infantile action. When writing about the causes of action in infants he referred to such things as desires, intentions, purposes, and effort. Not only is it not clear what any of these things might be, there is no understanding of how any of them is involved in the production of action, if at all. According to some philosophers, e.g. Taylor (1966), none of them is. This is vitally important because it is in the causes of action that the idea of a cause originates, under Piaget's account. Not only that, but whatever cognitive or other processes are involved in the construction of a concept of action, they can only work on information that is available to them about how action is produced. It follows that, if the actual producers of action are hidden from these processes, whatever that expression means, they cannot form the basis of a concept of action.

It is difficult to know exactly what can be salvaged from Piaget's account because problems of validity and interpretation remain, not to mention the general scarcity of evidence. If some things are not exactly as Piaget thought, this in itself does not imply that other things in his account are also inaccurate. It is fairly certain, however, that some things have been learned by the end of the sensorimotor period (or around eighteen months, if the notion of the sensorimotor period itself is contentious), and one can at least put upper if not lower limits on their age of acquisition.

THEORIES OF ACTION AND CAUSATION

I propose that, by the age of two years, the infant is in possession of two basic theories, of action and causation respectively. I propose that these theories have a common origin, and become differentiated through the gradual acquisition of concepts and rules of application. Once formed, the basic theories persist essentially unaltered throughout life. Two types of change occur: addition of new concepts to the theoretical structure (sometimes coupled with deletion or modification of existing concepts so long as these are not at the basic level); and addition and modification of rules for the application of the theories in the interpretation of behaviour and events. In expounding the infant's two theories I have three main tasks: (1) to outline the essential ingredients of the theories; (2) to look among the available evidence in order to ascertain their origin and (latest) age of acquisition; and (3) to set the two theories in the context of psychological metaphysics, the basic assumptions on which the theories depend and from which they draw much of their meaning. First, the common point of origin of the two theories.

Origin: The Production of Action

From earliest times, according to Piaget (1954), infants have experience, not of contingencies between actions and outcomes, but of efficacy in the production of action. In White (1993) I proposed that the experience of efficacy was the point of origin of the two theories of action and causation, the earliest ingredient around which all else is constructed. The main problem with this is that it is not precisely clear from Piaget's account what he supposed efficacy to be. It is clear that it is intimately associated with the production of action, and that it is located at the juncture between action and result, though at earliest times the infant does not differentiate between these two things. This still leaves much unclear about the nature of the experience, however. Rather than try to fathom out the full and proper meaning of efficacy, I shall therefore define the point of origin in a slightly different and hopefully unambiguous way, with the aid of Taylor (1966; 1974).

The aim of Taylor's analysis was to strip away from the concept of action all that is inessential to it. The outcome of this, as described in Chapter 1, is just that I, the actor, produce my actions. This is meant to reject and contrast with claims that something else, such as a mental state of mine or a concept of self, is the cause of actions. In addition it is understood to be up to the actor what he or she does (again as opposed to it being up to some desire or intention, for example). There are two justifications for this view. One is that, under Taylor's analysis, nothing else can be found that is essential and exclusive to action. The other is an appeal to experience; I know that I produce my own actions because I experience myself doing so. The knowledge is given in the experience. And this is not just the production of action viewed, as it were, passively, from the outside. It is the actor's active involvement in the production of action. That is the kind of experience it is. Moreover, this experience of production lies not in the relation between action and result, but in the relation between actor and action.

This, then, is what I now propose as the origin, the starting point, for development of theories of action and causation: the actor's (infant's) experience of actually producing his or her own actions. It is an empirical question exactly what counts as action. Presumably many behaviours exhibited by infants are not accompanied by the experience of production: reflex behaviours would be an example. It needs only some behaviours to be actions for the infant to have the experience of producing action. Also, let me remind readers of Taylor's caveat about the concept of self (1966, p.135, italics in original): "In saying that my actions are caused by myself, I mean *only* that I cause them or make them occur, and this is in fact inconsistent with saying that something else, to be referred to as my *self*, is the real cause of them". The present view therefore does not require infants to have a concept of self.

An attractive feature of the proposal is its simplicity. The production of action is a single feature of a single instance, and there is no need either for relation between two things or for the accumulation of a record of experiences. The origins of concepts are likely to lie with the most simple things, because these are most immediate for the infant. The job of relating two things, or of appreciating a relation between two things in such a way as to yield a concept, is surely more difficult than just appreciating a single common experience. It would therefore be easier to begin cognitive development with a single experience as a basis than with a relation made between two experiences; the latter requires that the infant notice both *and* notice that they go together, which is asking a lot more than experiencing the production of action asks.

Moreover, and this is the strongest available support for the proposal, it forms a plausible antecedent to the later notion of the causal relation as generative or productive. Indeed there is no other plausible antecedent; as I have already argued, relations between events only give the idea of contingency or diachronic structure, and perceived collision events only give the idea of transfer of properties. It is hard to imagine what could give rise to a notion of production other than the actual experience of producing. Without this, even the events involved in the smashing of a plate by a hammer would be understood as nothing more than mere temporal succession, not essentially different from the succession of notes in a tune.

At the beginning, then, we need not assume that infants have anything more or other than the experience of producing their own actions. During the first 18 months of life three main kinds of development take place in the theories of action and causation. One is the generalisation of the idea of production to actions and events not accompanied by the experience of production (e.g. the actions of others). The second is the acquisition of what might be called specifying conditions, which say in effect just what can happen or be made to happen, to what, how, and when. The third is the differentiation between action and causation as distinct theories of how things happen.

Generalisation of the Concept of Production

The concept of production or generation is common to the theories of action and causation (Shultz, 1982a), and is the clearest sign of their common origin. Somehow, infants must come to understand that production is involved in all sorts of events which are not accompanied (for them) by the experience of production. Infants have the idea of other centres of causation perhaps by stage 4 and certainly by stage 5 of the sensorimotor period (see pp. 52–54). Whether this understanding involves the concept of production, however, is not clear. Piaget's observations are consistent with the idea that the infant has merely learned that some things predictably behave in certain ways, and learning this much does not depend on mastery of a concept of production. There is evidence that this concept has been generalised to other, impersonal, causes by the age of two years (Shultz, 1982b), but other developments to be discussed shortly suggest that it could have been generalised much earlier.

How can infants make the inductive leap from their own experience to other events? The most straightforward way would be via the recognition of similarity between things they do themselves and other things they observe happening. For example, an infant might hit a toy xylophone with a hammer, producing a sound of a certain pitch; an adult might then do the same. The infant could in principle observe similarity between the movement–outcome complex in these two cases, and attribute the concept of production to the adult's action by inductive generalisation. This form of inductive generalisation depends on salient resemblance of features and on the modus operandi of mechanisms of induction in infants. Imitation is a good opportunity for generalisation because the temporal gap between action and imitation is small, thus making it easier for infants to notice the similarity without undue strain on memory, and the fact that there are often several iterations of imitation in one sequence enables a strong record of experience to be built up over a short period of time, further facilitating the abstraction of similarity information. It must be admitted, however, that little is known about induction by infants, so at present further speculation about generalisation of the concept of production is unprofitable.

Acquisition of Specifying Conditions

In any causal relation or action having some kind of outcome there are three classes of specifying condition, relating to the thing on the cause side, the thing on the effect side, and the relevant conditions under which the causal relation occurs. In the language of causal powers theory (White, 1989; 1992a; 1993) these are, respectively, causal powers, liabilities or resistances, and releasing conditions or opportunities. (In cases of mere action not involving other things, such as just raising one's arm, liabilities do not enter the account.) I shall deal with each of these in turn.

The concept of a causal power relates to production in that it is a capacity to produce an effect. The causal power of a hammer to smash a plate is a property of the hammer understood by adults as normally possessing two features: stability and specificity. A causal power is specific: a given power operates to produce a given kind of effect (or a range of effects varying along a specific parameter) and nothing else. The causal power of a hammer to smash a plate is a causal power to smash that plate, or plates of that kind. A power is also stable. Powers are not required to be permanently possessed by things, but we normally assume that they endure, particularly if the object possessing them undergoes no apparent change. The power of the hammer to smash a plate is possessed by the hammer at all times, even though it is only occasionally manifest.

A causal power is our concept of a cause (as opposed to a causal relation). The concept of a cause requires differentiation between cause and effect. According to Piaget (1954), this happens at stage 3 as a result of the development of secondary circular reactions. In this case the cause is located in the infant's action or its immediate precursors (Piaget mentioned such things as desire, purpose, and intention). The earliest observable sign of understanding of stability in a causal power is the tendency to repeat a specific efficacious action: repetition of the action, resulting in reproduction of its effect, engenders appreciation of the *continuation* of the power to bring about that effect. The idea of stability in a causal power may therefore be grounded in the tendency to repeat an efficacious action. The tendency to repeat efficacious actions has certainly begun by the time infants start to engage in causality by imitation. According to Piaget (1954) this happens at stage 3; if so, then at stage 3 infants have acquired part of the concept of a causal power, stability.

At stage 3, however, infants do not appreciate the specificity of the relation between action and result, behaving as if any action accompanied by the experience of efficacy could produce any effect. The earliest unequivocal evidence of specificity, according to Piaget's account, comes at stage 5, where infants have learned that not just any action that feels efficacious will do to produce a desired effect. By stage 5, then, infants have acquired the two main features of the concept of a power, stability and specificity. This is important because both, under this account, have their source in infants' experiences of their own action and the results of their actions.

In the theory of powerful particulars (Harré & Madden, 1975) a liability is a causal power, but passive rather than active. That is, it describes what an object can have done to it, as opposed to what it can do. For example, in saying that copper is malleable we are saying that it has the liability, the passive power, to undergo changes of shape when beaten with a hammer. Accounts of the understanding of causation and action in infancy have focused on causes and the causal relation, and have neglected liabilities. Cause–effect relations are, nonetheless, relations between active causal powers and liabilities. In a sense, understanding a power entails understanding a liability; saying that a hammer has the causal power to smash a plate implies that the plate has the liability to be smashed by the hammer. In this sense, therefore, infants presumably learn about liabilities as they learn about powers.

As in the case of powers, liabilities are stable and specific. Infants may have plenty of experience of things being acted upon: Possible examples include the object acted upon in launching effect stimuli, objects manipulated by hands (Leslie, 1984b), things acted upon by the infant, and infants themselves when acted upon by others. The last of these may be particularly important, because for the infant there is an unambiguous marker of the difference between acting and being acted upon, and that is the presence or absence of the experience of efficacy. Thus, in acting the infant experiences efficacy, but in being acted upon there is no such experience. It is tempting to suggest that this marks the origin of the conceptual distinction between active and passive powers. On the other hand, the infant's experience of acting upon objects is also likely to be important. Consider banging a rattle: Just as infants can learn about the stability and specificity of causal powers by learning the specificity of the action needed to produce a noise from the rattle, and its repeatability, so they can learn about the specificity and stability of the liability of the rattle by learning the specificity of the effect produced by their action, and the repeatability of that. In summary, there are several possible sources of a concept of liability in infancy, and it seems likely that the concepts of power and liability develop in tandem. Unfortunately, however, there is no direct evidence on this.

A releasing condition is a condition under which, in the adult concept of causation, a cause operate to produce its effect. For example, for a hammer smashing a plate, the releasing condition is forcible contact of hammer with plate; for acid turning litmus paper pink, it is immersion of litmus paper in the acid. The most likely point of origin of this concept in infancy is the appreciation of spatial relations. The earliest sign of understanding of spatial relations in causation occurs in perception of mechanical interactions, such as those studies by Leslie (1982; 1984a) and Leslie and Keeble (1987). That is, insofar as causal perception can be said to occur in these cases, it depends on spatial and temporal contiguity of cause and effect, where these are located in different objects. Infants seem to be perceiving such mechanical interactions as different from other sorts of stimuli at the age of four months, although whether they can be said to have a concept as such at that age is open to question. This differential perception may, however, constitute the source and origin of such a concept.

If it is true as Leslie and Keeble (1987) proposed that the launching effect represents the operation of a low-level visual module, then it is doubtful whether it could contribute to development in this way. As we have seen, however, this interpretation is still open to question. Particularly relevant is the finding by Cohen and Oakes (1993) that infants appear to learn associations between specific objects and types of launching. If this finding is valid then not only does it show the launching effect to be subject to learning, but it may even lay the ground for acquisition of beliefs about causal powers. Causal powers, after all, are beliefs specific to objects or types of object concerning what they can and cannot do to other objects: it is necessary for beliefs of this type to develop that infants or children learn associations between objects and effects to develop, and the findings of Cohen and Oakes may show the earliest stages in this process. If this is right, then causal perception as in the launching effect is fully integrated with the general development of causal understanding.

Although at the age of two years children still have much to learn about particular causal powers and liabilities of things, and conditions under which particular powers operate, there is therefore evidence that they have some grasp of the basic concepts of specifying conditions by the end of the sensorimotor period. The ages given in this account should of course be regarded as upper limits; in general, research since Piaget has tended to push back specific competencies earlier into infancy (e.g. Baillargeon, 1987), and it would not be surprising if infants had a grasp of ideas such as stability and specificity of causal powers before they developed much competence in the application of them to particular objects and tasks. One development remains to be discussed, and this is the differentiation between causation and action. This is primarily an issue of psychological metaphysics.

THE PSYCHOLOGICAL METAPHYSICS OF ACTION AND CAUSATION

Causal Perception and Psychological Metaphysics

In White (1993) I touched on the psychological metaphysics of causal perception, but in a purely theoretical analysis. Simply, the perception of a causal relation as in the launching effect depends on more basic psychological axioms. I emphasised the fact that we operate as if we had a naive realist metaphysics of primary substances with properties. This means, among other things, that we understand the world as composed of distinct objects possessed of (1) natural persistence in time (i.e. persistence is axiomatic and requires no explanation); (2) substance or solidity (best understood by contrast with mental things); (3) a kind of identity that transcends (some) changes in their properties. It is apparent that these axioms play a part in perception of the launching effect, for the effect depends on our understanding that two substantial and persisting objects with distinct identities are involved. In Michotte's studies this is an illusion, and the fact that it occurs helps to show the fundamental nature of these assumptions and the role they play in perception. If the illusion is broken (for example, when viewing conditions become degraded so that the boundaries of the objects in space are no longer certain) the launching effect does not occur (Michotte, 1963).

Since writing that book I have discovered more of Michotte's research on the fundamental understanding of the world as revealed in the phenomena of visual perception (several papers in Thinès, Costall, & Butterworth, 1991). The research carried out by Michotte and his colleagues revealed to him a set of fundamental concepts similar to those I outlined in my theoretical treatment: "the reality of things; the persistence of their substantial identity during change (displacement or transformation); the continuity of their existence despite the discontinuity of their presence in our experience" (Michotte, 1991d, p.224, italics in original). Michotte added phenomenal causality to this list, but it is clear that this must be less basic then the assumptions listed here: "our basic *concepts* concerning the physical world (such as causality) are represented at the strictly sensory level by characteristic, primitive *impressions* (such as 'pushing' or 'launching'). Furthermore, these impressions can be regarded as constituting an *actual prefiguration* of such concepts" (p.225, italics in original). In other words, the concepts that make up the psychological metaphysics of the physical owe something, if not everything, to primitive impressions produced by definable patterns of stimulation in an organism with a particular kind of visual system.

Michotte worked only with adult subjects, but there is a clear implication that such impressions, and the fundamental assumptions to which they relate, should be in operation from earliest times. More recent research supports this implication. For example, infants seem to have some appreciation of the solidity and persistence of objects at 2.5 months of age (Carey & Gelman, 1991). At three months infants appear able to perceive objects as unified, bounded wholes separate from backgrounds (Spelke, 1982). At four months infants can perceive the unity of a partially occluded object (e.g. a rod the central portion of which is occluded by a block) if motion properties of the visible parts of the rod conform to the Gestalt principle of common fate (Kellman, Spelke, & Short, 1986). In addition to these studies of perception there are also studies of object permanence (Baillargeon, 1987), showing that infants around four months of age have some understanding of the natural persistence and substantiality of physical objects (although this finding has been strenuously contested by Fisher and Bidell, 1991). The psychological metaphysics of physical objects are to a large extent established early in life. Spelke (1991) argued that in certain respects physical knowledge present in infancy (by four months) constitutes core principles of reasoning about physical objects that remain constant throughout life. These respects are: continuity of motion, solidity, rigidity, and mechanical causation (as she expressed it, no action at a distance). The similarity of this to Michotte's fundamental concepts and to my psychological metaphysics of the physical world is striking. Other things that may seem similar, such as concepts of gravity and inertia and other forms of inference, are developmentally and conceptually quite distant from these basic principles.

This research, and Michotte's arguments, bring into focus the most important issue for this topic. The launching effect, and the perceptual phenomena discussed in this section, are all phenomena of visual perception. I have been arguing that at least some of our most basic understanding of causation (and action) originates in action, both action in itself and action upon objects. It can hardly be denied that infants learn a great deal about the physical world not just through visual perception of it, but by acting upon it. The issue concerns how these two sources of knowledge come to be integrated in our mature understanding of the physical world and physical causation. While there is now a great deal of research on the relation between perception and conceptual development, and while there is the complementary Piagetian tradition of study of cognitive development in relation to action, little seems to be known about the integration between these two that must occur. Take solidity, for example. Is the solidity of objects an innate concept, or an invariance afforded through visual perception, or a concept grounded initially in tactile experience and the active manipulation of objects? If two or all three of these things contribute to our understanding of solidity, how do they come together? There is much still to be learned.

Understanding the Mental and the Physical

There is hardly anything more obvious to us as adults than the profound distinction between the mental and the physical. Our inner world of experience seems to us totally unlike the outer world of inanimate objects such as stones and tables. Yet there is a great deal that we have to learn about this distinction. We have to learn just what it is that distinguishes the mental and the physical from each other. We also have to learn what other sorts of things have minds—not necessarily minds possessing all of our own mental capacities, but minds nonetheless. Even as adults we have trouble with this. We cannot gain direct or trustworthy evidence of other minds, so we depend for our beliefs on criteria for attributing minds. Which of the following do you think have minds? Chimpanzees, dolphins, cats, birds, fish, computers. By what criteria are you making your judgements? Why those criteria?

At what age do children attribute mental states to others, and at what age do they understand the states they attribute as mental? According to Perner (1991) this question is properly answered by reference to three criteria.

1. Inner experience. We naturally understand inner experience as essential to mentality. But to attribute inner experience to others, Perner argued, just having inner experience ourselves is not enough. We must in some sense know or be aware that we have it. Attributing inner experience to others depends on us having this knowledge or awareness, whatever form it takes, in a form suitable for use in processes, such as processes of inference and attribution. According to Perner it is perhaps impossible to say when infants first achieve this, but he made a case for them having achieved it by the time they show empathic responses to others, around the second year of life.

2. Theoretical constructs. When children attribute such things as beliefs and desires to others they are certainly attributing concepts, or theoretical constructs. This alone, however, does not show an understanding of mind as such because, as Perner (1991) argued, children may have theoretical constructs relating to purely physical things as well. The assumption of continued existence of a thing that has gone out of sight is

an example. Perner argued that we can be sure that children have an understanding of states like beliefs and desires as mental when they show that they can link such theoretical constructs to inner experience. (One could add the corrollary, not mentioned by Perner, that they must also not be linking concepts of purely physical states such as substantiality to inner experience.) Perner again cited the occurrence of empathic reactions to others as evidence for this.

3. Intentionality (in the sense of "aboutness"). The Intentionality of, say, a desire concerns the sense in which a desire is about something or has an object. In this sense, children have some grasp of the Intentionality of mental states around the age of two years (Wellman & Woolley, 1990). A full understanding of Intentionality, however, seems not to be acquired until the age of four years or even later. It is only at this age, for example, that children appreciate that a belief may misrepresent its object; that is, represent something about an object that is not true of it (Perner, 1991).

Although children by the age of two years still have much to learn about the mind, it seems likely that they have succeeded in characterising the mental in terms of inner experience, a particular set of theoretical constructs, and Intentionality. Perner's analysis, although valuable for this contribution, leaves many questions unanswered. First, are these the right criteria for identifying the mental? Under the functionalist view the mind is understood as a set of capacities (Kenny, 1989). What matters about a mental state is not what it is (e.g. it is a desire, it has the intrinsic qualities characteristic of desire) but what it does, for example its dispositional relation to action. Having a certain desire amounts to a tendency to engage in a certain sort of action; knowing French enables one to utter meaningful and grammatical French sentences; and so on. By the age of two children do seem to have some understanding of the specificity of relations between desires and actions (Wellman & Woolley, 1990, and see Chapter 3). To understand these capacities or functions as *mental*, again it is presumably necessary that children link them to inner experience. Perner (1991) has argued persuasively that this link has been made by the age of two years. It is therefore possible to conclude that children have some understanding of mental capacities or functions by that age. There is, however, still much to learn about how that understanding originates and develops.

A second important question concerns how children understand the physical, as distinct from the mental. It is not enough to say that children understand the mental in terms of inner experience, theoretical constructs, Intentionality, and function, if they have the same view of the physical. In a sense we understand the mental much better than the physical by virtue of having our own inner experience. For our understanding of the physical we depend on the evidence of our senses and how we interpret that, or on the received wisdom of those around us. The problem, moreover, is not just to understand *this* thing at *this* moment, but to understand the essential and general features of the physical, those that all that is physical possesses in contradistinction to all that is mental. This is no trivial problem: certain traditions in both Western and Eastern philosophy have found it easier to deny the existence of the physical as such than to deny the existence of the mental or spiritual as such.

It seems natural to assume a priori that infants at earliest times would be solipsists, because the world of their own inner experience is the only world with which they have direct acquaintance. From this point of view, postulating a world outside their experience of which they are only part seems an impressive feat. Whether infants are in fact born naïve realists, or whether they become naive realists because of what they learn, may be an unanswerable question. It is clear, however, that infants and children possess beliefs about the physical quite different from those they possess about the mental. They come to believe, for example, that some things lack inner experience or the capacity for it, even if they are not sure which things do and which do not. This too is an impressive achievement. Strictly speaking, we never know that a thing lacks (or indeed has) inner experience. We just suppose that it does, on the basis of criteria that we accept as valid. This is one reason why the notion of mental capacities must be important to our understanding of the mental: the criteria we use to ascribe inner experience must make reference to observable things, and these must surely be the expression of capacities in behaviour. Ultimately, we infer that something lacks a mind from its persistent failure to exhibit things that we regard as enabled by possession of mental capacities, that are observable signs of the operation of those capacities—capacities that we understand as mental. The criteria by which infants and young children make these inferences remain to be discovered. Perhaps, for example, apparent self-movement is a criterion, at least at some stages of development. Perhaps a criterion of mere resemblance is used: "If it cannot do as I do, it does not have what I have". Whatever the criterion, it may be some time before infants or children realise that there are things in the world that lack minds, and even longer before they sort out what sorts of things have minds and what are merely physical in nature.

By the age of three years, children appear to have learned some fairly basic things about physical reality (Wellman & Estes, 1986; Estes, Wellman, & Woolley, 1989). They understand that physical things can be touched and seen (in contradistinction to things in the inner, mental world), that access to them is public (whereas access to mental things is private), and that one cannot transform a physical object just by thinking about it. These findings reveal a good deal about how children (and adults) conceive of the physical. The physical is characterised by substantiality, solidity, and persistence (White, 1993). Physical things have a substance that can be ascertained through touch. They naturally persist unless acted on in some way. They are solid. (There are exceptions, such as mist and flames; it is worthy of note that those physical things most often associated with the spiritual are exactly those that lack the subsantiality that we taken as defining the physical, such as fire and breath—see Onians, 1951, for many examples.) Their existence is, moreover, independent of being thought about or perceived. Each of these characteristics of the physical can be contrasted with our understanding of the mental (Wellman & Estes, 1986; Estes et al., 1989).

How does all this relate to the developing theories of action and causation? Eventually, infants and children understand the theory of action as relating to the mental, and the theory of causation as relating to the physical. Action and causation are differentiated, in part, by being understood as springing from the mental and the physical, respectively. It is not clear how this happens, however. The development of a mental–physical distinction may help the infant understand action and causation as different, and as operating in different ways. It is perhaps more likely that action is understood as relating to the mental (that is, to inner experience) from earliest times, because the first understanding of action is gleaned from the infant's own experience of producing action. If this is the case, then a proper understanding of causation cannot develop until the infant has successfully distinguished the physical from the mental, and knows that some things lack minds and therefore the capacity for action. Conversely, action itself may help the infant to understand the merely physical: observing that some other things cannot do what I do when I perform actions may tell me that they lack the capacity for action and therefore that they lack inner experience and mind in general. Observing what those things *can* do even though they lack minds may tell me that there are other ways in which things can be made to happen, and that may be the route to an understanding of physical causation. There are many such possibilities, however, and at present evidence does not allow us to choose between them.

In addition, as I have stressed repeatedly, in our understanding it is up to us what we do in cases of action. This is to be contrasted with physical causation, which we understand as involving necessity; that is, when appropriate conditions are set up for the operation of a physical cause, the cause *must* operate to produce its effect. For example, when a piece of litmus paper is dipped into a beaker of acid, the power of the acid must operate to turn the litmus paper pink (so long as the power of the cause is sufficient in relation to the resistance of the object acted upon—Harré & Madden, 1975). In the case of action, there is no necessity: actors can always choose whether to perform some action or not. Even if someone holds a gun to my head and orders me to sing the National Anthem, I have the capacity to choose not to do so. Situational pressures are never such as to necessitate action; if they were, the behaviour produced would, by definition, not be action. There is some evidence that children appreciate the principle of determinism, which relates to necessitation, by three years (Bullock, Gelman, & Baillargeon, 1982; Bullock, 1985b), but there is no evidence on the possibility that children much younger than this might appreciate the distinction between choice, in the case of action, and necessitation, in the case of causation. Evidence reviewed earlier in this chapter suggests that infants do have some understanding of self-movement (agency) between 12 and 18 months of age, but this need not reflect anything fundamental to their understanding of action and causation, nor does it show that they differentiate between action and causation as modes of occurrence of events: it shows only that they have learned things about the kinds of powers possessed or not possessed by different kinds of objects, the kind of learning of specific causal beliefs that continues throughout life. Agency is not action; there are many things in nature that move themselves or appear to do so, but people do not necessarily interpret such self-movement as action, in the sense of it being up to the thing what it does. At present, therefore, it is not clear at what age infants or children first grasp these distinctions.

Finally, many of the properties of objects are hidden and only manifest themselves in certain ways under certain circumstances. Causally relevant properties such as causal powers only manifest themselves when they operate to produce effects, and this may be quite infrequently. Yet we as adults understand these properties as persisting in objects even when they are not manifest. It is evident that infants younger than two years understand this too, because they clearly know what to expect when they call a causal power of a familiar object into operation (e.g. pulling a light switch or operating the remote control of a television). Not all properties of objects are stable: for example, many wet objects tend to become dry, and hot objects may become cool. Infants presumably therefore learn which properties are stable despite being hidden most of the time, and which are transient.

Understanding Persons

On reading the extensive literature on the child's theory of mind one is struck by a curious omission. A great deal of ingenious and fruitful research has been carried out on children's developing understanding of mental states such as beliefs and desires, of the mind as a representational system, and so on (Wellman, 1990; Perner, 1991; Astington, Harris, & Olson, 1988;

Frye & Moore, 1991; Whiten, 1991). There seems to be nothing, however, concerning children's understanding of the person whose mental states and representations they are. My idea of myself as a person, and of the human beings around me as persons, seems so basic that I suppose it must be acquired early in life, if not innate. As I understand it, there is an existential core to my being that I call "I"; I believe that other human beings also have an "I" as their existential core, even though I have never seen one; and that things such as trees, machines, and other objects do not have one. I am sure that other people share these beliefs. Whether this is direct knowledge of something real or whether it is a construct created during development and the object of a belief that has to be acquired, it may not be possible to discover. It is certain, however, that ideas about which other things have an "I" and which do not must be learned.

Moreover, we do not understand "I", the existential core of one's being as a person, as without characteristics. The characteristics of "I", one might say, are those that define the nature of a person for us in the most fundamental way. There are many characteristics that might be taken as defining a person, and it is for research to discover which ones make up our understanding of what a person is. A good case can be made, however, for including at least the following three. The case is that I cannot readily imagine myself denying that these are true of me, that to imagine that they were taken away from me would be to imagine that I no longer existed as a person. This constitutes at least a prima-facie case for each of them as basic to our understanding of persons.[1]

1. Persistence. We do not suppose that our minds consist merely of successions of individually transient mental states, unified only by the fact of their occurrence in the one body (a view famously propounded by Hume, 1739/1978a). It is our assumption that a person endures as the same, continuing being from moment to moment, day to day, and that this continuing being is some kind of substrate to, or at least the subject of, mental states and experiences. I would find it hard, if not impossible, to accept that yesterday a different person was in my body, that my memories of that day are not of me at all but of him, that I came into existence some time last night (or even five seconds ago!). I hold the same assumption for other human beings as well.

2. Being a centre of inner experience. Whether "inner experience" is the most felicitous term can be debated (see White, 1986 and 1993, for arguments about consciousness and conscious awareness). Despite this it is clear that I am, as I understand myself, a centre, the subject, of inner experiences in this body. Those experiences do not exist apart from me; indeed I would want to say that they would not occur at all if I did not exist to be the subject of them; they are only mine and can be shared by no one

else; and I am similarly remote from the inner experience of any other being. All this I hold to be equivalently true for other humans and their experiences too.

3. Being an originator of action. As we understand it, a person is the producer, the causal origin of his or her own actions. Actions are not produced impersonally: something that is not a person cannot act,[2] even though it may have causal powers to behave in various ways. As I understand it, my actions do not happen by themselves, nor are they members or end-points of a deterministic, impersonal chain of causation. I produce or perform them and it is up to me what I do, whether I do it or not, and when I do it. I also hold this to be true of other persons.

These ingredients of the concept of a person, and perhaps others as well, are obviously crucial and basic to common sense psychology. When we explain an action by referring to a certain belief–desire combination, for example, we do not have in mind impersonal inner states somehow causing action by themselves. We have in mind a person whose mental states they are, freely choosing to act on account of them. Choice is an essential part of this understanding: a belief–desire combination does not compel one to act; still less does it determine *when* one acts. I am in charge of my own actions, as I see it, and I choose whether and when to act on the combination of belief and desire that I hold. At the moment, however, we have no idea of when children come to have this concept of a person, or when they have it in distinction from their understanding of things that are not persons. This is, I suggest, the most urgent priority for future research in this area.

A child who has some concept of a person, no matter what sort of concept it is, still has to judge which things are persons and which are not. Let us suppose that the child's concept includes the three features listed above. In principle each of these serves to define a rule for attributing person-hood to things. In practice, since we cannot observe the relevant features of persons directly, any possible rule depends for its use on criteria for the interpretation of evidence. What, for example, would count as evidence for possessing the feature of being a centre of inner experience? We have a strong tendency to take verbal reports about what is going on in our minds as evidence about conscious awareness (White, 1993), which suggests that such verbal reports, or the ability to give them, may be taken as a criterion for inferring that the thing providing the report is a person.

In the case of the third feature, it may seem obvious that observed actions are a criterion for inferring that the thing producing them is a person. This, however, begs the question of how we identify actions, so as to distinguish them from behaviours and other occurrences not so identified. The criterion of apparent self-movement may help, at least at early stages of development: apparent self-movement does not give us the concept of action, as I argued earlier, but it may be useful as a criterion for identifying persons once one has a concept of action.

The first feature relates to the ancient philosophical problem of personal identity. Despite the quantity of philosophical literature on this topic, the criteria for ascription of personal identity in common sense remain obscure and neglected. One might be tempted to answer that any human being is taken to be a person, and that personal identity is inferred simply on the basis of identity and continuity of the physical body: one person per body, and the same person for as long as the body lives. But I think things are not so simple. Not wishing to dip more than a toe into murky philosophical waters, consider our common sense understanding of cases of multiple personality. We do not, I think, see such cases as one person with distinct and contrasting aspects or patterns of behaviour. Instead, and this is where such cases hold their fascination for laypeople, we imagine *two (or more) persons*, two centres of inner experience, two origins of actions, housed in the one body, perhaps one dormant while the other is active. How we come to see things this way is not clear: perhaps we are using some criterion related to stability, similarity, or psychological consistency in patterns of behaviour; perhaps we infer two persons from the fact that one aspect may claim not to know about the other, or not to know what the other thinks and does. In any case, how children acquire criteria for the ascription of personal identity to others is, like other important topics reviewed in this section, unknown.

DO YOUNG CHILDREN REALLY HAVE THEORIES?

The general orientation taken here is that, by the end of the second year, children possess two basic theories about how things happen: the theory of action and the theory of causation. In the introductory chapter I described Wellman's (1988, p.66) claim that subscribers to a theory share three things: "a basic conception of what phenomena are encompassed by the theory [ontological distinctions]; a sense of how these phenomena and propositions about them are mutually interdependent [coherence]; and, consequently, what counts as a relevant and informative explanation of changes and relationships among the various phenomena [a causal- explanatory framework]". Wellman was discussing the child's theory of mind, but it can be seen that the two theories of how things happen possess these three features. Taking the theory of action as an example, the ontological distinctions are evident in the concepts of causal power, liability, actor, and action that are the main ingredients of the theory; coherence is evident in the fixed interrelationship of these concepts; and the causal-explanatory framework is revealed in the use of the mental state concepts in the theory to explain actions.

Theories cannot be observed directly, so there is still room to argue for an alternative account of how infants appear to have a theory-like understanding. Johnson (1988) has argued that young children are intuitive and, although directed at the theory of mind literature, his argument is relevant here too. Johnson stated (p.48, italics in original): "Intuitive knowledge is distinctively marked by *first-order* conceptions, consisting of *primitive* elements that are self-explanatory. Such knowledge is *minimally abstract*, being closely tied to concrete experience, hence *phenomenological* in nature". Johnson argued that children do not need higher order concepts of the sort invoked in "theory of mind" explanations, but can work with their first-order intuitive knowledge. There are two main parts to this. First, experience has a kind of structure that is accessible to consciousness: thus, the nature and development of intuitive psychology are limited and defined by the limits on what is accessible to consciousness. Second, children can explain and predict the behaviour of others by constructing simulations utilising first-order representations of their own particular mental states, without concepts of the natures of those mental states.

In Johnson's account, the basic feature of the natural structure of experience is that it is dualistic; the distinction between experiencing and the content of experience, or between "I" the experiencer as psychologically primitive and everything else, is fundamental. Based on this are two types of relation between "I" and the world. One is direction of fit (Searle, 1983, p.50), which can be from mind to world or from world to mind: "The direction of fit has to do with whether the organism is oriented towards adapting (fitting) the world to the goals of the mind [world-to-mind direction of fit], or adapting the mind to the properties of the world [mind-to-world direction of fit]". For example, seeing has a mind-to-world direction of fit. The second type of relation between "I" and the world is causal direction, which may also be from mind to world (acting on the world) or from world to mind (perceiving or reacting). These two types are treated as orthogonal by Johnson, yielding a two-dimensional space in which psychological categories can be located. This structure of experience is given, and forms the basis for an intuitive psychology without concepts. Intuitive psychology is the creation of consciousness, which is (p.53) "a higher-order projection of information already available at lower levels of processing". According to Johnson it is an adaptive feature enabling the regulation of processing states, and is limited to episodic, intentional states and does not encompass processes (cf. Nisbett & Wilson, 1977; White, 1988). With this intuitive psychology, children can use simulations as a substitute for having a theory of mind. Children can note relations between objective conditions and their own experiences and use these as a basis for simulating the mental states of others from information about objective conditions, using only first-order representations.

Arguing that young children hold concepts and theories does not entail denying that the structure and content of experience is an important source of information about the mind, nor that young children can simulate the mental states of others. Wellman (1990), who supported the notion that preschoolers have a theory of mind, nonetheless agreed with Johnson about the importance of subjective experience. In the present account, too, experience of mental states and occurrences is fundamental to theory construction: The experience of producing action, for example, is the foundation of the infant's theory of action. One does not need to understand what consciousness is to concede this point.

The challenge posed by Johnson's account is to find some positive evidence that young children possess theories. Wellman (1990) found this evidence in research on blind children (Landau & Gleitman, 1985) and extrapolated from that: "If blind children commonly engage in [some] theoretical endeavour, it seems senseless to deny a similar sort of constructive-theoretical knowledge to ordinary three-year-olds" (Wellman, 1990, p.196). In the present case, for the core theory of causation Johnson's position is clearly untenable: the psychological metaphysics of causation include concepts that cannot be yielded by first-order intuitive knowledge because they refer to features of the physical world that mental states simply do not possess. These include solidity, rigidity, and continuity of motion (Spelke, 1991). It is not so easy to refute Johnson's claim in the case of the theory of action, since the psychological metaphysics of action could plausibly figure in first-order intuitive knowledge. However, the fact that children are almost certainly theorising about the mind by the age of three years (Wellman, 1990), and the fact that infants have a theory of physical causation and physical objects, are together sufficient to shift the burden of proof onto Johnson; it is now necessary to show that infants do not have a theory of action, given the strength of the case that they do. Claiming that infants possess theories does not mean denying that they can run simulations based on personal experience, or exercise imagination, or do many other things. Saying that infants have theories should not be taken as implying that infants are being viewed as a kind of scientist (see Kuhn, 1989). The child's understanding of human behaviour possesses coherence and incorporates ontological distinctions and a causal-explanatory framework: it is by virtue of these things, and these things only, that the young child can be said to possess theories.

To some extent, arguments over the appropriateness of the term "theory" are semantic in nature. Under one definition, "theory" is appropriate, under another it is not. I have chosen to define "theory" in terms of Wellman's three criteria. Perner (1991) has a fourth criterion, which is that a theory should provide a deeper explanation for how something works. For example, a theory might interpret a set of observable phenomena (such as behaviour) with the use of explanatory concepts referring to underlying and unobservable entities (such as mental states) and how those give rise to the observable phenomena. Clearly, the basic theories of action and causation satisfy this criterion as well. Since it is clear that, by the age of two years if not earlier, children have a kind of understanding which fits these criteria for the use of the term "theory", one can only argue about whether these are the right criteria for the use of the term or not, and this, as I have said, is a semantic problem, not a psychological one. By these criteria, infants have theories.

Conclusions

I propose that, by the age of two years, the child is in possession of two theories, of action and causation respectively, both originating in the experience of the production of action, but diverging during development, and having the following features:

1. Theory of action. "I" produce action, where it is understood to be up to the actor what he or she does. Action is limited by the range of causal powers at the actor's disposal; these do not cause action themselves, but are understood as instruments used by the actor. For actions upon other things, the actor produces a given effect by a specific kind of action upon a specific kind of thing under specific conditions; that is, actions upon things involve reference to the causal powers of the actor, the liabilities of the thing acted upon, and the releasing conditions which allow the action to have its effect.

2. Theory of causation. Causation involves some causal power of a thing operating to produce a given effect under a given condition. That is, the concepts of causal power, liability, and releasing condition apply as they do to action, but it is the causal power and not the actor that produces the effect, and the property of necessitation applies; if appropriate conditions are set up, the power must operate to produce its effect, and cannot choose otherwise. The causal relation is understood as generative, which is essentially the concept of efficacy without the actor.

These can be described as theories in the specific sense that they are coherent sets of concepts which can be applied in the interpretation of things that happen. They are the core theories of action and causation, which means two things:

1. All and only those things that are interpreted as action are interpreted in terms of the whole set of concepts making up the theory of action, and all and only those things that are interpreted as causation are

interpreted in terms of the whole set of concepts making up the theory of causation. Other concepts may be added to these theories during the course of development, but they are not core concepts because they are not used in the interpretation of *all* instances.

2. The theories, once formed, never change. They are, with additions and embellishments, the adult theories of action and causation. The theories in turn are underpinned by fundamental assumptions about the nature of the mental and the physical, persons and other things; the age at which these various assumptions are established is unknown but they, like the theories, never change once established, and constitute the psychological metaphysics of the understanding of action and causation.

Development from these core theories therefore consists of two kinds of thing. One is the addition and integration of new concepts (e.g. in the case of action, intention, desire, and so on). The other is the refinement of rules for their application. These rules may also be attached to concepts added to the theory—for example, there may be rules for identifying action as intentional (Shultz & Wells, 1985). The following two chapters are concerned largely with these two kinds of development, in the spheres of human behaviour and physical causation respectively.

This account is far from definitive. I offer it in the spirit that Wellman (1990) offered his model of adult belief–desire psychology (see Chapter 5): it is intended only to be useful, to be a target for future research. Although there have been other accounts of the origin of understanding of action and/or causation, summarised earlier in this chapter, it is clear that these accounts simply have not addressed many of the important questions, particularly concerning the psychological metaphysics of action and causation. If nothing else, I hope to have shown what must be included in a comprehensive account.

NOTES

1. It might appear that a better case could be made by appealing to philosophy. In fact the philosophical literature on the concept of a person is not very helpful. It is, as commentators generally acknowledge, one of the most discussed and most controversial areas of modern philosophy (Gill, 1990). Not only is the debate complex, it is also intimately related to other debates, concerning the nature of mind, of rationality, of human nature, of personal identity, the mind-body problem, and problems in ethics. The three characteristics discussed here have all been included in definitions of the person by philosophers (see Ayer, 1963a; Carruthers, 1986; McCall, 1990; Gill, 1990). So have other characteristics which are arguably less helpful to this developmental study. For example, Frankfurt (1971) defined the person

in terms of the capacity for second-order desires, that is, the capacity to want to have certain desires and motives. By this criterion, children before the age of four years are not persons because evidence suggests that they lack this capacity (Perner, 1991).

2.   This is not a claim about a matter of fact, but something that is true of action by definition.

CHAPTER THREE

The Child's Understanding of Action and Causation in the Realm of Human Behaviour

As adults we employ two different conceptual frameworks in the interpretation of human behaviour, and have a clear understanding of which framework to use for different kinds of behaviour. For most actions we employ the common sense theory of action, interpreting them as freely chosen, intentional, and underlain by reasons referring to such things as the desires or goals of the actor. For behaviours of other kinds we use a framework that owes more to the theory of causation. Emotional reactions, for example, we tend to interpret as caused rather than freely chosen, as representing liabilities of the actor called into operation by the powers of external things and events. There are probably grey areas between the two, behaviours interpreted as a mix of the two conceptual systems, or behaviours the interpretation of which is not clear even to adults (White, 1993). Children have a great deal to learn: although in possession of two basic theories of action origination and causation, children build on these theories and, presumably, acquire a keener sense of which theory should be used to interpret which kind of behaviour. The aim of this chapter is to review what little is known about this phase of development. I shall review each theory in turn.

THE THEORY OF ACTION

At the end of infancy the child's theory of action, which I have argued continues to be the core of the understanding of action throughout life, consists only of an idea about how action is produced, that is that it is produced by "I", the actor, and that it is up to the actor what they do. The actions of an actor are limited only by the range of causal powers possessed by the actor. Where actions are carried out upon other things, children also understand action as relating the causal powers of the actor to the liabilities of the thing acted upon and the conditions under which actions upon a thing may be carried out. For example, even infants understand sucking their thumb as an action they carry out upon their thumb, under the condition of having or putting the thumb in their mouth, the thumb in turn being understood as having the capacity (liability) to be sucked.

It is not unlikely that adults still understand some actions as nothing more than things produced by the actor. For instance, Taylor (1966) argued that he might just raise his arm in the air, not because of any desire or intention or purpose or for any reason at all; despite the absence of these things, it is still an action of his, something he did, something he could have chosen to do or not to do. Nonetheless, most instances of action are probably interpreted as involving, or assumed to involve, something more than just the actor carrying them out. Philosophers have argued that actions may owe something to a variety of mental states, including intentions, desires, and beliefs. Although some philosophers argue that these things cause actions, so that reasons explanations which make reference to beliefs and desires are a form of causal explanation (Smith & Jones, 1986), under the account favoured here it is proposed that people do not see these things as causes of action but as things which the actor might, so to speak, take into account in deciding how to behave, so that reasons explanations are fundamentally different from causal explanations. The reason for this preference is simply that people do not see action as necessitated; that, as they see it, it is always up to the actor how to act. The kind of necessitation that is associated with causation is missing from the understanding of action. One does not have to act in accordance with one's intentions.

In general, though, under this account people act as they do intentionally, and their intention reflects an appropriate combination of belief and desire. For example, one might say, John jumped into the shop doorway intentionally, meaning that he acted as he did because he desired to remain dry and believed that it was starting to rain and that the shop doorway afforded shelter. The belief most relevant to the action is the belief that by acting in that way one can achieve what one desires.

This is a complex and sophisticated account of action: one can imagine many other possible accounts of action no more complex but involving very different kinds of concepts. There is evidence, however, that children have this kind of understanding of action before the age of four years, and I shall begin by reviewing this evidence.

Intentions and Action

It is still not clear at what age children first interpret actions as underlain and guided by intentions. A concept of intention is different from, and not entailed by, an ability to act intentionally (Poulin-Dubois & Shultz, 1988), so it is almost impossible to ascertain whether a pre-verbal infant has a concept of intention or not. Once the child has begun to use language, use of a concept of intention can be sought in verbal expressions of intention. Brown (1973) found that children around two years of age start to use the auxiliary "gonna" in relation to the forthcoming actions. For example, a child might say "I gonna run", and then start running. Hood and Bloom (1979) studied spontaneous causal statements, that is, two events (clauses in a sentence) and a causal connective between them. All of the eight children in their sample started producing such utterances between two and two and a half years of age, and many of the clauses in the causal statements expressed intentions. The children concentrated on their own intentions, however (Hood & Bloom, 1979, p.36): "reference to the listener's actions or states generally took the form of directives in which the child requested the listener to do something". Dunn (1991) reported the use of expressions such as "I don't mean to" by children aged two years and under. Huttenlocher, Smiley, and Charney (1983) found that children aged around two years were beginning to use what the authors called "change verbs" such as "build", "get", and "give" in a consistent manner. Huttenlocher et al. argued that this could only be accomplished by a speaker who has a concept of an actor as an intentional causal agent acting to bring about change in the world. Studies of replica play, such as play with dolls, show that children begin to ascribe intentions to such figures around the age of 31 months (Wolf, Rygh, & Altshuler, 1984). Dasser, Ulbaek, and Premack (1989) have found that children ascribe intentions and goals to moving objects at the age of three. (This does not necessarily indicate animistic thinking, as adults are happy to do the same—Heider and Simmel, 1944.)

While these studies suggest possession of a concept of intention, they do not tell us what sort of concept it is, nor how children understand the relation between intentions and behaviour. For this it is necessary to study the ways in which children discriminate intentional behaviour from behaviour of other kinds. Early research suggested that young children might be rather limited in this respect. Berndt and Berndt (1975) studied children's understanding of motives as reasons for action in relation to consequences of action, and found that five-year-olds tended to see accidents as intended. Smith (1978) found that four-year-olds tended to judge everything an actor did as intentional, even when she stumbled over a box. By the age of five, however, children distinguished object-like movements (e.g. being pushed) and involuntary behaviours (such as sneezing) from intentional actions. They also showed some ability to judge the intentionality of an outcome by its desirability, by the actor's state of knowledge (specifically whether the actor was watching what she was doing or not) and by the nature of the act itself (i.e. only outcomes of intentional acts can be intended).

These studies were both concerned more with outcomes and consequences of action than with action itself. As adults we understand that not everything we do is intentional. For example, we do not regard reflex behaviours such as sneezes as intentional, nor mistakes such as slips of the tongue. Shultz and his colleagues (Shultz, 1980; Shultz, Wells, & Sarda, 1980) investigated children's understanding of these distinctions. The procedure involved asking children to carry out simple activities such as repeating sentences and making particular kinds of hand movement, some of which were designed to elicit mistakes. For example, children were asked to repeat "she lives in a house", which they were generally able to accomplish, and the tongue-twister "she sells sea shells by the sea shore", which reliably led to mistakes. After each attempt the child was asked "did you mean to say it like that?". Equivalent questions were asked for the behavioural tasks. Children also observed other children attempting these tasks and were asked equivalent questions about the behaviour they observed. The results showed the three-year-olds were able to distinguish intended actions from mistakes, and they could make this distinction for the behaviour of others as well as for their own behaviour.

Also at the age of three children showed some understanding of conditional intentions (Shultz et al., 1980). In one version, children played a card game in which child and experimenter both turned over a playing card at the same time. If the cards matched in colour the first player to slap his or her hand down on the table won both cards. The intended action, then, is slapping one's hand down and the condition under which the action is appropriate is matching colour of the exposed cards. In this game, children sometimes slapped their hands down appropriately and sometimes inappropriately. Behaviours of each kind were followed by the question "did you mean to slap your hand down?". All children tested at the age of three gave perfect answers to these questions. The proper interpretation of this result is obscure, however. The action is the same in all cases, and presumably intentional in all cases: the action of slapping one's hand down when the colours do not match is not unintentional, just wrong if the child wishes to win the game. Thus, while Shultz et al. (1980) may be right to emphasise the child's appreciation of conditionality, the results may show more about the child's appreciation of beliefs and desires underlying behaviour (see pp. 85–91). The child desires to win the game and believes that to do so it is necessary to slap one's hand down when the colours match and not when they do not; so what the child understands is that, when the hand is slapped down inappropriately, he or she didn't mean to do it, not because it was actually unintentional but because it was not the way to achieve the desired end. A grasp of belief–desire psychology entails some understanding of conditionality in relation to action; the belief effectively specifies the condition under which the action leads to fulfillment of desire.

Other aspects of the understanding of intentional action appear to be slower to develop. By the age of five years the child can distinguish intentional actions from reflexes and passive movements (Shultz, 1980). The reflex was the knee-jerk reflex. For passive movement, the experimenter held the child's arms down while the child tried to push upwards. After about ten seconds the experimenter let go, producing "a slow involuntary upward movement of the arms" (Shultz, 1980, p.141). Children aged five judged that there was more intentionality in intentional movements than in these movements, and they were able to do this whether judging their own behaviour or that of someone else. A trend for three-year-olds did not reach statistical significance.

It is important to distinguish, here, between intending an action and intending an outcome of action. For example, throwing crumbs to birds is an action; birds then eating the crumbs is a consequence of action. While children at three years can distinguish intended actions from nonintended behaviours, findings suggest that they are not able to distinguish intended from unintended consequences of actions (Astington, 1991; Shultz & Shamash, 1981). The evidence is consistent with the idea that children are judging intentionality of outcomes or consequences by use of the matching rule (Shultz & Wells, 1985; and see p.109); this rule leads to errors of judgement when there is a merely fortuitous match between intention or desire and outcome, and the findings show that children aged three tend to judge outcomes as intended when they fulfil a desire or an intention accidentally. By the age of four years (Astington, 1991) or five (Shultz & Shamash, 1981), children can distinguish intentional from accidental fulfilments of intentions. Having said that, the distinction between act and outcome is not entirely straightforward, as outcomes and consequences can very considerably in their distance from the action that brought them about. The action of lifting an object has the obvious outcome that the object gets lifted, and it is clear (see Chapter 2) that this is understood by infants at the stage of secondary circular reactions. The age at which a child shows understanding of the distinction between act and outcome therefore depends on the kind of outcome studied.

Perner (1991) has argued that, while children understand goal-directed actions at an early age, they do not understand an intention as a mental state representing that one will perform a certain action until the age of four years. His reason for arguing this is that such an understanding depends on the child having a general understanding of the mind as a representational system; that is, an understanding of the representational relations between mental states and states of the world. This understanding, according to a body of research findings reviewed by Perner, does not develop until around the age of four years. Children younger than four can understand intending an outcome that does not exist at the moment, because this depends only on the ability to construct multiple models and not on a concept of the mind as a representational system (see Perner, 1991, for more extensive arguments on this point).

The key test is to present a story describing an action and an outcome but not a goal. Can children distinguish an intended from an accidental outcome (holding the actual outcome constant) when information about the actor's goal is not presented? Perner (1991) reported a study by Astington in which three-year-old children were not able to do this, but four-year-old children performed much better. In one scenario, for example, one child jumped into a swimming pool while another fell in, and children were asked which child meant to get wet. Despite the use of pictures, the study does depend to a considerable extent on children's understanding of words like "jump" and "fall". Three-year-old children might understand intentions and intention-outcome relations without knowing whether "fall" is a word for an intentional action or not. In addition, success at the task depends on the simultaneous comprehension of two stories while pondering a particular question, and this may be cognitively demanding for younger children. The results are suggestive, but not conclusive.

Finally, Shultz and Cloghesy (1981) investigated recursive awareness of intention, that is, the child's understanding of others' knowledge of the child's intentions. This involved a card game in which one participant had to guess the colour of the next card to be turned up. The other participant knew the colour and pointed at either a red or a black card as a clue to the guesser. If the guesser guessed correctly, he or she won the card, and if the guesser guessed incorrectly, the pointer won the card. The pointer can choose to be truthful or deceitful, with the aim of winning the game thereby. The guesser can show awareness of the possibility of deception, by choosing the colour not pointed at. Children aged three years failed to show recursive awareness of intention in this game, but by five years such awareness was beginning to emerge.

As Shultz (1980, p.152) pointed out, recursive awareness of intention makes possible strategic acts, "acts that are performed in order to disguise one's intentions or to lead others to misinterpret one's intentions". This may therefore underlie some further developments in children's understanding of action. For example, around the age of six years children are able to distinguish a lie from a joke on the basis of whether the speaker intended the listener to believe the false statement, and around the age of seven years they assign responsibility for accidents on their assessment of what the protagonists know about each other's knowledge (Perner, 1988). At the age of six, children understand that people can seek to mislead others about their emotional state, putting on an appearance of having or not having a certain emotion because of a certain motive, such as not wanting to be laughed at. At the age of four, children do not understand this, and tend to see all emotion as unfeigned reaction to external events (Harris & Gross, 1988).

One problem with the study by Shultz and Cloghesy (1981), however, is that to show recursive awareness of intention in this situation the child has first to master the rules of a new game, and a kind of game with which they may not be familiar. Failure at the task may show difficulty in learning the strange new game (played, moreover, with strangers) rather than an inability to think about others' knowledge of one's intentions. Indeed, naturalistic observations have been made of deception by children aged less than two years (Dunn, 1991; Piaget, 1954); experimental studies have shown that children aged less than three years can engage in simple forms of deception (Chandler, Fritz, & Hala, 1989; Lewis, Stanger, & Sullivan, 1989). According to Perner (1991), however, genuine deception must involve an attempt to manipulate a belief held by some other person, and this in turn depends on an understanding of belief as a representational state. The forms of deception noted in the observations and studies do not depend on this, and are therefore not genuine deception; we need suppose only that the children were intending to bring about a desirable consequence (or avoid an undesirable one), and that they had worked out ways of doing this which did not depend on an understanding of belief. In support of this interpretation, Perner pointed to the fact that the young child's strategies of deception tend to be used rigidly, and sometimes in entirely inappropriate circumstances. Furthermore other research shows that understanding of the recursive nature of thinking develops gradually during middle and later childhood (Flavell, Miller, & Miller, 1993). It is therefore likely that deception as an intentional manipulation of beliefs emerges only after the age of four years.

The research by Shultz and colleagues (Shultz, 1980; Shultz et al., 1980) concentrated on immediate action. Intentions can also apply to the more distant future: one can, for example, sensibly express an intention to visit a certain country next year. There has been little research on understanding of intentions and plans in relation to behaviour not yet carried out, but one study by Astington (1991) may shed some light on this.

Astington presented children with pairs of pictures such as a girl standing in front of paints but not actually painting, paired with a picture of a girl painting. She then asked the children either questions about actions, such as "which girl is painting?" or questions about intentions, such as "which girl thinks she'll paint?". The appropriate response to the latter sort of question is to refer to the girl who is not painting. This response was actually given by 13% of three-year-olds, 44% of four-year-olds, and 61% of five-year-olds. Astington suggested that three-year-olds, although in possession of a simple concept of intention, do not recognise intention as a person's representation of the intended subsequent action, that is, they cannot represent intentions separately from goals. Thus, they answer the question about prior intention by pointing to its realisation in action, that is, the achievement of the goal specified in the intention. The findings are not conclusive, however; as Astington (1991) noted, it is not incorrect to point to a picture of a girl painting in response to the intention question, because that girl presumably does also intend to paint, intending both what she is doing now and the continuation of the same action into the future. This response was judged inappropriate because adults normally take intention questions as referring to action not yet begun, not because it is actually wrong. It may be, then, that three-year-olds have not yet learned an adult convention about the use of a word. Moreover, they may quite sensibly be adopting a conservative strategy in responding; after all, the girl who is painting clearly intends to paint, but who knows what a girl standing in front of paints might be going to do? The findings therefore do not show that three-year-olds do not understand prior intentions.

One final point about intentions is that they possess causal self-referentiality, that is, the mental representation of an intention is not just a representation of the goal state. An intention does not just state "I do X", but "I do X by way of carrying out this intention". Not all action has this property: to take Taylor's (1966) example, I might just raise my arm in the air, not with any particular intention to do so, but just as something I do. A child could therefore have a concept of action without having a concept of intentional action, and in fact a child could have a concept of intention without understanding the causal self-referentiality of intentions. Such children would make predictable errors in identifying actions and outcomes as intentional. They would not be able to distinguish between an outcome produced by the enactment of an intention and an outcome also intended and desired but produced fortuitously, such as accidental success on some task. This would happen if children identified outcomes as intentional only by use of the matching rule (Shultz & Wells, 1985), as this rule relates intentions to outcomes and takes no account of the means of production of the outcome. This is an important problem in the development of the concept of intention, but there is as yet no clear evidence concerning the age at which children understand the causal self-referentiality of intentions (Astington, 1991).

The term "intention" is very ambiguous in common usage. It can refer to an immediate intention, as when I intend to raise my arm and do so immediately; it can refer to a prior intention which may be formulated seconds, hours, or years before the action which fulfils it is carried out. An action can be intentional; so can an immediate or distant consequence of an action. An action (or outcome) can be intentional under one description and not under another (see Chapter 1). Not only children but also researchers have to master all of these distinctions: a study showing that three-year-olds do not understand what it is for a consequence to fulfil a prior intention does not thereby show that they do not understand intentions at all.

The main findings to date are summarised in Table 3.1.

Beliefs and Desires and Action

In Chapter 1 I discussed the intentional theory of action, the philosophical theory according to which an action is properly explained by reference to a desire (pro-attitude) and a belief that the action undertaken is a way of attaining the desire. A major line of developmental research shows the emergence of a view of action not unlike that, between the ages of two and five years. The findings suggest, if not exactly stages, four landmarks in this development.

Perner (1991) noted Piaget's observation that infants tend to repeat actions and seem not to be discomfited by repeated failures. Perner suggested that such infants may be capable of goal-directed action, but do

TABLE 3.1
Development of Understanding of Intentions

Development	Age
Verbal expressions of intention	Two years
Distinguish intentions from mistakes	Three years
Understand conditional intentions	Three years
Understand prior intentions/plans for the future	Four years
Distinguish intentional actions from reflexes and passive movements	Five years
Distinguish intended from unintended consequences of action	Five years
Use of goal explanations for action	Five years
Recursive awareness of intention	Five years

not yet conceive of having goals. One sign of such a concept is the tendency to cease an activity when a clear or specified goal has been achieved. This starts to happen around the age of two years (Bullock & Lutkenhaus, 1988). Children also show appropriate affective reactions to their completion of a task (or failure to complete it) before two years of age (Bullock & Lutkenhaus, 1988; Gopnik & Meltzoff, 1984). Around two years of age there is also evidence that children understand other human beings as intentional agents having desires and goals (Bretherton, McNew, & Beeghly-Smith, 1981; Huttenlocher et al., 1983). This can therefore be regarded as the first elaboration of the basic theory of action: the concept of desire or goal (pro-attitude) and of action as goal directed.

The second landmark is what Wellman and Woolley (1990) referred to as "desire psychology", that is to say an understanding of human action based on desires and not on beliefs. At first encounter this idea hardly seems possible, but consider the nature of desire in this theory. "Desire" does not refer to physiological drives or needs, but to a mental state, a pro-attitude (Davidson, 1968). A desire is a propositional attitude and must have an object. One can have a desire for an apple and this desire can underlie one's actions, without any particular belief being invoked: one might not know where to find an apple, for example, but one can still look for one, and know what it is one seeks.

According to Wellman and Woolley (1990, p.250), therefore, children see desires as leading the actor to do two things: (1) "to engage in goal-directed actions (seek water, avoid fire), including persisting in goal-directed actions (if the route to water is blocked, seek an alternative)"; (2) "to have certain emotional reactions (getting what you desire yields happiness, not getting it yields frustration, unhappiness, etc.)". If the child knows where an object is, he or she can predict that the actor will look for it there, but without attributing a belief to the actor. Their first study showed that children aged two had mastered these components of desire psychology. They were also able to understand the specificity of desire: it is only getting what you want that makes you happy, and not just anything will do.[1] In their second study, children aged from 2.9 to 3.3 years were able to predict an actor's action on the basis of the actor's desire even when it differed from their own, showing an understanding not only that desires may vary from one actor to another, but also that an actor's actions can make sense in terms of their desires, rather than the child's own.

The third landmark is the explanation of actions in terms of both desires and appropriate beliefs. There is little doubt that understanding of belief lags well behind an equivalent understanding of desire. For example, Wellman (1991) reported a survey of children's spontaneous use of terms for belief and desire. Wellman took care to select uses of belief and desire terms for psychological reference, excluding conversational uses (e.g. "you know") and uninterpretable uses. He found that use of desire terms (specifically "want", which accounted for 97% of expressions of desire sampled) for psychological reference was well established by the age of two years. By contrast, use of belief terms ("think" and "know", together accounting for 94% of expressions of belief sampled) did not commence until shortly before the third birthday, and developed gradually during the fourth year. Wellman also looked for utterances where children explicitly distinguished between their own desires and beliefs and those of others, and found a similar pattern. Two-year-olds were able to distinguish their own desires from the desires for others, but a similar tendency for beliefs did not emerge until the age of three.

Three-year-olds have begun, however, to understand belief–desire combinations. Bartsch and Wellman (1989) presented children with simple stories, such as: "Here's Jane. Jane is looking for her kitten under the piano. Why do you think Jane is doing that?". They then coded children's responses to these questions. In all, 65% of explanations given by three-year-olds were psychological. Of these, 60% referred to beliefs and desires. Thirty-seven percent of all explanations given by three-year-olds referred to an appropriate combination of belief and desire. No other category of mental state was mentioned as frequently as beliefs and desires. These frequencies increased when the experimenters prompted children with questions about the beliefs and/or desires of the actor. Bartsch and Wellman included a group of adults in their study, and found broadly similar results. Seventy-nine percent of explanations offered by adults were psychological, and 53% of all explanations (67% of psychological explanations) referred to a combination of belief and desire. Adults therefore referred to belief/desire combinations only slightly more often than three-year-olds did. The remainder of the psychological explanations given by both children and adults tended to refer to perceptions (less than 10%) and preferences (e.g. "she likes kittens", 17%).

The degree of similarity between three-year-olds and adults is striking. In this and other respects, "three-year-olds' theory of mind is commensurate with our own" (Wellman, 1990, p.319). By "commensurate", Wellman meant that children have the same paradigm for understanding action that adults have. Indeed this very similarity may lead us to imagine that there is something inevitable about the results of the study by Bartsch and Wellman (1989); how else could children have explained the actor's actions? Actually there are several other theories that children might have possessed and employed. They might have construed action in terms of conditioning history, in terms of physical (as opposed to psychological) causation, or as caused by the physical situation. In fact they did not. Some explanations by both children and adults did refer to features of the situation, but it is possible that these were elliptical references to beliefs,

beliefs about states of affairs so obvious that they need not be identified as beliefs. There was one clear age difference: More than half of the adults spontaneously referred to personality traits in their explanations, but only one out of forty-five children (aged three and four years) did so. Traits will be discussed later.

There is one problem with Wellman's model of belief–desire psychology, which I shall highlight here and then discuss more fully in Chapter 5. In the intentional theory of action, the important aspect of the antecedents to action is not the kind of mental state they are, or their intrinsic qualities as mental states, but the functions that mental states take on in the generation of action. These functions are, specifically, inclining an actor towards a certain action or towards the achievement of a certain outcome, and furnishing information about how the outcome might be achieved. I prefer the terms "pro-attitude", which avoids the misleading connotations of "desire", and "action belief", which distinguishes the particular function of belief in relation to action, and serves as a reminder that not just any belief will do. A model of the adult understanding of action using these functional concepts is presented in Chapter 5; the findings reviewed here conform to models of the sort presented in Fig. 3.1.

There are two things to note about these models. The first is that intentions are no longer present. This is because, in the intentional theory

FIG. 3.1. Modified models of the child's understanding of action.

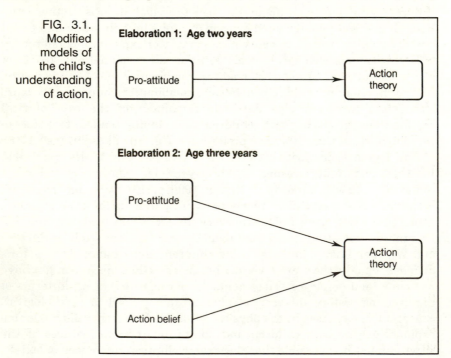

of action on which this model is based, there is no distinct mental state of intention as such: the pro-attitude–action belief combination is the only antecedent to action other than the fiat of the actor. This may or may not be an accurate reflection of people's understanding of action: that is for future research to ascertain. The second is that the arrows in this figure do not imply causal necessitation. In the intentional theory of action, the pro–attitude/action—belief combination is a cause of action, but in the child's understanding of action, as in Taylor's (1966) theory, the only cause of action is the actor. The actor can always choose to act or not to act on the basis of a given combination of pro-attitude and action belief. Moreover, not all actions need have any pro-attitude or action belief as their antecedent: only the actor's performance of action is necessary.

Children at the age of three years understand actions as intentional (Shultz, 1980; Shultz et al., 1980). A study by Nelson-LeGall (1985) shows that they also understand something of the relation between belief–desire combinations and intended outcomes of action. Nelson-Le Gall manipulated information about the actor's state of knowledge and reaction to an outcome of action: in the "unforeseeable outcome" vignettes, children were told that the actor did not know some state of affairs crucial to the eventual outcome of their action, and was surprised by the outcome ("surprised because he didn't know ...", p.334). The manipulation is therefore, in part, of the belief component of a belief–desire combination. Children aged three years judged the outcome more intentional when it was foreseeable than when it was not. It is possible that they relied for this judgement solely on the information about surprise but, as we shall see later, children of that age have some understanding of surprise as a reaction related to belief states (Wellman & Bannerjee, 1991), so this would still be sufficient for us to infer that these children understand something of the belief–intention–action link.

Wellman (1991) suggested that children make the transition from desire psychology to belief–desire psychology through predictive and explanatory failures of desire psychology. Desire psychology alone does not explain why two actors with the same desire engage in different actions, nor why actors do things that appear contradictory to their desires. The concept of belief, once mastered, can be used to explain these anomalies; actors with the same desire do different things because they have different beliefs about how to attain what they desire, and actors do things that thwart their desires because they have false beliefs about how to attain their desires. This does not explain, however, why children develop desire psychology first. If desire psychology is so poor at predicting and explaining action, why not develop a model of beliefs and desires together from the start? In other words, there must be something intrinsically more difficult for the child in mastering the concept of belief than in mastering that of desire.

An answer to this is proposed in Chapter 5. One can also ask why anomalies help the child to apply a concept of belief, in particular. Why not abilities (or lack of them), preferences, situational causation, or traits? Clearly, there is much still to learn.

Bartsch and Wellman (1989) reported that three-year-old children were also able to explain actions in terms of false beliefs. For example, they could say that Jane was looking for her kitten under the piano, when the kitten was in fact behind a chair, by referring to Jane's false belief about the kitten's location. Perner (1991), however, has argued that the results can be interpreted in other ways and do not show understanding of false beliefs. Moreover, Moses and Flavell (1990) failed to replicate this part of their results, finding very few references to beliefs in explanations for mistaken actions. Although three-year-old children can refer appropriately to beliefs in explanations of action when no false belief is involved, a full understanding of beliefs as representational states is probably not acquired before the age of four (Perner, 1991).

This marks the fourth elaboration of the theory of action. Children aged three years can hold multiple models of reality: for example, they can have a model of reality as it is now and also a model of reality in the future, following some goal-directed action. What they lack is an understanding of the mind as a representational system. That is, they do not understand that a mental state such as a desire or a belief has a representational function, that it can, for example, misrepresent its referent. Perner (1991) argued that this understanding begins to emerge around the age of four years, and that at this age children begin to understand that beliefs can be mistaken, even that they can implant false beliefs into the minds of others. This enables them to understand the actions of others in terms of the actor's mistaken beliefs. Also, and importantly in the present context, understanding the mind as a representational system enables the meta-representation[2] of desires. They can represent a desire as a propositional attitude with an object. This enables them to consider the prospect of manipulating their desires and goals (or those of others). They can want to want things: they have the freedom to want what they want to want. Perner (1991) called this metavolition, and it is in essence Frankfurt's (1971) definition of a person. As yet, however, there seems to be no evidence on the emerging ability to manipulate desires.

To summarise progress so far, we can identify four successive elaborations of the theory of action, occurring before the age of five years. In all these elaborations, "action" is understood in terms of the basic theory of action. In the first elaboration children understand action (some actions) as goal directed. In the second elaboration, they understand that attainment of a goal results in happiness and the cessation of the goal-directed action, and that non-attainment of a goal results in unhappiness, persistence, or giving up. They also understand the specificity of the goal–outcome–reaction relation. In the third elaboration children understand action as directed by specific belief–desire combinations (instead of just desires), so that actors with the same desires may undertake different actions if they have different beliefs. Finally, children represent beliefs and desires as representations or propositional attitudes, understanding that beliefs can misrepresent their referents and that desires can be manipulated. At some point, and certainly by the age of three years, children understand action as intentional, and intentions can perhaps be placed between belief–desire combinations and action (as in Wellman's model but not the intentional theory of action).

There has been research on four other kinds of addition or extension to the theory of action: (1) antecedents to beliefs and desires; (2) reactions to outcomes of action; (3) other mental states in relation to action; (4) personality traits in relation to action.

Antecedents to Beliefs and Desires

Wellman has proposed a simple model of children's belief–desire psychology which has guided much of his research on the topic. First presented in Wellman and Bartsch (1988), the model has also appeared in Bartsch and Wellman (1989) and Wellman (1990; 1991). The model is presented in Fig. 3.2, without the lists of mental states usually appended to the various components.

In this version Wellman did not include intentions between the belief–desire component and actions, but included as extras possible antecedents to beliefs and desires, and reactions following actions, the topics of this section and the next.

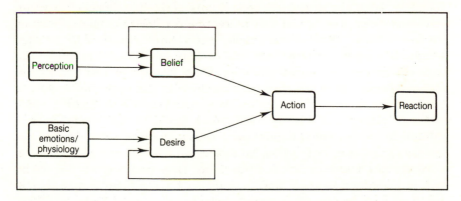

FIG. 3.2. Welman's model of children's belief–desire psychology.

As far as antecedents are concerned, Wellman has postulated two particular sources, one for beliefs and one for desires. The source proposed for desires is physiology and basic emotions. The distinction between emotions and desires, according to Wellman (1990), is that desires are propositional attitudes, which is presumably meant to imply that basic emotions are not. In this, Wellman is incorrect. Emotions are also propositional attitudes in that they have objects (Kenny, 1989); one is angry at something, afraid of something. Emotions combine mere affect with cognition, where the cognition concerns the object of the emotion. Something other than having propositional content is necessary to distinguish desires from their supposed antecedents. There does not appear, however, to have been any research on children's or adults' understanding of internal antecedents to desires, so this part of the model remains conjectural at present. As we shall see, when children first get ideas about antecedents to desires, they concern things that are not internal to the person who has the desire.

In Wellman's model beliefs have their source in perceptions. Wellman and Bartsch (1988) devised scenarios like the following: "There are magic markers on the desk and there are magic markers on the shelf. This morning Jane saw the magic markers in the desk, but she did not see the magic markers on the shelf. Now Jane wants magic markers. Where will she look for magic markers?" (Wellman, 1990, p.73). In this scenario children are told nothing about what Jane believes, but only about what she perceived. From this information, 14 out of 16 three-year-olds were able to predict that Jane would look in the location where she had seen the magic markers. According to Wellman and Bartsch (1988), these children were inferring a belief from information about perception, and using that in concert with the desire information to make an appropriate prediction about the actor's behaviour. Thus, they link perception to belief to action via desire; they understand that perception can lead to belief. A further study by Pillow (1989) showed that three-year-olds were able to judge whether a puppet character knew what colour a certain object was on the basis of whether the puppet had "seen" the object (which was in a box) or not, independently of whether they themselves had seen and knew the colour of the object. Other studies (Wimmer, Hogrefe, & Sodian, 1988; Wimmer, Hogrefe, & Perner, 1988) have failed to find evidence that children of this age understand the link between perception and belief, but this may be due to a methodological shortcoming. In these studies children were asked a double question, of the form "Does he know what is in the box, or does he not know that?". Children have difficulty with double questions even in otherwise straightforward situations (Wellman, 1990). In a study by Pratt and Bryant (1990) three-year-old children showed mastery of the perception–belief link when asked a simple question, but failed in the same situation when asked a double question. It is therefore very likely that, by the age of three years, children have some understanding of the way in which beliefs can be grounded in perception.

Reactions to Outcomes of Action

Reactions following outcomes of action tend to be specific, depending on how the outcome relates to the desire and belief underlying the action. As Wellman (1990, p.170) expressed it: "If you want something and get it, you are happy; whereas if you want it and fail to get it, you are unhappy. Similarly, if you believe something will happen and it does not, you are surprised; if you believe something will happen and it does, then you are not surprised". Research findings suggest that children have some understanding of the relation between desires and beliefs and reactions at the age of three years, though in the case of beliefs this understanding is barely beginning to emerge (Wellman & Bannerjee, 1991). These findings support that part of Wellman's model; they are further considered in the section on understanding of the causes of emotional reactions (pp. 101–105).

Other Mental States in Relation to Action

Most of the research on the child's theory of action has been driven by the intentional theory of action, as borrowed from philosophy. This theory is remarkably specific about the sorts of mental states that underlie behaviour and says nothing about the possible contribution of such states and internal factors as personality traits, ability, effort, interest, and so on, except insofar as these things can be said to function as desires (Davidson, 1968; Smith & Jones, 1986). The reason for this is that a philosophical theory has different objectives from a psychological theory: it seeks, for example, to ascertain the logical status of statements about action, or to identify what is essential and basic to action, in the sense of being involved in all and only those things that count as actions. The force of the intentional theory of action is that every action is underlain by a belief–desire combination, and that this is what makes something an action.

People in general, of course, may not have this kind of understanding of action. I have already argued that the lay understanding of action resembles Taylor's (1966) account, in which actions are often but not necessarily underlain by any or all of belief, desire, and intention, and in which actions are performed by the actor and not caused by mental states. If this is the case, then people may understand actions as underlain by all kinds of mental states, and beliefs, desires, and intentions may be important only in the sense of being the most usual concomitants of action. (There is a profound difference between what is usual to action and what is necessary to it.) This becomes easier to see if we bear in mind that action is usually not a monolithic, all-or-nothing occurrence. Jane searches for her kitten under the piano, but she may search more or less hard depending on how much she really wants to find her kitten, she may succeed or fail, depending on the amount of skill she has in searching for things, she may miss the kitten if she does not pay enough attention to what she is doing, and she may give up too soon if she is tired.

There is a smattering of evidence that children understand some of these things at the age of three years. Miller (1985) found that children aged three years were able to make correct predictions about the effect of a number of variables on performance at various tasks (e.g. learning the names of birds). These included four internal variables: interest (likes v. doesn't like), motivation (wants v. doesn't want), psychological effort (thinking hard v. not thinking hard), and intellectual ability (smart v. not smart). In a second study children aged three and four years showed similar understanding of internal factors affecting athletic performance, including energy level, strength, speed, and skill. Other studies have also shown that children understand the effect of interest on learning and attention (Miller, 1982; Miller & Zalenski, 1982).

It could be argued that these results are concerned with understanding of a special case of action, namely achievement-related behaviour, covering the same kind of ground as Weiner's (1985) theory of attribution for success and failure. But this would be to underestimate the sphere of application of these findings. Whenever an action is performed in respect of some intention or desire, the action can be said to succeed or fail, the intention is realised or not, the desire fulfilled or not. This is particularly true of young children, who are learning skills that adults take for granted. Thus, one can aim to open a door, and succeed or fail; one can find a lost kitten, or not; one can pronounce "she sells sea shells by the sea shore" (cf. Shultz, 1980) correctly, or not. Any variable that affects performance can, in principle, affect any attempt to carry out an intention or attain a desire. Miller's research shows that young children have at least an elementary understanding of how some internal variables may do so; what it does not show, unfortunately, is how children understand these variables as relating to their theory of action. In the absence of evidence from developmental research this question must be left hanging for the time being, but I shall return to it when considering adult understanding of action, in Chapter 5.

Personality Traits in Relation to Action

Ever since Heider (1958) the idea that adults tend to explain behaviour by reference to personality traits has been a mainstay of causal attribution theory. Indeed, some measures of personal attribution have only asked subjects about the extent to which an actor's behaviour was due to their personality, and have ignored most other mental states and internal variables (e.g. Storms, 1973). The idea that adults might explain action by referring to beliefs and desires has by contrast been almost completely neglected by attribution theorists and researchers; the findings of Bartsch and Wellman (1989) for adult subjects suggest that this is a serious oversight.

Developmental research presents a different picture. Studies of the use of trait terms in descriptions of others have found that children hardly use such terms at all before the age of six. Peevers and Secord (1973) reported a steady increase in the use of personal dispositional terms to describe others during childhood (as percentages of total terms used, 8% for kindergarten children, 13% for third-grade children, 22% for seventh-grade children, 33% for eleventh-grade children, and 30% for college students). These figures include references to mere behavioural consistency, however (e.g. "he is always fighting"), so are not reliable indicators of the use of trait terms. Other studies have suggested that use of trait terms emerges around the age of seven (Livesley & Bromley, 1973; Barenboim, 1981). Yuill (1992) has reported that the meanings of some trait terms are understood by five-year-olds. For a variety of trait terms, including cheerful, kind, greedy, nosey, and a few others, children of that age were able to give appropriate descriptions of the kinds of behaviour exhibited by people with the trait in question, and to give appropriate trait labels for various descriptions of behaviour. Although five-year-olds also failed with other traits, such as calm, trusty, fussy, and mean, ability at both the labelling and description tasks increased rapidly between the ages of six and ten. Eder (1989) reported some use of trait terms by children aged three and a half years, but her trait category very misleadingly included internal states such as emotions and cognitions, and in fact the examples given in her article are all feeling terms (e.g. "didn't feel very good", a notably occasion-specific attribution).

Of course, there is more to a concept of trait than simply knowing how to use trait labels. The essence of a personality trait as understood by adults is that it is a stable dispositional feature of a person, which enables predictions to be made about their behaviour in different situations by virtue of the tendency towards consistency that it is presumed to give to their behaviour. Two types of consistency may be involved: consistency in similar situations across times, and consistency across situations. Heller and Berndt (1981) assessed understanding of the former kind of consistency by asking children to predict an actor's behaviour on the basis of information about the actor's past behaviour, and found that children aged five years appeared to have mastered the idea of consistency across times. This does not imply, however, that they understand consistency as mediated by traits possessed by the actor. Bennett (1985) has pointed out that the children could have made their predictions simply by matching overt features of the behaviour, such as its positivity or negativity, without making inferences about personality characteristics. In Bennett's own study, children aged five years were more willing to predict consistency in an actor's behaviour when that behaviour was described as intentional than when the same behaviour was described as careless or unintentional. This does at least show that children are making use of information about the mental states of the actor in their predictions, such that they expect the actor's intentions to be consistent across time, but whether they understand this consistency in intentions as due to personality characteristics is not clear.

Rholes and Ruble (1984) tested children's understanding of the stability of traits across situations by looking at their expectations for an actor's future behaviour. The results showed that children aged five or six years do not expect cross-situational consistency in behaviour, but nine-year-olds do. Thus, the notion of a trait as stable across situations appears to be acquired between these ages. Newman (1991) found a similar result: indeed, his results suggest the possibility that Anglo-American children aged 10–11 years may predict greater cross-situational consistency in behaviour than college students do, although this trend was not significant. Newman reported unpublished research by Josephson (1977) apparently showing the same tendency. Rholes and Ruble (1984) also found that children aged five and six were able to use consistency and distinctiveness information (Kelley, 1967) to infer internal causation by making personal dispositional attributions, but they did not expect these dispositions to be stable across situations. They did, however, expect stability over time within situations. Older children expected both kinds of stability. Rotenberg (1980) told children stories about actors causing harm either intentionally or unintentionally. Children aged five years judged the actor as more mean when the harm was intentional than when it was unintentional, but there was no evidence that they used this attribution of meanness as a basis for predictions about the actor's future behaviour. Children aged seven years did so, however, suggesting that by then they have begun to appreciate stable dispositional properties as sources of cross-situational consistency. Rotenberg (1982) found a similar result, and also found that children aged eight to nine years understand that a personal disposition can be stable despite changes in the person's physical appearance or facial expression. Rholes and Ruble (1986) found that children aged five to six years did not seem able to sort out consistent individual differences in behaviour of actors on different occasions, an ability which is presumably necessary for an understanding of personality characteristics as stable individuating features of people. Children aged nine had acquired this ability.

The results of two studies by Ruble, Newman, Rholes, and Altshuler (1988) run somewhat counter to this. Children were given information about actor A's behaviour in situation A and actor B's behaviour in situation B, and were asked to predict actor A's behaviour in situation B. Even children aged five to six years used actor A's behaviour in situation A as a basis for prediction to some extent, contrary to the expectation that they would rely more on situational information at that age (as found by Ross, 1981). The authors commented (p.110), "young children's level of performance, however, appears to be dramatically influenced by seemingly minor variations in the context, such as the accessibility of previous behavioural information and the exact nature of that information". Also, since the situations used were similar, the results show appreciation of consistency across times, but not necessarily across situations; and there is no direct evidence that the children were inferring traits as mediators of behavioural consistency.

Finding a method which reveals the true extent of the child's understanding is a problem, and some methodological issues for this research should be noted.

1. Stipek and Daniels (1990) found that kindergarten children used trait labels to predict behaviour, but did not show sensitivity to situation characteristics. They seemed to be employing a global theory that a child possessing a positive trait (e.g. niceness) would do better than a child possessing a negative trait in all respects (including academic and athletic performance). Yuill (1993) commented that children at this age seem to have a simple theory that there are good people and bad people, and use only this for their behavioural predictions: this could account for many of the results obtained (e.g. by Heller and Berndt, 1981).

2. Most studies have given children only small quantities of behavioural information from which to draw trait inferences. Gnepp and Chilamkurti (1988) gave children information describing several instances of trait-related behaviour, and found that even six-year-olds used this to predict similar trait-related behaviour by the actor in a different situation. The children were also able to identify the trait from the behaviour descriptions, which is at least indirect evidence that their predictions were mediated by trait inferences.

3. In most studies the task set for children is abstracted from real life. Feldman and Ruble (1988) found that overt trait ascriptions by children aged five and six years increased in frequency considerably when the children were anticipating future interaction with the target, suggesting that pragmatic considerations are an important factor in trait ascription, even at this early age.

According to Secord and Peevers (1974), a final crucial milestone in the development of the child's understanding of other people (and of action) is the realisation that others behave in consistent, predictable ways, that is, the realisation that there are stable internal features of people that lend cross-situational consistency and predictability to their behaviour. The research reviewed here suggests that there are at least four stages on the road to this achievement. First, understanding of the relation between trait labels and behaviour (by five years, according to Yuill, 1992). Second, understanding of traits as underlying consistency in behaviour across times within similar situations (perhaps by six years, Bennett, 1985; Heller & Berndt, 1981; Rholes & Ruble, 1984; Ruble et al., 1988). Third, understanding of traits as underlying consistency in behaviour across different situations (perhaps by seven years, Rholes & Ruble, 1984; Rotenberg, 1980; 1982). Fourth, understanding of traits as differentiating actors from each other (by nine years, Rholes & Ruble, 1986).

It is less easy to judge, however, how personality traits become attached to the developing theory of action. When people explain behaviour by reference to personality, they typically omit any intermediate stages on the route from personality to action. This could mean that people see personality as causing action directly, but there is evidence that children understand the link as more indirect than this. This comes from a study by Millar (1984). In this study, actors who were described as either nice or bad were said to have acted in a way that led to either a good or bad outcome. The child was asked to judge whether the actor had produced the outcome intentionally or not. At both seven and nine years, children tended to judge that the action was intentional (i.e. that the actor intended the outcome that occurred) when there was a match between the characteristic of the actor and the outcome, i.e. nice actor with good outcome or bad actor with bad outcome. When there was a mismatch, i.e. nice actor with bad outcome or bad actor with good outcome, they tended to judge that the outcome was not intended by the actor. These results show a link between personality and intention: children believe that people intend things that are congruent with their personality, that personality in some way underlies the formulation of intentions. Personality, therefore, belongs somewhere among the antecedents to intentions in the developing theory of action, perhaps by shaping the desires which the actor aims to fulfill. As children grow older, they come to see personality as underlying consistent patterns in intentions, desires, and actions (Bennett, 1985). Ultimately, what personality characteristics explain is not some behaviour in itself, but the consistent and distinctive pattern of an individual's behaviour across time. By nine years, children are using the notion of stable personal dispositions as a theory of individuating consistency in behaviour.

One final caveat is that the idea of personality as the ultimate explanation for action is, to some extent at least, a cultural phenomenon. Evidence for this comes from a study by Miller (1984), who compared American subjects with subjects living in Mysore, India. Subjects were asked to describe and explain two deviant behaviours and two prosocial behaviours recently carried out by someone they knew well. The explanations were coded into several categories, but Miller concentrated on the comparison between general (personal) dispositions and situational factors. For present purposes, references to stable personal dispositions are most relevant. Such references were uniformly rare at the age of eight and increased with age. The rate of increase, however, was much greater for American subjects than for Indian subjects. How these results should be interpreted is not certain; Miller's interpretation reveals an inadequate grasp of the culture studied (Das Gupta, personal communication), and the extent to which a typically Western approach to social psychology can be validly applied in non-Western cultures is also questionable (Smith & Bond, 1993). The study does, however, serve as a reminder that children undergo enculturation, and that, at least from the age of eight years, the development of the theory of action is likely to be marked by the acquisition of culture-specific ideas and tendencies.

THE THEORY OF CAUSATION IN THE REALM OF HUMAN BEHAVIOUR

To recapitulate, in the theory of causation established by the end of infancy causal powers of things operate to produce effects under suitable conditions, the causal relation being understood as generative in nature. From the child's point of view (or from that of any person) there are in effect two versions of this, because the child or person could be on the cause or the effect side of the causal relation (or both). There is a dearth of evidence on children's use of the theory of causation in relation to themselves or to people in general, perhaps because researchers have construed it as more applicable to purely physical phenomena. This is clearly too sweeping. What most basically serves to identify action for the child is the experience of producing action; action is something I do, and I experience myself doing it (Piaget, 1954; Taylor, 1966). Many behaviours are presumably not accompanied by the experience of efficacy: a child may fall over when not very good at walking, cry when a family pet dies, jump in surprise at a loud noise, or make a mistake when trying to pronounce "she sells sea shells by the sea shore". Such things as these are not actions, but are effects of shortcomings in the child's powers, or external events acting on liabilities of the child. It is likely that children do not think of them as actions, because they lack the experience of producing them, and indeed may have a sense of them happening despite what they are trying to do. By the age of three years, we do have evidence that children regards some things of this sort as not intentional (and therefore presumably, although not absolutely certainly, as not being their own actions). The research by Shultz (1980) and his colleagues discussed earlier has shown that by the age of three years children can identify mistakes (including failures on the sea shore tongue twister), passive behaviour, and reflexes as not intentional, whether the actor is the child in person or someone else observed by the child. They also judge that an outcome was not intended when it does not match information they possess about the actor's motive or intention (Shultz & Wells, 1985) or when it was not foreseeable (Nelson-Le Gall, 1985). It is possible that young children may judge any behaviour or outcome as not intended when it does not fit any of their rules for judging intentionality (Shultz & Wells, 1985). Given the evidence, however, that young children judge behaviours such as sneezing, yawning, and even tripping as intentional (Smith, 1978), it seems more likely that they judge behaviour or outcome as intentional unless it positively contradicts their rules for attributing intentionality. For example, instead of using a matching rule to attribute intentionality, they use a non-matching rule to attribute lack of intentionality. The difference is that, in the latter case, they assume behaviour to be intentional in the absence of information about the actor's intention.

Children have two theories about what makes things happen: the theory of action and the theory of causation. By the age of three children have learned to apply the theory of action to things other people do, even though those things are not accompanied by the experience of efficacy. Shultz's research does at least make it clear that the theory of action is not applied indiscriminately to the behaviour of others, and I shall discuss later the rules children might be using to discriminate action from other behaviours in other people. One might infer from this that children understand everything that is not action as causation: that such things as mistakes, passive behaviours, and reflexes are interpreted under the theory of causation. This inference is not compelling, however, because children might just not interpret these behaviours at all. They might regard them as just things that happen, and nothing more. Consider an example. Astington and Gopnik (1991) reported an unpublished study by Gopnik and Seager in which children were shown two books, an adult book and a child book, and were asked which one an adult would choose. At the age of three, most children judged that the adult would choose the child's book, whereas this tendency was much reduced at four and five years of age. Astington and Gopnik suggested that three-year-olds may think that desirability is an objective feature of the world. Such a conceptualisation would imply that they understood desires as caused externally by features of objects, and if correct would therefore support the notion that children are applying the theory of causation to people's desires.

If correct, however, this would imply that children aged three should see everyone as having the same desires in relation to a given object. This is not the case: Wellman (1991) has reported a study of spontaneous utterances showing that children aged two are already able to distinguish their own desires from those of others, for example (p.35), "They think they are slimy. I think they are good animals". Flavell, Flavell, Green, and Moses (1990) also found that three-year-olds were capable of inferring from another person's behaviour that she didn't like a certain kind of biscuit, even though it was one that the child had selected as his or her favourite. Clearly, children at this age understand that, at least in some instances, desirability is not an objective property. The study by Gopnik and Seager (reported in Astington & Gopnik, 1991) may just show that young children are not very good at inferring the desires of others, despite recognising in principle that they may differ from their own. Where they have trouble, they could use their own desires as a kind of judgemental heuristic, in the absence of any better guide, for judging the desires of others. (The adult judgemental bias known as the false consensus effect—Marks & Miller, 1987; Ross, Greene, & House, 1977—could be a remnant of this heuristic surviving into adulthood.)

There has been no test of children's use of generative mechanism cues to make causal inferences in relation to human behaviour (analogous to the tests run by Shultz, 1982b, reviewed in Chapter 4). A case for use of the theory of causation in relation to human behaviour could be made, however, from evidence that children see some behaviours (or mental states) as externally caused, since this would at least show that they do not see such things as just happening, without any kind of causal analysis. Most such evidence concerns emotional reactions.

External Causation of Emotional Responses

There has been abundant research on children's understanding of the causes of specific emotional reactions, and it is clear that by the age of three years children already have a wide repertoire of beliefs about external causation of emotion. Even at 18 months children occasionally talk about antecedents to emotions, and "by 24 months the children engaged in conversations about the cause of feeling states, taking an active part in enquiring about antecedents and offering appropriate causal answers" (Dunn, Bretherton, & Munn, 1987, p.138). Bretherton and Beeghly (1982) reported some examples of spontaneous statements about causes of emotional states by children aged 28 months: "I give a hug. Baby be happy";

"I'm hurting your feelings cos I was mean to you"; "Grandma mad. I wrote on wall"; and "Bad dreams scare me". In three of these four examples, the emotional state is attributed to someone other than the speaker. Bretherton and Beeghly observed (p.919) that "children tend to speak of their own states before they label those of others, but the lag is relatively small". Not only are children of this age able to attribute emotional states to others, but they evidently have ideas about the causes of those states that make sense to adults. Further evidence of this with older children (aged three to five years) comes from a study by Fabes, Eisenberg, McCormick, and Wilson (1988). Observers in a school playground watched for naturally occurring emotions and then asked a child near the emotional child "Why is X (happy, sad, etc.)?". Children gave various explanations for anger, happiness, sadness, and distress, which were coded into various categories. Fabes et al. found close agreement between children's explanations and adult judgements. Moreover, children frequently referred to goal states in their explanations, and tended to explain anger in particular by referring to some action that thwarted a goal of the angry child. These results reinforce the notion that children have a sophisticated ability to make causal attributions for emotional reactions by the age of three.

I use the word "causal" deliberately here. To us as adults there is nothing surprising about the idea that emotions are caused by external events, just as there is nothing surprising about explaining actions in terms of the actor's beliefs and desires. But a young child could in principle have a variety of different ideas about emotions, which need not resemble adults' theories very closely. What is striking about these findings is not just that adults agree that children's causal attributions for emotions make sense, but that children do not see emotional behaviour as action. That is, they do not see angry behaviour or distress as something the actor does intentionally, or chooses to do. Indeed, at the age of four, external causation appears to be the only theory the child has about emotional behaviour: it is not until the age of six, for example, that the child is able to see emotional behaviour as strategic, as motivated by the goals and concerns of the actor (Harris & Gross, 1988). At the age of six children understand that one may put on an appearance of emotion because of certain motives (e.g. the actor didn't want other children to laugh at her)—in other words, they understand that under some circumstances emotional behaviour is action, performed intentionally, and explicable in terms of beliefs and desires. Before that age they do not understand this, and only see emotional behaviour as caused by events. Similarly, Lalljee, Watson, and White (1983) found that children aged five years tended to explain emotions by referring to past events or (more rarely) the current situation or some characteristic of the person concerned. They almost never explained emotions in terms of the person's goals, whereas they frequently explained actions in this way.

In fact, children's understanding is more sophisticated than this, because they see an emotional reaction as due to an interaction between external events and some state of the actor; not only that, but they have consistent ideas about the kinds of event–state interactions that result in particular emotions. Consider again the child's theory of action. In general, children by the age of three years tend to explain action in terms of relevant beliefs and desires: for example, Jane looked for her kitten under the piano because she wanted to find it and believed it was there. Adults understand certain kinds of emotional reaction as dependent on the outcome of Jane's action. In the case of desire, for example, attaining what one wants results in generally positive emotions such as happiness and satisfaction, and failing to attain what one wants results in negative emotions such as sadness, anger, or frustration. In the case of beliefs, an outcome that disconfirms a belief leads to what Wellman (1990) referred to as "cognitive" emotions such as surprise, puzzlement, and disappointment, whereas outcomes that confirm beliefs do not lead to these things, though it is less clear what they do produce in the way of emotions. Again, these emotions are not actions, they are reactions, which means specifically that they are produced by events acting upon a particular liability of the person who experiences the emotion. In principle, liabilities are stable: everyone has the liability to be made angry at any time. In practice, liabilities are more specific than that because of their dependence upon the mental state of the experiencer; whether an outcome acts on a person's liability to be surprised depends on what they were expecting about it. (Technically, the mental state acts as an enabling condition—a full account of this can be found in Harré & Madden, 1975.)

Research findings show that children around the age of three years already understand the specificity of some of these kinds of emotional reaction. Yuill (1984) found that children aged three judged an actor more pleased with an intended outcome than with an unintended outcome (in fact the phrase she used was "wants to do", which identifies a desire rather than an intention) when the motive for action was neutral, though not when the motive was bad. Wellman and Bartsch (1988) found that four-year-olds judged an actor happy when she got what she wanted and when she didn't get what she didn't want, and they judged the actor to be unhappy when she got what she didn't want or didn't get what she did want. Similar findings for children aged three years have been reported by Hadwin and Perner (1991) and Wellman and Bannerjee (1991). The importance of these findings is that the judgement of emotion did not depend just on the outcome, but on the relation of the outcome to the actor's desire, showing that children aged three or four understand something of the interaction between mental states and events in the production of emotional reactions.

Findings on the relation between belief and surprise are less clear. Since children appear to incorporate beliefs into the theory of action later than desires, one might expect an understanding of the relation between beliefs and reactions also to be slower to develop. Indeed, Hadwin and Perner (1991) found that children did not understand surprise as a reaction to mismatch between belief and reality until the age of five. There was evidence, however, that younger children have a specific understanding of the word "surprise" as something pleasant (as in a birthday surprise), and this may account for their poor performance. According to Hadwin and Perner, acquisition of the adult meaning of "surprise" comes about when children have a concept of belief sophisticated enough to give them the notion of something unexpected—that is, a concept of a belief as an expectation, which may or may not be violated. There is therefore a lag between understanding belief and understanding its role in bringing about emotional reactions.

Other studies, however, have found evidence that children do have some grasp of surprise at younger ages. Wellman and Bartsch (1988) found that four-year-olds were more likely to judge an actor as surprised if something happened that she did not think was going to happen, or if something did not happen that she thought was going to happen, than if something happened that she thought was going to happen, or if something did not happen that she did not think was going to happen. Again, this interactive pattern is important because it shows that children are not judging just from the outcome: they can only succeed at this task by integrating information about belief and outcome. Wellman and Bannerjee (1991) found, as Hadwin and Perner (1991) did, that three-year-olds understand surprise only as a pleasant reaction, but they went on to show that children of that age do understand both surprise and curiosity as reactions to unexpected events. Suppose a child is asked why a character is surprised. If they understand surprise as essentially similar to happiness, they might answer this question by referring to the character's desire. If, however, they understand surprise as related to belief, then they should reply by referring to the character's belief: for example, if the character is surprised to find that it is raining, they should tend to say "because he thought it wouldn't rain", rather than "because he likes the rain". Wellman and Bannerjee (1991) found that three-year-olds referred to beliefs more when explaining surprise than when explaining happiness, and this supports that idea that they have some understanding of suprise as a function of belief and outcome, as opposed to desire and outcome.

Understanding of a wide range of emotions appears to develop rapidly from the age of four. We have already seen that four-year-olds tend to explain anger by referring to the goals of the angry person in ways that adults judge appropriate (Fabes et al., 1988). By the age of six, children are beginning to understand other emotions in relation to specific causes of success and failure. For example, they tend to associate pride with success due specifically to effort, and surprise with success due specifically to luck (Stipek & Decotis, 1988). The same study found that children of the same age associate guilt with failure due to lack of effort as opposed to bad luck, but also associate it with lack of ability, as if they suppose that one is responsible for one's ability just as one is for the amount of effort one exerts. Children have essentially mastered these relations by the age of nine.

Here I have concentrated on children's understanding of the causes of emotions; research on their general understanding of emotions has been reviewed by Miller and Aloise (1989).

External Causation of Other Behaviours

Perhaps the least controversial evidence for beliefs about external causation of behaviour comes from studies of children's understanding of the effects of external variables on performance. In a study by Miller (1985) children as young as three years made correct predictions about the effects of several external variables on performance at a number of tasks. The variables included parental pressure, noise level, visual distraction, and external reward (money). Three-year-olds know that distracting noise interferes with remembering (Wellman, 1977), and five-year-olds know that memory is aided by help from others, written reminders, and external cues (Wellman, 1977; 1978). Three-year-olds also understand that noise can affect performance on a writing task (Miller & Zalenski, 1982).

Some studies have found evidence that children aged five (Ross, 1981) and eight (Miller, 1984) tend to attribute other sorts of behaviour to situational factors and objects. Other studies (Ruble et al., 1988) have found evidence contrary to this, and both the generality and validity of these findings are open to question (Miller & Aloise, 1989). One problem, for example, is that references to situational factors in explanations do not imply a view of the behaviour as situationally caused. When Jim says that he bought some flowers for his mother because it was her birthday, he does not mean that the situational factor caused his behaviour; he means that buying the flowers was an action of his, and reference to the birthday is an elliptical description of the belief, or part of the belief, that lay behind his action. Since Miller (1984) simply recorded references to situational factors in the explanations her subjects gave, her results do not show belief in external causation of behaviour.

In a study by Ruble, Feldman, Higgins, and Karlovac (1979) subjects watched an actor select an item from an array. They were then asked (p.602): "Does the person's choice tell you more about the object on the card, that it's really nice; or more about the person, such as his/her own personal taste?". The experimenters also manipulated consensus: the subjects watched four other actors being asked "who else likes that one best?", whereupon the actors either all nodded and smiled or all shook their heads and frowned. Ruble et al. ran three age groups: four to five years, eight to nine years, and adults. All three age groups tended to attribute more to the object than to the person when consensus was high than when it was low. The youngest group, however, tended to attribute more to the object under both conditions, whereas the other two groups tended to attribute to the person in the low consensus condition. A similar study was run by Higgins and Bryant (1982), and they found similar results. In this case they varied the age of the actor making the choice, and found that older subjects attributed more to the actor when the actor was their own age, and more to the object when the actor was of a different age; but the youngest group, again aged four or five years, attributed more to the object in both cases.

These studies show children aged four or five years tending to make causal attributions to objects, even for behaviour such as choices which they presumably see as intentional (Shultz, 1980; Smith, 1978), when slightly older children tend to prefer making causal attributions to the person for the same behaviours. It is not certain how this pattern should be interpreted, but there are two possibilities that fit well with the rest of the research evidence reviewed in this chapter. One is that children first acquire the notion of situational causes of behaviour (other than emotions) around the age of four, and initially tend to overgeneralise it, perhaps because at first they lack clear rules for applying the idea. We have seen that younger children do judge some behaviours as not intentional (Shultz, 1980; Shultz et al., 1980; Shultz & Wells, 1985), but this is not the same as saying that they have a positive idea about how unintentional behaviours are produced. Situational causation may be their first hypothesis about this.

The second possibility is that children of this age are just beginning to grapple with the problem of consistency across occurrences. They might have noticed, for example, that similar behaviours occur on different occasions, involving the same actor or different actors, the same situation or different situations, the same object or different objects. Perhaps at the age of four they begin to seek some unifying explanation for consistency in behaviour, and the first theory they formulate is a theory of object or situation causation. Behaviour is consistent across occasions because objects have stable and specific causal powers by virtue of which they tend to produce similar effects on people across occasions. This theory is therefore grounded in their understanding of physical causation, which is well developed by that age (see Chapter 4). It does not imply a rejection of their theory of action, however. Instead, objects are seen as causal antecedents to the elaborated theory of action that they possess at that age, exerting their influence not directly upon behaviour but upon the beliefs and desires in respect of which the person acts. After the age of six, when children have acquired the idea of personality characteristics as stable and enduring, they change theories, coming to see personality as the source of consistency in people's behaviour.

Although these possibilities are merely speculative at present, indirect support comes from a study by Rholes and Ruble (1986), who investigated children's ability to integrate information about behaviours separated in time. They commented (p.877): "To come to regard dispositions as stable entities, children probably must first become aware of (a) cross-situationally consistent patterns of behaviour and (b) individual differences in such patterns among the people whom they regularly observe". Their results showed that children aged five to six lack the latter (p.877): "individual differences in the actors' patterns of behaviour became obscured in the younger children's perceptions". Now if children aged five to six are aware of cross-situational consistencies in behaviour but not of consistent differences between individuals then it would be natural for them to see the situation, or things in the situation, as responsible for the consistencies they observe; they cannot interpret consistencies as a function of individuals if they are not sensitive to consistent differences in behaviour patterns across individuals. This may therefore explain why children aged five to six are going through a stage of being object or situation theorists. By the age of nine they are able to perceive consistent individual differences and have therefore become trait theorists.

RULES FOR DIFFERENTIATING ACTION AND CAUSATION

I have so far concentrated on the development of the child's theories of action and causation in the realm of human behaviour, showing that even by five years of age the child has a sophisticated, organised repertoire of concepts, particularly in relation to action. It is evident that children are able to differentiate action from causation in human behaviour, even if not always in the way that adults do; they identify mistakes and reflexes as being in the realm of causation (Shultz, 1980) and, when asked why Jane is searching for her kitten under the piano, they are able to decide without further information or cues that her behaviour is action, and explain it accordingly (Bartsch & Wellman, 1989). How do they do this?

In early stages infants identify their own actions as those things that they experience themselves producing. This differentiates things infants do from such things as passive behaviours, e.g. being picked up and carried by an adult. No doubt the experience of producing action continues to be an identifier of one's own actions throughout life; I certainly have a sense of my own actions as things that I do, and this comes, at least in part, from the actual experience of doing them. Things that I do not have the experience of doing do not seem to me to be actions. In this function, we can say that the experience of producing has the status of a rule—a rule for identifying one's own actions.

The experience of producing is not good enough on its own, however, for two reasons. First, it is clear that children soon come to identify things that other people do as actions, and they does not have the experience of producing in relation to these things. Children must therefore have developed ways of identifying actions by others which do not depend on the experience of production. Second, the experience of producing relates to actions, not to outcomes. Many things that can be identified as actions because they are accompanied by the experience of producing do not lead to the desired or intended outcome. The action of bringing a spoonful of food to the mouth is accompanied by the experience of production regardless of whether the food ends up in the mouth or on the nose. Therefore, once infants or young children have an idea of action as involving desires or intentions, the experience of production is no longer adequate as an identifier of actions because it does not differentiate those actions that lead to successful realisation of desires or intentions from those that do not.

The simplest way to identify things other people do as actions is by the cue of resemblance. That is, children can observe that things others do resemble things they can do themselves, and infer inductively that those things are actions and are accompanied by the experience of production for the person who carries them out. It is not clear at what age infants might start to do this, but the ground for this ability is laid early in life. According to Piaget (1954), infants recognise independent centres of action by stage 4 or 5 of the sensorimotor period: this does not imply that infants see those things that others do as being actions at that stage, but it is part of what is required for that to be possible. As far as use of the cue of resemblance is concerned, the ground for this is laid even earlier, at stage 3. At this stage infants master the game of imitation, and the game of imitation cannot be mastered except by one who can recognise resemblance between its own actions and those of others. Infants are therefore equipped to generalise the basic theory of action to things others do by means of the cue of resemblance before the age of 18 months.

Identifying whether outcomes are intended or not is a more difficult problem. For one's own actions, intentionality of an outcome can be judged by the match with some stored representation of the intention. That is, if infants remember their intention at least until the outcome occurs, then they can judge by match or mismatch whether the outcome was intended or not. This procedure has been proposed as a rule for identifying intentionality of outcomes by Shultz and Wells (1985; see also Shultz & Kestenbaum, 1985). To be precise, the matching rule specifies that "if there is a match between an intentional state and a behavioural outcome, then that outcome is intended. If there is not a match, then the conclusion is that the outcome is not intended" (Shultz & Kestenbaum, 1985, p.223). Although presumably originating in experience of one's own intentional action, the rule can be used in application to the behaviour of others if the judge has information about others' intentions. Use of this rule was tested by Shultz and Wells (1985). They used a game involving a ray gun. On depressing the trigger of the ray gun a beep was emitted and a light went off behind one of five target colours, indicating a "hit". Children either shot the gun themselves or observed others doing so; sometimes the shooter stated an intention prior to firing and sometimes not. Shultz and Wells found that children aged three years used the matching rule to identify intentionality of outcome (which light went off) all the time for their own actions, and for others when they had evidence of the actor's intention.

According to Shultz and Wells (1985) and Shultz and Kestenbaum (1985) the matching rule is the primary identifier of intentionality of outcomes because it deals with the essence of intentional states by employing direct awareness of intentions, in the actor's own case. In the case of others, however, the rule cannot always be applied because information about the intentions of others is not always available. For such cases, Shultz and Wells (1985, p.84) proposed three further rules.

1. Valence. "Outcomes that are positive for the actor are intended, whereas outcomes that are negative for the actor are not intended". Valence of outcomes can be judged by the actor's reactions, such as emotional expressions, so information about emotional expressions could also be used as a means of judging intentionality of outcomes (Shultz & Kestenbaum, 1985).

2. Monitoring. "An outcome is intentional insofar as the actor is observed to monitor, and thus presumably control, the relation between action and outcome".

3. Discounting. "Intentionality is discounted to the extent that a sufficient external cause of the behaviour is operational". This is a variant on Kelley's (1972b; 1973) discounting principle, and some of the evidence that children use that principle counts as support for this variant as well (Karniol & Ross, 1976; Shultz & Butkowsky, 1977; Shultz, Wells, & Sarda, 1980; Wells & Shultz, 1980).

In their experiment, Shultz and Wells (1985) found that children aged three years could use the matching rule for the behaviour of others, but that the other principles were not used at three years, used inconsistently at seven years, and used consistently only at eleven years. Other studies have suggested, however, that younger children can use these rules to judge the intentionality of outcomes for the behaviour of others when the matching rule cannot be used. Cues to valence can be used to judge intentionality of outcomes by the age of five (Rybash, Roodin, & Hallion, 1979; Smith, 1978) but apparently not at the age of four (Smith, 1978). On the other hand, this result may be specific to Smith's study, because several studies have shown that children understand the relation between desires and emotional reactions to outcomes by the age of three years (Hadwin & Perner, 1991; Wellman & Bannerjee, 1991; Yuill, 1984). Children also seem to become able to use the monitoring rule around the age of five (Smith, 1978). Children seem able to use the Shultz and Wells variant on the discounting principle by the age of three years under some circumstances (Shultz et al., 1980), though perhaps not under others (Shultz & Kestenbaum, 1985).

A child who has mastered the matching rule but not the others will have trouble making judgements about outcomes when not in possession of information about the actor's intention. The matching rule can be interpreted in two ways: Either the child only judges an outcome as intentional when a positive match is observed, or the child only judges an outcome as unintentional when a positive mismatch is observed. These alternatives generate different predictions for the child who has no other rules and no information about intentions: Under the former, the outcome in question should be judged unintentional, and under the latter it should be judged intentional. At present, evidence favours the latter: Smith (1978) found that children aged four years, who had not mastered the valence and monitoring rules, tended to judge everything the actor did as intentional, even such things as sneezing and tripping over obstacles.

These may not be the only rules that children could use for judging intentionality of outcomes. To give just one example, Heider (1958) suggested that intentional action is characterised by equifinality, meaning that if one route to a goal is blocked the actor will attempt to find another route to the same goal. Thus, action tends to be characterised (p.101) by "the invariance of the end and the variability of the means". Heider recognised that physical systems also sometimes exhibit equifinality, giving as an example a marble in a bowl, which will always come to rest at the lowest point regardless of its starting point or route (see also Taylor, 1966). Heider argued that, in the case of personal causality, equifinality is due to the person as a local cause, as a leader or possessor of power directing events towards the intended conclusion, whereas in the case of physical causality there is no centre of power but merely an entire system governed by universal physical laws. Whether children can appreciate and use this distinction is a moot point; there does not appear to have been any study of children's use of equifinality to infer intentionality.

IS THE DISTINCTION BETWEEN ACTION AND CAUSATION FUNDAMENTAL?

The content of this chapter is shaped by the particular theoretical orientation here, that is, the idea of a fundamental distinction in the child's understanding between action and causation. With this distinction, the primary task in the interpretation of behaviour is to judge whether it is action or not, and the rules described are devices which allow children to do that. It could be argued that this begs the question, in that there are other possible distinctions and perhaps one of these, and not the action–causation distinction, is truly fundamental. Traditionally in attribution theory the distinction between internal and external factors in the causation of behaviour has been treated as fundamental (Heider, 1958), and as we saw in the previous chapter some authors have postulated an agent–patient distinction as basic (Premack, 1990; Shultz, 1991). There are problems with both of these, however.

Research has shown that the internal–external distinction is not fundamental to our understanding of behaviour (Miller, Smith, & Uleman, 1981; White, 1991). The problem can be expressed quite simply. References to internal and external factors can be made within both the theory of causation and the theory of action. In the case of action, references to external factors can play the same roles as references to internal factors in reasons explanations, because they may serve to identify the content of the actor's desires or beliefs. Beliefs are especially likely to be identified elliptically by reference to external factors; when we say that John bought his mother some flowers because it was her birthday, we do not imply that the external factor, the birthday, was the cause of John's behaviour, but rather that we mean to identify it as John's true belief, and as part of his reason for action. In the case of causation, we explain behaviour as the elicitation of a liability of the actor, brought about by the causal power of something that may be either internal or external to the actor. We cannot know what a reference to an internal or an external factor means unless we know whether the behaviour in question has been interpreted as action or not.

Take as an example the studies by Ruble et al. (1979) and Higgins and Bryant (1982). In these, children aged four to five years tended to say that, when a person chose an object from an array, that told them more about the object, that it was desirable, than about the person making the choice. This does not imply, however, that they saw the choice as externally caused. They could have interpreted the properties of the object as an external cause, that is as causal powers acting upon liabilities of the actor so as to produce a reaction of liking, and the behaviour of choosing the object. They could also have interpreted the properties of the object as a reason in an account of the choice as intentional, that is to say an account which draws on the concepts in the theory of action. Liking may in fact pose problems of interpretation (for adults as well as children), in that it could be seen as akin to emotion and therefore interpreted under the theory of causation, or as akin to choosing and therefore interpreted under the theory of action. We cannot know what the children meant by their judgement without ascertaining which of these two interpretations they adopted. The internal–external distinction therefore confounds and is subservient to the distinction between action and causation as accounts of behaviour.

Turning to the agent–patient distinction, Premack (1990) and Shultz (1991) have suggested that agency or self-movement is basic to the developing concept of action; in effect, infants first have a theory of agency and an understanding of action develops from that. Premack (1990), for example, proposed that infants divide the world into two kinds of objects: those that are and those that are not self-propelled. The rules for attribution of agency proposed by Shultz (1991) are similar in that they are used to identify an object as being of a certain kind. Thus, the world becomes divided into agents and non-agents, or patients. This fails to be fundamental, however, because it is too global. Things that are agents may also be patients, as the infant must know from its own personal experience. It is likely that an understanding of how things happen develops on the interpretation of individual occurrences, not from the rule-based classification of objects.

As in the case of the internal–external distinction, rules to do with self-movement fail to distinguish action from causation. Self-movement can be understood either as action or as caused. To take a simple example, as adults we understand the movement of a battery-powered toy as caused and not as action, even though it counts as self-movement. It is possible that, at an early stage, infants interpret all agency as action and everything other than agency as causation, but there is no evidence for this. As we have seen, before the age of two young children already understand that some things that people do are not actions (e.g. emotional behaviours), so they have clearly learned something that goes beyond classifying things as agents. Moreover, judging whether something is self-movement or not is far from straightforward owing to the fact that many causes are not readily observable (see Chapter 2), so the use of self-movement as a rule for attributing a concept of action would be fraught with difficulties and uncertainty. For all of these reasons, it is to be doubted whether a notion of agency plays any role of importance in the development of understanding of how things happen.

To summarise, the distinction that is fundamental for young children is not that between agent and patient, nor that between internal and external causes. It is that between action and causation. Children have to learn these and other concepts and distinctions and how they interrelate; overlap between them is no better than partial. Internal and external causes can both be of different types. Self-movement can involve either action or causation. Even adults may not have mastered all of this, especially in an age where machines do things that look more and more like actions. But the basis on which an understanding of all these things is erected is the fundamental distinction between action and causation, and the organised network of concepts distinctively associated with each by middle childhood.

It is clear that the child's understanding of human behaviour and how it is produced develops rapidly during early childhood. This review has outlined the main steps in that development, as far as research has revealed them so far. It is less clear, however, how this understanding develops, by what means the child acquires a more sophisticated, elaborate, and discriminating set of beliefs about human behaviour. Several possible learning mechanisms have been proposed (e.g. Johnson, 1988; Kuhn, 1989; Shultz, 1988). Most relevant research, however, has been carried out in the sphere of physical causation: for this reason, a review of possible learning mechanisms will be reserved for the next chapter.

NOTES

1. Perner (1991) reports that a sample of slightly older children (3.2 to 3.5 years) performed less well than the sample studied by Wellman and Woolley (1990). At present there is therefore some doubt about the age at which children master desire psychology.
2. There is some ambiguity in the use of the term "metarepresentation". Perner used it to mean the representation of the representational relation itself, or the representation of something as a representation. This is the ability which, he argued, children develop from the age of four years.

CHAPTER FOUR

The Child's Understanding
of Action and Causation
in the Physical World

The aim of this chapter is to review the development of the child's understanding of the causation of events and occurrences in the physical world, from the end of infancy onwards. As in the previous chapter, the review will concentrate on the application and development of the two theories to the realm of physical causation. Most of this chapter will be concerned with the theory of causation. I shall first consider the extent to which the theory of action might be applied in the realm of physical causation.

THEORY OF ACTION

The theory of action is, in essence, a theory of how a being's movements are caused from the inside, that is, it is a theory of self-movement. The primary sphere of application of this theory, therefore, is apparent self-movement. The word "apparent" is relevant because many kinds of movement may appear to be self-movement when in fact they are not. Any movement which does not have an obvious or easily inferrable cause, or about the cause of which the perceiver has no belief, will appear to be self-movement. Even adults have problems with this,[1] and for children, who have fewer preconceived beliefs about the causes of movement, and whose inferential skills are more limited, interpreting apparent self-movement must be even more difficult and prone to error.

Consider the following examples. A child takes a biscuit from a plate. Another person does the same thing. The child jumps at a sudden noise. Another person does the same thing. A dog walks across the floor, or turns its head to look at something, or attacks something. The branches of a tree move (actually in the wind). Clouds move. A volcano erupts. A mechanical toy walks across the floor. The second hand of a clock moves around the dial. A wound-up piece of string unwinds. The sun moves behind the trees when the child walks. A balloon released from the hand flies across the room (actually propelled by the jet of air escaping from the nozzle of the balloon under pressure).

Most of these examples are not of action, but they are all of things which may appear to be self-movement, to a child if not to an adult. If the child is going to err in applying the theory of action too broadly, it is in cases of apparent self-movement where that error is most likely to occur. I have put the issue like this in order to distinguish it from the problem of animism, or of the child's concept of life, to tie it to the fundamental distinction between action and causation. The basic theory of action as outlined in Chapter 2 does not depend on a concept of life, and is in principle distinct from it. A child can apply the theory of action to a case of apparent self-movement without believing or judging that the thing that moved is alive. Even a child with no concept of life at all could do this. A child can also judge something to be alive without granting it the capacity to perform actions. Whether the child can interpret apparent self-movement using the more elaborated theory of action, involving concepts of intention, desire, and belief, without judging the thing that moved as alive is also an open question. It is very likely that children have to learn the set of relationships that pertain between these various concepts: that, for example, only living things can have minds, that only living things with minds can have desires and intentions, that self-movement is not confined to living things, and so on. Thus, if a child says that a piece of string "wants" to unwind, he or she may be applying part of the elaborated theory of action to the interpretation of the string's behaviour, but we cannot infer from this that the child believes that the string is alive, or that it has a mind, or thoughts. These are empirical questions. We think of these things as if they always go together, but, at least early in development, children may see them all as independent of each other.

There is evidence that young children apply the theory of action to some cases of apparent self-movement. Piaget (1930) claimed that, for young children, any movement involves force, and the concept of force is as life, will, and substance (p.174): "The child fills the world with spontaneous movements and living 'forces'; the heavenly bodies may rest or move as they please, clouds make wind by themselves, waves 'raise' themselves, trees swing their branches spontaneously to make a breeze". Inanimate things are endowed not only with life but with will: in other words, their movements are actions. Movement is regarded as intentional and is explained teleologically: for example, the sun is said to move along in order to give us light, the clouds move in order to give us rain. Piaget went so far as to claim that, in early childhood, every movement of a thing is interpreted as the thing moving itself, even a leaf moving in a breeze. This claim is too extreme, as we shall see later, but if Piaget was right and children attribute will to things and explain movement in terms of purposes then they must be using the theory of action for those things. Piaget (1974) added some further illustrations of this tendency in young children. He reported (p.69), for example, that children at the pre-operational stage (aged four to five years) have difficulty in understanding a yo-yo; in explaining why the spool goes back up when it reaches the end of the string, they would sometimes attribute the effect to the spool itself, "which wants to go back up".

On the basis of interview studies of the child's developing concept of life, Piaget (1929) postulated four stages of development of this concept. In the first, activity or usefulness of any kind is the criterion for attributing life. Thus, even poison can be said to be alive because of its power to kill. In the second stage, life is attributed to things that move, even to stones rolling down a slope. In the third, (apparent) self-movement is the criterion. In one of Piaget's examples, a child stated that a stream was alive because the water was moving all the time. In the fourth, only plants and animals are said to be alive.

Findings since then have been mixed: some investigations have lent further support to Piaget's claims, some investigations have failed to support the notion of stages in the development of the concept of life, and others have failed to find evidence of animistic thought in children at all (Looft & Bartz, 1969). As Looft and Bartz pointed out, methodological problems make interpretation difficult. For example, the word "life" or "alive" might just mean something different to a child. It might mean just "having the power to move" and nothing more. One study found that children would call a chipped dish dead because it was broken and of no use (Russell & Dennis, 1939). Perhaps the most serious problem is that children may say that things are alive, and even treat them as if they were alive, without believing it. Children as young as two years engage in pretend play in which they attribute desires and other mental states to dolls and other inanimate objects (Fenson, 1984; Shultz, 1991). Adults frequently use animistic metaphors when describing occurrences which they know are purely physical (Heider & Simmel, 1944; Michotte, 1963). Children may therefore be engaging in a kind of game with the experimenter, in which they make pretend attributions or play with metaphors, not meaning to be taken literally.

More recent research suggests that young children are not consistently or excessively animistic, and that self-movement is a key feature of the concept of life. Siegler and Richards (1983) found that even at four to five years children tended to judge that animals were alive but that plants and objects capable of movement were not. Even so, when they asked children to name those attributes that make things that are alive different from things that are not alive, children at all ages from four to eleven years nominated self-movement more often than anything else. This suggests that they treat self-movement as a necessary but not sufficient condition for something to be alive; on the other hand, if self-movement is used as a criterion, then it will lead to errors of attribution in cases of apparent self-movement by inanimate objects. Findings suggest that such errors may occur, but that they reflect specific areas of ignorance rather than a general tendency. Bullock (1985a) showed children videos of animate and inanimate objects, with movement either spontaneous or elicited, and then asked questions such as "does X have a brain?", and "if X breaks, can we fix it with glue?". Children aged three years were no more likely to give inanimate objects animate properties than vice versa, but merely seemed uncertain about the properties of objects in general. By the age of four, children were almost as good as adults. Gelman and Kremer (1991) looked at children's explanations of how things originate, and also suggested that errors of attribution reflected domain-specific ignorance rather than a general tendency to animistic thought. They argued that, when guessing, children make use of knowledge from domains with which they are familiar, and that these tend to involve reference to people because that is what children know most about.

Any of these points could be applied to Piaget's (1930) early work on the child's concept of physical causality. Children may be applying the theory of action to such things as celestial bodies and weather, but also they may just not know how else to describe the power of an inanimate object to move apparently by itself; they may knowingly be using the theory of action as a metaphor, or engaging in pretend play; or, being ignorant of how the cosmos and the weather actually work, they may just be making guesses by means of an analogy with the domain of human action, with which they are most familiar. As Shultz (1982b) pointed out, Piaget's strategy has consistently been to identify the limits on the child's understanding by finding questions to which the child does not know the answer, rather than by discovering what the child does know and understand. It is exactly under these circumstances that children will indulge in unconstrained guesswork, and their guesses cannot be taken as indications of what they actually believe. The available evidence is therefore inconclusive.

Nobody knows where the boundaries between action and causation lie. Does a cat have intentions, or act because of particular belief–desire combinations? But we can ask some sensible questions about the application of the theory of action in the non-human realm. As indicated in Chapter 3, the theory of action undergoes considerable development during childhood, in which further concepts are erected upon the basic theory of action. The basic theory of action comes to be associated with the concept of a person, and in Chapter 2 I suggested three basic characteristics of persons: persistence, being a centre of inner experience, and being an originator of action. Children also come to distinguish the mental from the physical in various ways. The sensible questions therefore concern the extent to which the concepts in or intimately related to the theory of action are applied outside the human realm at different stages of development. Thus, do children at any stage attribute the basic theory of action to beings other than human beings? Do they see any other beings as persons, or as having minds? Do they at any stage attribute any or all of the mental concepts associated with action to other beings (cats, trees, computers, balloons, etc.)—desires, intentions, beliefs, personality traits, and so on? Can these concepts be detached from the basic theory of action, so that even a being that is not a person can still be understood as having desires, beliefs, and so on? Due to the fact that research effort has been concentrated on animism and the concept of life, and to the methodological problems discussed above, we have no answers to these questions at present. One can only suggest that they are fertile ground for future work.

THEORY OF CAUSATION

To repeat from the end of Chapter 2, by the age of two years the child is in possession of a theory of causation with the following characteristics. Causation involves some causal power of a thing operating to produce a given effect under a given condition. That is, the concepts of causal power, liability, and releasing condition apply as they do to action, but it is the causal power and not a person or "I" that produces the effect, and the property of necessitation applies; if appropriate conditions are set up, the power must operate to produce its effect, and cannot choose otherwise. The causal relation is understood as generative, which is derived from the experience of producing action, but divorced from the actor.

This theory in itself undergoes little further development during childhood. Most of the development that takes place involves the acquisition and refinement of content-specific beliefs, such as beliefs about the causal powers of particular kinds of thing. The key set of experiments are those carried out by Shultz and his colleagues (Shultz, 1982b; Shultz, Altmann, & Asselin, 1986; Shultz, Fisher et al., 1986).

Shultz (1982b) ran a series of studies designed to test the idea that children understand the causal relation as generative, and that this understanding overrides the use of other rules and cues such as covariation, temporal and spatial contiguity, and similarity. The first study involved the transmission of sound and wind. For the sound transmission procedure, the experimenter held two tuning forks. One was made to vibrate by banging it against a hard surface, and then both were placed inside a box, which resonated audibly. For the wind transmission procedure, two blowers were used. The experimenter lit a candle, turned on one of the blowers, then removed a shield from between the blowers and the candle, whereupon the candle went out. In both versions, children as young as two years reliably identified which tuning fork made the box vibrate and which blower made the candle go out. Moreover, in versions in which generative transmission cues were in conflict with temporal contiguity and spatial contiguity cues, children relied on generative transmission for their causal inferences. When asked to justify their choices, most children referred to generative transmission (e.g. "The white one because it blowed it. The green one didn't because it didn't go", a five-year-old, quoted by Shultz, 1982b, p.13).

The second study was concerned with light transmission. Shultz used two flashlights, each aimed at a spot on the wall, and asked children to identify which flashlight was making a spot of light on the wall. A screen could be used to block the path of the light. The youngest children in this study were aged three years, and as in the previous study these children made consistently correct attributions, justified their choices by referring to generative transmission, and continued to rely on generative transmission when it was in conflict with temporal contiguity, spatial contiguity, and covariation cues.

A third study mixed the apparatus from the preceding two. For example, if a blower and a flashlight are both turned on, which will a child identify as the cause of a spot of light on the wall, and how will they justify their choice? Children could not use temporal contiguity, spatial contiguity, or covariation cues to solve these problems because each was equated across the two possible causes. As before, however, children as young as three years were extremely accurate in identifying the cause of the effect, and again tended to refer to generative transmission in their explanations.

Shultz's fourth study was a replication of the sound transmission version of study 1 and the light transmission study, using as subjects urban and rural schoolchildren living in Mali. These children had no Western schooling and virtually no contact with Westerners or Western technology. Even at age three, these children showed very similar performance to their Western counterparts, except that they were somewhat less inclined to give verbal justifications for their choices. Shultz commented that this could be due to the strangeness and novelty of the testing situation. The results clearly show that an understanding of causation in terms of generative transmission is not a product of Western education, and make a strong case for the universality of this element of the theory of causation.

In his final study Shultz (1982b) used a Crookes' radiometer. This comprises a set of metal vanes mounted horizontally on a pivot inside an evacuated glass bulb. The vanes rotate when a flashlight is shined on them, because of a physical mechanism (see Shultz, 1982b). Shultz established that educated adults (psychology students) were not familiar with this device, and could not explain the rotation of the vanes. The experimenter showed subjects the apparatus with a flashlight on and the vanes of the radiometer rotating. Subjects were asked what they thought was making the vanes rotate, and if they failed to mention the light the experimenter suggested this to them as a possibility. Subjects were then asked how they would test this possibility, and were given five alternative methods. These methods were based on the use of various cues to causation, including generative transmission, covariation, temporal contiguity, spatial contiguity, and similarity. Subjects fell into three age groups—four years, eight years, and adult—and subjects at all ages consistently tended to choose the method based on the cue of generative transmission. In all, 50 out of 75 subjects chose this method, against a chance expectation of 15. No other method was chosen by more than nine subjects. Subjects who chose the generative testing method were less likely than others to choose to continue their inquiry after the first test, and all of them concluded from their test that the light was the cause of the vanes' movement. Those using other methods were less likely to identify the light, and more likely to continue testing. This experiment shows what one would expect if generative relations are fundamental to the understanding of physical causation, a tendency to fall back on generative transmission when the causal mechanism is not understood, to rely on it as a means of finding out the cause of an effect.

In summary, these experiments show that children as young as two years are able to use generative transmission cues for causal inference, that they tend to refer to generative transmission when justifying their inferences, and that they consistently prefer generative transmission cues over temporal contiguity, spatial contiguity, similarity, and covariation when these cues are in conflict with generative transmission. These tendencies are also shown by young children in Mali who have not received a Western education and who are not familiar with Western technology, suggesting that an understanding of physical causation in terms of generative relations is universal. Moreover, the experiments consistently showed little if any developmental trend. Older children showed a somewhat greater tendency to prefer generative transmission over other cues in some of the studies, but in no case was this difference very marked. The oldest children used were 13 years (studies 1 and 2), and the responses of these children were very similar to those of the two- and three-year-old subjects in these studies. In study 5, there was no difference between four-year-olds, eight-year-olds, and adults in preference for the testing method based on generative transmission. These results support the claim that an understanding of physical causation in terms of generative relations is established by the age of two years and develops little if at all thereafter.

Later studies have reinforced this picture. Shultz, Altmann, and Asselin (1986) used stimuli based on Michotte's (1963) "entraining" effect, in which one object joins another and appears to push, pull, or carry it along. Subjects as young as three years used generative transmission cues to make appropriate causal inferences, whereas the cues of temporal priority and human intervention were only used by older children. Shultz, Fisher et al. (1986) also found that generative transmission was the primary and preferred identifier of causation for children as young as three years. Children used other cues such as temporal contiguity and covariation only when the generative relation was not obvious.

Although not directly investigating generative relations cues, Kaiser and Proffitt (1984) studied the ability of children to distinguish natural from anomalous collision sequences, using stimuli presented on videotape. In these stimuli the Humean cues of spatial and temporal contiguity and temporal priority were present in all the sequences, whether real or anomalous, and there was no covariation information. Despite this, children as young as five years were able to distinguish real from anomalous sequences with a fair degree of accuracy. As Kaiser and Proffitt pointed out, these results show that the conjunction of spatio-temporal contiguity and temporal priority is not sufficient for a causal impression. Although causal judgement depended in some way on the dynamic properties of the sequences used, it is not certain that children were using generative relations cues, because the sequences resembled those studied by Michotte (1963), and the causal impression may just represent the operation of a hard-wired visual mechanism using the motion properties of the sequence (Leslie & Keeble, 1987).

The theory of causation involves not just the generative relations concept but also the concepts of power and resistance (or liability). Where an effect is the outcome of an interaction between a power of one thing and a liability of another, causal judgement and prediction require integration of information about both of these things. Such judgements and predictions therefore depend to a great extent on acquired wisdom about object properties, and may be expected to undergo development with experience.

Zelazo and Shultz (1989) studied the judgements of three age groups (five years, nine years, and adult) about two simple physical systems. One involved blocks sliding down a ramp and striking other blocks at the bottom of the ramp. In this case, other things being equal, the movement of the blocks at the bottom of the ramp depends on the number of blocks sliding down (force or power) and the number at the bottom (resistance). The second system was a balance, in which the displacement of a given tray is a function of the number of objects of a given size placed in the other tray (force or power) and the number in the tray in question (resistance). Zelazo and Shultz found that even the youngest subjects demonstrated some competence in their judgements, but their judgements were less accurate than those of older children and adults because they had less differentiated notions of power and resistance, and had not yet mastered division models of the integration of power and resistance information. The findings suggest that development of causal understanding of this kind is basically a story of increasing differentiation: beliefs are not discarded and replaced by radically different ones, but undergo refinement in the light of experience and education. This is consistent with the view espoused here, that the basic theory of causation remains unaltered through development, and functions as a foundation on which increasingly sophisticated beliefs and judgemental competence are erected.

Shultz's findings contrast with those of Piaget (1930; 1974). Piaget claimed that the child shows little understanding of physical causation before the age of seven years; that early causal inferences tend to be animistic and finalistic, and dominated by phenomenal contiguity (i.e. any two events that are juxtaposed in experience may be seen as causally related, regardless of whether they are contiguous in fact); that causal understanding is transformed during development, and in particular that it is tied to the development of logical operations. Piaget (1974) argued that problems of mediate causal transmission (e.g. a rolling marble strikes the first in a row of contiguous stationary marbles, whereupon only the last marble in the row moves) can only be solved through the use of transitive inferences, and that children only develop the ability to make transitive inferences around seven years of age.

In this case, Piaget's findings do not withstand critical scrutiny. The problems he used make heavy demands on the child's comprehension and verbal ability (Fincham, 1983), so that failure to solve them may indicate a failure of comprehension or an inadequate command of the language necessary for a correct response. Children's responses on problems with which they are unfamiliar may show nothing about what they believe, but only that they are willing to make free uneducated guesses, e.g. by analogy with domains with which they are familiar (Gelman & Kremer, 1991). Understanding of physical causation is better shown by performance on problems at which they can succeed, such as the simple problems used by Shultz (1982b). The idea, fundamental to the Piagetian approach, that understanding of physical causation proceeds through distinct stages in which knowledge is thoroughly transformed, appears to be an illusion due in part to developments in the child's linguistic competence, in part to developments in domain-specific knowledge during childhood, and in part to the difficulty of the problems used.

Piaget's (1974) claim about the link between causal inference and logical inference has also been questioned. Bindra, Clarke, and Shultz (1980) set problems in reasoning about necessary and sufficient conditions. They compared causal versions of the problems, embodying a generative relation between events, with noncausal versions, embodying nongenerative, but still logical, relations, and found that the children consistently performed better on the causal problems. Thus, contrary to Piaget's claim, children can master logical aspects of causal relations before they understand the same logical relations in noncausal contexts. Other studies have shown that children understand mediate causal transmission in relatively simple, mechanical apparatus at three years, thus confounding Piaget's (1974) claim that such understanding does not emerge before the beginning of concrete operations, around seven years (Baillargeon, Gelman, & Meck, 1981, unpublished but described in Bullock, Gelman, & Baillargeon, 1982; Shultz, Pardo, & Altmann, 1982).

In conclusion, it appears that Piaget underestimated the child's understanding of physical causation, and that a theory of causation based on the concept of generative relations is established early in life, and forms the foundation for subsequent acquisition of more detailed and sophisticated domain-specific knowledge.

One of the crucial differences between action and causation is that, in cases of action, it is up to the actor how to act, whereas physical causation involves necessity. That is, if appropriate conditions are set up for some physical mechanism to operate, it must do so. If a piece of litmus paper is dipped into a beaker of acid, the acid must turn the litmus paper pink: it cannot elect not to do so. At some point this principle, which we may call the principle of determinism (Bunge, 1963; Bullock, 1985b), must be incorporated into the theory of causation. Obtaining relevant evidence is not easy, however, simply because of the generality of the principle. We can show that children have expectations about physical occurrences which seem to exemplify the principle of determinism. For example, Keil (1979) presented stimuli involving the removal of a support from an object, whereupon the object did not fall. Infants of 18 months showed surprise at this event, indicating some appreciation of what would normally happen. Evidence of this kind is not conclusive, however. Infants may show surprise when an adult does something unexpected, but this does not indicate that they regard the behaviour of adults as fully determined. Keil's infants may have dealt with their surprise by inferring that the object just chose not to fall, in other words that its behaviour is a matter of action, not causation. Even if infants regard the falling of objects as fully determined, however, this would not show that they understand the principle of determinism; it would show only that they understand something about falling. Understanding of specific mechanisms does not imply, or depend on, understanding of a general principle.

Bullock, Gelman, and Baillargeon (1982, p.236) reported that three-year-olds "claimed that what appeared to be an uncaused event required some explanation, even if they could not specify the details". Even this does not imply a grasp of the principle of determinism, because the children might have been satisfied with an explanation based on the theory of action. Bullock (1985b) argued that young children operate with the principle of determinism, but only on the grounds that preschoolers appear not to engage in probabilistic reasoning. Again, this does not rule out the possibility that children interpret events with the theory of action, or that their grasp of causation does not include the principle of determinism. The evidence is therefore inconclusive.

Causal Inference and Causal Belief Acquisition

Although the theory of causation undergoes little development after early childhood, it is evident that a great deal is learned about physical causation during childhood. I have argued (White, 1993) that our understanding of the physical world can be regarded as having a number of hierarchically related levels, from the level of individual causal relations through beliefs about stable causal powers of things and types of causal power, to what might be called the world view of common sense, comprising global assumptions about the nature of order in the world such as the principle of determinism. There has been very little developmental research focussing on the higher levels: the fact that Bullock (1985b) was unable to cite or report any tests of the child's grasp of the principle of determinism is an apt illustration of this deficit. It would in any case be inadvisable to use these hierarchical levels as a means of organising a review of the literature, because the levels are almost certainly related psychologically, and because the categorisation of research findings in respect of the levels is often unclear.

Consider an example. Shultz and Ravinsky (1977) showed children a beaker of clear liquid. The experimenter added to the liquid solution from a pink and a blue dropper bottle, whereupon the liquid turned pink. Children tended to identify the solution from the pink bottle as the cause (although older children tended to rely on covariation cues in preference to similarity). Now one could say that this is a study of an inference about a single causal connection, and shows that there is some tendency for young children to use similarity as a cue to causal inference concerning individual occurrences. Certainly no more than this can be inferred from the results with any confidence. But the results leave a number of questions hanging.

Having made the inference, how far are children willing to generalise it? A useful analogy can be drawn here with work on adult attribution. Many studies have presented subjects with a single behaviour carried out by some real or fictitious person, and have found that people are willing to attribute stable personal dispositions to that person on the basis of that single instance. This happens even when available information about situational constraints might be thought to preclude such attributions (Fiske & Taylor, 1991; Jones & Harris, 1967; Ross, 1977; White, 1992b). Clearly, in the sphere of human behaviour, people are not reluctant to make sweeping inductive generalisations from instances, for a multitude of possible reasons (White, 1992b). Might either children or adults show the same tendency in the realm of physical causation? For example, would the children in the Shultz and Ravinsky (1977) study attribute a stable causal power to the liquid in the pink bottle? How stable? Would they expect it to turn any clear liquid pink, or just water, or just the liquid (or kind of liquid) in the beaker, if that is identified for them? Would they expect it to turn any liquid pink, no matter what colour it was to start with? Would they expect it to turn other things pink, such as a piece of paper if spilled on it? Would they expect liquid from other pink bottles to have the same power? Would their attribution of the power to turn things pink be affected by information about the conditions under which the liquid acted? That is, would they expect the liquid to turn the solution pink under circumstances that were different in various ways, e.g. if they saw the experimenter shake the bottle before applying the liquid from it to the beaker, would they regard this as an important condition for the power of the liquid to operate?

In the sphere of human behaviour, we have seen that children's ideas about stability and consistency undergo considerable development. Children first understand traits as underlying consistency in behaviour across times within similar situations; then as underlying consistency in behaviour across different situations; finally as differentiating actors from each other. Is there an equivalent progression in the understanding of stable causal powers of things? Do children first understand the powers of a thing as underlying consistency in the behaviour and operation of that thing upon similar other things (or a single thing on multiple occasions) or in similar situations; then as underlying consistency in the behaviour or operation of that thing upon diverse other things or in different situations; then as differentiating otherwise similar things from each other? Objects are not individuals in the way that people are. To some extent, though, they do behave differently from each other. Not all pink liquids turn clear solutions pink. So, to pursue the analogy, children might first believe that the pink liquid turns other clear solutions pink; then that the pink liquid might turn all sorts of things pink, or the same solution pink under all sorts of circumstances; finally, that not all pink liquids have the same power, and that pink liquids can be differentiated (in part) according to whether they possess the stable power to turn things pink.

Generalising, then, one extreme is a view of the world as entirely capricious, in which things can do anything to anything else whenever they want, and no prediction is feasible. The other extreme is a world with fixed laws in which things have a limited range of stable powers and liabilities, the former operating only under specific appropriate conditions, and in which sufficient knowledge enables accurate prediction. (We can also ask whether the order in the world is imposed by causal laws, by static principles of order, or by fiat of gods, but this is another issue.) The understanding of the child lies somewhere between these two extremes, but where, and in which direction does it move during development?

There are few clues to this at present, but some enlightening findings have been reported by Karmiloff-Smith (1984; 1986; 1988; Karmiloff-Smith & Inhelder, 1974). These findings concern the development of the child's naïve physics, and suggest a developmental progression towards increasingly sophisticated generalisation. Initially (around four years) children tended to treat problems individually, showing sensitivity to data concerning a single problem and often, as a result, performing better than six-year-old children, but treating each solution or explanation as isolated. For example, having successfully balanced a block on a narrow support, children did not use information gained from that block in their attempts to balance another one. By six years, children behaved as if in possession of a simple theory, but were insensitive to disconfirmations of their theory and either treated such occurrences as insoluble, or interpreted them so as to fit with their preferred theory. By the age of eight, they had acquired a more sophisticated and successful theory. The limits on generalisability are hard to learn (or, to put it another way, it is hard to find the joints at which to carve nature); the child appears to progress from not enough generalisation, through too much, to just about right.

A second set of questions concerns the grounds for the causal inference made by the children. Inferring that the solution turned pink because of the addition of liquid from the pink bottle was taken by Shultz and Ravinsky (1977) as exemplifying use of the cue of similarity for causal inference. But why use such a cue? Many things that are similar are not causes of each other. One cloud looks much like another, but do children believe that one cloud causes another? In fact, many things are similar not because they cause each other but because they are effects of similar causes. This is entailed, after all, by the notion of stability in a causal power, and there is no doubt that young children have some understanding of this: such understanding is shown by infants who have learned how to reproduce an interesting effect by repeating an action upon a thing (Piaget, 1954; and Chapter 2). As a cue to causal inference, therefore, similarity is imperfect, to say the least. On the other hand, children might use similarity as a cue to causal inference when certain other conditions are satisfied. In the Shultz and Ravinsky (1977) experiment, the inferred cause (the addition of the liquid to the solution) and the effect were both spatially and temporally contiguous; the addition of the liquid to the solution had temporal priority over the colour change of the solution, and the actions of the experimenter in adding the liquid to the solution presumably suggested that some kind of causal mechanism was being put into operation, even if the mechanism itself was not apparent. Perhaps when, and only when, all of these cues to causation are present, similarity is used to discriminate between competing possible causes.

At the other end of the spectrum, the similarity of causes and effects could be a global assumption about the nature of order in the universe. Something like this was the case in the medieval world view (Debus, 1978), although people at that time thought in terms of order and harmony rather than causes. An example is the microcosm–macrocosm analogy, the idea that nature is a simple, harmonious system under which man is "created in the image of the great world, and that real correspondences do exist between man and the macrocosm" (Debus, 1978, p.12). Many kinds of correspondences were thought to exist. One kind was the Paracelsian doctrine of signatures, according to which "the correspondence of the name or shape of a plant to that of a human organ indicated the plant's proper medicinal usage" (p.53). Such correspondences were thought to be signs put into the world by God for men to use, and this was the ultimate justification for regarding similarities as more than mere coincidences. Of course, children do not literally possess the medieval world view in all its elaborate and comprehensive detail. On the other hand, our own adult view of the physical world is also to a considerable extent a cultural artefact, the diffusion into common sense of the mechanistic philosophy of the scientific revolution (Bronowski, 1951; Toulmin & Goodfield, 1961). We are therefore guilty of prejudging the matter if we view the development of understanding of physical causation as a progression from ignorance towards the view of twentieth-century Western adults. There is every likelihood that children may, at some stage in their development, possess a world view, or specific theories and beliefs consistent with a world view, radically different from ours, and there is no reason why relations of similarity might not be a key element of their world view. There is so much, after all, that must appear mysterious to children too young to have learned much about how things work. Even adults have trouble interpreting such things as coincidences (Marks & Kamman, 1980); to children, less conceptually bound by the world view of mechanism (Dijksterhuis, 1961), coincidences must seem like almost magical signs of hidden relations between things.

These are some of the most important questions to ask about the development of understanding of physical causation: it is therefore disappointing to report that there seems to have been little attempt to answer them. There has been research on the ways in which children make causal inferences and acquire causal beliefs, and this research will be discussed under the next series of subheadings. The research has not, generally speaking, been placed in context of the issues just considered, and it has, generally speaking, been guilty of treating the topic as a matter of cognitive development, to the neglect of relevant social and cultural considerations. Nonetheless, progress has been made.

Cues to Causation

Several studies have investigated the use by children of stimulus features as cues to causation. The cue of similarity has already been discussed: apart from the study by Shultz and Ravinsky (1977), which showed that children as young as three years use the cue of similarity, there has been little research on this cue. Shultz and Ravinsky (1977) found that older children relied more on covariation than similarity when the two were in conflict, and Shultz (1982b) found that children aged four and eight years preferred generative transmission to similarity as types of method for testing a causal hypothesis. It is unlikely, therefore, that similarity is fundamental to the understanding of physical causation at any age, although the place of similarity in the child's world view, as already stated, remains unknown.

Several studies have found that temporal contiguity is an important cue for causal inference by children (Mendelson & Shultz, 1976; Shultz, Fisher et al., 1986; Siegler, 1975; Siegler & Liebert, 1974). In fact the evidence for use of temporal contiguity is stronger than that, because many studies on other cues to causation (excluding those using verbal or pictorial stimulus presentations) have used cause–effect relations that are temporally contiguous (Shultz, 1982b; Shultz, Altmann, & Asselin, 1986; Shultz & Mendelson, 1975; Shultz & Ravinsky, 1977; Siegler, 1976; Sophian & Huber, 1984). In the study by Siegler and Liebert (1974), causal inferences based on covariation were successful when there was no delay between cause and effect. When there was a delay of five seconds, preschoolers failed, whereas older children succeeded. Siegler (1975) showed that the failures with the five-second delay were not due to insufficient number of trials, failure to draw the causal inference between the two test stimuli, problems with word meaning, or lack of appreciation of equal temporal intervals. The reason for the failure, almost certainly, was that young children were unable to relate events occurring five seconds apart, in a relatively complex field of stimuli. If this is correct, then the evidence on temporal contiguity is of two kinds. First, childen appear to use temporal contiguity as a cue to causation. Second, they are limited in their ability to detect relations between events that are separated in time by a few seconds or more, an ability that improves during childhood (Siegler & Liebert, 1974). In the latter case, temporal contiguity is a limiting factor rather than a cue. Causal inferences can be made by children aged four to five years despite lack of temporal contiguity when there is an apparent rationale for the delay between cause and effect (Mendelson & Shultz, 1976). In this study, however, subjects were not required to pick out the key events from among a number of competing stimuli. Presumably in this case the children are in effect dealing with a problem of mediate causal transmission, similar in form to the problems used by Shultz, Pardo, and Altmann (1982).

There has been little research on the cue of spatial contiguity. Lesser (1977) found that spatial contiguity was necessary for perception of the launching effect (Michotte, 1963) by children aged six and nine years, except when they had been instructed in the behaviour of magnets, and even then this exception did not hold for all subjects or all circumstances. On the other hand, the launching effect may be a special case of causal perception in that it is automatic and possibly impervious to effects of learning (Leslie & Keeble, 1987). It is therefore uncertain whether this finding can be generalised to causal inferences of other kinds. Bullock and Gelman (1979) found evidence for the appreciation of spatial contiguity in causation at three to four years, but temporal priority overrode this in their study when the two were in conflict.

The cue of temporal priority has been extensively studied. The rule of temporal priority is that causes must precede or co-occur with their effects in time. Bullock et al. (1982) and Bullock (1985b) list this rule as a fundamental assumption about causation, along with the principles of determinism and mechanism.[2] It is perhaps better regarded as a mere cue, however, because many events that have relations of temporal priority are not causally related, whereas the principles of determinism and mechanism are exclusively asociated with causation.

There has been some controversy over the use of temporal priority as a cue to causation. Bullock and Gelman (1979), Kun (1978), and Shultz and Mendelson (1975) all found that children as young as three years used temporal order information in causal inference. Corrigan (1975) and Kuhn and Phelps (1976) reported failures of children to use this cue. The latter two studies both used verbal materials, however, and Fincham (1983) and Sedlak and Kurtz (1981) both suggested that children were having difficulty with the understanding of syntax rather than with the temporal priority cue. Since then, however, two more groups of authors have reported failures of young children to use the temporal order cue with more concrete stimuli (Shultz, Altmann, & Asselin, 1986; Sophian & Huber, 1984). The failure in the Sophian and Huber study may have been due to the presence of alternative cues which overrode temporal priority or to the fact that their subjects had some trouble in identifying the temporal order of events. In their second experiment, in which the temporal order was unambiguous, some evidence suggested appropriate use of the cue by three-year-olds. In the study by Shultz, Altmann, and Asselin (1986), however, the temporal order cue was unambiguous and few if any alternative cues were available.

Evidence therefore suggests that, at the age of three years, appreciation of temporal order as a cue to causation is imperfect. By five years, children appear to have mastered it. How can one explain this relatively late mastery of a cue that seems basic to, if not actually entailed by, the generative relations theory of causation? The problem lies with the fact that the cue is not meant to be independent of other cues and rules for inferring causation. The original motivation for studying children's grasp of spatial and temporal contiguity and temporal priority as cues to causation was their presence in Hume's (1739/1978a) definition of a cause (see Chapter 1). But researchers have made two errors in acting upon this motivation. The first is that precedency and contiguity were not meant by Hume as cues for inferring causation; he meant only that when object relations possess those features (along with constant conjunction) the idea of a causal connection will tend to arise in the human mind. It is an associative model, not a rule-using model. For this reason, the psychological theories that come closest to capturing the spirit of the Humean approach are associative models of human instrumental learning, to be considered in Chapter 6.

The second error, more important for present purposes, is that of considering the features independently of each other. It is clear in Hume's definition that the idea of a causal relation arises only for object relations possessing all of the features of constant conjunction, precedency, and contiguity. An object relation possessing only precedency, or for that matter only spatial contiguity, or only temporal contiguity, will not give rise to the idea of causal relation. Nor should it. Hume's definition is already overinclusive (see Chapter 1): if its components are treated as disjunctive, rather than conjunctive, all sorts of object relations that are not causal will be treated as if they were. Asking whether children can use one of these cues independently of the rest, or when in conflict with one or more of the others, is therefore inappropriate because under those circumstances the cues are not reliable guides to causation.

Apply this to the problem of the apparently late acquisition of the temporal order cue. Take event X, for which one might want to find the cause. Consider all information about events and things anywhere in time and space that the person is able to scan (e.g. in memory) for possible causes. Only a very small proportion of those events and things is temporally contiguous with X. Only a very small proportion is spatially contiguous with X. But a considerable proportion is temporally prior to X, especially if X is a recent occurrence.This means that although temporal priority is a necessary condition for a thing to be a cause of X (and although it may be recognised as such by young children), it is far from being a distinctive cue. Many events prior to X are not causes of it. This may make it difficult for children to abstract temporal order as a cue to causal inference. Alternatively, it may make them understandably reluctant to use it independently of other cues to causation. This is true to some extent of the other Humean cues as well; children may use the Humean cues in concert for causal inference earlier than they can use any of them independently of the rest.

Researchers investigated children's use of Humean cues partly because of the possibility that children might be naïve Humean causal reasoners, that is, that causal inference is in fact much as Hume claimed it was. It is clear from much of the research reviewed in this book that infants and children are not Humean at all (Leslie, 1982; Leslie & Keeble, 1987; Piaget, 1954; Shultz, 1982b), but more nearly resemble singularists in the style of Harré and Madden (1975). If this is the case, why should children use Humean cues at all? In White (1988) I argued that use of these cues derived from their presence as invariable features of the continuity relations that are processed causally by infants according to the iconic processing hypothesis (see Chapter 2). That is, the Humean features (together with similarity in the motion properties before and after transfer) are present in every case of motion continuity relations processed causally, and because of this they are, at later stages of development, abstracted from their context in the motion continuity relation and used as guides to causation in cases that do not conform to the pattern of the motion continuity relation in all respects. It is worth adding that the same features are universally present in many of the infant's actions upon objects. Obviously an appreciation of spatial contiguity, for example, could develop from the need for actual contact with objects in order to manipulate them: The infant must learn that a given movement of the hand will only manipulate an object when the object is touched or grasped. Thus, cues to causation could be abstracted from any such experiences that contribute to the development of causal understanding in infancy. There are various ways in which this could be achieved, some of which are described under the following subheadings. At present, however, there is no evidence bearing directly upon this possibility.

An alternative possibility is that cues are used because, and when, they satisfy more fundamental considerations; we can imagine the child as being in possession of principles for selecting, or selecting between, cues to causal inference, these principles being shaped in respect of the more fundamental considerations in virtue of which causal inferences are made. This possibility is discussed under the next heading. A third possibility is that abstract rules are developed out of experience with concrete, specific, and familiar occurrences; this possibility will be discussed under the next heading but one.

Rules and Rule Selection

There are many cues or rules that children may use for making causal inferences: generative transmission, spatial contiguity, temporal contiguity, similarity, temporal priority, and covariation or regularity (to be discussed shortly). (In the case of human action, rules such as matching and valence, discussed in the previous chapter, can be added to this list.) On any given occasion on which a child seeks to make a causal inference, how does he or she choose which rule to use? Different rules may yield different inferences, and the use of several at once may be cognitively inefficient. These considerations led Shultz, Fisher, et al. (1986) to put forward a model of rule selection, comprising a set of hierarchically organised principles.

The overriding principle asserts the basic importance of generative relations and states that, if the generative mechanism is sufficiently obvious to the perceiver, it will be used for causal inference. This principle is supported by the findings of Shultz (1982b) and Shultz, Fisher et al. (1986), that generative relations cues are reliably preferred over several other sorts of cue for causal inference. It would be better, however, if the principle referred to the appearance or impression of a generative relation: for example, when perceiving the launching effect stimuli used by Michotte (1963), perceivers have the impression of a causal relation even though none is actually there, showing that such impressions can be illusory.

When no generative mechanism seems obviously present, Shultz, Fisher et al. proposed that five secondary principles come into operation.

The *fundamentality principle* states that rules that have better adaptational success are favoured. Adaptational success can be defined in various ways, of course: one way would be in terms of accuracy, in that some rules have greater validity than others as identifiers of causal relations; another way would be in terms of the perceiver's practical concerns (White, 1984; 1993), in that some rules make reliably better contributions to the perceiver's practical concerns than others. Shultz, Fisher et al. (1986) and Shultz and Kestenbaum (1985) opted for the former definition. Following a brief review of relevant studies, Shultz and Kestenbaum proposed that rules other than generative relations could be ordered in terms of decreasing fundamentality as follows: temporal priority, spatial contiguity, temporal contiguity, covariation, similarity. Defining adaptational success in terms of practical concerns would lead to a more flexible ordering, to the extent that the adaptational success of a rule varies across different practical concerns.

The *salience principle* refers to the fact that different rules require different items of information. According to this principle, the more salient some piece of information is, the more likely it is that the rule that operates on that kind of information will be used. Some support for the salience principle was found by Shultz, Fisher et al. (1986), but only for temporal contiguity information. Effects of salience on causal attribution have been found in adults (Fiske & Taylor, 1991; Taylor & Fiske, 1975), although the discussion of salience by Fiske and Taylor (1991) makes it clear that issues of salience are not straightforward. For example, salience is not an objective property: the salience of a stimulus can be manipulated by an instruction given to a subject, without any alteration to the stimulus itself (Quattrone, 1982). Part of what matters, for making something salient, must be the observer's active involvement in the situation. To a pedestrian trying to cross a road, all the cars in view are dynamic, but the only ones that are salient are those that are relevant to the judgement of whether and when to cross. As far as salience is concerned, the individual is not driven passively by features of the stimuli or by the mechanics of attentive processing, but actively by purposes, plans, and practical concerns.

According to the *facility principle*, if use of the required information for a particular rule exceeds the observer's processing capacities, the probability that the rule will be used decreases. Again, this principle relates to work on adult social cognition supporting the idea that adults are cognitive misers, seeking and preferring simpler and less effortful ways of dealing with inferential problems (Fiske & Taylor, 1991; Nisbett & Ross, 1980; Taylor, 1981). While the principle probably holds under some circumstances, the amount of cognitive effort people will devote to a task obviously depends on many factors. In general, more effort will be devoted to a task when such effort is justified by the contribution or potential contribution of the task outcome to the individual's concerns. Experimental research in social cognition probably gives a misleading impression because subjects have little of importance invested in the experimental tasks. Tetlock (1983; 1985) has shown that manipulations of practical concerns, in the form of accountability, make a difference to the way in which people perform on social inference tasks.

On the other hand, the principle has particular relevance to the use of covariation information for causal inference. While cues such as temporal contiguity are relatively easy to use, assessing covariation is often difficult and effortful, because of the quantity of information that is involved, and the problem of distinguishing covariates of an effect from other events (Siegler & Liebert, 1974). Consistent with this reasoning, Shultz, Fisher et al. (1986) found that increasing amounts of covariation information led younger children (three to five years) to abandon covariation in favour of temporal contiguity, to a greater extent than seven-year-olds.

The *plausibility principle* states that use of a rule must generate a causal attribution that is consistent with an imagined or hypothesised causal mechanism. That is, an attribution will only be accepted if it conforms to some preconceived idea possessed by the judge about the sorts of things that could cause the effect in question. The rule therefore asserts the importance of preconceived beliefs and hypotheses against the blind empiricism of Humean causal inference.

Finally, the *discriminability principle* states that rules which do not permit discrimination among competing possible causes will not be used.

The last two principles are both slightly odd in that the perceiver cannot use them to make an a priori selection between rules; the force of them is probably that a rule is used, but the outcome is rejected if it does not satisfy either the plausibility or the discriminability principle.

From Concrete to Abstract

Sophian and Huber (1984) ran a study involving a model train with an engine, middle car, and caboose (guard's van). Children observed movements of the train and had to judge whether the engine or the caboose was making the middle car move under various conditions. Although the study was designed to assess children's use of the temporal priority rule, Sophian and Huber observed that many children made their judgements by relying on concrete features of the stimuli, namely the type of car and its direction of movement. They seemed to be applying domain-specific beliefs, such as the belief that engines pull cars and cabooses don't, or that trains work by pulling rather than by pushing, instead of using abstract cues such as temporal priority or spatial contiguity. The children didn't all have the same theory, but were consistent in their use of whichever theory they had.[3]

Sophian and Huber therefore suggested that causal knowledge begins as an understanding of specific, familiar causal sequences and is based on concrete features of those sequences. That is, at early times, children just acquire a lot of particular, domain-specific causal beliefs, not based on or linked by any abstract cues or rules. Children later abstract rules and cues for causal inference presumably by identifying features common to the familiar sequences, and can then use these abstracted rules for causal inferences about unfamiliar occurrences. In support of this, they pointed out that younger children in their study (three years) were more likely to base their judgements on concrete features of the stimuli than were older children (five years), who were more likely to use abstract rules. A second study using a different kind of problem gave further support to this reasoning.

The proposal of Sophian and Huber (1984) implies a critique of previous studies of cues to causal inference. When a study finds, for example, that children use the cue of temporal contiguity in a particular causal inference task, it tends to be interpreted as support for the notion that children have the temporal contiguity cue, as an abstract inferential device. If Sophian and Huber are right, then in the case of younger children especially such results should only be interpreted as showing the kinds of beliefs that children have about the particular domain studied, and there are no grounds for generalising from the results to performance in other domains. Many causes and effects are related by temporal contiguity, so it would not be surprising if children possessed domain-specific beliefs that happen to conform to a temporal contiguity rule.

On the other hand, children must have some general concept of causation. Otherwise, there would be nothing to distinguish domain-specific causal beliefs from domain-specific non-causal beliefs. Children cannot abstract a rule from a set of causal beliefs if they do not have some appreciation that those causal beliefs form a set, distinct from beliefs of other sorts. It is therefore possible to propose a slight modification to the Sophian and Huber developmental hypothesis. Young children (by the age of two years) are in possession of the theory of causation, as described at the start of this chapter. They then acquire domain-specific causal beliefs which are identified as causal by being assimilated to the theory of causation. There are many ways in which they can do this. One way, for example, is by perceiving apparent or actual generative relations. Any child can get the idea that hammers can smash plates by observing a hammer being used to smash a plate and interpreting what they perceive in terms of the theory of causation. Another way is by direct teaching: Once a child has a general idea of what it is for one thing to cause something else, they can acquire limitless numbers of causal beliefs just by being told things. A parent might tell a child, for example, that eating a lot of chocolate causes stomach ache. The child might choose not to believe it, but in principle the use of appropriate causal terminology is sufficient for the child to acquire a belief that relates chocolate and stomach ache in terms of the theory of causation. The third stage is the abstraction of rules and cues from common features of specific causal relations about which the child has acquired beliefs. Of course, once this third stage has begun, the development of causal beliefs becomes a kind of dialectic process in which domain-specific beliefs contribute to the acquisition of abstract rules, and the application of rules to novel instances leads to the formation of new domain-specific beliefs, and so on. The force of the Sophian and Huber proposal is that, at early times, formation of abstract rules and cues depends on possession of a sufficient number of domain-specific beliefs, and their studies provide some supporting evidence for this.

Other studies have also shown that specific beliefs about causes can be used by young children to make causal inferences. Gelman, Bullock, and Meck (1980) tested children's understanding of object transformations, using three different kinds of case. In one case, children saw picture cards depicting before and after states of an object, such as a window intact and then broken, and were asked to infer how the breakage came about by choosing an object from an array that had the power to bring about the effect. In another case, children saw pictures of two objects, such as a window and a stone, or a broken cup and glue, and were asked to say how one might be used to transform the other. In a third case, children saw a picture of a transformed object, such as a sliced fruit, and were asked to infer what its original state was and how it got to be transformed. Children aged three and four years handled these tasks competently, although four-year-olds were generally better than three-year-olds and both ages had more difficulty with transformations that restored objects to canonical (e.g. unbroken) states than with transformations that did the opposite. Gelman et al. (1980, p.696) commented: "children found it rather easy to pick an instrument that could mediate two stages of an object, even when the sequence was an unusual one, as in the case of a needle and thread for an intact and a cut banana. This suggests that preschoolers' knowledge of event sequences involves more than a memory for contiguously associated events." In other words, children have beliefs about the causal powers and liabilities of objects which they can apply to novel instances.

Das Gupta and Bryant (1989) pointed out two possible interpretations of these results: Either the children were making genuine causal inferences by relating the initial and final states of an object, or they were just demonstrating their knowledge of the causal powers of agents and instruments. They argued that although some studies have shown the latter (e.g. Shultz, 1982b), none has unambiguously shown the former. The way to do this, they argued, was to "present a pair of sequences, both of which begin with an object in a noncanonical state. One sequence would begin with a wet cup and end with a wet and *broken* cup, and the other would begin with a broken cup but also end with a wet and broken cup. If the child can work out that a hammer and not the water is the instrument in one case, and the water rather than the hammer in the other, one can be quite sure that she has taken the object's initial state into account in both sequences and thus has made genuine causal inferences" (Das Gupta & Bryant, 1989, p.1139, italics in original). They found that children aged four were able to do this, but three-year-olds had more difficulty, although their performance was better than chance. These results suggest that knowledge of the causal powers of things develops slightly earlier than the ability to make causal inferences relating initial and final states of objects. Having said that, these studies used pictures and the results therefore depend to some extent on the ability of young children to read picture sequences. Gelman et al. (1980) trained their subjects to read the pictures from left to right, but if younger children were unfamiliar with this procedure they may still have experienced some difficulty in the experimental tasks. Despite this, it is clear that preschool children already have a repertoire of beliefs about causal powers and liabilities and can use those beliefs to some extent to make causal inferences.

Regularity Information

The essence of the Humean approach is the accumulation of a kind of record of experiences, in the course of which the impression of a causal relation arises for those object relations which possess the key features of constant conjunction, precedency, and contiguity. Causal inference is entirely passive and empirical; the impression of a causal relation arises only after multiple occurrences of a given object relation, and the arising of such impressions is unaffected by preconceived beliefs or biases in the mind of the perceiver. The chapter on infancy (Chapter 2) has already presented a strong case that infants and young children do not proceed like this: for example, that they can form ideas of cause and effect from single instances, and that they develop things that function as theories, often in clear violation of experienced empirical regularities (Piaget, 1954). I have elsewhere described in detail the reasons why people cannot be regularity theorists, and the uses to which regularity information might be put under the causal powers theory (White, 1988; 1989; 1992a; 1993), and there is therefore no reason to cover the same ground again here. I shall list briefly some problems with the specific idea that children use covariation or regularity information for causal inference in the realm of physical causation, then discuss some research which places the use, or misuse, of covariation information within a model of the child as a naïve hypothesis-tester.

There is evidence that children in the five- to nine-year age range can use covariation as a cue to causal inference (Kassin & Pryor, 1985; Mendelson & Shultz, 1976; Shaklee & Mims, 1981; Shultz & Mendelson, 1975; Siegler & Liebert, 1974). There are several problems with this evidence, however.

First, some of these studies have shown that children have difficulty in using covariation for causal inference (Shultz & Mendelson, 1975; Siegler, 1975; Siegler & Liebert, 1974). Siegler (1975) showed that children of about five years cannot use covariation as a cue when the cause and effect events are separated by more than five seconds, and that this is because children of that age cannot detect covariation in the absence of temporal contiguity. Shaklee and Goldston (1989) set problems in which children were able to choose what information to sample from a set presented to them. Third-grade children (approximately seven years old) performed barely above chance in terms of the use of covariation to infer causation, both failing to identify true covariates as causes and identifying noncovariates as causes. To some extent this was attributable to their sampling strategy; when given a hypothesis to test (e.g. whether the sun causes flowers to open), children preferentially sampled information about events in the presence of the supposed cause, neglecting information about events in the absence of the supposed cause. This led them into error when the event in question happened as often in the absence of the supposed cause as in its presence. Thus, error in the use of covariation information for causal judgement can be attributed in part to the use of a positive instance hypothesis testing strategy (Evans, 1983; Kuhn, 1989). Older children (approximately eleven years) and college students performed somewhat better, despite also drawing biased samples; Shaklee and Goldston (1989) suggested that the older subjects were better able to organise the information sampled before making a causal judgement. This highlights a crucial problem in the use of covariation information for causal inference: large amounts of information must be organised both accurately and usefully before accurate causal judgements can be made according to the covariation principle, and the use of pre-packaged information in many studies obscures the difficulty of this.

Second, some of the supportive evidence can be interpreted in other ways. Ruble and Rholes (1981) argued that covariation information is often confounded with information about mere magnitude of the effect, and that children may be responding to the latter. Children also appear not to use covariation information when to do so would place excessive demands on memory (Shultz, Fisher et al., 1986). This is particularly important in view of the fact that the demands placed on memory in research studies are often less than they would be under more naturalistic conditions.

Third, the evidence does not show much sophistication in the use of covariation as a cue to causal inference. Shaklee and Elek (1988) have pointed out that, in the studies by Shultz and Mendelson (1975) and Siegler and Liebert (1974), children were only required to distinguish between perfect covariation and zero covariation. Even simple and incorrect strategies for judging covariation, such as assessing only instances of co-occurrence, would lead to success on this task. In their own study, with older children (11–13 years), Shaklee and Elek (1988) found parallel age trends in covariation judgement and causal judgement. Only half of their subjects identified actual covariates as causes, but to some extent this was due to their use of imperfect strategies of covariation judgement. Their results suggested that males tended to associate covariation with causation, but that females did not. However, their study also used idealised presentations, in which subjects judged covariation from frequency data presented in 2 x 2 contingency matrices: that is, they were presented with clearly packaged information about occurrences, rather than being exposed to the occurrences themselves.

Fourth, some studies have set up contests between different cues to causation, and in these covariation generally comes off badly. Mendelson and Shultz (1976) showed that children preferred a causal candidate which had temporal contiguity but did not covary with the effect to be explained over one which covaried with the effect but lacked temporal contiguity with it. Shultz (1982b) showed in a series of studies that children preferred cues to generative transmission over covariation cues, and there is evidence that children and adults prefer generative transmission cues over all other cues to causal inference (Shultz, 1982b, study 5; Shultz, Fisher, et al., 1986). This point is important, because it shows that, not only is regularity information not necessary for causal inference, it is not even the preferred kind of information, at least in these experiments. If regularity was basic to causal inference, these tendencies and preferences would not occur.

Perhaps the most important point, however, is that when children do use covariation information, they use it in a way that is driven by their preconceived beliefs and hypotheses: that is, their ideas lead them to have expectations about covariation, and these expectations bias their search for and treatment of covariation information. This view of children has emerged from a body of research on the child's attempts to co-ordinate hypothesis and evidence (Karmiloff-Smith, 1988; Klahr & Dunbar, 1988; Kuhn, 1989; Schauble, 1990).

Kuhn (1989) has proposed that the child can be regarded as a naïve scientist, meaning specifically someone who holds theories, so that development can be regarded as a matter of interplay between theories and evidence. This can be applied as a framework for studying the development of causal understanding, given that the child can be presumed to hold causal beliefs or hypotheses which are in principle evaluated in the light of evidence, or applied in the interpretation of particular occurrences. Kuhn suggested that while the processes involved in hypothesis formulation, testing, and so on, differ between child, adult, and scientist (at least when engaged in scientific work), the basic involvement of theory and evidence in conceptual change is similar. The research discussed by Kuhn (1989) reveals a number of points about the use of covariation information in the interplay between theory and evidence.

When theory and evidence are compatible, "there is a melding of the two into a single representation of 'the way things are'. The pieces of evidence are regarded not as independent of the theory and bearing on it, but more as *instances* of the theory that serve to illustrate it" (p.679, italics in original). Around the age of eleven, children don't distinguish between theory and evidence in the role of support for a conclusion (p.676): "both theory and evidence point to the same conclusion, and one thus seems to be the same as the other for purposes of justifying the conclusion". Not only children but also adults engage in *proof by examples*. Having formulated a theory, a single example that conforms to the theory is enough: the theory is then regarded as unassailable *for that example*, and it is only the limits on the generalisability of the theory that are not known.

When theory and evidence conflict, children tend to use inferential strategies to interpret the evidence in such a way as to render it compatible with their preferred theory, such as selectively attending to confirming instances and ignoring discrepant instances. Children do not assess covariation. Examples that do not conform to a theory, if they cannot be reinterpreted to fit, merely support some other theory; they may serve to limit the generalisability of the original theory, but do not disconfirm it.[4] "Identical evidence was interpreted one way in relation to a favoured theory and another way in relation to a theory that was not favoured" (p.677). Where theory and evidence conflict, children only acknowledge the evidence, the covariation, when they have formulated a new theory which would account for it: they don't acknowledge covariation without a theory to explain it. Far from covariation driving beliefs, as in the Humean approach, beliefs drive the assessment and interpretation of covariation. Moreover, children are very free in their interpretation of covariation: They tend to see any covariate as causal if it fits their theory; they make causal inferences on the basis of lack of variation; they make different interpretations of the pattern of evidence for different levels of a variable, rather than co-ordinating them (for example, they will say that a thing "sometimes" makes a difference, when saying so fits their theory). These are all errors of confirmatory or positive instance testing. That is, once a hypothesis has been formulated, children seek positive instances of the hypotheses, appearing not to appreciate the relevance of negative instances (cf. Evans, 1983; Wason, 1960, 1968). This is consistent, of course, with their treatment of disconfirming instances as placing limits on generalisability rather than as threatening the validity of the theory.

Subsequent work by Schauble (1990) has extended this picture. Schauble set children aged eight to twelve years problems which required a series of tests of possibly causal features of things over an extended period of time. Although the children did make progress, they did so in a disorganised fashion, not recording covariation information, engaging in positive instance testing, and devising tests which in fact did not allow them to obtain the kind of information they were seeking. Those who did well succeeded by getting the right theory first and then testing it, not by using evidence to modify their ideas. Some children relied too much on their beliefs and then misread the evidence they obtained as supportive; others relied too much on evidence and changed to a new theory on the basis of just one observation, rather than by assessing covariation across multiple tests.

In summary, although children can use covariation information as a basis for causal inferences, at least when it is presented under near-ideal conditions and without conflicting with other cues, this is not characteristic of their ways of treating covariation information with respect to causation. They prefer to rely on other cues, particularly generative transmission, and, once they have a hypothesis or theory, they tend to adopt positive instance testing strategies which lead them to interpret, discount, or misperceive covariation information in ways which render it consistent with their hypothesis. Far from inferring causation from covariation, children more characteristically infer covariation from causation.

Researchers in this area tend to have an implicit (and sometimes explicit) theory about the proper use of covariation information for causal inference, namely the covariation principle. This principle underlies Kelley's (1967) ANOVA model of causal attribution, which is sometimes regarded as a normative procedure for causal attribution (Nisbett & Ross, 1980), as well as his causal schema notion (Kelley, 1972b). In the study by Shaklee and Elek (1988), causal judgements were deemed accurate if they conformed to the covariation principle, this time in the form of chi-square analysis of a 2 x 2 contingency table. In fact the covariation principle is wrong, and probably has no more than heuristic value. Researchers all know that, when interpreting data, covariation does not indicate causation, and there are many reasons for this (White, 1992a; 1993; and see Chapter 1). Two events may covary, for example, because they are common effects of another cause.

In research studies children are deemed to be performing incorrectly if they fail to use information about events occurring in the absence of a hypothesised cause (Shaklee & Goldston, 1989), but under many circumstances they may be quite right to take that approach. If the event occurs in the absence of the hypothesised cause, that could mean just that there is another thing that also causes it (White, 1992a), and this does not count against the causal hypothesis under test. Moreover, if an event fails to occur in the presence of a hypothesised cause, that might mean that conditions necessary for the causal mechanism to operate have not been met (Harré & Madden, 1975; White, 1992a), and this does not indicate that the causal hypothesis is wrong. Thus, the relevance of events involving either the nonoccurrence of the effect or the absence of the hypothesised cause is not at all clear. Given, therefore, that there is no clear relationship between covariation and causation, children can hardly be castigated for failing to use covariation information in conformity with the covariation principle; nor is it surprising that covariation is not fundamental to causal inference. It is right that it should not be.

Sources of Causal Beliefs and Hypotheses

With respect to causal understanding, the image of children that is emerging has two main features:

1. The theory of causation, that is, a stable, enduring set of fundamental assumptions about causation, comprising the concepts of causal power, liability, releasing condition, and of the causal relation as generative in nature, coupled (at some stage of development) with the principle of determinism or causal necessitation.

2. A large and rapidly growing repertoire of domain-specific beliefs about the causal powers and liabilities of things, which from an early age children are able to use in causal inference.

Children may also learn abstract cues to causation such as temporal contiguity which they can apply to make causal inferences under appropriate circumstances, but which are probably to be regarded as reserves, devices to be used only when their repertoire of causal beliefs and their ability to perceive generative relations fail them. It is apparent that children rarely, if ever, use covariation information as a means of forming novel causal beliefs. This being so, how do children develop beliefs and hypotheses about causes and effects? There are a number of possibilities.

Abstraction from a Record of Experiences

This involves the detection of features common (and/or exclusive) to a number of examples or instances. Shultz (1991) was dubious about this technique on the grounds that, as with covariation assessment, it places considerable demands on working memory capacity. This does not have to be a problem, however, because instances can simply be added to a record of experiences stored in long-term memory. This is, after all, the general idea of the associationist approach (Shanks, 1993). It is also exemplified by the notion of causal schemas (Kelley, 1972b; 1973), which are abstract, simplified representations of patterns of covariation among events, built up through experience. People can then create causal beliefs by pulling out associations in long-term memory which satisfy whatever criteria are being used—covariation, necessary and sufficient conditional relation, and so on. This strategy does not strain working memory capacity: it is simply a kind of retrieval process. The real problem for this technique is, as we have seen, that evidence does not support the contention that this is how people behave (Kuhn, 1989; Piaget, 1954; White, 1988; 1989; 1992a; 1993). Covariation and conditional relations are not passively registered and stored as a source of new causal beliefs, but are interpreted at input in the light of causal beliefs already held.

Use of Single Instances

There may be two ways in which new causal beliefs can be formed by generalising from single instances. The first way involves the direct perception of generative relations. As Shultz (1982b) has argued, perception of generative relations is the overriding cue to causal inference at least from the age of two years. Harré and Madden (1975) argued that causal relations can be perceived just as shape and movement properties of objects can. That is to say, such perception is not immune from error and illusion (the launching effect, Michotte 1963, is an example), but under normal circumstances it is a trustworthy guide to objective features. Someone who has never encountered a hammer or a window before can perceive the causal relation involved when a hammer is used to smash a window. Moreover, the occurrence also yields information about the properties of the objects involved, information which can be used as a basis for belief formation by generalisation. By observing the action of the hammer on the window, the perceiver can obtain at least a rough idea of the causal power of the hammer and the liability or resistance of the window, and the inductive generalisation that follows merely instantiates an assumption that causal powers and liabilities tend to be stable properties of things. Thus, from perception of the interaction between the hammer and the window, the observer can gain an idea of the strength of the hammer and the weakness of the window.

The second way, where no generative relation is perceived in a single instance, involves the formulation of a causal hypothesis. One instance can lead to the formation of a rule which fits the relevant features of the instance, and which is then used as a hypothesis, generating predictions for future instances. In cases considered in this and previous chapters (Piaget, 1954; Schauble, 1990), the rule is then tested on instances involving the same objects, which is the most limited form of generalisation possible. Generalisation to other objects can be accomplished by abstracting the features relevant to the rule and searching for other objects which possess the same feature (see Holland, Holyoak, Nisbett, & Thagard, 1986, and Holyoak & Nisbett, 1988, for more on inductive generalisation). Thus, if a child forms the hypothesis that a given car was fast because it possessed tailfins, the feature of tailfin possession can be abstracted into a causal hypothesis which is then generalised to, or tested with, other objects that possess tailfins (Schauble, 1990). The problem, as always, is judging the limits on generalisability: can one generalise to bicycles or only to other cars, for example (see Nisbett, Krantz, Jepson, & Kunda, 1983)? There is also evidence that children learn scripts, that is to say event descriptions in general form, from single specific instances (Hudson, 1993; Hudson & Nelson, 1986; Fivush, 1984; Fivush, Kuebli, & Clubb, 1992).

Analogy

According to Shultz (1991, pp 88–89), analogy "involves finding a similar problem where the rules are known, mapping the rules to the novel target problem, and then tweaking the rules to adjust for possible differences between the target and analogous problems". It now appears that children as young as three years can solve analogies, and that failures to solve analogical problems show specific difficulties with problem content rather than inability to engage in analogical reasoning (Goswami, 1993). Their use of analogy in the domain of causal judgement and causal belief formation remains to be investigated.

Chunking

Chunking refers to a technique in problem solving which involves searching through the problem space for instances which are then combined to form a new rule. Essentially, chunking is a form of pattern recognition, in which the new rule or concept represents features common to the instances chunked together. The involvement of chunking in problem solving has been studied extensively (Shultz, 1991; Simon, 1979), but again its relevance to causal thinking in children is unknown.

Heuristics

Heuristics are devices for restricting the area of a problem representation that is to be searched for a solution. They represent a trade-off between accuracy and effort, meaning that they are more likely to be used as effort becomes more important in relation to accuracy. The heuristics most often discussed in inference research are representativeness and availability (Kahneman & Tversky, 1972; 1973; Tversky & Kahneman, 1973; 1974), which are devices for making judgements of frequency and probability. Karmiloff-Smith (1988) has argued that children use heuristics such as spatial symmetry in naive physics tasks.

Creative thinking

It is safe to say that virtually nothing is known about creative thinking (Lesgold, 1988; Perkins, 1988). It is also probably true that nothing ever comes completely out of the blue; the most original ideas and creations are always to some extent reworkings of old ones. But when Picasso combined a pair of handlebars and the saddle of an old bicycle to make an image of a bull's head, he demonstrated the power of combinations as a source of new ideas. Every person has in long-term memory a huge store of beliefs, ideas, information about features of things, whether individual things or categories, and the number of possible paired combinations of those things is effectively infinite. A child could easily create new causal hypotheses (or new ideas of any kind) by juxtaposing any two things from this store, and then generalising from the outcome. There are many other procedures for creating things from large information stores (Perkins, 1988). The possibility that procedures of these kinds may be involved in the development of causal beliefs should not be ignored.

Simulation
Simulation involves setting up a model of reality and making judgements about some real situation by applying the products of the simulation. In the present context, the main question about simulation concerns the kind of knowledge or information that is used to construct the model. According to Johnson (1988), young children can run simulations without the aid of concepts or theoretical constructs, by relying on minimally abstract representations of their own mental states. Any kind of information, however, can in principle be used to construct a simulation. Simulation and its close relative counterfactual reasoning have been extensively investigated at the adult level (Kahneman & Tversky, 1982; Wells & Gavanski, 1989; Lipe, 1991; and see Chapter 6; Fiske & Taylor, 1991) but not with children. Simulation and counterfactual reasoning both depend heavily on pre-existing beliefs or knowledge; while one can see how they might be used to generate particular judgements in particular situations (such as a judgement of likelihood of an uncertain event), they are much less plausible as a source of new beliefs and hypotheses. Perner (1991) suggested that simulation may be an important source of children's understanding of emotional reactions in others, but even in this case the construction of the simulation depends on social and personal knowledge (e.g. scripts) and, according to Perner, cannot be completely atheoretical.

Deduction
Deduction can be characterised as the inference of valid and provable conclusions from premises by means of proper rules of inference (Langer, 1967; Lemmon, 1965; Rips, 1988). Although deduction is not often considered as a means of making causal inferences, it has been applied to causal inference within the framework of the theory of lay epistemo-logic by Kruglanski (1980) and Kruglanski, Baldwin, and Shelagh (1983). This will be discussed in Chapter 7.

Direct Teaching, Education, Socialisation, and Social Transmission.
As already stated, once children have the theory of causation, that is to say a set of general ideas about the nature of the causal relation and what sort of things causes and effects are, they can acquire new causal beliefs simply by being told about things. An adult can tell a child that too much chocolate

causes stomach ache, and the use of the word "causes" gives the child grounds for acquiring a new belief simply by assimilating the specific information in the statement to the general concept of causation, and storing the product in memory. No induction is involved here, because the generality of the causal relation is indicated in the adult's statement. Much the same could be said of education in such topics as the physics of motion. In both cases, of course, the child's mind is hardly a blank slate and education may involve clearing the child's mind of inappropriate beliefs as much as teaching them correct ones (e.g. Howe, Tolmie, & Rodgers, 1992).

Children may also learn about action-related concepts by hearing how adults make use of them in discourse about action. Smetana (1993) has argued that children learn about social rules through social interactions in which rules are invoked for various purposes by people around them. It also seems likely that children learn about structures in society through social transmission (Emler & Dickinson, 1993). As Emler and Dickinson pointed out, social transmission need not imply a passive recipient. Children may still actively construct the information they are given, and moreover interpret it according to their existing state of understanding, resisting that which does not fit with knowledge structures already held.

Conclusion

The acquisition of causal beliefs, and the operation of ways of acquiring causal beliefs, may be limited and constrained by genetically determined cognitive capacities which undergo maturation through childhood. Children of a certain age may simply not be capable of acquiring certain kinds of belief, or of doing certain kinds of thing with the beliefs they already hold (Carey & Gelman, 1991; Perner, 1991). It is clear, though, that in fundamental respects young children's understanding of physical causation is commensurate with our own, just as their understanding of beliefs and desires underlying action is. Our understanding may be more elaborate, sophisticated, functional, and accurate than theirs, but it is not of a different kind.

NOTES

1. Two examples will suffice. First, to what extent can the theory of action be applied to other animal species? That is, can other animals act as we do on intentions formulated (non-linguistically) in respect of desires and beliefs? And how far down the animal knigdom might this capacity extend? Second, how many adults have been frightened at night by the sudden movement of

a lace curtain in an unnoticed draught? Concepts such as fate and destiny, and the tendency to ask "why me?" when one has been the victim of a chance misfortune, hint at a persistent tendency to apply the theory of action, or to seek to apply it, in areas where physical causality and probability are not well understood.

2. As expressed by Bullock (1985b), this is the idea that causes must do something to bring about their effects. This idea perhaps finds better expression as the concept of the generative relation (Bunge, 1963; Harré & Madden, 1975; White, 1989).

3. A similar idea was proposed by Lepper, Sagotsky, Dafoe, and Greene (1982) in the social domain. They suggested that children first acquire concrete scripts concerning familiar social situations and episodes, and later generalise these into more abstract principles such as the discounting principle (Kelley, 1973; see also Kassin & Pryor, 1985).

4. Disconfirming instances tend to lead not to rejection of the old theory but to creation of a new theory to explain a class of exceptions of which the disconfirming instance is a case. Processes of this sort have been studied in the context of stereotype change in adults (Johnston & Hewstone, 1992) but, as with so many other things, not in application to children's understanding of physical causation. This is also related to specialisation, the creation of exception rules that have a more limited condition than the parent rule to which they relate (Holyoak & Nisbett, 1988).

CHAPTER FIVE

The Theory of Action in Adulthood

The main purpose of this chapter is to address the possible development of the theory of action in adulthood. It is first necessary to distinguish two senses in which people may "explain" action. In one sense, to explain action is simply to give meaning to it. In the other, to explain action is what I have termed (White, 1993) "action origination attribution", which is to say how one came to perform a particular action, or to give one's reasons for action. The theory of action as I have treated it in this book relates mainly to the latter sense, and the latter sense is the predominant concern of this chapter. A comprehensive account of action origination attribution, however, requires that it be set in the context of the meaning of action, and I begin with an account of that.

GIVING MEANING TO ACTION

The study of the meaning of action has been called "ethogenics" by Rom Harré, and this account summarises some of Harré's views on ethogenics (Clarke & Crossland, 1985; Harré, 1976; 1979; 1983; Harré & Madden, 1975; Harré & Secord, 1972).

According to Harré, people understand persons as having, among other things, powers. A power is a capacity or tendency to produce or generate a specific kind of behaviour or a specific effect. All kinds of things may have powers: for example, acid solution has the power to turn litmus paper pink. In the case of powers of material particulars other than persons, powers operate to produce their effects only under specifiable conditions. For example, acid only turns litmus paper pink when the paper is brought into contact with it. When suitable conditions are met, the power of a thing operates as a matter of necessity. The powers of persons are different in this respect; they constitute a resource for the construction of action, but the way in which they are used in the production of action is largely up to the actor. In the case of action, powers do not operate as a matter of necessity under suitable conditions. There are conditions which can be thought of as opportunities for the exercise of powers (e.g. the presence of a charity box is an opportunity for the action of donating money), but opportunities do not compel powers to operate. The powers of persons are in effect a kind of competence, a resource drawn upon not only for the construction and performance of action, but also for the interpretation of the actions of others. They enable us to make an action appropriate to its synchronic and diachronic context, and to give informative accounts which lay bare the meaning of an action or a set of actions. An account of action is not necessarily accurate, however, because it may be drawn from a different part of the resource than the action to which it refers.

This account differs from mere generative causal mechanisms in two important respects. First, it allows that, in the case of human action, it is up to the actor how to act. Rules guide action, but they do so through the actor's awareness of the rule and what it prescribes. Second, it involves the capacity to monitor the control of one's actions. Awareness and self-monitoring underlie a kind of equifinality that is unique to human action: awareness of rules and meanings ascribed to situations, and monitoring of behaviour in order to ensure that it continues to be appropriately directed towards the end the actor has in mind, in the light of rules and meanings. These aspects of Harré's account are well captured by the following quotations, from Harré and Secord (1972):

> Social behaviour is meaningful behaviour. It involves an agent with certain intentions and expectations, an agent capable of deliberating and choosing from a variety of courses of action, and whose words and actions are understood by his fellows (p.35).

> In general, social behaviour is the result of conscious self-monitoring of performance by the person himself, in the course of which he contrives to assess the meaning of the social situation in which he finds himself, and to choose amongst various rules and conventions, and to act in accordance with his choice, correcting this choice as further aspects of the situation make themselves clear to him (p.151).

With respect to the explanation of action, Harré (1976) identified three levels at which behaviour may be described:

1. Behaviour: the movement itself, described in purely physical terms.
2. Action: action is sometimes referred to as movement plus meaning, and an action is a socially meaningful unit of behaviour.
3. Act: a higher level description making reference to the broader social context of an action. For instance (and see Chapter 1), a man's action of putting a ring on the fourth finger of a woman's left hand is part of the act of marriage, but the act of marriage is not to be identified with that action because, for example, in different cultures the same act of marriage is accomplished by different actions. There may be many different actions which, under different circumstances or in different cultures, count as the performance of the same act.

This tripartite division has been criticised by Ginet (1990) and is probably too simple in many cases, as the famous example of assassinating Archduke Franz Ferdinand illustrates. At the bottom level, the physical movements involved in this action can be described, but there are several levels of describing it as an action above that: pulling the trigger, firing the gun, shooting the Archduke, assassinating the Archduke, striking a blow for freedom, and starting the Great War. It has been shown that people recognise multiple levels of action identification (Vallacher & Wegner, 1987). Irrespective of the number of levels there may be, however, the idea of levels of description and explanation of action is important to ethogenics. To avoid confusion, I shall use the term "action" for all levels of description above that of mere physical movement.

As the example of sealing an agreement suggests, the explanation of action involves reference to a surrounding context, the identification of which helps to render an individual action meaningful. Mainly, this context is a more extended behavioural configuration or episode of which the action is a part. One can think of an episode as governed by a set of procedures or rules for arranging actions in meaningful (perhaps functional or purposeful would be better terms) sequences or strings; these rules or procedures may define a kind of syntax of action (Clarke, 1983).

In Harré's account there are two types of meaning of action, each with two orthogonal subdivisions. One type is called internalist, and is an adaptation of the Saussurean grid (Harré, 1976). Saussurean linguistics distinguishes between syntagmatic and paradigmatic relations. Syntagmatic relations specify "the combination of units into larger constructions over time" (Clarke & Crossland, 1985, p.72). In linguistics this was a way of referring to acceptable grammatical structures, and in ethogenics it is a way of referring to acceptable, that is meaningful, sequences of actions. This is easiest to see in cases of sequences that relate to scripts. For example, a sequence in which a bargain was sealed before the terms had been agreed would probably not be regarded as meaningful, and represents a violation of syntagmatic rules. Paradigmatic relations are relations of substitutability: that is, given a certain action in a certain place in an episode, what other actions could be substituted for it without damage to the meaningfulness of the episode? For example, at a certain point in a church service it is normal to sing a hymn. There is no particular hymn that must be sung, however: The hymn chosen on one occasion could be substituted by another without loss of meaning. Substituting a hymn with a tap-dancing session, however, would be a violation of paradigmatic rules.

The other type of meaning of action is externalist, that is, referring outside the system. Again there are two types of externalist meaning. One is referential semantics. This refers to the way in which something can stand for, represent, or symbolise something else. For example in medieval art the chi-rho figure stands for or represents Jesus Christ. Actions do not usually have this kind of meaning, but there are instances, for example in rituals, where actions have a symbolic significance of this sort. The other type of externalist meaning is prescriptive semantics. This refers to the social force of an action, covering such things as the laying down of obligations or instructions or expectations for the future.

This account therefore reveals several ways in which an action may be explained, in the sense of being given meaning. One can explain an action by giving information about its location in an episode or sequence of interaction, or about its function in that context; one can explain by saying what the action stands for or symbolises; one can explain by elucidating its social force; one can explain by redescribing the action or identifying it at a different level (e.g. "Why did you fire the gun?"; "Because I was assassinating the Archduke").

A number of accounts to be found in social psychology are variations on this general theme. Some of them straddle the boundary between meaning attribution and origination attribution, but they are included in this section because of their apparent similarities with Harré's ideas.

Lalljee and Abelson (1983)

Lalljee and Abelson argued that explanations are derived not from an empirical analysis of regularity (see Chapter 6) but from knowledge structures such as scripts, personae, and plans (Schank & Abelson, 1977). These are stereotyped representations of social events and episodes. The fact that they are stereotyped means that they can be used to fill in gaps in available information with standard details. In this sense, to explain action is to fill in a gap in information, and knowledge structures such as scripts provide one way of doing that.

Lalljee and Abelson claimed that when people are asked to explain why a scripted action took place they usually refer either to enablement (i.e. an action is explained as enabling the person to perform the next action in the script) or to the satisfaction of goals, using expressions such as "in order to". Other knowledge structures have a similar relation to explanations.

For unscripted actions Lalljee and Abelson suggested two types of explanations. One type they called constructive explanation, and they suggested that this has three stages: (1) identify the actor's goals; (2) identify the plan being used to satisfy the goal; (3) connect the action to the plan.

The other type they called contrastive explanation. This involves contrasting the action with some standard, an idea of a normal action "with reference to which the action is seen as in need of explanation" (p.74). The notion of contrastive explanation has appeared in several accounts of the explanation of action since Lalljee and Abelson (Hesslow, 1988; Hilton, 1990; Hilton & Slugoski, 1986; McGill, 1989) and has antecedents in the philosophical literature (Gorovitz, 1965; Hart & Honoré, 1959). Lalljee and Abelson suggested that there may be many types of contrastive explanation, and they listed six. These include such things as planning failure (e.g. lacking the means to satisfy a goal) and external interference (e.g. the route to the goal being blocked). Knowledge structures can be used in the development and testing of plausible explanations.

Lalljee and Abelson emphasised, as Harré did, the importance for explanation of detailed contextual information; for them, however, the role of contextual information is primarily as a means of identifying goals and plans, rather than the meaning of action in the sense to be found in Harré's work (Harré & Secord, 1972). Their account implies that people should often refer to goals when asked to explain actions, and there is some evidence to support this. Lalljee, Watson, and White (1982) reported that goals were referred to in 38% of explanations for actions given by adults, and Lalljee, Watson, and White (1983, study 1) reported that goals were referred to in 37% of explanations for action given by children. By contrast, in the same study Lalljee et al. (1983) found that only 0.4% of explanations for emotions referred to goals. These findings suggest that goals are only considered appropriate for explaining actions, although not that they always are.

Read (1987)

Read's account resembles that of Lalljee and Abelson, although in some matters Read has gone into more detail. His first point is that a single action occurs in the context not only of a situation but also of a sequence of behaviour: an action is an element in a sequence. Making sense of it therefore involves relating it to the other actions in the sequence. Read took an analogy with the construction of a story, and suggested that people are naive storytellers, rather than naive scientists. He went on to argue that we make sense of action with the aid of knowledge structures. Generally, explaining an action involves relating it to goals and plans, and people work out: "(a) how the individual actions form a plan, (b) what the goals of the sequence are, (c) how that particular plan could achieve the individual's goals, and (d) what conditions initiated the goal" (p.289). People use their knowledge of the world to work these things out. Read argued that a lot of this interpretation ("causal reasoning", as he rather misleadingly called it) goes on automatically and is part of the comprehension of action. The result is a mental representation in the form of a story that can be used to answer questions.

Read then gave a detailed list of social knowledge structures. These include traits and stereotypes, but Read concentrated on the following, drawing on the work of Schank and Abelson (1977):

1. Scripts. These are stereotyped action sequences comprising a stereotyped plan to attain a certain kind of goal. A familiar example is the scripted stereotype of the actions involved in having a meal at a restaurant. With respect to scripts, people can explain several things:

   (a) A whole script (e.g. Why did X go to the restaurant?), explained by reference to initiating conditions.
   (b) A script deviation or failure: the script provides a source of hypotheses which can be tested, for example by contrastive analysis (Lalljee & Abelson, 1983).
   (c) A behaviour that is part of a script: "people probably explain action in one of three ways: (a) by the immediately following action that it enables, (b) by the subgoal of which the action is a part, or (c) by the overall goal of the script" (Schank & Abelson, 1977, p.290).

2. Plans. These concern knowledge about the general kinds of action that can be used to attain different goals.
3. Goals. This includes relations between different goals held either by the same person or by different people in interaction, which may result in goal conflict.
4. Themes. Themes are collections of goals, and may be of three types: (a) role themes (e.g. the typical goals of a police officer), (b) interpersonal themes—goals related to relationships, and (c) life themes, "the general position or aim that a person wants in life" (Schank & Abelson, 1977, p.144).

According to Schank and Abelson (1977), relations between elements in sequences are limited by a kind of causal syntax defining permissible relations among actions, events, and mental states.

Read proposed a model in which we construct a scenario for an action sequence, based on the idea that input activates knowledge structures through a spreading activation process. Read outlined six steps in the construction of a scenario.

1. Categorise people (and situation). This gives a basic scenario.
2. Connect subsequent actions with the current scenario.
3. To do this, we see "whether the action could be part of a plan suggested by our scenario" (Read, 1987, p.293). We use world knowledge to generate possible plans to see whether they fit the scenario or not.
4. Once we identify a plan, try to identify the goal if we have not already done so.
5. See whether the goal is part of a larger plan or not.
6. Try to identify a source of the goal.

Presumably things are not required to occur in this exact order: it is likely that people iterate one or more of these steps, continuing until they have constructed a scenario they regard as complete, or perhaps until their interest runs out.

In addition to this, Read summarised some general principles of scenario construction, which are in fact principles of story comprehension (Wilensky, 1983) adapted for Read's purpose:

1. Principle of coherence. People aim for the most coherent interpretation possible.
2. Principle of concretion. People prefer concrete to abstract information and explanations.
3. Principle of least commitment. People aim for the minimum number of assumptions necessary to make a coherent scenario.
4. Principle of exhaustion. People aim to account for as much of the data as possible.
5. Principle of parsimony. Simple explanations are to be preferred, subject to satisfaction of the preceding principles.

Read's account shares with Harré's the emphasis on explaining action by embedding it in a context consisting primarily of a behavioural episode or sequence. The account draws heavily on previous work by various authors (Lalljee & Abelson, 1983; Schank & Abelson, 1977; Wilensky, 1983); on the other hand it is a useful illustration of the likely complexity of any account of the explanation of action that takes seriously the idea that knowledge structures and episodic context are crucial to the way in which people interpret actions. Testing a proposal of this sort would be extremely difficult, but it would be regrettable if this difficulty acted as a barrier to the development of thought along these lines. There are many things that count as explaining action, in the sense of giving it meaning, and there is a great deal to be lost by neglecting these issues.

Hilton (1990)

Hilton (1990, p.66) has added a further sense to the word "explanation", as something that goes on in conversations, or interpersonal interaction in general: "The conversational model of causal explanation states that explanations identify the factor that makes the difference between a target event and a counterfactual contrast case. It also states that explanations are constrained by general rules of conversation". The first sentence refers to the abnormal conditions focus model (Hilton & Slugoski, 1986), which will be discussed in Chapter 6. The second sentence identifies the main concern of this section, the idea that explanation is often a part of conversation.

Hilton proposed a two-stage model. The first stage, causal diagnosis, involves identifying a causal connection between two events. The second stage is interpersonal explanation, the aim of which is to make use of the causal diagnosis to close a gap in the explainee's knowledge. The person giving the explanation selects from the full diagnosis the element that closes the gap in the explainee's understanding. For the sake of this function, causal explanations in conversation must "be *relevant* to a question as well as *true* of the target event" (p.67, italics in original). To fulfil its interpersonal function, a conversational explanation should satisfy Grice's (1975) four conversational maxims. These are:

1. Quality: say something that you know not to be false and for which you have some kind of support.
2. Quantity. Say enough to be informative but not more than is needed for this purpose.
3. Relevance. Answer the question asked.
4. Manner. Avoid being obscure, ambiguous, long-winded; be brief and to the point.

This is relevant to what subjects do and say in experimental studies of causal attribution, because in these studies they are engaging in a kind of interpersonal interaction with the experimenter. This means that they expect what the experimenter says to them or asks of them to be bound by the conversational maxims, and they themselves generate answers to those questions in conformity with the maxims. For example, they interpret a causal question asked by the experimenter as being of a certain type, and aim to give an answer to the question as they have interpreted it, in accordance with the principle of relevance (for an illustration, see McGill, 1989). "Subjects may omit factors from their explanations not because they believe that these factors do not have any causal role in producing an event, but because they consider them irrelevant to the question that they have been asked" (Hilton, 1990, p.73), or at least irrelevant to the question they *think* they have been asked.

Hilton applied this analysis to attribution biases, and speculated that such biases may result from conversational factors and implicit questions: an unbiased answer may appear biased to the experimenter because experimenter and subject have different ideas of what is relevant to answering the question asked. In particular (p.76), "response formats may serve as an important informational cue for subjects". For example, formats may tell the subject what kind of question the experimenter wants answered. It could be added that the information presented to subjects may tell them what is supposed to be *relevant* to the question asked, and that they should therefore use it; subjects not unreasonably assume that the experimenter gives them information in accordance with the principle of relevance, and that they should therefore use whatever information is presented. Exactly this argument has been used in a critique of the dispositional bias literature by Funder (1987), and supported empirically by Miller, Schmidt, Meyer, and Colella (1984) and Wright and Wells (1988). In short, *anything* that the experimenter gives the subject may be a cue to causal questions and how to answer them.

Hilton's analysis is a valuable reminder that giving meaning to action is not purely an intrapersonal process, but is itself part of a social and interpersonal context including a sequence of actions. The kind of explanation that people give for action depends on the interpersonal function that the explanation is meant to fulfil, and is constrained by interactional factors such as the conversational maxims. The easiest way to see this is to compare explaining an action to a child and to an adult; one naturally takes account of what either party is likely to know and understand (not to mention what one thinks they *ought* to know or not to know) and shapes the explanation accordingly. These points apply equally to action origination attribution, the topic to which I now turn.

EXTENSIONS TO THE THEORY OF ACTION

In Chapter 3, I showed that the basic theory of action was gradually elaborated during childhood. By the age of three years children are probably in possession of a version of the intentional theory of action as shown in Fig. 5.1. By the age of nine years, possibly earlier, a notion of personality as an antecedent to beliefs and desires, and functioning as a source of individuating consistency in individual behaviour, has been added. Here I am concerned with the adult elaboration of the theory of action, as building on and revising the structure shown in Fig. 5.1. The literature yields only a small number of proposals on this important topic.

Heider (1958)

Heider (1958, p.1) recognised the importance of inferences about mental states in interpersonal behaviour: "Generally, a person reacts to what he thinks the other person is perceiving, feeling, and thinking, in addition to what the other person may be doing". In consequence, Heider's book was an attempt to elucidate the key concepts, including mental state concepts, crucial to the understanding of interpersonal relations, and how they relate to each other. He mainly used word explication as his means of achieving this. His investigation was guided by a number of orienting principles, which have continued to influence the study of attribution.

1. Heider regarded the ordinary person as a kind of naïve scientist, not able to employ the sophisticated experimental methods of professional scientists but sometimes relying on naïve versions of those methods, such as the covariation principle (see Chapter 6). He emphasized the primacy of understanding, prediction, and control as the goals of attribution. Understanding is the most important of these, as it is presumed to provide a foundation for accurate prediction and effective control.

2. In accord with the primary goal of quasi-scientific understanding, Heider argued that people seek to explain the transient phenomena of the world by reference to stable underlying dispositional properties; it is the stability of these properties that makes accurate prediction a feasible goal. Although dispositional properties are now commonly taken to refer to stable properties of persons, especially personality characteristics, any kind of thing can have dispositional properties. Glass, for example, has the dispositional property of brittleness. Indeed, dispositional properties are

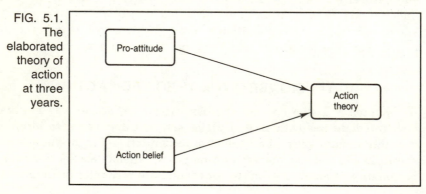

FIG. 5.1. The elaborated theory of action at three years.

Pro-attitude

Action theory

Action belief

not necessarily stable, although stable ones are presumed to have greater value with respect to the goals of attribution.

3. Heider also emphasised the importance of the internal–external (or person–situation) distinction for attribution. For example, in his analysis of the attribution of pleasure, Heider wrote (p.150): "If we know that our present enjoyment is due to the contribution of the object because it is an intrinsically desirable one, then we can expect anyone who has contact with it to enjoy it; on the other hand, if the enjoyment is attributed to our own personality, then at most we can expect only persons who have a similar personality to enjoy it". This exemplifies the role of understanding as a generator of predictions. The presumed importance of the internal/external distinction is one reason for supposing that the covariation principle has an important role to play in attribution (see Chapter 6).

Heider's discussion of the naïve analysis of action is not directed at the production of action in itself, but at the determination of outcomes of action. As such, it is confined to actions such as achievement-related behaviour, in which the individual's actions are in a kind of contest with environmental factors, the outcome depending on how the contest works out. Environmental forces can be facilitatory or inhibitory: opportunity, luck, obstacle, resistance, and so on. Here, I am concerned with Heider's analysis of factors within the person.

There are two main determinants of actions directed towards a certain outcome: power and trying. These are related as a multiplicative combination. In other words, both are necessary if the outcome is to be achieved. Power is often, and to a large extent, a function of ability. According to Heider, several sets of factors can contribute to power. These include personality traits and attitudes (e.g. self-confidence); temporary states and factors such as fatigue and mood; and various motivational factors such as fears, needs, wishes, and will. Trying, on the other hand, is a function of just two factors, intention and exertion. Heider made it clear that intention is the central factor in personal causality, and he related this to goals. The essence of personal causality is "where p tries to cause x, where x is his goal" (p.100). Where the attempt is successful, the outcome of action is the achievement of the goal. We infer want from trying. Want relates to intention, but lies behind it, as a reason. Wanting (desire) does not figure prominently in this analysis, but is mainly treated in a separate chapter in relation to pleasure. The reason for this is Heider's belief that desire is only loosely co-ordinated with action because (p.128):

1. "The same wish may lead to very different actions according to the requirements of the environment".
2. "A wish may exist long before a specific action is taken to satisfy it, or without its ever being actualised in action".

3. "Wishes can have other effects besides action" (e.g. affective reactions).

Heider did not discuss the role of desires in reasons explanations. He also made little mention of personality characteristics, except insofar as they are implicitly included in references to stable personal dispositions.

This summary of Heider's account of the naïve analysis of goal-directed action can be expressed diagrammatically in Fig. 5.2.

In this figure, "ability" is in bold type to indicate that it is the main determinant of power. The diagram is slightly misleading in its implication of a causal sequence from exertion through trying to action; it might be better to regard exertion and trying as components of the production of action, rather than as antecedents to it, and as acting in the face of inhibitory environmental factors, rather than independently of them. Also, the model is not complete, because it takes no acount of beliefs as mediators between desires and action. Heider did make brief mention of beliefs, but in a way that does not resemble their role in the intentional theory of action, as the following sequence (extracted from his Fig. 1 on p.162), illustrates:

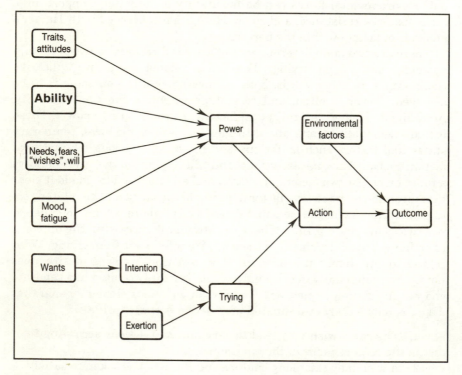

FIG. 5.2. Heider's elaborated adult theory of goal-directed action.

Desire of p for x→Belief that p can cause x→Exertion

where "p" refers to the person, not to the person's action. Finally, in the case that p likes x, Heider added the following causal links (p.297):

p–x contact→pleasure; belief in losing x→fear
p–x separation→desire; belief in achieving x→hope
desire→contact→pleasure

Summarising the book, Heider commented: "The interpretation does not consist merely of arbitrarily connecting meanings to data; that feature which is characteristic of science—namely that a network of concepts that are systematically defined is fitted to the empirical manifold, and lends the terms in which the manifold is encoded—is already present in naïve perception and judgment. One might say that we are much more implicit Newtonians than implicit Baconians".

Perhaps insufficient attention was paid to that passage, because following Heider there was a period of fragmentation: the account of goal-directed action became the model for Weiner's taxonomic model of achievement-related attribution; Heider's remarks on intention stimulated the correspondent inference theory of dispositional attribution (Jones & Davis, 1965); and Kelley (1967) developed Heider's references to the use of the covariation principle in distinguishing internal and external causes. Correspondent inference theory is a theory of dispositional attribution and therefore falls outside the remit of this book. Kelley's models will be discussed in Chapter 6. Brief comments on Weiner's model are appropriate here, however.

Weiner's Attribution Model

Weiner's model (Weiner, 1979; 1985; 1986; Weiner, Frieze, Kukla, Reed, Rest, & Rosenbaum, 1972) is in principle a model of attributions for the outcome of any kind of goal directed behaviour, though achievement situations have been the usual example. The full model places causal attribution in a context of outcome, reaction, expectations, and subsequent achievement-related behaviour; here I am concerned only with the causal attribution part of the model. Weiner argued that, following a behavioural outcome (success or failure), the person (or an observer) may attempt to make a causal attribution for the outcome. In Weiner's model the attributer searches three dimensions for possible explanatory factors. One of these is a dichotomy rather than a dimension: Heider's internal–external distinction (called locus in Weiner's model), and Weiner shared Heider's view that it is fundamental to causal attribution. The other two, although really dimensions, are conventionally treated as dichotomies as well. One is the stable–unstable dimension, and the other, a later addition to the model, is controllability (Weiner, 1979). These three factors yield, conventionally, eight cells, and possible causes of success and failure are located in one of these cells. For example, ability is categorised as internal, stable, and uncontrollable. Adventitious help from others would be categorised as external, unstable, and controllable. Weiner's model has stimulated a great deal of research, as well as some critical analysis (see Fiske & Taylor, 1991); here, I want to concentrate on one feature of Weiner's approach.

Weiner's model instantiates the rather odd assumption that it is the place of a factor in a set of dimensions or dichotomies that is important in the context of causal attribution, rather than the identity of the factor. The model is, in fact, an attempt to explain causal attribution by creating a taxonomy. Strictly speaking, taxonomic models cannot be models of causal attribution. A theoretical taxonomy is an attempt to elucidate the fundamental differences in kind between things: in the classical example of plants, a valid taxonomy uses criteria that lead to correct identification of plant species in terms of their relatedness to each other. This is different from using a taxonomy as a theory of causal attribution. There are two reasons for this:

1. The most valid taxonomic principles—i.e. those that generate correct classifications and relations—are not necessarily of the highest causal relevance, or indeed of any causal relevance at all.

2. Not all properties of things represent taxonomic principles; the whole point of taxonomy is to select those few properties that are important for classification by type and to ignore the rest as irrelevant or unimportant. It follows that properties of highest causal relevance need not be involved in taxonomic principles at all.

In summary, whether a property of a thing is of taxonomic significance is independent of whether it is of significance for causal attribution. Weiner (1985) made a good case for the three dimensions of his model as having the highest causal relevance of any taxonomic principles. This begs the question, however, of whether there are any properties of possible attributed causes that are not possible taxonomic principles but which have higher causal relevance than stability, locus, and controllability. It is arguable that there are two such properties. One is the particular identity of a given factor—the concept of ability, the concept of effort, and so on. Clearly, identity is not revealed by location in taxonomic structure: ability is stable, internal, and uncontrollable, but so might many other kinds of factor be. The other property is causal relatedness—that is, the location of a possible attributed cause in an organised system or network of causal relations. That is to say, the important feature of a factor is its function in relation to an outcome—how it interacts with other factors in the production of the outcome. For an example of a model proposing a network of causal relations, look at Wellman's model in Fig. 5.3, and compare it with Weiner's taxonomic model.

There are two main reasons why taxonomic principles are of less relevance to causal attribution than causal relatedness. First, taxonomic principles do not reveal beliefs about causal interactions between possible attributed causes; indeed they can be misleading in their apparent implication that different causes are seen as operating independently, that is, without one influencing another. Second, they take the causal interpretation of success and failure only one step back. In doing so they may fail to elucidate the factors that are of fundamental importance in being believed to be ultimately responsible for the particular immediate causes of success and failure. Questions of the form "what brings about effort?" or "on what does ability depend?" cannot be answered by reference to taxonomic principles, and yet these exemplify precisely the sort of question that must be addressed in order to reveal what is fundamental to people's understanding of the causation of success and failure.

A hypothetical illustration may be of some use. Suppose we look at how people make causal attributions for variations in the population of zebras. We may find that they can list several causes: for example, climate and weather, varying levels of zebra food, changes in the lion population, and so on. Now there are two things (among others) that we can do with this set of possible causes. One is to elucidate taxonomic principles, such as biological v. non-biological, things that zebras eat v. things that eat zebras, and so on. The other is to build up a structure depicting causal relations among these things, discovering for example that people believe that the population of zebras rose because there was more grass and there was more grass because more rain than usual fell in the rainy season and the local cattle herders moved elsewhere. This structure represents not just the identity of individual causes and effects but also the specific causal powers and liabilities of the things involved: not just what kind of thing heavy rain is, but what it can do. Taxonomic principles can be of causal relevance, but they cannot be a complete theory of causal attribution because they omit this crucial information about how different factors are causally related to each other, and about factors causally antecedent to the immediate causes of the effect. What matters about grass, as far as explaining the rise in the zebra population is concerned, is not its taxonomically relevant properties but how it affects and is affected by other things. It is for this reason that a theory of causal attribution, whatever use it makes of taxonomic principles, must make reference to causal structure.

None of this is to deny that properties that can be used as taxonomic principles are of any relevance at all to causal attribution, or that Weiner's three-dimensional model is the most successful one based on taxonomic principles. It is important to know whether a possible attributed cause is viewed as long-lasting or transient, regardless of its involvement in causal structure. Fundamentally, however, a theory of causal attributions for success and failure is a theory of causal structures, of the causal relations believed to hold between the constructs that people believe are relevant to the causation of success and failure.

Wellman's Model

Wellman (1990) has developed a model of adult belief–desire reasoning as an extension of the child's belief–desire psychology. The aim of this extension is not to be definitive but to offer a plausible account of the kinds of mental antecedents to beliefs and desires giving rise to action in common sense. The model proposes a set of categories of mental state, and various kinds of links between them. Wellman's categories are as follows:

1. Thinking. Thinking is a relatively basic category of mental activity in common sense (Rips & Conrad, 1989). In Wellman's account, thinking includes such things as dreaming, reasoning, learning, imagining, and remembering. These activities have a number of kinds of product, of which beliefs are one; beliefs emerge from formative thinking processes such as reasoning and remembering.

2. Intention. Wellman had not included intention in his model of the child's belief–desire psychology. In this extension he recognised that intentions are plans to actualise desires, made in the light of relevant beliefs. He did not, however, distinguish between momentary intentions formulated and actualised immediately and prior intentions which may be held in mind for a considerable length of time. Terms such as plan, goal, and aim, generally refer to prior intentions rather than to immediately actualised intentions. For this reason it may be that intention, with this ambiguity in its common-sense usage, belongs in more than one part of the elaborated model of action.

3. Cognitive emotions. This term is meant to encompass cognitive states with an evaluative or affective loading. Cognitive emotions include attitudes or values, but also mental states such as surprise, boredom, and puzzlement.

4. Perception.

5. Physiology and basic emotions. Physiological states such as sexual arousal, hunger, and thirst, are bracketed with basic emotions such as love, hate, fear, and anger.

6. Sensations. These include such things as dizziness, nausea, and pain, and are located between perception and physiological states, though the nature of their link to these is not clear.

7. Traits. Wellman supposed that traits (including not only personality characteristics but also intelligence) organise and ground many states and events in other categories: thinking, cognitive emotions, beliefs, desires, intentions, and to some extent physiological states and basic emotions as well. As such, they formed "an additional layer laid on top of the core schema" (p.114).

Figure 5.3 presents these various elements of Wellman's elaborated model of action, and the links between them (from Wellman, 1990, Fig. 4.3, p.115).

The location of various categories in this model is in accord with a loose two-dimensional space. One dimension, from left to right, marks efferent–afferent relations, moving from proprioceptive bodies through more receptive parts of the mind to action-oriented parts of the mind and afferent bodies, producing action. The other dimension, from bottom to top, marks a shift from passive experiencing to active processing. As Wellman noted,

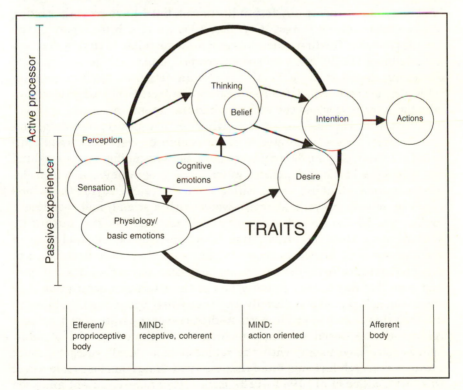

FIG. 5.3. Wellman's elaborated adult model of belief–desire reasoning.

this dimension is not exact; we can, for example, exert some control over our basic emotions, and we are not always fully in control of our thinking.

Wellman was careful not to claim too much for this model, and argued that its main value was as a stimulus to research on the development of adult belief–desire psychology. It is readily apparent that Wellman's model is different from Heider's. The main reason for this is that Wellman was concentrating on mental states underlying freely chosen actions, such as searching for a lost kitten, whereas Heider was concentrating on mental states underlying goal-directed action, such as trying to pass an exam, and the determination of outcomes of such action. It is important to ask how these two types of behaviour might be integrated in a comprehensive model of common sense psychology, and moreover how other types of behaviour such as emotion-related responses might be integrated. No one has yet attempted anything so ambitious, but this surely stands as an ultimate goal for research and theory in this tradition.

A Modified Model of Action Origination

Wellman did not report any test of his model, but I have recently carried out two experiments to test it (White, 1994), and a brief report of the findings follows. The first study was essentially similar to that by Bartsch and Wellman (1989). Sixty subjects were presented with sentences each describing an actor as performing a certain action or having a certain intention, desire, or belief. For each sentence, subjects were asked to explan why the actor performed the action or had the intention, desire, or belief. There were 12 core sentences, from which action, desire, intention, and belief versions were generated. The 12 sentences were concerned with going to a party, playing football in the park, helping mother do the washing up, solving a crossword puzzle, watching a programme on television, buying a dress, climbing a tree, eating some ice cream, tidying the actor's bedroom, saying prayers, sharing sweets with a friend, and mending a broken toy. In the second study, written questions asked a further 60 subjects about their intentions, desires, actions, and beliefs, and those of some person well known to them. In each case they were first asked to describe some desire they (their friend) had, some action they (their friend) had done that day or very recently, and so on. After each description they were then asked to explain briefly *why* they (their friend) had that desire, did that thing, and so on. In both studies responses were coded using a coding scheme based on the categories in Wellman's model of adult belief–desire psychology, with the addition of a "goal" category, since previous research has suggested that many explanations for action are of this sort (Lalljee et al., 1982; 1983). Explanations were content analysed by two blind coders, and high levels of reliability were found.

The results of both studies clearly showed that Wellman's model cannot be sustained. The model predicts that different categories should be favoured depending on whether the thing to be explained is a desire, an intention, or an action. In fact these differences were not found and people explained these three things in almost identical ways. Moreover, the way in which they explained them is not the way predicted under the model. The favoured categories of explanation were goals, desires, and attitudes (the term used for Wellman's cognitive emotion category). Across the two studies, these three categories together accounted for 86.2% of psychological explanations for actions, desires, and intentions; the remaining five psychological categories accounted for the rest. For beliefs, the model fared slightly better in that explanations often made reference to perceptions and to other beliefs, as the model predicts. The cognition category was rarely used, however. In addition, a substantial proportion of explanations for beliefs referred to attitudes (especially in study 1) and emotions (especially in study 2). References to emotions were just as frequent for beliefs as for actions, intentions, and desires, and there was little sign of the special association between emotions and desires predicted by the model. In both studies subjects were making free verbal responses. There is therefore a possibility that their explanations were constructed in conformity to the co-operativeness principle (Grice, 1975), and in particular the maxim of quantity (see p.156). In this case subjects would be selectively omitting parts of explanations which readers, or the experimenter, are assumed to be able to infer for themselves. This could bias the pattern found in the results, preventing it from being a fair test of Wellman's model. To test this, in a third study subjects were given explanations exemplifying each of the categories in the model and asked to rate how good each explanation was as a possible reason for a given intention, desire or action. The results showed that any given explanation was thought to be equally acceptable, whether it was being used to explain an intention, a desire or an action: correlations between these three different things across explanations were close to perfect. These results strongly suggest that people explain actions, desires, and intentions in the same way, and there is no case to be made, not only for Wellman's model, but for any model in which different antecedents are proposed for actions, desires, and intentions.

Wellman's model has its roots in the intentional theory of action. According to this theory an action is intentional if it can be explained by reference to a relevant belief and desire of the actor: a desire which the action was intended to fulfil, and a belief that the action in question was a means by which the desire could be fulfilled. The results of these studies are not incompatible with the intentional theory of action. The interpretation of the term "desire" by Wellman is both too narrow and incorrect, and it would be less misleading to use Davidson's (1963; 1968) term "pro-attitude" instead. Pro-attitudes can include desires, wantings, urgings, moral views, aesthetic principles, goals, and values, so long as these conform to the characterisation in terms of inclining the actor towards a certain action. They can also include permanent character traits and passing fancies (Davidson, 1963; 1968; Smith & Jones, 1986). Interpreting "desire" as referring to wants and wishes is therefore too narrow. In fact, of the psychological categories used in these studies, desire, physiology, emotion, goals and plans, attitude, and trait can all be subsumed under the general notion of a "pro-attitude".

The word "can" is important because none of these things is necessarily a pro-attitude. What makes something a pro-attitude is not its intrinsic quality as a mental state but its function. Wants, goals, attitudes, and so on are pro-attitudes when they function as part of a reason for action, and in virtue of the fact that they do so. A person can have a want, or a goal, or an attitude, and it is possible to describe these mental states *per se*, and it is also possible to say what kind of mental state they are, perhaps by referring to their distinctive intrinsic qualities. But in and of themselves they are not pro-attitudes. They become pro-attitudes when they function as a reason for action, and at no other time.

The other component of a reason for action under the intentional theory of action is a belief: not just any belief, but a belief that the action in question will lead to the fulfilment or attainment of the thing desired. In these studies such beliefs were almost never mentioned in explanations for action; most of the items coded as beliefs were beliefs of other kinds. We cannot conclude from this that the intentional theory of action is wrong as an account of the naïve understanding of action, however. In understanding action, the action belief is necessarily dependent on the desire. One can know what one wants without knowing how to attain it, but one cannot know how to attain it without knowing what it is one wants. It is therefore not surprising that people refer to beliefs less than to desires when giving explanations: the belief alone would make no sense to an audience who did not know the desire. For the same reason it is not surprising that young children master desire psychology before they master belief–desire psychology (Wellman & Woolley, 1990); the understanding of belief in relation to action depends on understanding desire, and cannot precede it. Moreover, the belief is usually less relevant to the understanding of an action. Usually, the reason for a journey lies in its destination, not in the means of travel; likewise, the reason for an action usually lies in the desired outcome, not in the means by which it is attained.

There is a compelling logic to the belief–desire combination; one cannot attain what one wants without knowing both what it is that one wants and how to attain it, except by accident. I therefore maintain beliefs in the modified model, but designate them as "action beliefs" to single out the special function of beliefs in relation to action.

The concept of an intention is more problematic. Under the intentional theory of action an action is intentional if it is carried out because of an appropriate desire–belief (or pro-attitude–action belief) combination; there is no separate mental state of intention between the belief–desire combination and the action. Wellman's model is again slightly inaccurate in this respect, and intentions were included in the materials for these studies because it was Wellman's model, not the intentional theory of action, that was under test. There are, however, such things as prior intentions (such as an intention to go to New York next week). These are more distant from the action in time and function as pro-attitudes, just as plans and goals and purposes do. Although even young children can distinguish intentional actions from various kinds of unintended behaviours (Shultz, 1980; Shultz & Wells, 1985; Shultz, Wells, & Sarda, 1980) it therefore remains unclear whether people have an understanding of an intention as a distinct mental state immediately antecedent to action.

These experiments have shown that beliefs are explained by reference to a variety of mental states: perceptions, other beliefs, attitudes, emotions, and so on. As in the case of pro-attitudes, however, what matters about these mental states with regard to what they explain is not what they are but what they do. In other words, they work as explanations for a belief by being ascribed a particular function in regard to the belief they explain. It is this function, not their intrinsic nature or quality as mental states, that carries the explanatory force. It is not likely that the function is that of a pro-attitude: this would be to claim that people explain beliefs in terms of some desired end that the belief attains or enables them to attain, and this appears implausible, at least under most circumstances. In science and philosophy beliefs (or knowledge-claims) are supported by justification: some argument, evidence, or antecedent claim is advanced as giving ground for the belief in question. The explanations given for beliefs in experiments 1 and 2 certainly appear to have the character of justifications, although the function is never explicitly identified as such. It therefore seems likely that the function served by mental states referred to in explanations for beliefs is also that of justification. This naturally raises many questions about how particular mental states subserve the function of justification, but that is for future research to investigate.

Putting all this together with the finding that people explain actions, desires, and intentions in the same way enables us to construct a new model of the naïve analysis of freely chosen actions. The model is presented in Fig. 5.4 In this model, the term "action" in the final box should be understood as referring to the basic theory of action proposed in Chapter 2: in other words, the pro-attitude–action belief combination does not cause

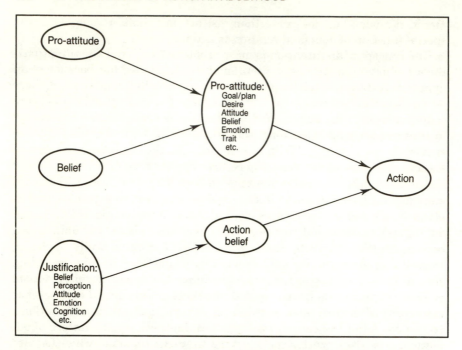

FIG. 5.4. A modified model of adult belief–desire reasoning.

the action, because between it and the action comes the actor's choice to act, and it is the actor who performs the action. The model is not complete: indefinite chains of pro-attitude/belief combinations can be attached to any pro-attitude, and indefinite chains of further justifications can be attached to any belief. The point of the model, though, is partly to reflect what has been learned from the experiments, and partly to reinforce the notion of pro-attitudes and action beliefs as functions rather than mental states *per se*, functions which in the case of pro-attitudes many kinds of mental state may take on. This model can be regarded as the new target for future research.

As I have already intimated, traits were rarely mentioned in either study: overall, in study 1 only 3.9% of explanations were coded as traits and in study 2 only 2.6%. This is a striking finding. Traditionally in the attribution literature stable personal dispositions such as traits have been accorded a pre-eminent place in causal attribution research. Some dependent measures used in attribution studies have asked subjects about personality characteristics and little or nothing else (Storms, 1973; White, 1993). This tradition perhaps owes something to Heider's (1958) contention that people seek to explain the diversity of manifest events by referring to the stable dispositional properties that give order and predictability to phenomena. Wellman (1990, p.114), despite giving pre-eminence to belief–desire psychology, also claimed that "traits figure prominently in causal explanations of actions". The results of these studies do not support this claim.

One possible reason concerns the level of analysis chosen. Subjects were asked to explain single actions. For this level, an explanation pitched at an equivalent level may be deemed most appropriate: that is, subjects favour explanations referring to occasion-specific factors, of which goals and desires are examples. Traits may be seen as having more of a role at a different level of explanation: the level of individuating consistency across occasions and situations. This is indeed the role suggested by developmental research reviewed in Chapter 3. If this is correct, then traits would be expected to figure more prominently in explanations for multiple actions than for single actions. One problem with this is that although attitudes are not usually regarded as occasion-specific, this category was the most popular category for explanations in the present study. If the reason for the infrequent use of traits as explanations is that they are more commonly used to explain multiple observations, then attitudes should have been infrequently used for the same reason. Moreover, one study using a similar method to the present study found results more closely in agreement with the traditional estimation of the importance of traits. Miller (1984) applied content analysis to free verbal explanations given by children and adults for prosocial and deviant behaviours. For American subjects, stable personal dispositions accounted for 20% of explanations at the age of 15 years, and for 40% of explanations given by adults. (For Indian subjects equivalent frequencies were significantly lower.) Why should the present results look so different?

An answer can be found by looking more closely at patterns for individual scenarios in study 1. The results show a remarkable degree of specificity between categories and scenarios. For example, all 14 physiology explanations (excluding data for belief version) were given for the eating scenario. Fifteen out of twenty-one trait explanations were given for the sharing scenario. Seventeen out of twenty-eight belief explanations were given for the prayers scenario. Seventy-six percent of explanations for the television scenario were coded as attitudes, but only eight percent of explanations for the prayers scenario were so coded. Fifty-seven percent of explanations for the party scenario were coded as goals, but only five percent of explanations for the eating scenario were coded in this way. Similar scenario-specific trends were noted by Lalljee et al. (1982). For example, stealing was explained mainly in terms of person characteristics (62.7% of explanations); for lying, an action with a similar moral quality, person explanations accounted for only 18.6%, whereas the goal category was favoured (42.4%). Lalljee et al. observed (p.183): "The moral quality of the act may be less important than the nature of the event itself".

The model in Fig. 5.4 is a general model of the naïve understanding of action. These findings suggest, however, that there is much more to the understanding of action than this general framework. They suggest that people possess specific variants of the model for particular kinds of action, specific mental state–action pairings which they use in explaining action. For example, they have in mind a pair consisting of a trait of generosity and the action of sharing; a pair consisting of a certain kind of belief and the action of saying prayers; a pair consisting of a liking for a certain television programme and the action of watching that programme. In each case, as an explanation for action the mental state takes on the function of a pro-attitude (or, permissibly but probably more rarely, an action belief). In each case, however, the kind of mental state in the pair is different, and the exact content of the mental state is specific to the kind of action being explained. If this is correct then the general model of action functions as a basic framework which accommodates a multitude of specific mental state-action pairings in common sense understanding.

Several authors have postulated that people explain actions with the aid of knowledge structures which may be specific to certain kinds of action; Lalljee and Abelson (1983) and Read (1987), summarised previously, are examples. The meaning of an action is to a large extent the role that the action places in the episode of which it is part (see also Harré, 1976; 1979; 1983). Script knowledge also offers a means of dealing with deviations from scripted actions, by suggesting plausible hypotheses. The kind of knowledge structure suggested by the present findings is script-like in that it is both specific and stereotyped, but also different from scripts as usually understood because it makes reference not to the surrounding episode but to the mental antecedents of an individual action. In this respect it resembles the notion of "paradigm scenarios" developed by de Sousa (1987).

De Sousa presented paradigm scenarios as a theory of emotion. Under this theory an emotion is not a particular mental state, nor a particular pattern of behaviour, but a constellation of elements which together make up the "character" of an emotion. These elements include subject and object of emotion, which are slots in the script that may be filled by particular things. They include the "feel" of an emotion, the cognitive aspects of the emotion (e.g. the subject's appraisal of the situation and relevant events), and the behaviours that characteristically go with the emotion. Whether this is a good theory of emotion or not, it may well represent the common sense construction of emotion. As such, and as with other scripts, it is a knowledge structure that people can use to interpret emotion-related behaviour by others, and perhaps even to tell themselves what sort of emotion they ought to be feeling or exhibiting on any given occasion.

The notion of a paradigm scenario or script suggests that people may possess elaborate stereotyped knowledge structures for mental state-action links; in addition to a mental state and an action, these knowledge structures may provide other information such as the cognitive state of the actor, the typical situation in which the action may be exhibited, and slots for actor and target. The use of such a knowledge structure would be in providing the attributer with a stereotyped explanation for an action given only minimal information: in study 1, the tendency for subjects to generate similar explanations for given scenarios despite the paucity of information presented strongly suggests that they were drawing on shared knowledge structures of this kind. The present findings show only links between mental states and actions, but future research could explore this notion in more depth. What is important about these knowledge structures is that, despite their variability in matters of detail, they are consistent in general because of being based on a common, general theory of action, perhaps resembling the sketch presented in Fig. 5.4. When explaining their own actions or those of people well known to them, attributers presumably discard the stereotyped features of knowledge structures in favour of specific knowledge of the person whose action they are explaining (and the situation in which the action occurred, and so on). Knowledge of this kind would still be constructed with the aid of the framework provided by the general theory of action, however; because of this, explanations based on individual knowledge lie in the same conceptual world as those based on stereotyped knowledge structures.

The hypothesis of specific state–action linkages can explain the divergent results of the studies discussed here. Miller (1984) asked her subjects to explain only prosocial or deviant behaviours. No deviant behaviours were included in this study, but it is noticeable that the one action that was peculiarly associated with trait explanations (sharing) is a prosocial behaviour. Lalljee et al. (1982) found a high proportion of person explanations (57.6%) for their sharing scenario as well. The relatively high proportion of trait explanations found by Miller (for American subjects) may therefore reflect the fact that people tend to explain prosocial behaviours peculiarly in terms of traits. In other words, the pattern of results in her study reflects specific beliefs about prosocial (and deviant) behaviour, but does not generalise to actions of other types.

Bartsch and Wellman (1989) used only three basic scenarios, concerned with looking for something under an item of furniture, buying something at a shop, and putting something in one's mouth. Different versions were used for neutral stories and stories in which the actor did something apparently contrary to his or her desires or beliefs. The looking scenario has no parallel in study 1. The putting in mouth scenario appears to have a parallel in the eating scenario, but putting something in one's mouth is not at all the same as eating something (one may, for example, put the reed of an oboe into one's mouth, but not in order to eat it). The buying scenario does have a parallel, however, and it is noteworthy that, in study 1, the buying scenario elicited the highest proportion of desire explanations of any scenario. It may be, therefore, that the scenarios used by Bartsch and Wellman are of a sort that tend to lead to desire explanations more than most. It should also be noted that the results of the Bartsch and Wellman study include explanations given for anomalous beliefs and desires, and it is not clear that these will be explained in the same way as ordinary actions.

The idea of specific state–action links has significant implications. Consider, for example, lay prediction of behaviour. Kunda and Nisbett (1986) found that people overestimated the consistency of trait-related behaviours across a variety of individual occasions. Does this imply that people generally overestimate behavioural consistency? It may depend on the type of action being predicted. Sharing, as we have seen, tends to be explained by reference to traits, and people may therefore see this kind of behaviour as highly consistent across occasions and situations. Other actions were not explained in terms of traits in this study. Attitudes are regarded as stable, therefore actions typically explained in terms of attitudes (such as eating a particular food and watching a given programme on television) may also be regarded as highly consistent across occasions, at least across occasions where the attitude object is present. Other mental states such as desires and goals are often more occasion-specific, however. Actions that are typically explained in terms of these things, therefore, may not be seen as so consistent across occasions or situations, because people see them as varying with the varying desires and goals of the actor. So, while it may be true, as the findings of Kunda and Nisbett suggest, that people overestimate consistency for trait-related behaviours (behaviours typically explained in terms of traits), it remains an open question whether this is also true for desire-related and goal-related behaviours (or belief-related behaviours, or physiology-related behaviours, or emotion-related behaviours). This would appear to be worthy of further investigation.

Towards a Functional Analysis of Explanations

I have been emphasising the fact that a pro-attitude is a function that a mental state may take on, and not a kind of mental state in itself (or at least not as defined by intrinsic nature or content). Thus, wishes, desires, attitudes, and other kinds of state may function as pro-attitudes at some times and not at others. Despite this, the category system used in the studies discussed here, and based on that proposed by Wellman (1990), is a system of intrinsic kinds of mental states. Arguably, such a system misses the point about mental states. The fact that something is an emotion, for example, doesn't tell us what role it plays in action. Doing something because one is elated is quite different from doing something because one is unhappy; the latter is, often, an attempt to correct the negative state, whereas the former may just be an expression of the positive state. If what is important about a mental state is its function, then it should be possible to interpret all the explanations given by subjects in terms of their functional significance, that is, the function served by the thing referred to in the explanation in relation to the action, desire, intention, or belief being explained. To this end I scrutinised the explanations given in study 2 for possible functional categories.

Table 5.1 shows the categories that seem to be present for the explanations given for actions, desires, and intentions. I emphasise the

TABLE 5.1

Functional Categories of Explanations for Actions, Desires, and Intentions

1. Negative feature of or feeling about present (past) state, which action, desire, or intention is to correct.

2. Further end or goal of action or thing intended or desired.

3. Value of action or thing desired or intended: general statement of values as opposed to feeling specific to action, etc., in question.

4. Opportunity—i.e. the actor has the opportunity to do the action or attain the thing desired or intended now.

5. Constraint or lack of opportunity—i.e. there has been no opportunity until now or will be none in the future, or no opportunity to do anything other than the action in question.

6. Duty or obligation.

7. Negative consequence of not doing action or attaining desire/intention.

8. Causal relation—e.g. situational cause of something in actor (such as emotional reaction) which is then part of a reason.

9. Habit, routine, or action tendency.

10. The action or thing desired or intended as an end in itself.

11. A state of mind such as a wish or an attitude which inclines the actor away from some alternative(s) to the action, desire, or intention given.

12. Other personal characteristic related to action, desire, or intention, but not as a pro-attitude—e.g. ability, or internal determinism of traits, etc.

13. Action belief or other relevant cognition.

14. Incidental information—information about past deeds of actor or other people, actor's role (e.g. student), states of other people, situation, etc., giving meaning to a reason's explanation but not itself the reason.

word "seem" because, so far, these categories have not been subjected to a reliability check, nor any further test other than my own judgement. They are offered merely in the spirit that Wellman offered his model of adult belief–desire psychology, in the hope that they, and the idea of functional analysis, may be useful to future theory development.

Most of these categories were used comparatively rarely in study 2, by my categorisations. Of the total of 671 explanations, 295 fell into category 2, further end or goal. Category 1, negative feature of present state, accounted for a further 97, and category 10, end in itself, for 80. The remaining categories were used much less frequently.

For beliefs a different set of categories seems to be useful, and these are summarised in Table 5.2. Out of the total of 213 explanations, the evidence

TABLE 5.2
Functional Categories for Beliefs

1. Categories of evidence relative to belief:
   1a. Positive evidence as support for belief.
   1b. Further belief or knowledge-claim as support for belief.
   1c. Personal experience with thing believed in.
   1d. Evidence against, or lack of evidence for, alternative to thing believed in.
   1e. Further belief or knowledge-claim counting against alternative to thing believed in.
   1f. Personal experience as reason for rejecting alternative to thing believed in.

2. Categories of thing belief leads to:
   2a. Positive function, end, or goal of belief (as opposed to object of belief), such as beneficial effect on actor or thing enabled by belief.
   2b. Positive effect or consequence of thing believed in being the case.
   2c. Explanatory value of belief, things explained by it.
   2d. Negative function or effect of alternative belief, such as detrimental effect on others of believing thing actor does not believe.
   2e. Negative effect or consequence of thing not believed in being the case.
   2f. Lack of explanatory value of alternative to thing believed.

3. Positive or negative feeling as reason for belief.

4. Value or ethical or moral principle.

5. Causal relation—e.g. situational cause of something in actor which is part of reason for belief.

6. Belief as effect of upbringing—influence of parents, school, etc.

7. Process of reasoning (inference, cognition in general) leading to belief.

8. Belief explained as a consequence of group membership/affiliation.

9. Trait or other stable personal disposition.

10. Incidental information.

categories account for 79 and the effect categories for 45. Values and upbringing were also commonly mentioned. It was striking, however, that subjects tended to use the effect categories to explain their own beliefs but not those of others, and the upbringing category to explain the beliefs of others but not their own. It seems possible that people have a somewhat more deterministic view of others' beliefs than their own.

The functional categorisation is far from being antithetical to the modified model of action in Fig. 5.4; on the contrary, as I have emphasised, the concept of a pro-attitude is itself functional, and is therefore perhaps best integrated into a model where the other components are functional categories rather than categories of intrinsic mental states. Almost all of the explanations givem, in fact, relate to pro-attitudes (as opposed to action beliefs) in some way.

In the case of action (and desires and intentions, which are explained in similar ways), one can see points of contact between the functional categories and the analyses of giving meaning to action reviewed at the beginning of the chapter. The emphasis on goals and plans in the account by Lalljee and Abelson (1983) clearly finds support in the frequency of reference to further ends and goals. Their idea of contrastive explanation also makes an appearance in the form of references to constraint or lack of alternative possible actions. Read (1987) also emphasised the importance of goals in explanations of action. Equally, though, these accounts seem to give only part of the story, in that there are several functional categories which have not been mentioned in them. A clear priority for future work is to develop a model of functional explanations for action that pays due respect to the variety of functional categories elucidated here.

The first category, negative feature of present state, relates to a simple model of the role of judgement in action that I have proposed elsewhere (White, 1993). The core of this model is what I termed the JEA sequence (judgement—evaluation—action). In this, the subject assesses some feature of their present state of affairs, evaluates it, and if the evaluation is negative, describes some intention or plan or actual action meant to correct the negative feature of the state. For example (White, 1993, p.265): "It makes me very sad to feel that I am being carried along by events and if I feel this at any time I try to change things, either the events or my approach to them." Many of the explanations for actions given in the above studies were of a similar kind, placing the action in the context of a JEA sequence. The JEA sequence is recursive, in that a person may continue with judgement, evaluation, and action, until such time as a satisfactory state is achieved, or the current state is deemed uncontrollable. The alleviation of a negative state is, of course, a kind of goal, but it is nonetheless to be distinguished from the mere attainment of positive goals, and has been rather neglected by previous authors. Clearly, JEA sequences may provide the core of complex functional accounts of action, incorporating judgements, feelings, and many other kinds of mental state.

Conclusion

In conclusion, adults have a general understanding of action, perhaps along the lines depicted in Fig. 5.4. Supplementary to this is a store of multifarious paradigm scenarios, making specific links between particular kinds of mental state and particular kinds of action. These are, in a sense, action stereotypes and may be used to give an initial characterisation to actions about which little is known. Supplementary to this in turn are more complex and idiosyncratic constructions of particular actions, reflecting the actor's special knowledge of themselves or those close to them, and perhaps best described in terms of functional organisations such as JEA sequences. Paradigm scenarios and idiosyncratic constructions both draw on the basic understanding of action which is, for adults, the metaphysical underpinning of all constructions of action, and which rests ultimately on the core theory of action laid down in infancy.

CHAPTER SIX

Regularity-based Models of Adult Causal Judgement

In contrast to the sparse literature on the naïve analysis of action, there is a considerable body of research on the methods people use to make causal attributions for behaviour. It might be thought that a method for making a causal attribution would depend on the kind of theory about behaviour held by the attributer, so that proposals about methods would follow from proposals about naïve theories of action and behaviour in general. In fact this has not been the case: Proposals about methods of causal attribution have mainly concentrated on the use of empirical cues as guides to causal loci, and have treated them as if people used them in an atheoretical manner. Whether this can be right will be considered later in the chapter. I shall begin with a review of the main proposals.

THE KELLEYAN TRADITION OF MULTIPLE OBSERVATION MODELS

Kelley (1973) distinguished two cases for attribution theory: cases in which the attributer has information from multiple occasions, and cases in which the attributer has information from a single occasion. Cases of the latter type were addressed by Kelley's (1972b; 1973) causal schema notion, to be considered later. Cases of the former type were addressed by Kelley's ANOVA model, and are the topic of this section.

In formulating his ANOVA model, Kelley was following Heider's (1958, p.297) suggestion that causal analysis is "in a way analogous to experimental methods". In fact, Kelley was following two specific ideas put forward by Heider. One was the idea that the goals of lay inference and understanding are essentially similar to those of science, namely understanding, prediction, and control. Heider emphasised the search for stable dispositional properties, the underlying constancies which explain the manifest diversity of phenomena, as a means of achieving this. Kelley followed this idea in proposing a model for the attribution of effects to loci of stable dispositional properties.

The other was the idea of a method which people often use to attribute a phenomenon to one kind of dispositional property rather than another. For example, Heider argued that we seek to ascertain whether the cause of pleasure is in the person experiencing it or in the object. This aim reflects Heider's contention that the distinction between the person and the situation, or internal and external causes, is of fundamental importance in attribution, a point of view also adopted by Kelley in his attribution theories. For the purpose of distinguishing the person and the object as contributers to enjoyment, Heider (p.152) argued that we use what is now generally called the covariation principle:[1] "that condition will be held responsible for an effect which is present when the effect is present and absent when the effect is absent". Heider (p.151) emphasised that the use of this principle is in the service of understanding, prediction, and control: "If we know that our present enjoyment is due to the contribution of the object because it is an intrinsically desirable one, then we can expect anyone who has contact with it to enjoy it; on the other hand, if the enjoyment is attributed to our own personality, then at most we can expect only persons who have a similar personality to enjoy it". Heider (p.82) stated that the covariation principle is also used to distinguish the contribution of the forces of the person and the environment to outcomes of action, and of the perceiver and object or conditions to a percept (e.g. one person might not hear something heard by others because of a personal characteristic, deafness). As Heider used it, the principle was quite flexible and could be used to distinguish between variations in the state of a thing, between one thing and another, and between classes of things.

In developing these ideas, Kelley (1967; 1972a; 1973) suggested that people use a naïve version of analysis of variance for causal attribution. In this, the cause of some effect is identified by sampling information along each of three orthogonal dimensions and applying the covariation principle to the information obtained. The effect is always described as a relation between a person and an object (hereafter called the "stimulus"). For example, the effect to be explained might be "John laughs at the comedian". The three dimensions are consensus, concerning how other people respond to the same stimulus; distinctiveness, concerning how John responds to other stimuli of the same type; and consistency, concerning how John responds to the same stimulus on other occasions.

Most tests of the model have followed the format used initially by McArthur (1972), in which two levels of each variable are used. Typically, subjects see a target event such as "John laughs at the comedian", followed by prepackaged representations of covariation information such as the following:

> Hardly anyone else laughs at this comedian (low consensus).
> John laughs at most other comedians (low distinctiveness).
> In the past, John has almost always laughed at this comedian (high consistency).

Subjects are then asked what caused the target event to occur and are given seven options, representing the main effects of person, stimulus, and circumstances, and the four possible interactions of these three loci (though McArthur, 1972, did not present all four separately). Subjects are not required to make a specific attribution (such as, "John has an easily tickled sense of humour"), but only to identify the locus of causation.

The covariation principle generates three predictions for information of this sort. For the combination of high consensus, high distinctiveness, and high consistency, the stimulus is the sole covariate and should be chosen as the cause. For low consensus, low distinctiveness, and high consistency (as in the example above) the person is the sole covariate and should be identified as the cause. For low consensus, high distinctiveness, and low consistency, occasions or circumstances are the sole covariate and should be identified as the cause. In most studies (e.g. McArthur, 1972) a majority of subjects have chosen the predicted causal locus in each case.

The Template-matching Model

The predictions just listed are obviously of limited value, and it would be desirable for the model to be extended to cope with a greater range of stimulus configurations. What happens, for example, when a subject only has high consensus information? To deal with extensions of this sort, Orvis, Cunningham, and Kelley (1975) developed the template-matching model. Taking persons, stimuli, and circumstances as possible causes, Orvis et al. suggested that people develop expectations about the pattern of information that corresponds to each of them as causes. These templates are causal schemas, which Kelley (1972b, p.2) defined as "an assumed pattern of data in a complete analysis of variance framework". The expectations conform to the patterns of covariation that identify each causal locus, and are given in Table 6.1.

TABLE 6.1

Information Patterns for the Three Attributions (from Orvis et al., 1975)

	Information pattern		
Causal locus	Consensus	Distinctiveness	Consistency
Stimulus (S)	High	High	High
Person (P)	Low	Low	High
Circumstance (C)	Low	High	Low

These templates allow some attributions to be made from just one type of information. For example, from high consensus information we tend to infer that the stimulus (S) is the cause because the stimulus template is the only one in which high consensus appears. Conversely, given low consensus we can infer that the stimulus is not the cause because low consensus is incompatible with the stimulus template. Thus, under the template-matching model, consensus information is used to make inferences about the stimulus, distinctiveness information to make inferences about the person (P), and consistency information to make inferences about the circumstances (C). Any configuration of information can be used to generate predictions about choice of causal locus, through its consistency with one template and inconsistency with the others. If a configuration is consistent with more than one template, as in the case of low consensus, then the prediction is that both causal loci will be identified as causal. In the case of low consensus, this would mean that a causal attribution should be made to person and circumstances.

Although the template-matching model generates predictions for all configurations of consensus, distinctiveness, and consistency, most tests have confined themselves to the eight standard configurations involving all three types, and the model's predictions for these types are listed in Table 6.2.

This table also lists the predictions generated by other models, to be reviewed in the following pages.

The Inductive Logic Model

This model was put forward by Jaspars (1983), Jaspars, Hewstone, and Fincham (1983), and Hewstone and Jaspars (1987). These authors pointed out that a large proportion of causal attributions in the studies by Orvis et al. (1975) were made to causal loci not predicted by the template-matching

TABLE 6.2
Predictions of Various Models for Standard Information Combinations

Information pattern			Template-matching model	Inductive logic model	Abnormal conditions model	True ANOVA model	Counter-factual model
Cs	D	Cy					
H	H	H	S	S	S	S	S
H	H	L	SC	SC	SC	ST	SC
H	L	H	PS	NP	PS*	NP	P or S or C
H	L	L	PSC	C	C	T	C
L	H	H	PSC	PS	PS	PS	PS
L	H	L	C	PSC	PSC	PST	PSC
L	L	H	P	P	P	P	P
L	L	L	PC	PC	PC	PT	PC

Note: Cs = consensus, D = distinctiveness, Cy = consistency. S = stimulus, P = person, C = circumstances, T = times. H = high, L = low. NP = no prediction.
*In this case, PS means specifically P + S, and this prediction applies only for unscripted events.

model. For example, for the combination of high consensus, low distinctiveness, and low consistency, the template-matching model predicts a PSC attribution (Table 6.2), but Orvis et al. found a significant preference for circumstance attributions in their study 1, and no preference in their study 2. This led Jaspars and colleagues to propose a different model, not as a competitor to the ANOVA model but as a different formalisation of it. This formalisation is in terms of empirically necessary and sufficient conditions, and instantiates Mill's definition of a cause as the set of conditions jointly necessary and sufficient for an effect. With the standard Kelleyan combinations of information, the attributer is supposed to look for the condition that is both necessary (the effect does not occur in its absence) and sufficient (the effect always occurs in its presence), and identifies that as the cause. The predictions generated by this principle are presented in Table 6.2.

Where the inductive logic and template matching models differ in their predictions, the findings generally favour the inductive logic model (Hewstone & Jaspars, 1983; 1987; Jaspars, 1983). The problem configuration for the inductive logic model is the combination of high consensus, low distinctiveness, and high consistency. In this case no causal locus covaries with the effect because the effect occurs under all conditions. The inductive logic model therefore generates no prediction for this combination.

The Subjective Scaling Model

Jaspars (1983) conducted a test of the inductive logic model and found that the match between predictions and results, although better than chance, was not very close. Jaspars also commented that, although the inductive logic model represents relations between stimulus combinations and attributions, it does not specify a process by which attributions are generated from stimuli. These things led Jaspars to propose a model of the causal attribution process as the construction of a mental model, a subjective scaling model which represents relations. The model was worked out with the aid of an example of cases of success and failure, where multiple case information is represented as a network of dominance relations yielding a rank order of persons and tasks in terms of dominance. For example, if person A succeeds at task X, this is represented as a relation in which person A is dominant over task X. The model is extended by the addition of further pieces of outcome information. Kelleyan types of information allow the model to be filled out in various ways. For example, if everyone succeeds at the task (high consensus) then everyone is represented as dominant over the task in the model. Jaspars applied this analysis to the results of his experiment, and concluded that it fitted. The model does not appear to have been tested since then, however.

The Abnormal Conditions Focus Model

The basic propositions of the abnormal conditions focus model (Hilton & Slugoski, 1986) consist of two criteria for selecting the cause of some effect. The first criterion selects as causal candidates conditions that are necessary for the effect, given the scenario within which the effect occurred. This qualification is important, because many causes are not necessary conditions except in the context of a particular scenario. To use the example that Hilton and Slugoski (1986) used, a faulty rail is not a necessary condition for the derailment of a train, because derailments can occur in the absence of faulty rails, but it may be necessary given other features of the scenario on the occasion in question. This criterion is called the counterfactual criterion.

The second criterion selects from the set of factors identified by the first criterion the condition (or combination of conditions) that is abnormal in the context of the given subject-matter. Hilton and Slugoski (1986, p.76) expanded the derailment example as follows: "In explaining a train derailment, one can refer to any number of necessary conditions but for which the accident would not have occurred, such as the presence of a faulty rail, the weight of the wagons, and the speed at which the train was moving". The faulty rail is selected from these as the cause of the accident because it is the one feature from that set which is abnormal with regard to trains. Abnormality is judged by comparison with a contrast case, consisting in this example of occasions on which trains run normally without going off the rails. This criterion, called the contrastive criterion, was derived by Hilton and Slugoski (1986) from the legal philosophy of Hart and Honoré (1959), where it was put forward as a methodological principle for identifying causes (see Chapter 1). The contrastive criterion is empirical (and is in effect the identification of a sufficient condition from within the set of scenario-specific necessary conditions) and implies no evaluative judgement, although it does reflect the idea of Hilton and Slugoski (1986) that causal processing occurs in response to departures from some notion of what is usual.

Although the abnormal conditions focus model presents a different set of concepts from the inductive logic model, in application to Kelleyan information combinations they work in the same way, because the counterfactual criterion corresponds to the identification of empirically necessary conditions, and the contrastive criterion corresponds to the identification of empirically sufficient conditions. Hilton and Slugoski extended the model, however, to account for performance on the troublesome combination of high consensus, low distinctiveness, and high consistency (the HLH combination). For this, they drew on the notion of scripts.

Scripts are shared ideas about normal occurrences (Schank & Abelson, 1977). For example, "Sally bought something at the supermarket" is a scripted action, because it conforms to a notion of what people normally do at supermarkets. "Sally bought nothing at the supermarket" is a script deviation, because it violates that notion. Unscripted events are events which carry no shared notions of what is normal. For example, "Sue is afraid of the dog" is an unscripted event because people generally assume that some people are afraid of some dogs. In this case, HLH information is informative about both person and stimulus: low distinctiveness says that Sue is one of those people who tend to be afraid of dogs, and high consensus says that this dog is such a one as people tend to fear. Because of this, Hilton and Slugoski predicted a P + S attribution (as opposed to a P x S attribution—in P + S both parties are independent contributors to the effect, whereas P x S indicates an interaction). For scripted events, however, HLH is uninformative: Sally bought something at the supermarket, but so do most other people and so does Sally at most other supermarkets. The information does not individuate either Sally or the supermarket, and the combination does not enable the identification of an abnormal condition because the effect always occurs. For such scripted events, therefore, Hilton and Slugoski predicted that subjects would prefer to make no attribution. The results of their experiment 2 supported both predictions.

The Diamond Model

Pruitt and Insko (1980) suggested that Kelley's model was incomplete in its specification of information relevant to causal attribution. This incompleteness, and their additions, can best be comprehended by comparing the diagrammatic representations of the models in Fig. 6.1.

The diamond model depicts four additions to Kelley's model, two of which are further kinds of covariation information.

1. Comparison-object consensus. Kelleyan, or target-object consensus concerns the reaction of other people to the stimulus. Pruitt and Insko proposed that the reaction of other people to other stimuli was also relevant. In the case of "John laughs at the comedian", then, comparison-object consensus concerns the responses of other people to other comedians.

2. Other forms of consistency. In the Kelleyan model (Fig. 6.1), consistency is represented by multiple lines connecting person and stimulus. Pruitt and Insko filled out the model by including the three other possible forms of consistency: person to comparison objects (is John consistent in his reaction to other comedians?), other people to target object (are other people consistent in their response to this comedian?), and other people to comparison objects (are other people consistent in their reactions to other comedians?).

The other two additions represent relations between opposing points of the diamond.

3. Target object to comparison object relations. Kelley seems to have assumed that the comparison objects will be moderately similar, but Pruitt and Insko suggested that increasing dissimilarity can affect attribution.

4. Person to other people relation. Pruitt and Insko again suggested that similarity makes a difference, and predicted that with high consensus more object attributions will occur when this type of similarity is low.

These four additions present something of a quandary. It is plausible that they should affect causal attribution, but they cannot be accommodated within the covariation principle. Consider comparison-object consensus. For "John laughs at the comedian", comparison-object consensus might be, "most other people laugh at most other comedians". Neither the template-matching model nor the inductive logic model suggests any way in which this can be used to generate a causal attribution. The reason for this is that none of the causal loci considered under the ANOVA model is mentioned in the comparison-object consensus statement, so the statement says nothing about covariation with any of those loci.

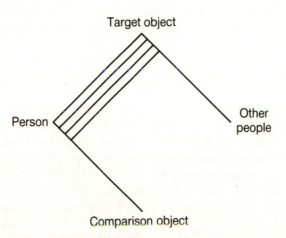

Presentation of the Kelley model in terms of specified and unspecified relations between four elements: person, target object, other people, and comparison object. (The multiple person to target object lines symbolise the consistency of that relation.)

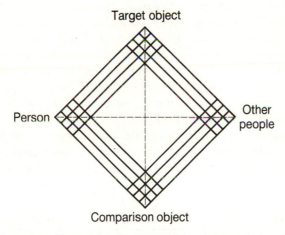

The diamond model specifying all possible relations between the four elements: person, target object, other people, and comparison object. (Multiple lines symbolise the consistency of a relation.)

FIG. 6.1. Diagrammatic representation of Kelley's ANOVA model and the diamond model (Pruitt & Insko, 1980).

Pruitt and Insko suggested that comparison-object consensus is used to establish the credibility of the target person, by assessing their behaviour against what amounts to a norm, represented in the form of empirical information. The concept of credibility lies outside the realm of covariation reasoning, however.

The True ANOVA Model

Forsterling (1989) argued that previous models had not succeeded in capturing the intended analogy with analysis of variance, because of an inappropriate conceptualisation of independent variables. He first distinguished between times and circumstances, pointing out that in a true ANOVA the three independent variables would be persons, stimuli, and times, not circumstances. A circumstance attribution would be an attribution to an interaction involving all three variables, not to just one of them. Following this reasoning, under high consensus, low distinctiveness, and low consistency, an attribution to times is predicted (compare with the other models in Table 6.2).

Although Table 6.2 presents predictions for the standard eight combinations, according to Forsterling these are not the correct combinations. He argued that previous authors erred in compiling the combinations, in that they treated consensus, consistency, and distinctiveness as the independent variables. In fact the independent variables are persons, stimuli, and times. Under this scheme, the combination of another person, another stimulus, and another time is relevant, even though it is not represented in the standard eight combinations. Forsterling presented the eight combinations that are possible under his true ANOVA model, assuming just two levels of each variable. These are depicted in Table 6.3.

Following the numbering in this table, case 1 is the event in question. Case 2 corresponds to consistency information. Cases 3 and 4 correspond to distinctiveness information, incorporating Pruitt and Insko's notion of

TABLE 6.3
Information Combinations in the True ANOVA Model (Forsterling, 1989)

Person 1				Person 2			
Stimulus 1		Stimulus 2		Stimulus 1		Stimulus 2	
Time 1	Time 2	Time 1	Time 2	Time 1	Time 2	Time 1	Time 2
1	2	3	4	5	6	7	8

consistency in the relation between person and comparison object. Cases 5 and 6 correspond to consensus information, incorporating Pruitt and Insko's notion of consistency in the relation between other person and target object. Cases 7 and 8 correspond to comparison object consensus, incorporating Pruitt and Insko's notion of consistency in the relation between other person and comparison object.

Forsterling then analysed the abnormal conditions focus model. The key here is the different predictions made under this model for scripted and unscripted behaviours. Forsterling argued that script notions function by filling out the missing cells in the traditional pattern—cases 7 and 8 in his model. Because of this, they should be thought of as covariation information, and the script terminology is misleading. This part of the abnormal conditions focus model is therefore functionally similar to comparison object consensus. Forsterling's model also solves the problem of incorporating comparison object consensus within the general logic of the covariation principle.

Using the covariation principle in application to the true ANOVA model, Forsterling was able to make predictions for combinations not covered by the other models, and these predictions were mostly supported by the results of his experiment.

Counterfactual Reasoning

Lipe (1991) proposed that the notion of counterfactual reasoning can be used as a framework for attribution theories. This kind of reasoning uses counterfactual information, which is information about what would have happened if something that happened had not happened: for example (p.457), "would the goblet have shattered if the opera singer had not sung the high note?". Lipe argued that people use this kind of information to make causal attributions by comparing it with what actually happened. When counterfactual information is not available, people make use of two substitute kinds of information or "proxies": covariation data and alternative explanations. These substitutes are used to assess a likely answer to a counterfactual question, which is the route to a causal attribution.

Lipe proposed that a general model of the causal attribution process has three stages: generating a hypothesis, assessing the strength of it, and considering alternative explanations. Her account deals only with the second and third stages. At stage 2 people assess the strength of a causal hypothesis with the aid of covariation data, and Lipe also suggested that similarity, temporal order, and contiguity may be relevant cues here. For stage 3 Lipe presented a formula under which the judged probability that the hypothesised cause was responsible for the outcome is a function of the judged strength of the hypothesised cause and the strength of alternative explanations. This is an anchoring and adjustment model (Tversky & Kahneman, 1974): the anchor is the initial assessment of the strength of the hypothesis, and the adjustment phase is the integration of the alternative explanations.

Applying the model to Kelleyan combinations involves rendering covariation data in a series of 2 x 2 contingency tables. Each type of information and each combination of types has its own contingency table, making seven in all. To make an attribution, people integrate information from all seven tables. For most of the standard eight combinations, Lipe's predictions match those of the inductive logic model (see Table 6.2). The exception is the HLH combination, for which the counterfactual reasoning model predicts P or S or C.

General criticisms of models in the Kelleyan tradition will be discussed later, but some specific difficulties with Lipe's model should be mentioned here. The key to the model is counterfactual reasoning, a concept not found in any other model in this tradition. Under Lipe's account, covariation information is not used directly for causal attribution, but to construct counterfactual information, which is then used for causal attribution. Covariation information is said to be used when counterfactual information is not available.

The first problem with this is that, strictly speaking, counterfactual information is *never* available because it is by definition hypothetical and can only be constructed *ex hypothesi*. Counterfactual information is not information about nonoccurrences.[2] The difference between these two things corresponds to the grammatical difference between negatives and subjunctives. A negative statement would be "X did not happen", which can be ascertained in principle by consulting the environment in the right way. A subjunctive statement would be "X would not have happened" (or "would have happened"), which cannot be ascertained at all. If people reason with counterfactual information, one has to ask how they construct it, since they cannot obtain it from the environment. Viewed from this perspective, the use of covariation information to construct counterfactual information seems a laborious and unnecessary step. Moreover, since counterfactual information is never available, if people wished to use it for causal inference they would always have to construct it, and it is therefore of crucial importance for a counterfactual reasoning model to explain how people do this. Lipe does give an account of how Kelleyan information might be used to construct counterfactual information, but there are many other possible ways of doing this. One could, for example, use existing beliefs about causal powers and releasing conditions to construct counterfactual information; on the other hand, if one has such beliefs, then causal inferences can be made directly from those and the intermediate step of constructing counterfactual information is again unnecessary. What this problem shows is that Lipe has things the wrong way round. As I argued in Chapter 1, causal inference is not dependent on counterfactual reasoning, but counterfactual reasoning is dependent on causal concepts. We could construct a model of how people use their understanding of causation to engage in counterfactual reasoning, but we cannot do the opposite.

The application of the model to Kelleyan configurations seems to avoid counterfactual information altogether. Lipe did not suggest that people pose counterfactual questions in Kelleyan studies, but merely that they use covariation information as a substitute for counterfactual information. The novelty of her approach lies in the presentation of covariation data in the form of a series of contingency tables; these, however, are only a different formal representation of covariation logic and, with the exception of the HLH combination, function in a manner indistinguishable from the inductive logic model. In fact, the procedure for dealing with Kelleyan information appears to violate her own general model; instead of one causal hypothesis being assessed first, and subsequently compared against alternative explanations, all causal loci appear to be considered together, and the attribution emerges from an analysis of contingency.

The Probabilistic Contrast Model

This model was proposed by Cheng and Novick (1990; 1991; 1992). Instead of assessing covariation, people using this model would estimate and compare proportions. According to Cheng and Novick (1992, p.367), "everyday causal inference is based on contrasts (i.e. differences or differences between differences) between the probability of the effect conditional on the presence versus the absence of (single or multiple) potential causal factors. These contrasts are computed for selected factors in a focal set". The model can be applied to a variety of domains, but Cheng and Novick (1990) concentrated on the application to the Kelleyan tradition.

Consider first main effect contrasts. These correspond to effects of P, S, or C (or T) in the Kelleyan tradition. To assess whether a given causal locus is a cause of some effect, people compare the proportion of instances on which the effect occurs in the presence of the possible cause to the proportion on which it occurs in the absence of the possible cause. If the former proportion is greater than the latter by a significant amount, that amount being "an empirically determined parameter that defines a noticeable difference" (Cheng & Novick, 1990, p.549), then the causal locus is identified as a cause of the effect. In keeping with this, Cheng and Novick (p.549) defined a cause probabilistically as "a factor, the presence of which (relative to its absence) increases the likelihood of the effect". The main effect contrast can be expressed as follows:

$$\Delta p_i = p_i - p_{-i}$$

where i denotes some possible cause, p_i denotes the proportion of cases on which the effect occurs in the presence of i, and p_{-i} denotes the proportion of cases on which the effect occurs in the absence of i (Cheng & Novick, 1992, p. 367).

For interactive causes an equivalent logic applies. For two-way interactions four proportions need to be considered, representing proportions of cases on which the effect occurs under each combination of presence and absence of the two factors. Let i denote a person and j a stimulus, and suppose we are considering whether the conjunction of i and j is the cause of an effect on occasion k. Then the four proportions are: $p_{[i,j]}$ (i.e. the proportion of cases on which the effect occurs when i and j are both present), $p_{[i,-j]}$, $p_{[-i,j]}$, and $p_{[-i,-j]}$. This gives:

$$\Delta p_{ij} = (p_{ij} - p_{-ij}) - (p_{i-j} - p_{-i-j})$$

(from Cheng & Novick, 1992, p.367). Again, if Δp_{ij} is greater than zero by a noticeable amount, then it will be identified as a cause of the effect. According to Cheng and Novick (1990), the following version is also permissible:

$$\Delta p_{ij} = (p_{ij} - p_{i-j}) - (p_{-ij} - p_{-i-j})$$

This simply means that the identity of i and j is immaterial, as far as the computation of probabilistic contrasts is concerned.

If Δp_i (or Δp_{ij}) turns out to be negative, then i (or ij) is identified as an inhibitory factor. The computational logic is the same. The model also enables Cheng and Novick to distinguish multiple independent causes from interactive causes: the former are any causes identified by main effect contrasts (where more than one cause is so identified), and the latter are identified by interactive contrasts.

The notion of a focal set is crucial to this approach. It is a formalisation of a kind of concept found in a number of philosophical treatments of causal analysis (see Chapter 1), including the causal field (Anderson, 1938; Mackie, 1965; 1974), a dimension for comparison for identification of abnormal conditions (Hart & Honoré, 1959), a standard for comparison for identification of a differentiating factor (Gorovitz, 1965; 1974), and a given state of affairs in which only two changes occur during a given period

(Ducasse, 1965). The definition of a focal set can make a profound difference to causal selection. In Mackie's (1974) example, a man seeking an explanation for his cancer may construct a focal set consisting of events from his own past life, whereas a factory owner seeking an explanation for the same man's cancer may construct a focal set consisting of other men at the same moment in time, with implications for the factor each identifies as the cause (see Chapter 1). Cheng and Novick did not discuss how people construct focal sets; their purpose was to provide a computational formulation of the concept. Despite this, the allowance for flexibility in focal set construction marks a major advance over other models in this tradition, which generally specify a particular set of comparisons or dimensions as appropriate for all causal attributions.

Cheng and Novick (1992) used the concept of a focal set as a means of distinguishing between causes and enabling conditions; an enabling condition is a factor constantly present in a focal set (that is, present across both occurrences and nonoccurrences of the effect in question within that set) so long as it covaries in a different focal set. If it does not covary in any other focal set then it is just causally irrelevant.

Cheng and Novick (1990, p.550) stated that "our model is a probabilistic interpretation of the covariation principle ... It is a general procedure that is not committed to particular dimensions". Because it is general, the model can predict effects not predicted by the other models, and the test reported by Cheng and Novick (1990) leans heavily on this fact. The idea of probabilistic contrasts leads them to consider regions of covariation data not included in Kelley's original three dimensions. These include the cases specified by Forsterling (1989). Forsterling's predictions for combinations involving these regions, however, are generated by the definition of a cause as a necessary and sufficient condition for an effect. Under many such combinations, this definition yields no prediction because no causal locus or combination of causal loci is necessary and sufficient for the effect to occur. Probabilistic contrasts can still be computed for these cases, however, so the probabilistic contrast model generates predictions for combinations with which no other published model can deal.

In the stimulus sets they constructed, a given combination of Kelleyan information (e.g. LLH) was held constant, while information about other regions of the cube was varied. This enabled them to use the model to predict variations in causal attributions even though the Kelleyan information presented did not vary, variations which no other model predicts. On the whole, these predictions were supported by the results. Cheng and Novick also concentrated on the HLH combination, constructing six stimulus sets having this combination, but varying information from other regions. These variations were also associated with predicted differences in causal attributions.

This lays the ground for a possible explanation of a puzzling trend in the literature. Some models make no prediction for the HLH combination, and others make predictions which are not well supported by the data. The results of several studies illustrating this are presented in Table 6.4, and these can be compared with the predictions for the HLH combination given in Table 6.2. Any model that predicted the choice of any locus other than the four including C (or T) would be well supported by these results, but no model makes that prediction. Cheng and Novick argued that the results can be explained in terms of the probabilistic contrast model, if people are drawing on their world knowledge to make assumptions about other regions of covariation. By presenting information about those regions, Cheng and Novick were able to predict variations in choice of causal locus for the HLH combination. In some cases, they successfully predicted choice of loci including C (or O for occasions, which matches Forsterling's T for times).

Cheng and Novick also focussed on two supposed causal attribution biases reported in some previous studies, a bias in favour of P explanations, and a tendency to neglect consensus information. They pointed out that one must distinguish bias in the data from bias in the process; if there is bias in the data then even a normative process can lead to error and bias in attribution. They suggested that the two biases were due to the fact that previous studies had constructed incomplete stimulus sets, leaving the possibility that subjects were making assumptions about the information they were not provided with, and that these assumptions might vary from problem to problem, and from combination to combination. In their study Cheng and Novick constructed stimulus sets that were symmetrical across the three dimensions of person, stimulus, and time. If the inference process is normative, each main effect attribution should occur equally often, and so should each two-way interactive attribution. Deviations from this would

TABLE 6.4
Percentages of Attributions to Particular Causal Loci
for the HLH Combination

Study	Most popular choices
McArthur (1972)	P (46%), PS (36%) (also C 4%, S 1%)
Orvis et al. (1975) study 1	PS (56%)
Orvis et al. (1975) study 2	P (43%), PS (31%), S (19%)
Jaspars (1983)	PS (27%), P (23%), S (20%) (also C 3%)
Hewstone and Jaspars (1983)	S (41%), PS (25%), P (18%) (also C 5%)
Hilton and Jaspars (1987)	P (31%), PS (24%)

show bias in the process. The results showed no evidence for a person bias, as each main effect category was chosen equally often. They also found no neglect of consensus information, in terms of proportion of variance accounted for. The biases found previously could therefore be explained in terms of the varying assumptions that subjects might make about information missing from the stimulus set they see.

Novick, Fratianne, and Cheng (1992) tested this directly. In their study a given Kelleyan configuration was presented with different subject matter, which the authors assumed (and found) would lead to different background assumptions about the occurrence of the effect on occasions not specified in the information given. These different assumptions were associated with predicted differences in the causal attributions made: Subjects were using their knowledge of the subject matter to make assumptions about patterns of occurrence, and then making causal attributions from these (together with the explicit information) in a rational manner, following the rules of the probabilistic contrast model. Novick et al. were even able to account for individual differences between subjects. Tendencies in causal attribution that appear to be biases sometimes at least, therefore, emerge from rational use of a model and in a way that is predictable once one knows the individual's background presumptions.

Evidence

Many studies have been carried out to test the various models, and all of them can claim some degree of support from the findings (Cha & Nam, 1985; Ferguson & Wells, 1980; Forsterling, 1989; Hansen, 1980; Hazlewood & Olson, 1986; Hewstone & Jaspars, 1983, 1987; Hilton & Jaspars, 1987; Iacobucci & McGill, 1990; Jaspars, 1983; Major, 1980; McArthur, 1972; Orvis et al., 1975; Pruitt & Insko, 1980; Ruble & Feldman, 1976; Smith & Miller, 1979; Zuckerman, 1978). That is, these studies have found significant trends in support of the predictions of the models, either predicted effects of information types on causal attributions or preferences for predicted causal loci for a given combination.

On the other hand, a number of authors have commented that the fit of data to predictions has not been close (Iacobucci & McGill, 1990; Jaspars, 1983). The consistent tendency of subjects to favour P, S, or PS attributions for the HLH combination, which is not predicted by any model, has already been discussed. A number of other points can also be made.

First, most studies have found not only that some predictions are not supported by the results but also that a high proportion of attributions are made to loci not predicted by any model for various combinations and configurations. For example, Orvis et al. (1975) used 26 different combinations of Kelleyan information in each of two studies, and used the template-matching model to predict a single favoured attribution for each combination. The predicted locus was the most popular choice for 18 combinations in study 1 and for 16 in study 2. Although these results constitute some degree of support for the model, the mismatch between predictions and outcomes is too great for the model to be convincing. In six cases (study 1) and seven cases (study 2) an unpredicted locus was significantly preferred to the predicted locus. Jaspars (1983) reported similar shortcomings in predictions generated by the inductive logic model, although that model has performed better than the template-matching model in most studies (Hewstone & Jaspars, 1987; Hilton & Jaspars, 1987).

Iacobucci and McGill (1990) have pointed out that statistical analyses in previous studies, which have used univariate analysis of variance and/or have considered combinations independently of each other, have lost information about the three-dimensional factor structure of the data. They argued that a more complete picture can be obtained by the use of log-linear analysis, which allows, for example, the effects of a given type of information (e.g. consensus) on specific response components (P, S, etc.) to be tested. They used this method to reanalyse data from four published studies (Hewstone & Jaspars, 1983; Hilton & Jaspars, 1987; Jaspars, 1983; McArthur, 1972), and found that only four effects were consistently represented in all four data sets:

> Consensus information was used for attributions to the person.
> Distinctiveness information was used for attributions to the person.
> Distinctiveness information was used for attributions to the stimulus.
> Consistency information was used for attributions to the circumstances.

These results do not precisely fit any model. Moreover, significant effects occur in some studies that also do not fit the models. Iacobucci and McGill (1990) noted that findings vary a lot from one study to another.

Second, all models imply that the different types of covariation information should be equally weighted, and that the weighting of a given type should not vary across stimulus combinations. Jaspars (1983) and Hewstone and Jaspars (1983; 1987) all reported that variations in weighting of information across combinations do occur. Jaspars (1983) suggested that the weightings correspond to different conceptions of a cause for the different causal loci: that stimuli are regarded as a cause when they are necessary and sufficient for the effect, persons when they are sufficient for the effect, and circumstances when they are necessary for the effect. The other studies found minor variations on this pattern: Hewstone and Jaspars (1983) found that the stimulus was treated as a cause when it was just sufficient for the effect, but Hewstone and Jaspars (1987) attributed this discrepancy to a change in the way consensus information was presented. Also, Hewstone and Jaspars (1987) found that the person was treated as a cause when either sufficient or necessary and sufficient for the effect. Such differences in weightings are not predicted by the models.

Third, even in studies which appear to give reasonable support to the models, the predictions of the models often account for less than half of the attributions actually made. In Orvis et al. (1975), the predicted causal loci captured more than half of the attributions in only 13 cases out of 26 in study 1, and 14 out of 26 in study 2. In Hilton and Jaspars (1987), ignoring the HLH combination for which the inductive logic model makes no prediction, that model predicted only 31.1% of attributions made for occurrences, and only 26.8% of attributions made for nonoccurrences.

The probabilistic contrast model fares somewhat better (Cheng & Novick, 1990). For the configurations and problem sets presented in Table 3 of their article, nine tests of predictions are reported. For eight of these the predicted causal locus was the most popular choice, but in only five of the nine was the predicted locus chosen by more than 50% of subjects. Cheng and Novick also reported stimulus sets using the HLH configuration, with additional information from other regions of the full ANOVA cube. For three of these (problems 10–12, reported in Table 4 of Cheng & Novick, 1990), 73% of subjects chose only causal loci predicted by the model. Four loci were predicted for each problem, however, and a reasonable percentage of attributions to these loci would be expected by chance alone. For the remaining problems (13–15, reported in Table 5 of Cheng & Novick, 1990) only 28% of subjects chose only the predicted causal locus, but many more made attributions that were consistent with the model (57%, 76%, and 74% for each problem), for reasons discussed in detail by Cheng and Novick (1990). No other model can match this general level of success for the predictions it makes, but there are still a large number of attributions made to loci not predicted by the probabilistic contrast model.

A different way of evaluating the evidence concerns the generality of application of the models. All models are based on regularity notions, most on the covariation principle. They differ, however, in specifying what sort of covariation information is used or how. Kelley's (1967) original formulation is the most specific, because it makes predictions only for appropriate combinations of consensus, distinctiveness, and consistency information. By this means of evaluation, the best model is the one that can account for findings predicted by other models and also make predictions not made by the other models. By this criterion the probabilistic contrast model is clearly preferred, because it successfully predicts differences in responses to given Kelleyan configurations (e.g. HLH) depending on extra information presented about other regions of the ANOVA cube.

The superiority of this model in this respect is due mainly to two features. First, the model does not specify particular dimensions of covariation information, and can in principle be applied to any information about multiple occurrences and/or nonoccurrences of some effect. Second, it does not give an exact definition of a cause. Under the inductive logic model, for example, a cause is defined as a necessary and sufficient condition for an effect, and if there is no condition that is necessary and sufficient for an effect then nothing can be identified as a cause under that model. The probabilistic contrast model is less exacting: anything can be identified as a cause that makes a noticeable difference to the likelihood of the effect occurring, even if it is neither necessary nor sufficient for that effect.

All of the studies discussed so far have investigated how subjects behave when presented only with covariation information, usually concerning the three Kelleyan dimensions. There have been studies of use of other types of information for causal attribution, but there appears to have been only one which has posed a direct contest between Kelleyan and other types of information. Hilton and Knibbs (1988) presented scenarios with conventional Kelleyan combinations of information. Included in these scenarios was information designed to elicit script information from the subject's store of world knowledge. In some scenarios, the causal attribution implied by the Kelleyan combination was at odds with that implied by the script-relevant information. In these cases, subjects tended to compromise, producing causal attributions that reflected both kinds of information. The results therefore appear to show that information other than covariation data is used for causal attribution, and is not swamped by covariation data when the two appear together. On the other hand, some authors have argued that script information effectively encodes consensus information, so that it is just another kind of covariation information in disguise, so to speak (Forsterling, 1989). Also, there is a danger that subjects might have been responding to an implicit demand, common to experiments of this sort, that they should use all the information they are given. For this reason, it is relevant to look at the kind of information subjects prefer to have when they are given the opportunity to seek it.

Information Search

The criticism has often been made of these studies that they present covariation information in prepackaged form, and moreover prepackaged in the form of single summary sentences (e.g. "most people laugh at this comedian") rather than as a series of instances (Hewstone, 1989; Hewstone & Jaspars, 1987; Kassin & Baron, 1985; Major, 1980). While people may apply the covariation principle to information in this form, and in a way resembling one or other of the models, this does not imply that they will do the same when required to seek and assess covariation data for themselves; nor does it imply that they prefer to seek and use covariation data over other types of information for purposes of causal attribution. The hypothetical covariation reasoner does not prefer one type of covariation information over another; all types should be sought and used equally in an inductive procedure, in which the causal attribution emerges from the record of covariation compiled by the attributer. A number of studies have shown that people do not behave in this way, but instead direct their search for information in consistent ways.

Major (1980) allowed subjects access to an array of pieces of information about consensus, distinctiveness, and consistency. Twelve pieces of each type were available, and subjects could see one piece at a time. Subjects continued to sample information until they were ready to make a causal attribution. In her first experiment people sampled consensus information less often than distinctiveness or consistency, and in her second experiment, using a different scenario, consistency was preferred to the other two types. Causal attribution tendencies in these two experiments did not match predictions of the models very closely. For example, in study 1, attributions to the person were more likely with low distinctiveness, in accordance with the template-matching model (Orvis et al., 1975), but were also more likely with high consistency, an unpredicted fnding. In study 2, attributions to circumstances were more likely with high distinctiveness, an unpredicted finding, and the predicted effect of consistency on attributions to circumstances was not found. Not only that, but the particular scenario used seemed to make a considerable difference to the amount and type of information sampled, and to the causal attributions subsequently made. All models in the Kelleyan tradition are content-free devices for using covariation information, meaning that they should be used in the same way under all circumstances. The particular content of a scenario should not affect the causal attribution process in this way. Only the probabilistic contrast model could potentially account for these findings, because of the possibility that subjects might have defined focal sets that included instances stored in memory.

Bassili and Regan (1977) argued that the usefulness of different types of Kelleyan information varies according to what they called the attributional focus. For example, the observer might be interested in finding out more about the person, or more about the stimulus. If the former, they will want to find out whether the person was the cause of the effect and will therefore be particularly interested in distinctiveness information. If the latter, they will want to find out whether the stimulus was the cause of the effect and will therefore be particularly interested in consensus information. The observer actively searches for "the information most suitable to his needs" (Bassili & Regan, 1977, p.115). For example, if you are going to see a film, you might want to know whether other people like it (consensus), but you might not be so interested in people's reactions to other films, because that is less relevant to your practical concerns. Bassili and Regan tested this reasoning by giving subjects a particular attributional focus and asking them which kind of information they would prefer to have. The results supported their hypothesis.

A similar study was carried out by Garland, Hardy, and Stephenson (1975). These authors posed problems in which a specific event was described, and subjects were then asked what further information they would require in order to be able to answer a particular causal question, concerning either the person or the stimulus (e.g. for a person question, having been told that Mary got an A in an exam, wnat further information would they need in order to say that Mary is intelligent?). Four categories of events were used: accomplishments, opinions, emotions, and actions. Garland et al. found that requests for different types of Kelleyan information varied with both person v. stimulus focus and event category. People were more likely to request consistency information for person questions than for stimulus questions, and, within person questions, for actions more than for any other category. People were more likely to request consensus information for stimulus questions than for person questions, and, within stimulus questions, more for accomplishments than for any other category. People were more likely to request distinctiveness information for person questions than for stimulus questions, and within person questions were less likely to request it for accomplishments than for any other category. The pattern for person v. stimulus questions fits the use of each type of information predicted under the template-matching model (Orvis et al., 1975), but no regularity-based model can account for the variations across type of event.

Alicke and Insko (1984) replicated the findings of Bassili and Regan (1977), and also found that the similarity of preferred object comparisons (distinctiveness information) and preferred person comparisons (consensus information) varied predictably according to the generality of the attributional focus. For example, if someone wanted to find out whether

Joe is a mystery-movie lover (relatively specific attributional focus), they would prefer information about his reaction to other mystery movies (similar object comparison), but if they wanted to find out whether Joe loves movies in general (relatively general attributional focus), they would prefer information about his reaction to movies of other types (dissimilar object comparison).

These findings can be interpreted within the framework of the probabilistic contrast model (Cheng & Novick, 1990; 1992). The observer's attributional focus serves to define a focal set, that is to say a set of cases within which the observer assesses causality by means of probabilistic contrasts. For example, where the observer's attributional focus is on the person, as opposed to the stimulus, this leads them to define a focal set consisting of other relevant occasions involving the person (rather than other relevant occasions involving the stimulus). They then make a causal attribution by applying probabilistic contrast reasoning to the occasions sampled from the defined focal set. The explanatory power of the model is to some extent illusory in this case, because the focal set notion is just a means of formalising ideas about information selection; it does not seek to explain why people define one focal set rather than another. Other tendencies in information search are harder to reconcile with the model, however.

According to Hansen (1980), information search is directed not only by attributional focus but also by naïve hypotheses about where the cause of some effect is likely to be found. Specifically, Hansen proposed that a naïve hypothesis about the person leads to a preference for distinctiveness information (information that tells the observer whether a possible stable cause resides within the actor), and a stimulus hypothesis leads to a preference for consensus information.

In his first experiment, Hansen (1980) posed three different kinds of effect and found that people had different naïve hypotheses about the likely cause of each. For achievement the naïve hypothesis was the person; for a therapeutic outcome, the naïve hypothesis was a mixture of person and stimulus; and for an emotional response it was the stimulus. In experiment 2, Hansen found that causal attributions made by subjects tended to confirm the naïve hypothesis in each case, and in experiment 3 Hansen found information preferences that matched those specified in his argument. Hansen viewed the attribution process as a confirmatory testing procedure: subjects begin with a naïve hypothesis, they then seek information designed to test that hypothesis by sampling positive instances of it, and the outcome tends to be confirmation of the initial hypothesis. Furthermore, Hansen (1980, p.1008) found that adding more information of different types did not strengthen the attributions made:

Personal attributions made by perceivers possessing only low distinctiveness information were as strong as those made by perceivers with low consensus and high consistency in addition. Entity attributions made by perceivers possessing only high consensus information were as high as—in fact higher than—those made by perceivers who also had high distinctiveness and high consistency information. Thus, a perceiver holding a naïve hypothesis of personal cause would be expected to seek distinctiveness information to directly confirm the hypothesis. Once having obtained confirmatory distinctiveness, the perceiver would be expected to make a strong personal attribution and to discontinue the information search.

These findings were extended by Lalljee, Lamb, Furnham, and Jaspars (1984). In two studies, Lalljee et al. asked one group of subjects to write down common explanations for a given event. Another group of subjects wrote down questions they would like to ask in order to explain why the event occurred. Lalljee et al. categorised each explanation and each question into a set of categories. They found close resemblance between the kinds of explanations given and the kinds of question asked for a given event; but, in most cases, such resemblance was not found when explanations for one event were compared with questions asked about another. These findings are consistent with the idea that people begin the process of explaining an event by formulating specific hypotheses about the possible cause, and their information search is then directed by the hypotheses formed; that is, they seek information relevant to evaluating the status of the hypothesis.

Perhaps the most revealing study is that by Shaklee and Fischhoff (1982). These authors considered the case of multiple possible independent causes of an effect. They compared three possible strategies of causal analysis in such cases:

1. Parallel search. This involves simultaneous consideration of a whole set of possible causes, collecting and reviewing evidence on all causes before passing judgement on any. As Shaklee and Fischhoff argued, this is the strategy embodied in Kelley's ANOVA model: All three causal loci are considered equally, and evidence relevant to all is collected before a causal attribution is made.

2. Serial search. This involves consideration of one possible cause at a time, collecting and reviewing evidence relevant to that possibility before moving on to the next. This too is an exhaustive strategy.

3. Truncated search. This is a serial search strategy which stops as soon as the causal role of one possible cause has been confirmed. Under this strategy people only search for the kind of evidence relevant to the hypothesis under test.

Over several studies the results supported the hypothesis that subjects were using truncated search strategies. For example, in experiment 4 (p.526), subjects "continued to prefer questions about an implicated cause even when its implication was certain, consistent with a truncated information search". They did not investigate other possible causes.

Directed information search in accordance with a truncated hypothesis testing procedure is not compatible with models in the Kelleyan tradition, under which causal attributions emerge from an undirected process of information sampling in accordance with the covariation principle. The notion of a focal set does not encompass these findings; a focal set can be defined in accordance with some practical concern or attributional focus, but not in accordance with a preconceived notion of the cause, or of where the cause is likely to be found. Restriction of information search in this way lies outside the spirit and scope of regularity-based devices.

These results show that the kind of information people prefer depends on the particular causal hypothesis under test. This implies that people would prefer, say, consistency information if that was the kind most relevant to the causal hypothesis, but not if it was not. If the type most relevant to the hypothesis does not happen to be Kelleyan information at all, then Kelleyan information will not be sought, unless the subject has no choice. It is fundamental to regularity-based devices that people should prefer to sample regularity information over information of other types, because regularity information is required for a regularity-based device to generate a causal attribution, and information of other types is irrelevant to it. Some studies have shown, however, that people prefer kinds of information other than regularity information, for purposes of causal attribution.

In the question-asking study described above, Garland et al. (1975) attempted to code subjects' questions into requests for information from each of Kelley's three categories, but were able to do this for only 23% of the questions asked: 3% of questions were requests for consistency information, 7% were for consensus, and 13% were for distinctiveness. Garland et al. found that an additional 15% were requests for more information about the person, and 29% were requests for more information about the stimulus. Lalljee et al. (1984) ran two studies in which subjects were asked to write down questions to which they would like to know the answers in order to explain an event. In study 1 the events used concerned stealing, giving something away, lying, and being truthful. The percentage of subjects asking distinctiveness questions varied from 18% (giving) to 37% (stealing), though these do not represent percentages of questions asked because subjects were allowed to ask as many as they wished. Lalljee et al. recorded no consensus or consistency questions. In study 2, using a different set of events involving either actions or emotions, 8.4% of questions were explicit requests for covariation information, but Lalljee et al. added to these questions which implied covariation (e.g. asking whether the actor was good at history). These accounted for a further 11.02% of questions. Questions of all three Kelleyan types were asked, but in proportions which varied with the scenario used.

An even more extreme result occurred in the study by Clarke, Wright, and White, reported in White (1989). Here, subjects were not given a specific attribution, but were simply instructed to write down questions they would like to ask to find out what caused a car accident. In this case, 97% of questions were coded as requests for more information about the particular accident in question (including questions about the people, things, and circumstances involved). Only 4 questions out of 350 were coded as questions about other occasions (a category designed to include, but not to be confined to, requests for Kelleyan information) by both coders; the coders disagreed about the coding of seven others.

Finally, Lalljee et al. (1984) made the point that subjects may not generate Kelleyan questions because they do not readily think of such questions, not because they regard them as unimportant. In their third study, therefore, they asked subjects to rate the importance of several questions, including questions formulated in terms of each of Kelley's dimensions. Subjects consistently rated these questions as relatively unimportant.

Failing to request covariation information does not mean that people do not use the covariation principle for causal attribution; they could be using covariation information stored in a mental structure such as a causal schema (Kelley, 1972b). More serious for the models reviewed here is the finding that people predominantly request and prefer information of other types. What people want to know, for purposes of causal attribution, is not empirical data concerning regularity or covariation, but specific properties and facts about the entities involved. This strongly suggests that, although people do not regard covariation as irrelevant to causal attribution, they assess causation primarily by ascertaining causally relevant properties of things.

Actions and Occurrences

Zuckerman (1978) reported that the use of Kelleyan information for causal attribution varied according to whether the event to be explained was an action or an occurrence (Kruglanski, 1975). The items categorised as occurrences by Zuckerman included achievements such as passing an exam, opinions, and attitudes (likes and dislikes). Zuckerman found that consensus information made a greater difference to attributions for occurrences than for actions, and this difference was found for each of the possible causal loci. Consensus information had a significant effect on attributions for actions, but accounted for only 1% of the variance. Zuckerman and Evans (1984) extended these findings, showing that subjects relate distinctiveness information more readily to actions and consensus information more readily to occurrences.

Zuckerman (1978) concluded that Kelley's model (and by implication other models in this tradition) is more appropriate for occurrences, that is to say in his study behaviours not considered voluntary, than for actions. Generally speaking this conclusion is correct. Take the example of a purely physical occurrence. Such physical occurrences exhibit regularity because they conform to physical laws; causal relations of this sort are necessary, meaning that the cause does not have an option as to whether it produces its effect or not, so long as the conditions are appropriate. Under these circumstances, causation implies regularity and covariation. Such covariation is likely to be imperfect, because there may be other independent causes of the same effect, and because conditions may not always permit the cause to produce the effect. In principle, however, the necessity in physical causal relations means that sampling covariation information is a reasonable way of inferring causal relations.

The case of action, as people generally understand it, is different because action is not produced as a matter of necessity. It is always up to the actor what he or she does: All sorts of appropriate conditions might be satisfied, and the actor might have all the mental states that usually precede the action in question, and yet the actor could still refrain from acting in that way. If different actors act in the same way, this does not imply that a causal mechanism was at work, only that they all chose to act in the same way. With this understanding, people might expect covariation to say very little about causation. Distinctiveness information might reveal causally relevant stable properties of the actor, thus encouraging a causal attribution to the actor. Even this is not an appropriate conceptualisation, however, because stable personal characteristics do not cause actions.

These arguments imply that Kelleyan information is less relevant for actions than for occurrences, if by occurrences one means to refer to causal relations exhibiting some kind of necessity. The distinction between action and physical causation has never been seriously considered by proponents of models in the Kelleyan tradition. In fact, such models are certainly more appropriate for causal attributions in cases of physical causation (or occurrences) than in cases of action, yet all studies have included actions in their stimulus materials, either solely or mixed in with occurrences. I shall show later, however, that the relation between actions and Kelleyan information is not quite as simple as this.

Critical Perspective

To summarise, several experiments have shown that people do make use of covariation information for causal attribution in roughly predictable ways. The best account of these findings published to date is the probabilistic contrast model: The model accounts for findings on the standard Kelleyan combinations of information as well as previous models, and successfully predicts findings not predicted by any other model. The notion of a focal set is a useful formalisation of a concept which helps to account for apparent deviations from so-called normative uses of covariation information. A number of critical observations can be made, however.

1. Most of the studies have used carefully packaged information. In many cases, information of the sort specified by Kelley has been presented to subjects in the form of single summary sentences. Findings obtained under these circumstances do not sustain generalisations to other circumstances. Even under these near-ideal circumstances, the fit between findings and predictions is not very close. When subjects are invited to sample individual instances of Kelleyan information, they do not do so in the manner prescribed by theory, and their causal attributions deviate markedly from the predictions of the models (Major, 1980). Even this situation is kind to the models, because subjects were not permitted to ask for any other kind of information, whether other kinds of covariation information or any other relevant information. Showing that people can make appropriate use of Kelleyan information when they have it and nothing else effectively overlooks the possibility that it may not be their preferred type of information, and that using it in a covariation analysis may not be their preferred way of making causal attributions. When people are free to ask for any information at all for purposes of causal attribution, they rarely ask for Kelleyan information and prefer information about the event in question, rather than about other events.

2. Several authors (Hewstone, 1989; Kruglanski 1980; Lalljee & Abelson, 1983) have made the point that studies in this tradition use artificial materials and methods, rendering the generalisability of the findings questionable. Cheng and Novick (1990) pointed out that it is extremely unlikely that subjects were using methods of causal inference in the studies that they do not use in real life, because of the observed consistency across subjects and agreement with the authors' predictions. If subjects were inventing methods *ad hoc* to suit the artificial circumstances of judgement, their attributions would surely show much greater variability than they do. This misses the point of the artificiality criticism, however. The point can be made most clearly with the aid of a

parallel. Harré and Secord (1972) critically analysed research on the similarity–attraction hypothesis: Typically, tests of this hypothesis involve exposing subjects to supposedly written responses of another person on an attitude questionnaire, following which they make a rating of their liking for the person. Subjects behave consistently in these experiments too: the more similar the other person's responses are to their own, the more liking they report for that person. The point is not merely that the materials and responses are artificial. Rather, the judgement of liking is taken out of context and expressed in unnatural ways. Liking is part of an interactive process involving two active participants and an extended episode of interaction. It changes and develops, and its change and development themselves contribute to the progress of the interaction. An equivalent point can be made about studies in the Kelleyan tradition. A causal attribution is part of an extended social episode. The material that goes into it is not a set of written summary statements, but actual observations of behaviour in all its variety and interactional complexity; the attributer is likely to be actively involved in the episode; and the attribution itself contributes to and has a role in the episode. This is the point of the artificiality criticism. People may use learned quasi-scientific procedures to deal with quasi-scientific problems presented on paper, but whether they use such methods for causal attributions in interactional contexts is another matter altogether.

3. Studies in the Kelleyan tradition do not ask subjects to make a specific causal attribution (Lalljee & Abelson, 1983). That is, when explaining why John laughed at the comedian, subjects are not required to identify something particular about a causal locus (such as, John has an easily tickled sense of humour), but only to identify the locus (something about John). Such attributions do not reflect everyday practice: people do not just identify the locus of causation, they identify the actual cause (or reason). Models in the Kelleyan tradition do not attempt to explain how people do this. This feature of Kelleyan models can also be criticised on empirical grounds. Smith and Miller (1983) presented single sentences describing behaviours and took response time measures of responses to various questions about the sentences. In two studies they found that Kelleyan questions ("Did something about the person (situation) cause the action described in the sentence?") were answered significantly more slowly than a question about intentionality ("Did the person intend to perform the action described in the sentence?") and a trait attribution question ("Does the adjective describe the person?"). There were two versions of the latter: a specific adjective was presented, which was either appropriate or inappropriate in relation to the action. These results suggest that models of attribution should be concerned more with (1) judgements of intentionality and (2) attributions to specific characteristics, not to causal loci.

4. Regularity-based models can only assist in the identification of stable causes. This was the aim of Kelley's model because he was following Heider's idea that people seek stable dispositional properties as explanations for transient occurrences. It is a severe limitation, however, because it rules out attributions to transient, occasion-specific factors. All such factors are covered by the dustbin category "circumstances", but when one considers that such factors may include temporary states of the person, such as mental states, or of the stimulus, the vague and misleading nature of this category is readily apparent. What do subjects do when they infer from low consistency that the cause may be a temporary state of the person? Do they make a P attribution, which appears incompatible with the covariation data, or do they make a C attribution, which appears to rule the person out as a cause? Models in this tradition do not allow people to give an accurate report of such an attribution. When one considers that people often explain single actions by referring to occasion-specific beliefs and desires of the actor (Bartsch & Wellman, 1989), this is a significant weakness.

5. The most pernicious feature of models in this tradition is their relative ease of testing. Since the models generate clear predictions about the relation between specific combinations of covariation information and causal attributions, it is straightforward to present those combinations to subjects and test the predictions. This ease has led to a flood of tests, and the resulting dominance of this tradition in the research literature gives a specious appearance of importance and generality to the models. Kelley (1973) was sufficiently aware of the limitations of the ANOVA model to point out that it was idealised, and would be used only for a minority of causal attributions in everyday life. Kelley's alternative model, the causal schema notion, is in principle of much wider applicability but has received less attention from researchers because of the greater difficulty of testing the ideas involved.

6. Although the notion of a focal set helps to explain some deviations from so-called normative use of Kelleyan information, other deviations fall outside the scope of the focal set notion. The initial formulation of naïve hypotheses which then direct information search is not compatible with a true regularity-based approach to causal attribution. Also, the kind of event to be explained makes a considerable difference to the sampling and use of Kelleyan information; the difference between actions and occurrences appears to be particularly important in this respect.

This last point brings us close to the nub of the matter, as far as regularity-based models are concerned. There is no single method of using regularity (or covariation) information for causal attribution: the way in which it is used, and the kind of covariation information which is used, both depend on several factors. These factors, to be detailed below, are not incidental features of causal attribution, but help to reveal its fundamental characteristics: it is the manner of use of regularity information that is incidental, as we shall see.

OTHER REGULARITY-BASED MODELS

Kelley's Causal Schema Notion

To deal with cases in which the attributer had access only to a single observation, Kelley (1972b; 1973) proposed that people made used of a kind of structure in memory called a causal schema. This use of the word "schema" is not to be confused with the content-specific schema notion used in other areas of psychology. A causal schema is a formal structure which may house a variety of specific contents. Kelley (1972b, p.2) defined a causal schema as: "an assumed pattern of data in a complete analysis of variance framework".

This definition makes clear the essential feature of a causal schema, that it is a record of experience in the form of summary statements of empirical regularities. It does not represent experience instance by instance, but summarised into a record of covariation. It uses no causal concepts other than regularity. It is therefore to be contrasted with beliefs about causal powers, which are also held in long-term memory but are different in that, although they may have been derived from experience, they do not represent covariation as such and depend on the fundamental causal concepts of generative relation, causal power, releasing condition, and liability (White, 1989; 1992a; 1993).

Kelley (1972b, p.2) also stated that a causal schema "is a conception of the manner in which two or more causal factors interact in relation to a [given] effect". A causal schema therefore never encodes a relation between a single cause and effect.

In the two causal schemas most commonly discussed, covariation is represented in terms of relations of empirical necessity and sufficiency. These are the causal schemas for multiple sufficient and multiple necessary causes, shown in Fig. 6.2.

Consider someone who succeeds at an easy task. One might have the idea that success at an easy task requires either ability or effort but not both. That is, someone who has ability can succeed without trying very hard, and someone who tries hard can succeed even if they lack ability. This set of beliefs matches the causal schema for multiple sufficient causes, where the effect is shown as occurring in the presence of either one of the two possible causes. Under this scheme, the occurrence of success does not permit an unambiguous causal attribution: The observer cannot say whether the actor succeeded because of ability or because of effort, because

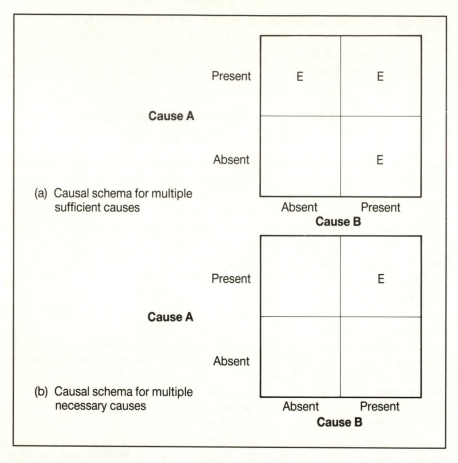

FIG. 6.2. Causal schemas for (a) multiple sufficient and (b) multiple necessary causes.

either would be enough. The schema therefore illustrates the circumstances under which Kelley's discounting principle applies (1973, p.113): "the role of a given cause in producing a given effect is discounted if other possible causes are also present". Thus, in a case to which the multiple sufficient cause schema applies, an attributer is less likely to attribute to one possible cause if the other possible cause was also present than if it was not.

   Now consider someone who succeeds at a difficult task. In such a case one might believe that success is only possible given both ability and effort. This belief matches the causal schema for multiple necessary causes, where the effect only occurs in the presence of both causes. In this case attribution is straightforward; since success is only believed possible given both ability and effort, the observation of success leads, by application of the causal schema, to the attribution of both ability and effort to the actor. Kelley hypothesised that this schema would be invoked more for extreme or unusual effects. In fact, this follows as a matter of logic, since effects that require more than one causal factor to occur are bound to be rarer than effects that only require either one of the two causal factors. Several other types of causal schema were discussed by Kelley (1972b; 1973), and in fact many types are possible, depending on number of causes and on the particular pattern of covariation represented.

As already noted, the causal schema notion has received less attention from researchers than the ANOVA model. There have been a number of tests of specific ideas such as the discounting principle (Fiske & Taylor, 1991), but tests of these ideas do not directly attack the notion of a causal schema; the discounting principle is not tied to the causal schema notion and would be expected to hold under many circumstances no matter what kind of causal understanding people possess. It is for this reason that I have not reviewed the developmental studies of the discounting principle or the multiple sufficient cause schema (Fincham, 1983). Such studies test the ability of children to deal with causal inference problems when more than one possible cause of an effect is present, but they do not address the fundamental question concerning the mental representation of those causes: Whether children have in their heads causal schemas, or sets of beliefs about causal powers and their possible interactions, cannot be discovered in such studies.

The causal schema notion is a specific proposal about the way in which causal beliefs are represented in memory. As such, it is almost impossible to test. It is easy to test competing theories about the use of information sampled from the environment, which is one reason why there are so many models in the tradition of Kelley's ANOVA model, but it is less easy to test theories about kinds of structure in memory because those structures are not directly accessible. A given causal schema may make exactly the same prediction for causal attribution as a set of causal beliefs of other types (powers and releasing conditions, for example); and, unless one knows which particular causal schema a person holds for some effect, no predictions can be made at all (Fiedler, 1982; Hewstone, 1989). This is unfortunate, because the causal schema notion has in principle a much greater range of application than the ANOVA model. Difficulty of testing yields a literature with an unacceptably lop-sided view of causal attribution.

Different theories do, however, make different predictions about violations of the discounting principle. Under the causal powers theory, the discounting principle will not apply when the actual generative mechanism is obvious: under such circumstances people should prefer to rely on the generative relations cue for causal inference and identify the cause by use of that cue, regardless of the presence or absence of other possible causes, and there is plenty of evidence that even young children do just that (Shultz, 1982b; Shultz, Fisher et al., 1986). The point about these studies is that what matters for causal inference is not the pattern of covariation across a number of instances (unless no better information is available), but the perceiver's ability to discern the interconnections between things and events on the occasion in question. If they can do the latter, they have no need of the former.

Contingency-based Models and Human Instrumental Learning

A number of authors have proposed models that are essentially devices for interpreting data in the form of a 2 x 2 contingency table representing instances of the presence and absence of two events. Two tasks are distinguishable: detection of covariation or contingency (e.g. Jenkins & Ward, 1965), and inference of causal relation. Here I am concerned only with the latter. It is convenient to identify the cells in the contingency matrix as shown in Table 6.5.

Causal inferences can be made by combining information from these cells. The normative assumption is that causal inference is linearly related to contingency: that is, judged strength of causal relation is a simple function of degree of contingency in the data. It should also be noted that the kind of contingency that is of interest in studies of causal judgement is unidirectional contingency, that is, the probability of one event given the presence or absence of another (Alloy & Abramson, 1979). This is to be distinguished from the kind of contingency represented in a chi-square table, which does not encode temporal relations. The point of this is that temporal priority or precedency of cause over effect is considered a necessary feature of the causal relation.

Although any contingency or covariation data can be represented in one or more contingency matrices, two complications are of particular interest.

TABLE 6.5
Use of Letters to Identify Cells in a Contingency Table

	Effect	
Possible cause	Present	Absent
Present	a	b
Absent	c	d

One concerns the evaluation of more than one possible independent cause. For example, Wasserman (1990a) constructed contingency matrices representing three possible causes of an effect. The effect was the occurrence or nonoccurrence of an allergic reaction, and the possible causes were items present or absent in 16 dinners eaten by the patient. One of Wasserman's matrices is shown in Table 6.6.

The other complication concerns variations in the degree of contingency between two factors. For example, in the same study, Wasserman varied the degree of contingency between strawberries and occurrence of allergic reaction, from 0.0 (four instances in each cell) through 0.25, 0.5, and 0.75 to 1.0 (shown in Table 6.6).

In principle, any kind of contingency can be represented in this way. Wasserman used entirely impersonal relations between items of food and allergic reactions. A particularly important strand of research, however, is concerned with human instrumental learning, in which the contingency concerns an action of some kind and an event that may be an outcome of the action. For example, in a study reported by Shanks and Dickinson (1987), the action was pressing a space bar on a computer keyboard and the outcome was the flashing of a triangle on a video screen.

With reference to Table 6.5, it is possible to construct a variety of models which integrate the information in the table to generate a causal judgement. In principle, all such models have a similar form. Frequency of occurrence of events in each cell can be treated as a variable. For causal judgements about one possible cause represented in a contingency table, five variables are possible: four represent the contributions of each of the four cells, and the fifth represents the contribution of information about other possible causes. Linear combination heuristics can then be described by regression equations giving weights to each of the variables. That is, research data can reveal the weights that people assign to the different cells in making causal inferences, and these weights contribute to the formulation of a regression equation designed to account for the maximum possible variance in judgements (e.g. Schustack & Sternberg, 1981).

TABLE 6.6

Example of Contingency Matrix Representing Multiple Possible Causes
(from Wasserman, 1990a)

Meal	Allergic reaction	No allergic reaction
Shrimps and strawberries	8	0
Shrimps and peanuts	0	8

The main research issue has been the extent to which human judgement matches the use of objectively correct equations for assessing unidirectional contingency. The correct rule is generally regarded as being the ΔP rule (Alloy & Abramson, 1979):

$$\Delta P = P(O/A) - P\ (O/-A)$$

where P(O/A) is the probability of a certain outcome given the event being considered as a possible cause, and P(O/–A) is the probability of the outcome in the absence of that event. Some studies have suggested that human causal judgements are not close to judgements generated by use of this rule, either because people are poor at assessing contingency or because they assign inappropriate weights to different cells in the table (Schustack & Sternberg, 1981). These results may reflect methodological weaknesses or problems other than the assessment of contingency or causation, however. For example, Schustack & Sternberg (1981) presented contingency information in the form of highly abstract verbal descriptions of events. It has been suggested that abstract summaries, shorn of competing information and not requiring subjects to assess contingency for themselves, may make causal judgement easier: in fact it is more likely that such information is either ambiguous or difficult to use for causal judgement because of the fact that individual instances are lost in a global description. Studies from the field of human instrumental learning show a much closer approximation to use of the ΔP rule (Alloy & Abramson, 1979; Chatlosh, Neunaber, & Wasserman, 1985; Shanks, 1993; Wasserman, Chatlosh, & Neunaber, 1983). In these studies, subjects are exposed to a series of individual instances. Again, such instances are generally shorn of competing information, so that possible effects of context and other information are minimised, but with this caveat subjects appear well able to make appropriate use of contingency information for causal judgement. In the strongest finding of this kind, 98% of the variance in subjects' judgements was attributable to the actual contingency as described by the ΔP rule (Chatlosh et al., 1985).

A case can therefore be made that subjects make causal judgements from unidirectional contingency information by use of the ΔP rule, at least in instrumental learning situations (Wasserman, 1990b). Against this, however, Shanks (1993) has listed five serious problems for this or any other rule-based model.

1. One plausible hypothesis (Wasserman, 1990b) is that subjects are computing P(O/A) and P(O/–A) and basing their causal judgements on these estimates. If this is the case, where their estimates deviate from the correct values according to the ΔP rule, the estimates should be better predictors of causal judgements than the values derived from the ΔP rule.

Wasserman, Elek, Chatlosh, and Baker (1993) found the opposite: the values derived from the ΔP rule were better predictors than subjects' estimates of P(O/A) and P(O/–A). Shanks (1993) argued that this result shows that subjects are not computing the probability values, but that the contingency is affecting their judgements in a different way (see later). This argument is not conclusive however. Subjects may have had difficulty in expressing the probabilities they computed in the format used in the study: having something in one's head and communicating it to the outside world are quite different accomplishments. Also, the discrepancy between their estimates and the actual values can be eliminated if one assumes that they are giving different weights to different components of the judgement; Wasserman (1990b) argued that weights of 1.00 for P(O/A) and 0.80 for P(O/–A) give the most accurate predictions. The question here, therefore, is still open.

2. The definition of ΔP depends on specifying a window of time. How long after a given event can another event occur and be judged to be an outcome of the first event? There seems to be no way to determine this objectively, and it probably varies from one judgemental task and situation to another. Given this, a window can always be defined to fit the data, which would mean that the ΔP rule is virtually unfalsifiable.

3. A series of studies of human instrumental learning have shown that causal judgements exhibit acquisition profiles, that is, they change as the subject gains more experience with the contingency. The ΔP rule predicts no such change, because the contingency to which subjects are exposed is constant throughout a series of trials, except for minor random fluctuations when the number of trials is low.

4. A number of studies have found effects of manipulating the value of the outcome. For example, Chatlosh et al. (1985, experiment 2) found that causal judgements were more extreme when the outcome was associated with monetary gain than when it was associated with monetary loss or was neutral, other things being equal. The ΔP rule does not predict differences of this sort. Since such results do not actually contradict the ΔP rule, it may be that this problem could be resolved by adding an account of motivational effects, rather than by rejecting the idea that subjects are using the rule, but this has yet to be done.

5. The ΔP rule does not account for selectional effects in causal judgement. There are several of these, reviewed by Shanks (1993). An example is the phenomenon of blocking. In an experiment by Dickinson, Shanks, and Evenden (1984), subjects were presented with a scenario that involved firing shells at tanks (represented by icons on a computer screen) by pressing a space bar on a keyboard. The shell might or might not cause the tank to blow up, and subjects were told that there were mines which might also cause tanks to blow up. In this situation subjects have to

distinguish the effects of their own actions from the effects of the competing cause, the mines. In one condition, subjects spent a preliminary period watching while the outcome occurred in the presence of the competing cause, a period to which control subjects were not exposed. Both groups then assessed the effects of their own actions, and judgements were significantly lower for the group that had spent a period merely watching. This effect of the preliminary stage on their judgements is termed blocking. The problem for the ΔP rule is that the contingency during the test phase is the same for both groups, so the rule predicts no difference between them. In short, the hypothesis that subjects are using the ΔP rule does not account for blocking or for other selection effects (Shanks, 1993).

The probabilistic contrast model (Cheng & Novick, 1990; 1991; 1992) is similar in that their formula for main effect contrasts is the ΔP rule, and the formula for interactive contrasts is a more complex version based on the same idea. It has the advantage, however, that the notion of a focal set enables the set of instances included in the contingency assessment to be defined in a different way. Some instances that have to be included under the ΔP rule can be excluded under a defined focal set. Because of this, the probabilistic contrast model can explain some phenomena, such as the signalling effect (Shanks, 1989) which the ΔP rule cannot. Shanks (1993) argued, however, that the probabilistic contrast model still suffers from the first four of the problems listed above, and in fact it cannot explain blocking effects either. In the experiment by Dickinson et al. (1984) described earlier, there is no way to define a focal set so as to predict the observed difference between the two groups, because ΔP was the same for both groups regardless of whether the action was performed or not.

Shanks and Dickinson (1987) included in their stimuli schedules in which the outcome was not contingent upon the action, that is, the outcome was just as likely to occur in the absence of the action as in its presence. For such schedules, Shanks and Dickinson found that causal judgement was affected by the prevalence of the outcome, $P(O)$. The more prevalent the outcome, the stronger the judged causality. Rule-based models can account for this by postulating that different kinds of instances are weighted differently; specifically, if occurrences of the effect in the presence of the action are given more weight than occurrences of the effect in the absence of the action (as claimed by Wasserman, 1990b), then the observed effect of prevalence on causal judgement follows. The finding does, however, conflict with the probabilistic contrast model. According to Cheng and Novick (1992, p.378) the probabilistic contrast model predicts that "the prevalence of neither the [potential causal] factor nor the effect will have any impact in situations in which the effect is not simultaneously produced by multiple alternative causes". The reason for this is that the different probabilities in their formulae are weighted equally. This prediction is clearly disconfirmed by the findings of Shanks and Dickinson (1987).

In the area of human instrumental learning, there is therefore a strong case that people are not making causal judgements by assessment of unidirectional contingency according to the ΔP rule. It is clear that any model of causal judgement in this area must be able to account for acquisition profiles, and the strongest candidates are learning models that describe the change in strength of an associative bond over the course of experience. Under such accounts causal judgement follows the accumulation of a record of experiences, forming an association between mental representations of action and outcome. In the model proposed by Dickinson and Shanks (1985) and Shanks and Dickinson (1987), causal judgement can be expressed as follows:

$$J_A = V_{AB} - V_B$$

where J_A is the causal judgement, the judgement of effectiveness of the target event A, V_{AB} is the associative strength of the compound of the target event and the causal background, and V_B is the associative strength of the causal background alone. The causal background stands for all potential causes other than the target event.

The associations V_{AB} and V_B are strengthened or weakened on a trial-by-trial basis according to a learning algorithm. An example would be the delta rule, which can be expressed as follows:

$$\Delta V = \alpha(\lambda - V)$$

where α is a learning rate parameter which can vary from 0 to 1, λ is a measure of the strength of the outcome, and V is the expectancy or associative strength of action and outcome.[3] ΔV then represents the change in associative strength following the trial. For example, where the outcome can either occur or not occur, if the expectancy (or judged strength of cause) is weak, then an occurrence yields a relatively large change in expectancy; if the expectancy is strong, then an occurrence yields a relatively small change in expectancy. Where the outcome is positively associated with the action, associative strength rises rapidly over trials and levels out as it reaches an asymptote.

The delta rule model can account for all the phenomena that are problematic for the ΔP rule (Shanks, 1993; Shanks & Dickinson, 1987). The model accounts for the finding that the actual contingency is a better predictor of judgements than subjects' estimates of the contingency, because the growth of an associative bond is not governed by a process of computation of probabilities. The problem of defining a window of time is dealt with by the claim that the ability of an event trace to form an associative bond is a function of trace strength, and the model includes an equation describing the decay of event traces in short-term memory. Having said that, there are some findings which the trace decay equation does not appear able to explain: for example, causal judgement is affected by the presence or absence of some intervening event which functions as a subjective link between cause and effect (Anderson, 1990; Shanks, 1989). The most conspicuous success of the delta rule model is in its very accurate prediction of the acquisition profiles observed in many experiments (see, for example, Shanks, 1993, Figs. 2 and 3). Shanks (1993) has also explained how the model can account for effects of the value of the outcome and selection effects such as blocking. It is noteworthy that many of these findings come from experiments designed as analogies to experiments in animal learning, and in the case of effects of value, blocking, signalling, and so on, human instrumental learning phenomena are strikingly similar to animal learning phenomena. The suggestion is that the same mechanisms may be at work in both.

Shanks (1993) did, however, identify one finding as a problem for the delta rule model. If the procedure used in a blocking experiment (such as that by Dickinson et al., 1984, described earlier) is reversed, so that exposure to instances of the competing event causing the outcome occurs after trials in which subjects have performed the action, it appears to lower causal judgements significantly (Shanks, 1985). This is a problem because, by this stage, there is an established associative bond between action and outcome and, under the delta rule model, the associative strength of the action should not be altered by the series of instances in which the action does not occur.

Despite the problems, associative learning models clearly give the most successful account of phenomena in human instrumental learning. The main weakness of such models is that they do not generalise to other phenomena in causal perception and judgement. Some of the limitations in this respect have been noted by Shanks and Dickinson (1987). In particular, they acknowledged that associative models do not apply to judgements based on summary representations of covariation, such as those used in research in the Kelleyan tradition. None of the models in this section can apply to causal perception of the sort investigated by Michotte (1963; Schlottmann & Shanks, 1992). Perhaps most important, the models do not cover the involvement in causal inference of beliefs and knowledge structures: Shanks and Dickinson admitted that, in some circumstances, causal beliefs (to be more exact, generative transmission cues) override contiguity and contingency (Shultz, 1982b). They suggested that associative processes might interact with inferential processes in various ways.

Few studies outside the field of human instrumental learning have investigated how a causal judgement is acquired from a series of instances, rather than derived from a summary or abstract representation. The delta rule model is Humean in spirit: Hume (1739/1978a) described how a causal impression should emerge as a function of event relations satisfying the conditions of constant conjunction, contiguity, and precedency. Hume's analysis, however, was directed not at action–outcome relations but at sense-impressions, or at least at objects constructed in the processes of visual perception. White, Milne, and Hatziyiannis (1993) therefore set out to discover whether a causal impression is acquired from stimuli meeting Hume's definition. We used stimuli essentially resembling the launching effect (see Chapters 2 and 7), except that object B moved off in a direction perpendicular to object A's direction of motion. This stimulus possesses both temporal and spatial contiguity and precedency, as defined by Hume. Repeated presentations satisfy the main requirement of constant conjunction. Over a series of 16 trials with this stimulus there was no evidence for the emergence of a causal impression; indeed the mean causal judgement was slightly lower on the last trial than on the first, and the slope of the curve resembled the visual adaptation effect observed by Powesland (1959). It appears from this experiment that the associative learning account does not generalise to associations between events in perception.

Even within the realm of action–outcome relations, however, the generality of the associative learning account is severely limited. Under the associative account, the causal impression never emerges with a single instance of an action–outcome relation: multiple instances are required. Developmental research has shown, however, that children can use various rules to judge the intentionality of an outcome of action on a single trial. These include the matching rule (Shultz & Wells, 1985), under which an outcome is judged to have been produced intentionally if it matches information about the actor's intention. Children can use this rule at the age of five, and use of other single instance rules develops later in childhood (Shultz & Wells, 1985). The matching rule has its counterpart in physical causation, where the single-instance cue of similarity is sometimes sufficient for causal inference: Anderson (1990) gave the example of a footprint, where similarity between the print and a shoe (compared to a different shoe) would suffice for inference of a causal link.

The most striking feature of the human instrumental learning research is that the link between action and outcome is hidden from the subjects. Typically, the action is the depression of a key on a keyboard, and the outcome is an event on a computer screen. In many real-life cases, action–outcome relations are not hidden, and generative relations cues are available. This is obviously true in action–outcome relations involving the manipulation of objects or tools by an actor. In such cases, accurate causal judgements can be made of single instances, and there is no need for a record of experience to accumulate. Not only that, but other phenomena of human instrumental learning also appear specific to situations in which the action–outcome link is hidden. As noted by Shanks (1993), research evidence shows that judgements of causality are reduced as the action–outcome interval is increased. But consider as an alternative case a snooker player potting snooker balls. The amount of time it takes for a ball to reach a pocket varies greatly from one shot to another, but it is hardly plausible that judgements of action–outcome contingency are affected by this, unless there are intervening events (e.g. the ball cannons off another ball and into the pocket).

Generative relations cues are not always available. Sometimes in real life people do not know whether an outcome is due to their action or not, but when this happens the reason is often not that the link is hidden from them but that the link is mediated by other causally relevant factors, and they have to judge the contribution of those factors. This is a different kind of problem.

Associative accounts of human instrumental learning therefore apply to a limited set of conditions: where people cannot use single-occasion rules and cues such as the matching rule; where the link between action and outcome is hidden from them; and where they are asked to judge a general pattern across a large number of events rather than to make a causal inference for a single event.

We must now consider the prospects for general rule-based models of causal judgement from unidirectional contingency. It has to be said that the failure of such models in the area of human instrumental learning is a damaging blow to their chances of accounting for any phenomena in human causal judgement. Even if a rule-based model, such as the probabilistic contrast model, accurately predicts causal judgement from contingency matrices, it cannot be correct as a general account of causal judgement if its predictions conflict with evidence about the acquisition of causal judgements. The clear superiority of single instance rules such as the generative transmission cue (Shultz, 1982b) and the matching rule (Shultz & Wells, 1985), and the fact that causal judgement is driven by general causal concepts (White, 1993) and acquired causal beliefs and hypotheses (Kuhn, 1989) are also serious drawbacks.

The models reviewed in this section all suffer from the weakness common to regularity-based models, that they cannot operate on single instances, and require at least a small sample of instances before any judgement can be generated. Use of occasion-specific cues such as generative transmission, the matching rule, and similarity falls outside the domain of application of these models. What the models give, in fact, is an assessment of the strength of a cause in producing an effect (compared to that of other possible causes), or the proportion of occurrences of an effect attributable to a known possible cause. The models do not generate an inference about a single occasion: They do not enable a person to say of one occasion, "this caused that". As I shall show later, this means that the models address only one among many types of causal question.

For example, Schustack and Sternberg (1981, p.104) set subjects problems in which they were asked to evaluate the strength of the causal relationship between an outcome and a specified possible cause of that outcome: "In each problem, subjects were presented with the hypothesis that a particular event was responsible for some outcome, and were asked to use a given body of evidence to estimate the likelihood ... that the hypothesized causal event, present in isolation, would produce that outcome". In experiment 3 the judgement was a prediction, but otherwise similar. Stimulus materials contained information about the contingency between the possible cause and the outcome, and also about the contingency between other possible causes and the outcome. Schustack and Sternberg (1981) reported a number of biases which resemble those reported by Kuhn (1989) in research on causal hypothesis-testing by children (see Chapter 4): subjects appeared to be using confirmatory or positive instance testing strategies and gave less weight to negative instances than to positive instances; they paid little attention to other possible causes; and they tended to ignore information about the base rate of occurrence of the effect and sample size information. Most relevant for present purposes is the finding that subjects gave most weight to cells a and b (refer to Table 6.5), and particularly to cell a, occurrences of the effect in the presence of the possible cause.

These findings have been interpreted as indicating bias in causal inference from contingency data. This interpretation depends on the assumption that the ΔP rule, with equal weighting of each component, is the correct way, not just to assess contingency, but to infer causation from contingency. This assumption is false. The strength of the relation between the possible cause and the effect is supposed to be weakened as relative frequencies in cells b and c increase (refer to Table 6.5), that is, as there are more and more instances in which the effect occurs in the absence of the possible cause or fails to occur in its presence. In fact, such instances are ambiguous.

Take cell b. Causes require appropriate conditions (enabling conditions, releasing conditions, opportunities; Harré & Madden, 1975) to produce their effects. If those conditions are not met, then the cause will not produce its effect, thus leading to an entry in cell b. This does not count against the causal hypothesis, however. For example, eating a lot of ice cream may be a cause of stomach ache, but it may only produce stomach ache when appropriate conditions are satisfied (e.g. a relatively high level of acidity in the stomach). Cases in which stomach ache does not follow consumption of a lot of ice cream do not unambiguously count against the causal hypothesis because of the possibility that conditions required for the power of the ice cream to operate were not met. It is perhaps relevant to note that the stimulus materials used by Schustack and Sternberg (1981) contained no information about enabling or releasing conditions. In the absence of this information, it is rational for people to neglect information about events in cell b, because it is uninterpretable.

Now consider cell c. Occurrences of the effect in the absence of the possible cause do not weaken the causal hypothesis either, because there may be other causes of the effect. People may suffer stomach ache on occasions when they have not eaten a lot of ice cream, but that only tells us that other things also have the power to cause stomach ache. Such evidence does not weaken the case for ice cream having that power. Schustack and Sternberg (1981) did present evidence about the presence and absence of other possible causes of the effect, and found that subjects gave relatively little weight to this information. However, the subjects were instructed to evaluate one specified possible cause, which amounts to an instruction not to evaluate the others. Neglect of information about cell c may therefore represent compliance with this instruction (Beyth-Marom, 1982), which would make it an artefact of the task characteristics.

Perfect unidirectional contingency between cause and effect can only be expected where there is one unconditional cause of an effect. Since most if not all causes require at least some conditions to operate, and since many effects have more than one possible cause, contingency is therefore an imperfect guide to causation. In any situation, but especially in situations where available information is incomplete, it is not wrong or irrational to give unequal weights to the different cells when making causal inferences. Subjects who do this cannot be accused of bias, unless the investigator is absolutely certain of the true causal structure of events in the domain under investigation. Similar arguments have been made by Einhorn and Hogarth (1986) and Anderson (1990) (see Chapter 7).

Where multiple possible causes are under consideration, the normative interpretation of contingency data is even more problematic. Consider again the matrix used by Wasserman (1990a) and presented in Table 6.6. The normative interpretation of the data in this table is that the strawberries are the cause of the allergic reaction, because the reaction always occurs in the presence of the strawberries and never in their absence. This prediction would follow from any rule-based device, as well as the probabilistic contrast model and the associative learning account, and Wasserman's results show it to be supported by subjects' causal judgements.

The problem is that at least two other causal interpretations are possible. One is that the shrimps are the cause of the allergic reaction and the strawberries, but not the peanuts, provide a releasing or enabling condition for the power of the shrimps to operate (Harré & Madden, 1975). The other is that the shrimps are the cause of the reaction and the peanuts, but not the strawberries, are an inhibiting factor which prevents the power of the shrimps from operating. Wasserman only asked his subjects to assess the likelihood that each item of food was the cause of the allergic reaction, and did not give them the chance to make either of these other interpretations. Contingency does not indicate causation: given this, the ways in which people interpret contingency data are likely to vary, depending on the causal beliefs they have about the domain in question.

I have recently run some studies to test this (White, in press), using stimulus presentations formally similar to Wasserman's, and with 1.0 contingency in all cases. In one scenario, for example, the effect was an upset stomach, the positive covariate was a pint of lager, the constant factor was eating a hot curry, and the negative covariate was the consumption of an indigestion tablet. In this scenario subjects showed a strong preference for the interpretation in which the constant factor was the cause and the negative covariate prevented the cause from producing the effect. Similar results were found in each of three different scenarios. These results contradict all rule-based contingency models, as well as the probabilistic contrast models; in any such model a perfect positive covariate must be preferred as the cause of an effect, and no such model predicts a preference for a constant factor under any circumstances. Cheng and Novick (1992, p.378) stated that a constant factor would not be identified as a cause in their model: "Our model predicts that a potential causal factor that covaries with the effect in the focal set will be considered a cause and will be distinguished from necessary factors that are constantly present in that set".

There is one possible means of escape for the probabilistic contrast model, however, and it is implicit in the phrase "in the focal set". It is possible that subjects were supplementing the information given in the stimulus materials with relevant information retrieved from memory. In effect, they could have defined a focal set in such a way as to include both the stimulus materials and the memorial information, and then judged causation from some integrated representation of the two. The probabilistic contrast model and the causal powers theory both allow the use of preconceived beliefs in causal judgements of the experimental stimuli. The difference between them lies in the kind of preconceived beliefs used. Under the causal powers theory it is causal beliefs, meaning beliefs about causal powers, liabilities, and so on. Under the probabilistic contrast model it is experience of empirical relations, of a sort from which probabilistic contrasts could be calculated - unidirectional contingency information. This is the key to discriminating between the two theories.

In a second experiment (White, in press), I assessed people's beliefs about covariation between relevant ingredients of the stimulus materials. By doing so I was able to set up contests between two possible causes of an effect: cause (a), highly associated with the effect both in the stimulus materials and in subjects' preconceived beliefs, but generally believed not to have the causal power to produce the effect in question; and cause (b), relatively weakly associated with the effect both in the stimulus materials and in subjects' preconceived beliefs, but generally believed to possess the causal power to produce the effect in question. Subjects gave significantly higher causal ratings to the latter than to the former in two out of three scenarios (there was a non-significant trend in the same direction in the third). These results support the causal powers theory and tell decisively against the probabilistic contrast model, and indeed all regularity-based models. Beliefs about causal powers override information about empirical regularities in causal judgement.

A further problem is that people sometimes prefer non-causal to causal interpretations of unidirectional contingency. This finding emerged from several studies by White (1994). In one scenario, for example, subjects were told about a hypothetical toy consisting of a model lighthouse and windmill mounted on a base. They were given information describing perfect unidirectional contingency between the light coming on and the vanes of the windmill rotating. Rather than judge the light to be the cause of the rotation, 80% of subjects preferred an interpretation in which both light and windmill were operated by a mechanism in the base of the toy. In other scenarios subjects interpreted perfect positive covariates as representing social conventions, and signs or indicators, rather than causes of the effects in question. No rule-based model predicts non-causal interpretations of perfect unidirectional contingency: if one event exhibits perfect association with another, especially if it also satisfies the cues of temporal and spatial contiguity, and if there are no other possible causes, then every rule-based model must predict that a causal interpretation will be made. The results of White (1994) clearly show this to be false.

The fundamental problem for all the approaches discussed in this section, therefore, is that they are simply content-independent models of the relation between empirical regularities, as represented in a contingency matrix, and causal inference. They do not take account of the role of causal beliefs in this process, or of the many possible causal interpretations of a given contingency. The precept that covariation, even in the form of unidirectional contingency, does not imply causation cannot be repeated too often. When people observe contingency or covariation, they might infer that something more than chance is involved, but this does not tell them exactly what causal interpretation to make. Consider the contingency between sunspot counts and the price of corn. Suppose that the "events" are samples taken at one month intervals, and that the sunspot counts are assigned to one of two categories, high and low, and prices of corn are also assigned to one of two categories, high and low. This yields a contingency matrix: let us suppose that the matrix represents a strong association between sunspots and corn prices, such that high sunspot counts tend to be associated with high corn prices. People detecting this correlation will see that there is something to explain, though they might decide that it is mere coincidence; but this does not imply that they will opt simple-mindedly for a direct causal relation between sunspots and the price of corn. Instead, they will seek a causal mechanism that could plausibly mediate the effect. By "plausibly" I mean one that is congruent with causal beliefs already held, or one that can be generated from such beliefs by inferential devices such as analogical reasoning. The mediation might be complex and have multiple stages: for example, people might imagine that sunspots affect climate which affects crop yield which affects crop prices, and indeed each of these links could be further analysed. When people detect contingency between two variables, X and Y, they will seek to explain this contingency, but that does not mean that they will infer that X is the cause of Y.[4] The models reviewed in this section therefore do not account for the ways in which people infer causal relations from contingency data.

INTERPRETATION 1: THE RELATION BETWEEN REGULARITY AND CAUSATION

The length of the foregoing review gives a fair indication of the dominance of regularity-based approaches in the adult literature. This dominance is at odds with the picture presented by developmental research, and a few key points from that literature will help to reveal the true and subordinate role played by the use of regularity information in adult causal understanding.

1. Regularity-based approaches have ignored the basic distinction between action and physical causation, and treat actions as if they were fundamentally similar to physical causation. There are signs from a few studies that the ways in which people use regularity information for causal attribution vary depending on whether the event to be explained is an action or not (Zuckerman, 1978; Zuckerman & Evans, 1984), but the extent to which the naïve understanding of action undermines the role of regularity information has yet to be realised. Differences in the

understanding of action and causation exist at the most basic levels, which is why I have talked throughout this book of two theories: any theory or model that ignores these basic differences is therefore bound to be inadequate.

2.   Research has shown that young children and adults tend to explain actions by reference to beliefs and desires of the actor (Bartsch & Wellman, 1989). The sorts of beliefs and desires that are invoked in explanations of action tend to be short-lived or occasion-specific. For example, suppose someone is asked to explain why Jane is looking for her lost kitten under the piano, and that they refer to her desire to find the kitten and her belief that it is under the piano. This desire and belief combination is occasion-specific: Jane has no desire to find her kitten when it is not lost, and no belief that it is under the piano when she can see that it is somewhere else.

Regularity-based models of causal attribution, on the other hand, deal in attributions of stable dispositions to the person or stimulus. In fact, such models only identify the person as the causal locus when the event to be explained covaries to some extent with the person. If an event does not covary with the person because the true explanation for it lies with occasion-specific beliefs and desires, then the models reject attributions to the person: models in the Kelleyan tradition would predict an attribution to the stimulus, or to circumstances or times, depending on what other regularity information is available. Clearly, this would be wrong. The fact that Jane is looking for the kitten under the piano may owe something, indirectly, to the actual presence of the kitten under the piano, but this hardly counts as an explanation: Jane would still look there even if the kitten were somewhere else, if she believed that the kitten was there; and she would not look there if she lacked the desire to find the kitten. To explain actions such as Jane's search for the kitten, people require information about Jane's mental states: They do not require information about other occasions, because no other occasion is relevant. This is where regularity-based models fail.

3.   Developmental research has shown that the use of regularity information for causal inference is a relatively late development, and that children experience considerable difficulty with it. Early on, children do not appear to be able to use regularity information for causal inference when temporal contiguity is violated (Siegler, 1975); later, they have difficulty making proper use of regularity information in the testing of causal hypotheses (Kuhn, 1989). At all ages, people prefer other cues to causal inference, particularly generative transmission cues (Shultz, 1982b), over regularity, and it is noteworthy that this applies in the case of physical causation, to which regularity information might be thought to be more relevant.

I have elsewhere critically reviewed the idea that regularity might be basic to causal attribution (White, 1992a; 1993). I defined basicity in terms of necessity and sufficiency: If something is basic to causal inference, then it must be both necessary and sufficient for causal inference. So if the intended claim is that our causal inferences, attributions, and causal understanding in general are based on regularity, however defined, then (perceived) regularity must be both necessary and sufficient for causal inference, attribution, etc. There is ample evidence, however, to show that regularity is neither necessary nor sufficient for causal inference

In the case of necessity, I argued (White, 1992a; 1993) that regularity information is not necessary for causal inference or attribution because such inferences are often made from single observations (Michotte, 1963; Piaget, 1954); made on the basis of similarity without regularity (Shultz & Ravinsky, 1977), on the basis of temporal contiguity when in conflict with regularity (Mendelson & Shultz, 1976), and on the basis of evidence about generative transmission when in conflict with regularity (Shultz, 1982b).

In the case of sufficiency, I argued that regularity information is not sufficient for causal inference because regularity is often interpreted as non-causal, whether as a sequence governed by an overriding cause, as relating sign or indicator to thing signified, as governed by procedural or other social rules, or as just part of the natural order of things. For example, a flashing right indicator on a car is (usually) reliably followed by the car turning right. People do not, however, interpret this regularity as indicating causation, even though it satisfies the Humean requirements of contiguity and precedency as well as regularity: the use of the indicator is interpreted as a sign that turning right is about to come, not as a cause of it (White, 1994).

Models based on the mere idea of covariation, contingency, or any other kind of empirical association inevitably fail the sufficiency test because many empirical associations are non-causal, and cannot be discriminated from empirical associations that are causal by empirical cues. The probabilistic contrast model, for example, is a model based on nothing other than contingency detection, and fails because non-causal relations such as "red apples are sweet" may show the same contingency relations as causal relations do. They fail the sufficiency test, in other words, because they try to make do without causal concepts, and this cannot be done.

Philosophers and scientists recognise that some regularities are spurious and do not indicate causation. The point of the sufficiency criterion is that it makes it the job of a good regularity theory to distinguish those regularities that constitute causal relations from those that do not. Likewise, the point of the sufficiency criterion in psychology is that it makes it the job of a regularity-based account of causal inference to distinguish those regularities which people interpret as causal from those which they interpret in other ways. It is important to note that we are not just asking how people distinguish spurious correlations from those that indicate causation: we are asking how they choose between various kinds of causal and non-causal interpretations of regularity.

It is now possible to make some definitive statements about the relation between regularity information and causation, and about what regularity-based theories actually concern. The key term in what follows is "diachronic structure" or "diachronic relations": Such relations are relations between things in time, as opposed to space. In principle, any kind of relation between things in time is a diachronic relation.

One can list a number of phenomena in causal perception, judgement, and inference:

1. The launching effect.
2. The production or performance of action by the actor.
3. Causal perception utilising generative relations cues.
4. Causal inferences, judgement, and beliefs utilising basic causal concepts (causal powers, etc.).
5. Causal learning: the use of regularity cues for judgements of causation (e.g. Shanks & Dickinson, 1987).

This list is not intended to be exhaustive. These things look very different and might be of quite separate origin. For example, Leslie and Keeble (1987) have argued that the launching effect may represent the operation of a low-level visual mechanism present from birth and relatively impervious to subsequent learning; as such, it may be unconnected with other, more deliberative forms of causal inference. But they cannot be completely separate because we recognise them as being all of a kind, as having something in common by virtue of which they are of a kind; something that we equally well recognise is not shared by other kinds of diachronic structure such as the relation between a flashing right indicator and a car then turning right. That something is the idea of a causal relation, specifically the generative relation. That is why the generative relation, and not some notion of regularity, must be basic to a theory of causal understanding.

By contrast, all regularity-based theories are theories of the perception, judgement, or inference of diachronic relations exhibiting unidirectional contingency. A number of kinds of such relations can be listed:

1. Causal relation.
2. Sequential relations in a process or as determined by an overriding cause.

3. Regular temporal relations between sign and thing signified, such as the relation between a flashing right indicator and a car then turning right, or between a red sky at night and fine weather the following day.
4. Relations governed by procedural or other social rules (such as scripts).
5. Relations understood as just part of the natural order of things.

Particular relations falling under any of these types may show any kind of regularity. For that reason, regularity-based theories do not distinguish between them. Such theories are theories of how people integrate multiple instance information to assess patterns in diachronic relations. By this I mean to exclude as fundamental to them any cue that can be assessed in a single instance, such as temporal contiguity: such cues may have a role to play in regularity-based theories, but are not fundamental to them.

All the models included in this chapter are models of the judgement of patterns in diachronic relations. Such theories may have a place in accounts of causal judgement, but that place is only part of their domain. The overlap between regularity and causation is only partial: many instances of causal perception and judgement do not depend on regularity, many instances of regularity in diachronic relations are not causal, or judged as causal. Models of patterns in diachronic relations are in the causal domain when applied to relations about which people hold causal rather than non-causal beliefs or hypotheses. Diachronic relations can be interpreted in many ways, and causal interpretation is just one. When people perceive a pattern across multiple instances of diachronic relations, this may suggest to them that there is something to explain, but they will not know how to explain it until they form a hypothesis as to what kind of diachronic relation it is.

INTERPRETATION 2:
THE USE OF REGULARITY INFORMATION
UNDER THE CAUSAL POWERS THEORY

Although regularity is not basic to causal understanding, and although regularity-based accounts of adult causal understanding have some serious inadequacies, it does not follow that people do not use regularity information at all for causal inference and attribution. On the contrary, the evidence reviewed here shows that people do use regularity information in roughly predictable ways, and this rough predictability needs to be explained.

Causal Questions

To begin with, the research reviewed here has revealed a rough sketch of the ordinary person's general approach to causal inference. When given some event to explain, the attributer begins by constructing a causal hypothesis. They then search for information of a kind suitable for testing that hypothesis: This information search is basically a confirmatory or positive instance testing strategy, with the inherent danger of falsely confirming the initial hypothesis. The kind of information sought varies according to the hypothesis under test; it may or may not be regularity information, and may or may not be some particular dimension of regularity information. When sufficient confirming evidence has been found, the attributer is unlikely to continue testing hypotheses; generally, people are content with truncated searches.

This sketch leaves many questions unanswered, and I have attempted to answer them elsewhere (White, 1992a; 1993). The key point is to imagine causal attribution or inference as an attempt to answer a particular implicit or explicit question. I have proposed two general hypotheses about this process:

1. When people seek more information in order to make a causal attribution, the information they prefer is information about the occasion or occasions implicit or explicit in the causal question posed.
2. The basic requirement for causal attribution is identifying something that answers the causal question posed.

The power in these hypotheses depends upon the fact that causal questions can be regarded as being of different types. Thus, the way in which people go about answering a causal question depends on the type of question posed. The usefulness of regularity information varies across types of causal question. I have proposed a simple typology of causal questions, outlined in Table 6.7. Those things that count as answers to each type of question are listed in Table 6.8.

This is a simple typology because (1) it does not purport to be exhaustive and (2) more complex types can be made by combining elements from the types given. It is sufficient, however, for the purpose of analysing the place of regularity-based accounts of causal understanding. I shall now analyse the types of causal question addressed by the models and research reviewed in this chapter. For the purposes of this analysis, I shall ignore the distinction between action and causation; action will be considered in a later section.

TABLE 6.7
Types of Causal Questions (from White, 1993)

A. Single occasion single effect question. What caused this (single) effect? or Why did X happen?

B. Single occasion cause question. What effect did this have?

C. Single occasion connection question. Did this cause that?

D. Multiple occasion occurrence question. What causes these similar effects? or What causes all effects of this type? or How can all (or a given set of) occurrences be causally explained?

E. Single occasion multiple effect question. What caused all of these things on this occasion?

F. Multiple occasion various effects question. What caused all these things across these occasions/all occasions/this particular time-span?

G. Comparison question. Why did this happen now when then (one or more occasions) it did not? or Why did this happen now when that was expected?

H. Selection question. Why did X happen when X and Y (etc.) both (all) seemed equally likely beforehand?

I. Single occasion nonoccurrence question. Why did X not happen?

J. Single occasion state question. What brought about this state? or What maintains this state?

K. Single occasion cause discrimination question. Was X caused by A or B (etc.)?

L. Multiple occasion effect discrimination question. What proportion of occurrences of X is/was caused by A? or Which occurrences of X from this set were caused by A?

M. Multiple occasion nonoccurrence question. How can all (or a given set of) nonoccurrences of X be explained?

N. Multiple occasion occurrence and nonoccurrence question. For all (or a given set of) occasions on which X might happen, how can its occurrences and nonoccurrences across these occasions be causally explained?

O. Intervention question. If possible cause A is changed (or substituted with B or prevented or introduced) what difference does this make to X?

Models in the Kelleyan Multiple Observation Tradition.

Research in this tradition has invariably posed single occasion single effect questions, such as "Why did John laugh at the comedian?". The problem with this is that most Kelleyan models (Forsterling, 1989; Hewstone & Jaspars, 1987; Kelley, 1967; 1972a; Pruitt & Insko, 1980) are models of how one might construct an answer to a multiple occasion occurrence and nonoccurrence question. Analysis based on the covariation principle takes a number of instances of occurrence and nonoccurrence of a given effect, and identifies one or more causal loci by assessing covariation across a number of specified dimensions. That is, use of the covariation principle reveals that, on the whole, across the sample of occasions in question, the effect is associated with possible cause X (for example) and not with possible cause

TABLE 6.8
Things that Count as Answers to Causal Questions (from White, 1993)

A.	Causal power.
B.	Effect believed possible for causal power in question.
C.	Yes/no.
D.	Factor common to all effects in question.
E.	One or more causal powers.
F.	Factor or factors common to all occasions in question.
G.	Differentiating factor.
H.	Occasion-specific addition to causal structure not known in advance.
I.	Causal power—presence of power to prevent or absence of power to produce.
J.	Causal power.
K.	Choice of one from candidates in question.
L.	Proportion or weight or list of chosen occurrences.
M.	Factor common to or factor(s) absent from all occasions in question.
N.	Covariate.
O.	Difference identified by comparison of X before and after change.

Y. It says nothing about any single occasion. Researchers know this: No one makes inferences about individual subjects from F ratios. Even if one could infer causation from correlation, one can certainly not deduce the cause of a single effect from a general pattern or tendency. Yet this is what subjects in tests of these models are asked to do. The models say nothing about how people might infer answers to single occasion single effect questions from covariation data. There are in fact several ways in which subjects might do this: They might, for example, reformulate the single occasion single effect question as a comparison question, which would entail comparing the occasion in question with other occasions on which the effect did not occur. None of the possible ways is normative, or known to be correct. This might help to explain why predictions of the main models in this tradition account for a relatively small proportion of attributions.

The Abnormal Conditions Focus Model

As applied to research findings from the Kelleyan tradition, this model instantiates the possibility described in the last paragraph: The contrastive criterion is in effect a proposal that people treat single occasion single effect questions as comparison questions and identify a differentiating factor as a cause. It is dubious whether people usually do this under normal circumstances. The reason for this is that the answer to a comparison question may often be a subset of the answer to a single occasion single effect question. For example, if I ask "Why did the car crash?" and decide that it crashed because the driver was going too fast on an icy road in a car with defective brakes, this is quite compatible with answering a comparison question, "Why did it crash this time when it has never crashed before?", by referring only to the fact that the brakes were all right in the past but failed on this occasion. This answer is a selection from the whole causal interpretation of the incident. It is, however, a feasible strategy for generating an answer to a single occasion single effect question when only regularity information is available. Other authors have also discussed ways in which comparison questions might be answered (Hesslow, 1988; McGill, 1989).

Counterfactual Reasoning (Lipe, 1991)

The fundamental idea of this approach is that a causal inference is generated by comparing the occasion in question with counterfactual information, which is information about what would have happened if some event that happened (or factor that was present) had not happened (or had not been present). This also is a model confined to comparison questions: If it is intended as a general account of causal reasoning, then it amounts to a proposal that people treat every causal question as a comparison question. This is implausible, as I have already argued, because comparison questions are ways of making selections from a more comprehensive causal interpretation of an event. Moreover, the model begs the question of how the comparison (counterfactual) information is constructed (see earlier comments on Lipe's model).

The Probabilistic Contrast Model

In general, this model applies to multiple occasion occurrence and nonoccurrence questions: The definition of a cause as a factor that makes a noticeable difference in likelihood of occurrence of an effect is a multiple occasion definition. It cannot be applied to a single instance. People using this model (or a process for which this model is a good computational simulation) are faced with the same problem faced by users of ANOVA-type models, that the model does not tell them how to generate a causal attribution for a single occurrence of an effect. Moreover, the model can only generate a causal inference when information is available about nonoccurrences of the effect: If information presented covers only occurrences of the effect, the attributer must find a way of constructing a focal set that contains at least some nonoccurrences of the effect. Since the model generates a judgement of causal strength, however (this is a function of the difference between p_i and p_{-i} in the case of main effect contrasts), it can also be used to answer multiple occasion effect discrimination questions, so long as the answer is only required to be a proportion, and not a list of particular cases. For the same reason, and with the same quali-fication, the model can also generate answers to multiple occasion cause discrimination questions. (These are not listed in Table 6.6 but are questions of the form "Were these many instances of X caused by A or B (etc.)?".)

The Causal Schema Model (Kelley, 1972b, 1973)

This is a record of multiple instances of occurrence and nonoccurrence of some effect. As in the case of ANOVA-type models, and for the same reason, it is not clear how a causal schema can be used to answer a single occasion single effect question, and there are again many ways in which people might do so.

Contingency-based Models

Since contingencies concern both occurrences and nonoccurrences of an effect in the presence and absence of one or more possible causes, these models also concern answers to multiple occasion occurrence and nonoccurrence questions. Like the probabilistic contrast model, these models can also be applied to multiple occasion cause discrimination questions (as in Wasserman, 1990a) and multiple occasion effect discrimination questions. This is explicit in Shanks and Dickinson (1987), in whose experiments people were asked to judge the strength of a given possible cause in producing an effect over a number of trials. The strength of the cause is assessed against a causal background, covering all other possible causes of the effect. Some experiments in this tradition, however, have posed a different kind of causal question for their subjects. An example follows.

Schustack and Sternberg (1981)

In the studies by Schustack and Sternberg (1981), the causal question posed (p.106) was: "use the evidence in each problem to determine the likelihood that a particular one of the possible causes, in isolation, leads to the outcome". Subjects addressed this question in respect of a particular causal hypothesis that was specified for them. In experiment 3 this was changed to a predictive judgement, but in other respects the problem was the same. The "outcome" was not, or not necessarily, a single occurrence but something that might be depicted as happening more than once in the stimulus materials. This, therefore, is a multiple occasion occurrence question. It is not a multiple occasion effect discrimination question because subjects were constrained by the instructions to treat the causal candidate as applying to either all occurrences of the outcome or none. The observed preference for joint presence information is a simple consequence of the type of question asked.

In general, regularity-based models are models of how people might answer multiple occasion questions. This is because regularity by definition is information about more than one instance. The particular type or types of multiple occasion question addressed vary from one model to another. The exception is the case of comparison questions, which are single occasion questions answered by use of a particular type of information about other occasions, information about factors absent from nonoccurrences of the effect in question. With this exception, regularity-based models fail to address the issue of how a single occasion question might be answered with the aid of any type of multiple occasion information.

In many cases, models do not compete with each other because they are models of how people might answer different types of causal question. In practice, however, such models may still compete with each other when (1) the causal question posed for subjects is ambiguous or (2) the type of information preferred for answering the causal question posed is not available, so that subjects must fall back on less preferred types, as in tests of Kelleyan models. This problem is discussed in more depth by White (1992a).

The typology presented here is a typology of causal questions, and I have throughout treated these models as if they were directed only at causal questions. Needless to say, there is an equivalent typology of action questions. So, for example, instead of asking "What caused this effect?", one could ask "Why did person X do this?", and this is a single occasion single effect action question. An important point about this is that, although the way in which people go about answering questions depends on whether the question concerns action or physical causation, this in turn depends on the kind of question asked. For example, for single occasion single effect questions, a causal question may lead to a search for a generative mechanism, whereas an action question may lead to an enquiry about relevant beliefs and desires of the actor. Comparison questions, however, specifically concern a comparison between an occasion on which something happened and one or more other occasions on which that thing did not happen, and the procedure for answering a question of that kind, involving the identification of a differentiating factor, is essentially the same regardless of whether the occurrence is an action or a physical event. In other respects, however, there are profound differences between causal questions and questions about action, and I now turn to those.

Action

In a sense, regularity information has no direct relevance to the explanation of action; in the theory of action, it is up to the actor how they behave, which means that similar actions by other people, or by the same person on other occasions, are logically independent of the action in question and reveal nothing about it. This is different from the case of physical causation, in which the occurrence of similar events on different occasions may represent the operation of a causal law, governed by a kind of necessity. In fact, however, things are not so simple and regularity information can have a number of different kinds of relevance to explanations of action.

First, a reminder that it is necessary to distinguish two ways in which action may be "explained". In one sense, to explain an action means to give meaning to it (Clarke & Crossland, 1985; Harré & Secord, 1972). Often, this is accomplished merely by identifying the action. For example, when someone asks "Why are you raising your arm like that?", I may reply, "I am hailing a taxi", or "I am making a bid for that lot". This is to emphasise the point that the same physical movement may be two different actions: action is, at the least, movement plus meaning. Action can be explained in this sense not only by mere identification but also by reference to its social context, invoking concepts such as rules, social situations, and the place of a single action in an interactive sequence (Clarke & Crossland, 1985; Harré & Secord, 1972).

In another sense, to explain action means to give an account of its origination. I use the term "action origination attribution" to refer to explanations of this type, to distinguish them from the giving of meaning to actions. In explaining the origination of action, we refer to the actor's reasons for action. An action origination attribution is, usually, an identification of some belief or desire or belief–desire combination constituting part or whole of the actor's reason for acting. Such an attribution may optionally enquire further into the antecedents of action, for example by identifying some stable personal disposition underlying the actor's desire. For example, we might say that Jane is looking for her kitten under the piano because she wants to find it and think it is there, and she wants to find it because she is very fond of it.

The use of regularity information in action origination attribution depends primarily on the type of action question that has been posed. For example, a comparison question addresses a difference between the event in question and other occasions on which something different was done. One might ask, "Why did John do this now when in the past he has usually done that?". The type of information preferred for answering a question of this sort is information about the occasions implicit or explicit in the question, and the thing that counts as an answer is something that differentiates the occasion in question from the comparison occasions. It makes no difference to this whether the event to be explained is an action or not. Answering the question therefore requires regularity information of a particular kind: information about the presence or absence of possibly relevant factors on occasions of nonoccurrence of the event in question. The information is used in a slightly different way, however, because the differentiating factor is located in the conceptual scheme for actions, not that for causes. That is, it may be identified as a reason, a belief, a desire, an opportunity, but not as a causal power, a liability, or a releasing condition. It is also important to note that the search for a differentiating factor is directed by specific hypotheses, and that the nature and content of these hypotheses differs in the cases of action and physical causation.

It is possible to distinguish three ways in which regularity information might be relevant to action origination attribution.

1. For what might be called freely chosen actions. These are to be distinguished from the case to be considered next, power-resistance relations; the latter concern interactions between one or more powers of the actor and one or more resistances or liabilities in some thing acted upon, so that the outcome of the action depends on the relative strength of the two. For example, taking an examination is a freely chosen action, but passing it is not, because it depends on the relation between causally relevant properties of the actor and the exam (and other factors such as circumstances). In the case of freely chosen actions, then, the use of regularity information depends on the type of action question asked, on the availability of preferred kinds of information, and on the specific hypothesis being tested.

Ideally, regularity information is only used for action questions for which it is the preferred type of information. For single occasion single effect action questions, the type of information preferred is information about the single occasion implicit or explicit in the question, and regularity information will therefore not be sought. For comparison questions, as we have seen, a particular type of regularity information is preferred, covering the presence or absence of a hypothesised factor on occasions of nonoccurrence of the effect in question. For a multiple occasion occurrence question a different type of regularity information is preferred, covering the presence or absence of a hypothesised factor on occasions of occurrence of the effect in question. The answer to such a question will be a factor common to all such occasions (or all those implicit or explicit in the question).

Where information of the preferred type cannot be obtained, then information of less preferred types is sought. In such cases regularity information may be one of those types. A detailed account of the use of regularity information for answering single occasion questions is given in White (1992a; 1993).

Finally, the use of regularity information also depends on the particular causal hypothesis under test. Suppose the action to be explained is Jane's search for her kitten under the piano. This is a single occasion single effect question, and the attributer will prefer more information about that one occasion, leading to the attribution of a specific belief and desire. The attributer may wish to take the matter further, however, and explain Jane's desire in terms of a stable personal disposition of caring for the kitten. That is, the attributer may hypothesise that Jane is looking for her kitten under the piano because she is very fond of it. Such a hypothesis can be tested in a number of ways (e.g. by asking Jane how she feels about the kitten, or by testing other implications of the hypothesis for her treatment of the kitten). Regularity information could be used to test it, however: presumably the hypothesis implies that Jane will look for the kitten every time it goes missing, and the attributer could test this implication as well.

2. In cases of power-resistance relations. Many statements of causation by ordinary people are properly interpreted as implying, if not stating directly, relations between causal powers and liabilities or resistances. Saying that Susan passed the exam, John laughed at the comedian, or Paul liked the painting he saw in the art gallery, is in each case to specify a relation between a power and a resistance. Susan's power to pass exams was greater than the difficulty of the exam to be passed; the comedian's power to make people laugh was sufficient to evoke John's liability to laugh; the power of the painting to evoke liking was sufficient to evoke Paul's liability to like things. ("Sufficient" is meant here not in the sense of a sufficient condition, but specifically in the sense of a power being sufficiently great to produce an effect, given the liability of the thing in which the effect is produced. It is a matter of strength, not conditionality.) As may be ascertained from the examples, success and failure attribution covers one type of power–resistance relation: that is, all success and failure attributions are power–resistance relations, but not all power–resistance relations are success and failure attributions.

Clearly, regularity information has a role in explaining outcomes of power–resistance relations, in that it is one way of ascertaining the strength of either the power or the resistance or both. For example, suppose we are told that Susan passed the exam, and we wish to find out whether this was due to the fact that the exam was an easy one. There are many ways in which we could assess the difficulty of the exam: having a look at the questions might be sufficient, or asking the people who set it. But we could also use regularity information. Specifically, we could assess consensus: If many people pass the exam, then it is probably an easy exam, and this supports our hypothesis; if few people pass the exam, then it is probably a difficult exam, and this does not support our hypothesis. Information about the kind of people in the comparison is also relevant: if they all possess high ability, then high consensus does not necessarily indicate an easy exam. Again, a more detailed version of this account can be found in White (1992a; 1993).

3. Opportunities. In many cases the occurrence of an action depends not only on the actor but also on the presence of an opportunity for action. In the case of physical causation, the operation of a power depends on environmental considerations termed releasing conditions (Harré & Madden, 1975; White, 1989, 1992a). These are conditions such that, when they are met, the causal power of a thing must operate to produce an effect. The word "must" indicates the causal necessity in the operation of the power. In the case of action there is no causal necessity: The term "opportunity" indicates that environmental considerations may act as conditions permitting, but not compelling, an action to be performed. For example, the presence of a charity box is an opportunity for a person to donate money to charity. If the box had not been there the person would not have been able to donate the money; but the presence of the box does not cause or compel the act of donation.

Clearly, particularly where the attributer is attempting to assess stable personal dispositions of the actor in relation to action, regularity information can be useful in this context. In assessing a disposition relevant to the donation of money to charity (e.g. generosity), the attributer may seek information about the availability of opportunities for donation. The attributer would not withhold an attribution of a generous disposition if the actor never had such opportunities: information about occasions on which such opportunities occur is the only relevant kind. For example, one actor might donate less money to charity and less often than another because the former has less money to give; this does not imply that the former actor is also the less generous of the two.

In summary, it can be seen that regularity information may have a number of uses in action origination attribution. The tendency to use regularity information, however, is not general, and it is not always used in the same way. In particular, its use depends on (1) the type of action question posed, (2) the availability of other, preferred types of information, (3) on whether what is being assessed is a freely chosen action, a power-resistance relation, or the presence of opportunities for a given kind of action, and (4) the particular causal hypothesis under test. Variations in the use of regularity information may reflect variations in any of these things.

NOTES

1.   It is sometimes asserted that this is Mill's method of difference. This is not correct, as can be seen in Chapter 1, where the method is described. The covariation principle is also frequently regarded as "normative", which means that deviations from use of it tend to be regarded as in error or biased.

This is unjustified: All scientists know that covariation does not imply causation, from which it follows that people may be quite right not to conform to the covariation principle on all occasions; also, a glance at Chapter 1 again shows that there are many ways in which covariation or regularity information might be properly used for causal inference, and that it remains uncertain whether any of them is valid. Hewstone and Jaspars (1987) suggested that the inductive logic model is a normative model, but this claim is subject to criticism on the same grounds. The covariation principle should not be regarded as a standard for assessing accuracy of causal attributions.

2.   For this reason, the term "counterfactual criterion" (Hilton & Slugoski, 1986) is misleading, because the information used under this criterion is nonoccurrence information, not counterfactual information.

3.   Different versions of this equation are presented in Shanks and Dickinson (1987) and Shanks (1993). The latter includes an equation with a value for the trace strength of the cue in short-term memory; this quantifies the effects of temporal contiguity, modelling the observation that the effect on associative strength decreases with increasing delays between action and outcome, so that more trials are required for the learning curve to reach asymptote.

4.   Personal experience provides a useful illustration. I catch the train to work, and I have observed that a relatively high proportion of people who smoke on the train are parents with infants or toddlers, whereas a relatively small proportion of people who do not smoke on the train fall into this category. I have not yet made a causal inference from this observation of contingency, because I have not thought of a hypothesis that makes sense to me. Contingency tells me that there might be something to explain, but it does not give me the explanation.

CHAPTER SEVEN

Other Approaches to Adult Causal Understanding

Surprisingly little work has been carried out on the adult understanding of causation, other than the regularity-based models of causal judgement reviewed in Chapter 6. It is hard to understand this neglect, as causation is constantly around us and the variety of causal beliefs and judgements that people make must be considerable. We perceive causal connections in mechanical causation; we attribute causal responsibility for minor car accidents; we have common sense beliefs about the causes of illness; we see certain kinds of causal order in nature; we wonder whether human activities are affecting global climate; we think about the role of fate in human affairs, and whether some apparent coincidences indicate hidden causal connections; and so on. At one level, one could simply catalogue the diverse beliefs and theories that people have about causal relations in the physical realm, the surface understanding of causation. At this level a considerable list of findings could be compiled. For example, there have been many studies of naïve physics (e.g. McCloskey, 1983), and of lay theories and beliefs about causes of illness (Cowie, 1976; Furnham, 1988; Kelley, 1983). For the purposes of this chapter, however, I am more concerned with the basic level of understanding in adulthood, with understanding at a level that can be applied to any particular domain of causal belief, or at least to a large number of domains. This is the level that has been neglected. I begin with research on the launching effect because of its relevance to the origins of causal understanding in infancy (see Chapter 2); I then discuss the few attempts to model adult causal understanding at a fundamental and general level.

PERCEIVED CAUSALITY

Imagine two small black rectangles some distance apart. As you observe, one rectangle (A) moves in a straight line and with uniform speed towards the other (B). When it contacts B, A remains at the point of contact and B immediately moves off, continuing the direction of A's movement, at the same or slightly lesser speed. This is a rough description of stimuli presented to observers by Michotte (1963). The observers usually report that they perceive A kick, push, or launch B. In other words, they have the impression that the movement of B is *caused* by A. In the actual stimuli there is no causal relation: in the type experiment, A and B are not even true objects but the visible parts of thick black lines painted on a rotating disc which is obscured, all but a narrow slit. The "rectangles" are the parts of the lines visible through the slit at any moment. The causal impression is therefore a perceptual phenomenon.

The causal impression that occurs with the stimuli just described is called the "launching effect". Michotte also used stimuli in which A continued to move after striking B, so that the two formed an effective unit. With this stimulus observers still report a causal impression, and A and B remain perceptually distinct objects after contact has occurred. Michotte called this the "entraining effect". Michotte (1963) studied many forms of perceived causality, identifying no less than 18 "Effects". He argued, however, that launching and entraining are the fundamental forms, and all the others are derivative of or variations on one or other. In fact, he concluded: "The Entraining Effect is thus the *basic form* of the causal impression, while the Launching effect is only secondary in relation to it" (1963, p.265, italics in original). This is because instances of entraining "are not only the most frequent forms of causal impression found in ordinary life; they are also the most perfect or complete ones from the point of view of structural organisation, and those in which the character of necessity is most marked" (p.265). Despite this, most of the many studies since Michotte's work have concentrated on the launching effect.

Michotte's methods have been sternly criticised, mainly by Joynson (1971) and Runeson (1983). In addition to the general absence of statistical analysis, in most of his experiments the subjects were not naive, and a small number of experienced observers, including Michotte himself, provided most of the responses throughout the series. Throughout Michotte's research, subjects gave free verbal responses. Michotte usually classified these simply as causal or non-causal, although in some experiments other categories were also used. Most of the results reported are therefore Michotte's interpretations, not the subjects' reports, and there is uncertainty about the extent to which these interpretations may have been prone to influence from his own expectations (Joynson, 1971).

Doubts have also been expressed about the immediacy of the causal impression. Some studies found that a significant proportion of naive subjects did not perceive the launching effect on the first trial (Boyle, 1960; Beasley, 1968), and Michotte himself reported that the occurrence of the causal impression depended to some extent on the attitude adopted by the observer, a phenomenon also reported by Gemelli and Cappellini (1958). These problems may have been exaggerated, however. Although Boyle (1960) excluded 50% of potential subjects on the basis of preliminary responses, there were three criteria for exclusion, of which failure to report the launching effect was one, and Boyle did not report how many subjects were excluded by that criterion. The stimuli used in those studies did not closely resemble naturally occurring collisions, and the quality of stimuli generated by Michotte's disc and projection methods can also be questioned (Runeson, 1983; Kassin and Baron, 1985). The use of free verbal responses, and indeed any dependent measure, causes problems because subjects may be unable to report what they have actually perceived, or their reports may be influenced by what they were thinking, as well as by what they saw.

Problems with assessing subjects' visual impressions are bound to dog this line of research to some extent, but many other studies have found much higher proportions of subjects reporting the launching effect, and there can now be little doubt about the occurrence of the phenomenon (Natsoulas, 1961; Schlottmann & Shanks, 1992; Gordon, Day, & Stecher, 1990; Thinès, Costall, & Butterworth, 1991; Costall, 1991; Michotte & Thinès, 1991; Powesland, 1959). Most of Michotte's other experiments, however, have not been replicated, and the findings of these must be regarded as in need of confirmation. This applies not only to the phenomena reported in the main experiments, but also to reports of failures to find a causal impression under various conditions. For example, Michotte (1963) claimed that features of the objects such as their size made little or no difference to the causal impression, but no experiment testing this was reported in the book, so it can only be regarded as an anecdotal observation.

Michotte distinguished between inferred causality, or the use of knowledge in causal inference, and just "seeing" causality, and his aim was to reach some understanding of why people speak of knowing in one case and seeing in the other. His ultimate answer to this was the elucidation of a perceptual structure which he regarded as innate. Here I shall describe the later version of Michotte's theory, presented in Appendix II of Michotte (1963). Michotte argued that, objectively, there are two stages in the typical launching effect sequence. In the first stage A is moving and B is at rest, and in the second stage B is moving and A is at rest. Michotte contended that the transition from the first stage to the second arouses a conflict between a perceptual tendency towards continuation of the kinematic state of the first stage (i.e. the movement of A) and the change of stimulus conditions which occurs at the start of the second stage. This conflict is resolved in perception through a transition stage, so that, phenomenologically, the sequence has three stages, not two.

This transition stage involves kinematic integration and phenomenal duplication. Taking the latter first, there is a phenomenal duplication of B's movement such that B undergoes passive displacement but is perceived as executing A's movement. For Michotte movement and displacement are different. "From the phenomenological point of view movement always appears as to some extent a manifestation of activity" (p.316). Displacement lacks the character of activity and is change of a purely spatial kind. B is displaced, therefore, but has no movement of its own: it has, or participates in, A's movement. Eventually B is perceived as having its own movement. The boundary between the transition stage and this third stage is what Michotte called the radius of action.

In the case of the Entraining Effect kinematic integration is due to the action of the Gestalt principle of common fate: A and B move together after contact, therefore have common fate, and because of this the two stages of the movement are kinematically integrated. In the case of the Launching Effect kinematic integration is due to the action of the Gestalt principle of good continuation: it occurs because the displacement of B continues A's movement. According to Michotte's findings, the causal impression in the Launching Effect is strongest when B's motion characteristics are the same as A's, or when B moves a little more slowly than A had done. These are the characteristics that maximise good continuation.

The essential perceptual structure of the causal impression corresponds to the transition stage. It was designated by Michotte "ampliation of the movement" ("l'ampliation du mouvement" in the original), and defined as follows: "a process which consists in the dominant movement, that of the active object, appearing to extend itself on to the passive object, while remaining distinct from the change in position which the latter undergoes in its own right" (p.217, italics removed).

Michotte argued that ampliation has the specific function of accounting for the impression of productivity in the causal relation. He argued that stimulus conditions alone cannot account for this. It might be thought that this much is obvious, because there is no actual causal relation in the stimuli. Michotte pointed out, however, that something is actually produced even in the stimuli he used, that something being the spatial displacement of B. Now if the production of B's displacement were sufficient for the causal impression to occur, then the causal impression would occur under many conditions in which, in fact, it does not. One example is a sequence in which the onset of B's displacement is delayed by 150ms after contact from A; another example is a sequence in which the direction of B's movement is discrepant from A's. Michotte reported that only small differences in direction of A's and B's movement were sufficient to destroy the causal impression: "When the angle is... only 25° off a straight line, there is already considerable weakening of the Launching Effect" (p.102). To explain the impression of productivity we therefore need something more specific than the mere production of B's displacement, and that something must account for the pattern in the occurrences and nonoccurrences of the causal impression. That is what the ampliation theory accomplishes.

The perceptual structure is not to be identified with the stimulus conditions under which the causal impression occurs. For example, Michotte reported that a causal impression can still occur, even if A does not come into contact with B (experiment 31). The size of the gap depends on the speed of A's movement, but according to Michotte even a gap of 500mm did not necessarily make the causal impression disappear. He argued, however, that this is not fatal to the ampliation theory, and that the phenomenal extension of A's movement onto B can still occur despite the gap between them. Apparently the gap is not sufficient to preclude kinematic integration due to good continuation.

If this is the case, how could the ampliation hypothesis be falsified? One way would be through Michotte's own method, experimental phenomenology (Thinès, 1991): if one could find a case where a causal impression was reported but, at the same time, the observer reported that A's movement was not phenomenologially extended onto B, that would count as a falsification of the ampliation theory. If the ampliation theory really explains perceived causality, rather than merely describing it as some have claimed (Piaget, cited in Michotte, 1963; Runeson, 1983) such an occurrence should at least be possible. Michotte's dependence on verbal reports has been criticised to such an extent, however, (Joynson, 1971), that it is doubtful whether this method is now viable, or how much faith one could have in results produced by use of it.

The ampliation theory does tie itself to stimulus conditions to some extent, however. In the case of the launching effect, as already described, kinematic integration is due to good continuation, which depends upon B's displacement continuing the direction of A's movement. If ampliation is the structure underlying the causal impression, then the causal impression should not occur when conditions do not favour kinematic integration; and conversely it should always occur when they do. Nonoccurrence of a causal impression under any conditions in which A and B move in the same direction (and in which other conditions are also favourable for kinematic integration), and occurrence of a causal impression when B's direction of movement is grossly discrepant from A's, would both constitute falsifying cases.

Michotte (1963) did describe several instances where people report a causal impression but where ampliation could not be involved because conditions were not right for kinematic integration or phenomenal duplication (e.g. p.361, where Michotte commented that "there could not have been ampliation since the movements were in entirely different directions"). His argument was that people do not really "see" causality in these cases, but use acquired knowledge to interpret what they see. For example, stimulus conditions suggest that the movement of B is dependent on contact from A, and they interpret that dependence as causal with the aid of acquired knowledge. Michotte denied that this was happening in Launching or Entraining, and he discussed the differences at length. He concluded: "The essential difference between the Launching Effect and the Entraining Effect on the one hand and cases of simple dependence on the other thus consists, in the last analysis, in the fact that the causal significance is immanent and intrinsic to the perceptual structure itself in the first case, while it is acquired and has an extrinsic origin in the second" (p.368).

Ultimately, therefore, the theory hinges on the claim that the perceptual structure common to Launching and Entraining is innate, and that other forms of perceived causality are not. If a causal impression occurred when B's direction of motion was very different from A's, Michotte could presumably argue that this was a case of causality inferred from perceived dependence, and therefore not fatal to the ampliation theory. If Michotte cannot prove his case here, it is at least very difficult to prove him wrong. What grounds are there for supposing the perceptual structure to be innate? Michotte and Thinès (1991) presented a number of relevant arguments:

1. They claimed that there was a high correlation between different observers, of the sort usually associated with psychophysical functions, in the variation of the causal impression over variations in the pattern of stimulation. They argued that the link between stimulus and response is usually much weaker for responses based on acquired meanings, presumably because experience varies a good deal from one person to another.

2. The causal impression in the launching effect has an immediacy which is not characteristic of interpretation with the aid of acquired meanings. This is the "immanence" referred to above.

3. Appeal to meaning acquired through experience cannot explain negative and paradoxical cases. In negative cases, the causal impression does not arise even though the observer knows that a causal relation is really present (Michotte, 1963, pp.152-153). In paradoxical cases, the causal impression arises in cases where the conditions conflict with anything that could be in the record of experience. For example, the causal impression occurs when "Object B, which is already moving at the moment of impact, slows down following the blow it received" (Michotte and Thinès, 1991, p.75).

Unfortunately none of these points carries much weight. It is not clear exactly how much consistency there is across observers because of the methodological problems discussed above. Findings such as those of Gemelli and Cappellini (1958) suggest that there may be sufficient variation across observers for causal perception to be a function of experience. In addition, the immediacy of the causal impression does not mean that it is non-inferential, for the interpretive process could be automatic, in which case it would be fast, effortless, and not conscious (Weir, 1978). The argument about negative and paradoxical cases was refuted by Runeson (1983). Runeson correctly pointed out that actual causal interactions are not limited to the idealised linear collisions of classical mechanics, and that other factors enter into real collisions. For example, if A and B are cars, and A strikes B, then B would very often slow down after the collision, but observers would still see A causing B to slow down. In any case Gemelli and Cappellini (1958) also showed subjects films of paradoxical cases, and found that those subjects who reported a causal impression did not perceive the change in B's velocity correctly: in other words, the case is not phenomenally paradoxical because observers who have the causal impression do not perceive B as slowing down.

Despite the failure of these three arguments, there are two lines of evidence in support of the idea that the launching effect is not learned. One is the series of studies showing that infants around four to six months of age make perceptual discriminations, such as to suggest that they perceive launching effect stimuli in much the way that adults do, reviewed in Chapter 2. Discussing these findings, Leslie and Keeble (1987) proposed that the launching effect is mediated by a low-level visual mechanism. Such a mechanism would be present and operative from birth, and would persist relatively unaltered throughout life. It would account for the immediacy of the causal impression by virtue of being automatic and therefore fast and effortless. Variations in the occurrence of the causal impression across observers could be explained, as already argued, by imperfections in the stimulus conditions and by the vagaries of observer reports which are, after all, voluntary, no matter what the observer perceives.

The other line of evidence comes from a study by Schlottmann and Shanks (1992). In one experiment they used stimuli in which the impact of A on B was a poorer predictor of B's movement than another feature of the stimuli. The launching effect appeared undiminished by this. A second experiment replicated this finding and showed apparent independence of the causal impression from other causally relevant judgements. Schlottmann and Shanks (1992) interpreted these results as showing that perceived causality in the launching effect is distinct from and independent of judged causality. They argued that their results supported the idea that the causal impression in the launching effect is mediated by a visual mechanism of the sort proposed by Leslie and Keeble (1987), and not affected by subsequent learning about causality nor by other kinds of causal judgement.

Despite the supporting evidence, the idea of a mechanism present from birth appears implausible. One reason for thinking so is that nature does not provide good examples of collision sequences. The stimuli used in experiments are modelled on artificial objects and events, typically billiard balls rolling across an artificially flat surface low in friction. Such objects and surfaces are recent innovations into our visual environment, on an evolutionary time scale. It does not seem likely that there would be an inbuilt visual mechanism for perceiving event sequences that would rarely if ever be encountered in a natural, as opposed to human-made, environment, unless such a mechanism conferred some very strong advantage. On the other hand, the infants who were the subjects in those studies were already several months old, and this could be sufficient time for them to gain relevant perceptual experience from the various artifical objects they encounter. The experiment by Schlottmann and Shanks (1992) is not decisive because independence of perceived causality and judged causality can occur for other reasons. For example, perceived causality may result from the operation of acquired but automatic processes (Weir, 1978), whereas judged causality emerges from the operation of controlled processes: both processes may have a common origin, but be operationally distinct.

At present it therefore appears that Michotte has not succeeded in proving his case for the primacy of ampliation of the movement over perceived causality occurring for stimuli where there could not have been ampliation. Although this is not sufficient to refute Michotte's claims, it can be argued that a theory that can account for the full pattern of occurrence and nonoccurrence of perceived causality should be preferred to one that can account only for some cases, and depends for its explanatory force on a claim that those cases are special. Consider some findings from a study of multiple object interactions (White and Milne, 1994). Figure 7.1 shows an example of the stimuli used in these experiments. The left-hand diagram of Fig. l shows the first frame of the sequence, with object A at the left of the screen and four initially stationary objects in the centre of the screen. As subjects watch, A moves horizontally across the screen until it contacts the lowest of the four objects. At that moment all four objects *simultaneously* begin moving in the directions shown by the arrows in the right-hand diagram, continuing to move at the same speed and in the same direction until they leave the frame. Observers typically report a very strong impression that A causes the movement of *all* the other objects. This strong causal impression occurs despite the facts that (i) A only contacts one of the four objects, (ii) there is a considerable spatial gap between each

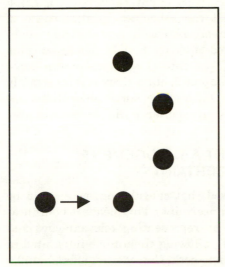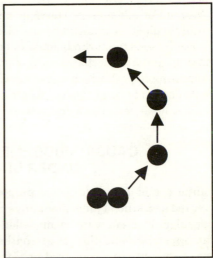

FIG. 7.1. Example Stimulus Sequence (from White & Milne, 1994).

adjacent pair of objects, amounting to twice their diameter (edge to edge), and (iii) the movement directions are grossly discrepant from A's, a condition which precludes ampliation of the movement (Michotte, 1963).

Our explanation for this was based on the notion, central to the causal powers theory, that the core of our concept of causation is the generative relations notion. Under this, causal relations involve the transmission of energy from cause to effect. In our stimuli several cues suggest that the four initially stationary objects are connected by energy transmission channels or are components of a physical system. These cues include the orderly array of initially stationary objects and the co-ordination in the time of onset and direction of their movement. Comparison with an imaginary sequence in which the same number of objects were arranged randomly in the frame, began to move at random times after contact from A, and moved in randomly chosen directions, gives an indication of just how much information these cues provide. Our proposal, therefore, is that the strength of the causal impression is determined by the extent to which the movement of the objects can be accounted for by the transmission of energy through the system from the point at which A contacts the array. A second experiment in which we systematically varied each of these cues to energy transmission gave support to this hypothesis. For example, when the objects moved off in randomly chosen directions, with everything else as in Fig. 7.1, the causal impression was virtually destroyed.

These findings suggest that the causal powers theory may offer the most satisfactory account of perceived causality. Much more work is necessary to confirm this, but one final observation is pertinent. To suppose that there is an inbuilt visual mechanism that can construct interpretations of multiple-object stimuli in terms of co-ordinated physical systems would surely be to stretch the bounds of credibility too far. There may be some kind of inbuilt mechanism, though currently I still prefer the iconic processing hypothesis discussed in Chapter 2, but if there is it is certainly not immune from effects of learning. Our findings surely show that automatic causal perception draws heavily on experience with collision events.

CAUSAL JUDGEMENT AS JUDGEMENT UNDER UNCERTAINTY

Einhorn and Hogarth (1986) proposed that causal judgement could be treated as a kind of judgement under uncertainty. This means in effect that causal judgement can be modelled by representing relevant cues and factors as probabilities (or strengths), allowing them to be integrated in what amounts to a computational framework. Consider an effect Y and a possible cause of Y, X. Einhorn and Hogarth distinguished between the gross and net strengths of the evidence that X causes Y. Gross strength is assessed for a single cause in isolation: net strength is assessed for a given possible cause against other possible causes. I shall first discuss judgement of gross strength. Einhorn and Hogarth treated judgement of gross strength under two main headings, the causal field and cues-to-causality.

The causal field is a notion taken from Mackie (1965; 1974; and see Chapter 1): it simply refers to a defined context within which causal analysis takes place. Causal fields can be defined in different ways, and the definition of a causal field has implications for causal judgement. The central point is that a causal candidate should be a difference-in-a-background; whether a factor is part of a background or not depends on how the causal field is defined. A factor may be a potential cause in one causal field, but part of the background or a mere condition in another, by virtue of being present in all cases within the causal field. Causal fields may define different dimensions of cases (e.g. consistency versus consensus), but as Einhorn and Hogarth pointed out they may also define different levels of enquiry. At one level, for example, a lightbulb coming on can be explained as due to the depression of a switch; at another level, it can be explained as caused by electric current flowing into the bulb; and so on. The kind of thing identified as the cause may therefore be determined in part by the causal field defined by the level of enquiry adopted. The causal field also affects the range of alternative explanations that will be considered, for the same reason: things that are conditions or part of the background in a given causal field will not be considered as possible alternatives.

Einhorn and Hogarth then stated (p.6): "once a causal field or context has been evoked, the gross strength of a causal link between X and Y depends on various cues-to-causality". In principle, anything might be used as a cue and incorporated in the calculation of gross strength, but Einhorn and Hogarth focused on those which subjects have been shown to use in experiments. Considering covariation, Einhorn and Hogarth asked why covariation need not be perfect for people to infer causation, and answered this by advocating a probabilistic formulation of Mackie's (1965; 1974) INUS condition notion (see Chapter 1). This formulation led them to an analysis of 2 x 2 contingency tables. The cells of a contingency table can be identified by letters as in Table 7.1.

Einhorn and Hogarth argued that cell b represents information about the conditionality of causation: for example, it includes cases in which X would have produced Y but for the lack of an enabling condition, or prevention by some other factor. Cell c represents information about alternative possible causes. These are the kinds of information that covariation data give us. For this reason (p.8), "the weights accorded the off-diagonal cells [b and c] should differ in causal judgements depending on whether multiplicity or conditionality is of greater concern. For covariation judgements, on the other hand, there should be more equal allocation of attention to all cells". In other words, while equal weighting is valid for covariation judgements, it is not necessarily valid for causal judgements. They cited studies suggesting that subjects have some sensitivity to this difference.

Einhorn and Hogarth also discussed the representation of temporal order, contiguity, and similarity in probabilistic formulations. They distinguished two types of similarity: physical similarity, and congruity of duration and magnitude of cause and effect. Einhorn and Hogarth argued that people may use these cues, despite their imperfect validity, because they have sufficient validity to reduce uncertainty in judgement. Uncertainty can be further reduced by the use of several cues, so long as they are complementary. They also discussed causal chains, and

TABLE 7.1
Use of Letters to Identify Cells in a Contingency Table

Possible cause	Effect	
	Present	Absent
Present	a	b
Absent	c	d

constructed a formula for assessing the strength of a causal chain from the strength of its component links.

Summarising the foregoing, judgement of the gross strength of possible cause X in producing Y is made with the aid of the variables listed in Table 7.2.

Three of these variables (Q_B, Q_T, and Q_L) are necessary in that if any of them has value 0, gross strength will also be judged as 0. As such, their effect on judgement of gross strength should be multiplicative. For the other variables this need not be the case. Einhorn and Hogarth therefore proposed the following equation for judging the gross strength of X as a possible cause of Y:

$$s(X,Y) = Q_T Q_B Q_L (\lambda_C Q_C + \lambda SQ'S)$$

where $s(X,Y)$ is the judged gross strength of X as a possible cause of Y, and λ represents attentional weight. Note that X may still be judged to be a probable cause of Y even if there is no correlation between X and Y. The equation does not include contiguity or congruity; Einhorn and Hogarth argued that these contribute to Q_L.

Net strength is calculated by taking account of alternative possible causes. The gross strength of any specific alternative can be calculated as for the cause under consideration. Einhorn and Hogarth noted that, under this process, a causal hypothesis is not disconfirmed but replaced by an alternative hypothesis. They proposed the following model of a process for updating the judged net strength of a possible cause:

$$S_k(X,Y) = s(X,Y) - \sum_{k=1}^{k} w_k s(Z_k,Y)$$

where $S_k(X,Y)$ is the judged net strength of X as a possible cause of Y after K alternatives have been discounted, $S(X,Y)$ is the judged gross strength of X as a possible cause of Y, $s(Z_k,Y)$ is the gross strength of alternative Z_k as a possible cause of Y, and w_k is the weight given to the Z_kth alternative. As they pointed out, this model can be interpreted in a variety of ways, one of which is as a Bayesian model. It is not a model of the adjustment of beliefs in the light of new evidence (a Bayesian model of this is discussed in the next section): rather, it is a model of the adjustment of causal judgement in the light of consideration of alternative hypotheses.

This is not a regularity-based theory. In principle, any cue could be incorporated in this approach, because any cue, variable, or factor can be formalised as a value in an equation for judging probability. The aim is to use the notion of causal judgement as judgement under uncertainty as a

TABLE 7.2

Variables Incorporated in Judgement of Gross Strength of
a Possible Cause (from Einhorn & Hogarth, 1986)

Variable	Definition
Q_B	Degree to which X is a difference-in-the-background
Q_C	Covariation of X with Y
Q_T	Temporal order of X and Y
Q_G	Contiguity in time and space
Q_S	Similarity of cause and effect Congruity of duration and magnitude Physical similarity (Q's)
Q_L	Causal chain strength

way of integrating diverse and fragmented strands of the literature under a common framework. The framework also holds the promise of using computed values for variables included in the equation to predict causal judgements.

Einhorn and Hogarth made no attempt to explain why some things are treated as cues to causality and others are not; in this sense, the model does not address causal understanding at all. This was not the intention. But if they are not guilty of throwing the baby out with the bath water, they can perhaps be accused of failing to put the baby in the bath in the first place. The model falls foul of the sufficiency problem that I have discussed elsewhere (White, 1993). Cues to causality are not used blindly to infer causal relations: The judgement made from a given pattern of evidence depends not on the weighting of cues but on their interpretation. This can be seen most clearly if I repeat my parody of their example of causal judgement. Here first is their example (p.4):

Imagine that a watch face has been hit by a hammer and the glass breaks. How likely was the force of the hammer the cause of the breakage? Because no explicit context is given, an implicitly neutral context is invoked in which the cues-to-causality point strongly to a causal relation; that is, the force of the hammer precedes the breakage in time, there is high covariation between the glass breaking (or not) with the force of solid objects, contiguity in time and space is high, and there is congruity (similarity) between the length and strength of cause and effect. Moreover, it is difficult to discount the causal link because there are few alternatives to consider.

This quotation makes reference to the factors identified in the formula for judging gross strength. If this were a valid account, then satisfaction of the cues listed would be sufficient for causal inference. This is not the case, as can be seen with the example of two consecutive strides in a walk. How likely is it that the first stride was the cause of the second? Assume, as Einhorn and Hogarth did for their example, a neutral context because no extra information is given. In this case, as Einhorn and Hogarth put it, the cues-to-causality point strongly to a causal relation; that is, the first stride precedes the second in time, there is high covariation between the occurrence of one stride and the occurrence of the next (moreover, it is possible to observe repeated conjunctions of strides); contiguity in time and space is high, and there is congruity between the length and strength of cause and effect (i.e. one stride looks very much like the other). In short, the two strides fit the criteria for ascription of a causal relation just as well as the hammer and breaking watch glass do, yet people do not ascribe a causal relation. The cues listed are, therefore, not sufficient as an account of causal inference. The reason they are not sufficient is that causal judgement is not a matter of integrating cues as weighted variables in an equation: It is a matter of interpreting cues, and interpretation depends on specific acquired beliefs. Equations do not capture interpretations.

Take a slightly closer look at the examples. In both, congruity and contiguity are high, and Einhorn and Hogarth argued that Q_L, causal mechanism or causal chain strength, is in part a function of congruity and contiguity. The strides example shows that this cannot be the case: However people work out what sort of causal mechanism is operating, or indeed whether there is one at all, it is not simply by relying on cues such as congruity and contiguity. In the strides example, a causal relation is not inferred even though both congruity and contiguity are high. In other examples, used in research by Shultz (1982b; Shultz, Fisher et al., 1986) and Anderson (1990), causal connections *are* inferred even though congruity and contiguity are low. Where contiguity and generative relations cues clash, people reliably prefer generative relations cues as a basis for inferring causal relations. Clearly, use of abstract cues such as contiguity is subordinate to use of beliefs about the particular things involved.

The Einhorn and Hogarth approach is limited in two further respects. It is comparatively deliberative, and it is hard to imagine how it could account for automatic causal perception. To return to the hammer and watch glass example, perceiving the relation between hammer and watch glass as causal is surely not a matter of weighing up and integrating cues in the manner they describe; one simply perceives the relation as causal. Such causal perception is underpinned by the basic concept of causation as involving the production of effects by the operation of causal powers of things, and it depends on a single cue—the perception of a generative relation (Shultz, 1982b; White, 1989). Einhorn and Hogarth did not include or account for generative relations cues and this is a serious failing.

In addition, the model does not account for causal learning: the equation for adjustment of judged gross strength of a cause deals with the consideration of alternative causal hypotheses, not with the integration of new evidence. This particular objection is not fatal to their approach because it seems feasible to model causal learning in a Bayesian framework, using an equation similar to their equation for calculating net strength. The next approach to be considered incorporates something very like this.

THE ADAPTIVE CHARACTER OF CAUSAL INFERENCE

Anderson (1990) has treated causal inference under a general approach to human cognition as adaptive. Under this approach we attempt to determine what would be optimal behaviour given the structure of the environment and the goals of the actor: Anderson claimed (p.3) that "we can predict behaviour of humans by assuming that they will do what is optimal". The ground for assuming this is the claim (pp.26–27) that the human being is "a construction that has been, to some degree, optimized to its environment by evolution. The behaviour computed by our cognitive mechanisms must be optimized to some degree and in some sense. If we could only specify that degree and sense, we would be in a position to place enormous constraints on our proposals for cognitive mechanisms". Cognitive mechanisms are not perfectly optimised because of constraints that depend on evolutionary history: For this reason the assumption of optimisation will explain more in some areas than in others. Nonetheless, Anderson set out to explore what he called the "general principle of rationality" (p.28): "The cognitive system operates at all times to optimize the adaptation of the behaviour of the organism". The term rationality is being used in a specific sense here: To be rational in this sense is to be optimal in terms of achieving human goals. This is to be distinguished from rationality in the sense of conformity to normative rules of deductive inference.

Anderson (1990, p. 29) proposed that developing a theory in a rationality framework involved the following steps:

1. Precisely specify what are the goals of the cognitive system.
2. Develop a formal model of the environment to which the system is adapted ...

3. Make the minimal assumptions about computational limitations. This is where one specifies the constraints of evolutionary history. To the extent that these assumptions are minimal, the analysis is powerful.
4. Derive the optimal behavioural function given items 1 through 3.
5. Examine the empirical literature to see if the predictions of the behavioural function are confirmed.
6. If the predictions are off, iterate.

In the case of causal inference, the first step is accomplished by assuming that the goal of causal inference is accurate prediction. This seems a dubious first step. The corresponding tenet from the Heiderian tradition of causal attribution research is that the goals of causal attribution are understanding, prediction, and control. It is not difficult to think of cases where causal inference is in the service of control and not prediction: for example, when I observe a decline in my performance on the squash court, the point of causal analysis is not to predict how I will do in the future, but to remedy the problem. However, the assumption of the goal of prediction is useful to Anderson, because it enables him to model causal judgement as a kind of likelihood judgement. It is difficult to develop a precise formal model of the environment because the structure of the world relevant to causal inference is rather complex and, more to the point, not known in many cases. While acknowledging this problem, Anderson proceeded by developing a Bayesian model of causal judgement.

As we have seen in Chapter 6, most other regularity-based approaches such as the probabilistic contrast model are essentially models of inference from contingency data. The Bayesian approach is different in that it integrates evidence with prior beliefs; that is, any belief the judge may have about the causal relation before the data in question are added. Essentially, it models change in belief as a function of evidence, and quantifies prior beliefs and the weight of evidence, expressed as conditional probabilities. This can be seen in Anderson's equation for generating a prediction:

$$P(E/C) = \sum P(i/C)\, P(E/i)$$

where $P(E/C)$ is the probability of a given event (E) occurring conditional on a set of cues (C), $P(i/C)$ is the probability of causal rule i applying in the presence of cues C, and $P(E/i)$ is the probability of the event E occurring when causal rule i applies. The use of the term $\sum$ is noteworthy: $P(i/C)\, P(E/i)$ is calculated for every causal rule under consideration, including the possibility that there is no (known) causal rule. Anderson illustrated the use of the equation with an example in which there were two possible rules:

(1) flipping a switch would cause a light to go on, and (2) stomping our feet would cause a house of cards to collapse. We can then use the equation to predict the probability of either effect (the light going on or the house of cards collapsing) in the presence of the act of flipping the switch (the cue), once we have assigned probabilities to each of the terms in it.

Anderson's second equation concerns the derivation of P(i/C) (for example, the probability that the rule that flipping a switch would cause a light to go on applies in the presence of the act of flipping the switch):

$$P(i/C) = \frac{P(i)\ P(C/i)}{\sum P(i)\ P(C/i)}$$

where P(i) is the probability of the rule holding irrespective of any cues (i.e. its base-rate) and P(C/i) is the probability that cues C would occur in an application of i. The terms in the equation can be modified slightly to take account of instances where we are uncertain about a possible causal rule.

What these equations imply is that accurate prediction—the goal of rational causal inference—depends upon accurate values for P(i) (or Con(i) where degrees of uncertainty are involved) and P(C/i). For P(i), Anderson developed a Bayesian model describing, as already stated, the modification of the probability of a causal hypothesis holding as a function of the prior probability (belief) and evidence. Anderson applied this model to the analysis of 2 x 2 contingency tables, and argued that evidence supports the contention that people interpret contingency data in a rational Bayesian manner. Studies such as that by Schustack and Sternberg (1981) have shown that people tend to give unequal weights to the cells of a contingency table. This is often interpreted as showing bias or inaccuracy in causal analysis, but Anderson argued that unequal weighting can be rational, depending on the prior model that is adopted. It is, of course, the prior model that contingency-based models neglect, and for that reason such models are in no position to assess whether causal judgement is rational or not.

Anderson (p.155) then discussed P(C/i), which concerns "the match of the rule to the context". Essentially, a rational rule is a rule that is well matched to the context. Anderson therefore considered various cues to causality, including temporal contiguity, spatial contiguity, and similarity, in an attempt to ascertain whether the use of such rules is rational, in the sense of matching the context in which they are called upon. Because the Bayesian approach incorporates prior beliefs, Anderson is able to accommodate any sort of beliefs and cues in his analysis. He argued that the use of cues such as temporal contiguity depends on the person's model of the situation, and that people are rational in their matching of cues to situations. For example, in a situation where the causal hypothesis concerned a possible cause producing an effect by vibration, subjects tended to rely on temporal and spatial contiguity cues. In an otherwise similar situation where the possible cause was a ball rolling along a passage from an entry point to the location of the effect, subjects abandoned temporal and spatial contiguity and judged causation in accord with cues to the velocity of the ball. Anderson concluded (p.162): "the right analysis of spatial and temporal contiguity is not that they are absolute cues to causality, as some have argued; rather, it is that they are rational cues to causal attribution when a transfer of force model is appropriate, and such models are most typically appropriate".

Anderson also reported a simulation of an experiment originally carried out by Siegler (1976). Siegler's results had seemed to show that children aged five did not discriminate between necessary conditions, sufficient conditions, and necessary and sufficient conditions when identifying the cause of an effect. Anderson's analysis showed (p.172), however, that these children were "behaving as optimally as we can expect, given their prior assumption about which was the more plausible cause and given how often they chose to attend to the computer as a possible cause". In other words, the children had prior beliefs which they modified in the light of evidence, but their scanning of the evidence was also affected by those beliefs. Given this, their modification of their beliefs was rational, in the sense of conforming to Bayesian principles.

In general, then, people's use of cues to causation accords well with the actual validity of those cues, once allowance is made for the role of prior beliefs and general cognitive limitations. Anderson's argument is that such use of cues is part of rational causal inference, and that the evidence about cue use supports the claim that people make causal inferences in a rational, adaptive manner. Although this account may have much to offer the study of causal judgement, two problems can be identified at present. First, although beliefs are incorporated into the model of judgement, Anderson's account says nothing about the origins of causal concepts. One cannot create a concept by Bayesian analysis; the weighing of probabilities, no matter how it is done, generates nothing other than judgements of probability. The conceptual foundations of such judgements must be explained in some other way, therefore.

Second, under a Bayesian approach, causal judgement is responsive to evidence. People may select cues in a rational manner, and they may weight prior beliefs and evidence in different ways but, despite this, causal judgement should change in response to evidence in a manner that is predictable if one has appropriate information about weightings and the selection of evidence or cues. Not only is it predictable, it is also gradual if the record of experience is incremented on an instance-by-instance basis. An instance consistent with a certain causal hypothesis shifts the judged probability of that hypothesis being correct by a small amount. Further instances shift it by further small amounts. The problem with this is that it does not fit much of the evidence concerning changes in causal judgement. Kuhn (1989) showed in her review that children and, in some cases, adults treat evidence in a less formally predictable way. They select evidence in accordance not only with cues but also with the hypothesis under test. Their causal judgements are not so much judgements of probability as judgements of the range of application of a hypothesis: a hypothesis holds, for example, for these confirming instances, and does not hold for those disconfirming instances. Instances that do not conform to the hypothesis do not lead to reduction of the judged probability of that hypothesis, but are interpreted as exemplifying some other hypothesis. Schauble (1990) found that shifts in causal hypotheses are not gradual but abrupt: often a small amount of evidence, such as a single instance, would prompt the generation of an entirely new hypothesis. Also important, from the point of view of the idea that people are rational Bayesian judges, is Schauble's finding that the subjects who did best, in terms of discovering the causal rules that governed the system under test, did so by getting the right hypothesis and testing it, not by using the evidence to modify their prior beliefs. At present it seems dubious whether these findings can be accommodated within a model of people as rational Bayesian judges.

LAY EPISTEMO-LOGIC

Kruglanski (1980) has proposed a theory of lay epistemology. The theory provides a general framework for inference, and causal attribution is treated as a special case. The general framework is the epistemic process, which comprises two steps: problem formulation and problem resolution. In the first stage, "the epistemic problem is conceived of as a set of mutually exclusive propositions whose validity a knower might wish to assess" (Kruglanski, 1980, p.76). Kruglanski emphasised (p.71) that the epistemic problem must be teleologically functional: "the knower assumes that the problem's resolution will serve some (intrinsic or extrinsic) end of importance to the individual".

Once an epistemic problem has been formulated, it is resolved by deductive inference. Information is relevant to the epistemic problem, and used in its resolution, if it is consistent or inconsistent with the implications of the alternative propositions in the problem. The key to problem resolution is non-common deducibility (p.73): "*An implication is noncommonly deducible from a set of propositions if the state of affairs it affirms is consistent with some of the propositions and inconsistent with the remaining propositions*" (italics in original). People therefore seek evidence that is validationally functional, in other words (p.73), "noncommonly deducible from the problem's constituent propositions". "In the course of problem resolution, the knower is assumed to (a) deduce from the alternative propositions (as he/she understood them) implications that might differentiate among them, (b) seek evidence regarding those implications, and (c) come to feel greater confidence in propositions consistent with the evidence and lesser confidence in those inconsistent with the evidence" (p.77).

An extension to the theory was presented by Kruglanski, Baldwin, and Shelagh (1983, p.83): "At some point along the line the individual stops generating hypotheses and attains 'closure' on a given belief". They called this "freezing". The occurrence of freezing depends on (1) the individual's capacity to generate hypotheses and (2) the presence of three motivations relating to three features of beliefs: the need for structure (beliefs provide structure and organisation); the need for specific conclusions (beliefs have specific content); and the need for validity (beliefs are assumed to be valid). These needs are not ends in themselves, but arise out of other needs and motives: They are teleologically functional. The first two needs tend to freeze the epistemic process, but the third tends to unfreeze it, because of the danger that premature closure on an epistemic problem may result in an invalid belief.

Kruglanski (1980) and Kruglanski et al. (1983) then applied these general ideas to the specific case of causal attribution. Kruglanski (1980) made two proposals about causal attribution theories: (1) different attribution theories address different kinds of epistemic problem; and (2) the relevance and use of different attribution criteria or cues to causal inference (e.g. covariation) depend on their value with respect to noncommon deducibility. The theories of Kelley (1967), Jones and Davis (1965) and Weiner et al. (1972) differ because they apply to different specific content areas. All of them can be modelled within the terms of lay epistemo-logic: "the general principle for ascribing causality is that of deducibility. And the 'attributional criteria' are nothing more than premises some people might generate to evaluate plausible causes for some effect" (Kruglanski et al., 1983, p.88).

Causal inferences are rendered in basically the same way as non-causal inferences: specific causal hypotheses are generated in accordance with the knower's generative capacity affected by the person's past knowledge and the momentary availability of various ideas. The tendency to continue generating different hypotheses also depends on the individual's epistemic motivations for structure, validity, and conclusional contents. Once generated, the causal hypotheses proceed to be validated in accordance with the principle of deducibility, or logical consistency. (p.94)

The theory of lay epistemo-logic is an ambitious attempt to construct a general framework for inference processes, and is particularly welcome for its emphasis on teleological relevance, as opposed to the content-free aim of understanding which lies at the heart of traditional approaches to causal attribution. The theory does suffer from a number of problems, however.

First, a central claim of the theory is that problem resolution always proceeds by means of deductive logic. In fact, Kruglanski et al. (1983, p.86) stated even more specifically: "all knowledge is validated deductively from propositions of the general form 'only if x then y' ". Even if one can accept that all knowledge is validated deductively, the particular form of the propositions on which problem resolution operates rules out most of deductive reasoning, apparently arbitrarily. Deductive logic works on several forms of proposition and with many and complex rules of inference (Langer, 1967; Lemmon, 1965). The deductive inference rules most commonly utilised in psychological investigations are *modus ponens* and *modus tollens* (Evans, 1982): these rules both operate on propositions of the form "if x then y", which is not the form favoured by Kruglanski et al. Asserting not-x allows one to infer not-y from "only if x then y", but allows no valid inference about y from "if x then y" (inferring not-y would be the fallacy of affirming the consequent).

Leaving this aside, the general claim that people always use deductive reasoning is implausible. Lay command of deductive logic is notoriously imperfect (Evans, 1982), and it appears unlikely that people proceed by inferring conclusions with the use of rules of inference at all: instead, evidence tends to favour the idea that people read off conclusions from patterns of representation of information in mental models (Johnson-Laird, 1983). Mental models can be constructed for many kinds of inference, and there is no reason to suppose that people use them only for problems formulated in a manner appropriate to the use of deductive inference rules. In any case, the claim that all inference is deductive is not supported by evidence. There are many ways in which people make inductive inferences, and moreover some of those ways are put to use in causal inference (Holland et al., 1986; Holyoak & Nisbett, 1988; Kunda & Nisbett, 1986; Locke & Pennington, 1982).

The distinction between problem formulation and problem resolution is also difficult to sustain. The key to the problem lies in Kruglanski's (1980, p.70) assertion that "the epistemic problem is conceived of as a set of mutually exclusive propositions whose validity a knower might wish to assess". Validity is then assessed with the aid of non-common deducibility. The difficulty here is that the assertion entails a requirement for the propositions included in the problem to be formulated in parallel, that is to say before the problem resolution stage begins. There is strong evidence that people do not approach causal attribution problems in this way. In several studies Shaklee and Fischhoff (1982) found evidence that people were proceeding with truncated serial search strategies. These are strategies in which one possible cause is assessed at a time. Under this type of strategy people only search for evidence relevant to a single possible cause under test, which of course need not be the kind of evidence necessary for alternatives to be eliminated by the criterion of non-common deducibility. The strategy is truncated because the search stops when the role of one possible cause is confirmed to the judge's satisfaction. For example, in experiment 4 (Shaklee & Fischhoff, 1982, p.526) "subjects continued to prefer questions about an implicated cause even when its implication is certain, consistent with a truncated information search". The subjects did not investigate other possible causes. This clearly violates the logic of the epistemic process, and therefore disconfirms the hypothesis that people are proceeding in the way postulated by Kruglanski.

A further problem with Kruglanski's account is that the meaning of the word "implication" is not clear. Although the reference to deductive logic suggests that the word ought to be meant in its formal sense, referring to the use of valid rules of formal inference, it is apparent from Kruglanski's account that it cannot be meant that way. For example (p.73), "one implication of the concept of causality (as intuitively grasped by most people) is covariation of the cause and the effect". But causality does not logically imply this: what Kruglanski means must be a kind of psychological implication. The problem of defining psychological implication has been with us since the days of cognitive dissonance theory (Aronson, 1969; Festinger, 1957), and its consequence is that, in the absence of correct definition, it is impossible to generate exact predictions about how people will draw inferences in particular epistemic problems.

Kruglanski did report some evidence supporting some of the propositions of the theory. For example, Kruglanski, Hamel, Maides, and Schwartz (1978) presented subjects with one of two objectives and asked them which of two epistemic problems they preferred to resolve. In accordance with the principle that the epistemic problem must be teleologically relevant, subjects tended to prefer to resolve the epistemic problem that was teleologically relevant to the objective they had been set. This evidence is not strong, however. Hilton (1990) pointed out that the subjects were engaged in a social interaction with the experimenter, and that such interactions are governed by Grice's (1975) conversational maxims. One of these is the maxim of relevance, which states that people should answer the question they have been asked. Hilton's point was that the subjects of Kruglanski et al. (1978, p.77) were simply conforming to this maxim, by expressing "most interest in the information that was relevant to the question that they had been asked". Conformity to rules of conversation carries no implications for intra-individual inference processes.

CONCLUSIONS

I chose these particular approaches to causal judgement not only because they have been worked out in most detail and depth, but also to illustrate the diversity, not to say divergence, detectable in what strikes me as a rather sparse literature. Despite the diversity, certain common tendencies are detectable. The approaches tend to emphasise, in different ways, the importance of the *function* of causal judgement for the individual, in the form of rationality defined as adaptiveness, teleological functionality, or as rendering the world comprehensible and predictable. They incorporate procedures for updating causal beliefs and judgements by some form of *hypothesis-testing* or integration of evidence with prior beliefs. They tend to conceptualise causal judgement as operating within a defined problem space or *causal field*, which may affect the judgement generated. They tend to exhibit, in different ways, a desire to model processes in *computational formulations* in such a way as to enable quantitative predictions for causal judgement.

I have perhaps said enough already to betray my view that the last of these is doomed to fail because people are not blind empiricists, but instead operate with a sophisticated set of causal concepts by means of which they assign multiple causal roles in the causal interpretation of events. It is the common weakness of these approaches that they fail to address what makes causal judgement *causal,* and that they fail to account for the variety of causal concepts that people employ in the interpretations of events. For example, people are capable of judging that a football smashed a window, not only because the event itself supplies *generative relations* cues, but also because they use their understanding that a football has the *causal power* to smash a window (i.e. its power to smash is great enough to overcome the window's *resistance* to being smashed) under the *releasing condition* of forcible contact between them, but that the smashing could have been *prevented* if the window had been made of reinforced glass, or if certain *enabling conditions,* such as the ball's being inflated, had not been met. There cannot be a computational formulation of the multiple causal roles in this example, because a given causal role does not have a fixed empirical relation to the effect being explained (White, in press).

Having said that, the first three characteristics of the approaches, emphasising function, hypothesis testing, and the causal field, are undoubtedly valuable advances in our understanding of causal judgement. Different models may disagree on just what the functions of causal judgement are, on how people test hypotheses, and on how the causal field is defined, but it seems unlikely that any successful model of causal judgement could afford to neglect any of these things. To make a link with earlier parts of the book, while research has made progress in understanding how hypothesis testing develops (Kuhn, 1989), there is plainly a need for more developmental research on the issues of function and the causal field. People surely learn how to define causal fields for causal judgement, even if the definition is strongly affected by salience and attentional factors, and investigating this should be a priority for future research.

CHAPTER EIGHT

The Naïve Theorist and Causal Powers: A Synopsis

I shall begin this chapter by painting a general portrait of the naïve theorist. Recent developments in several areas of research suggest that it is appropriate to depict people as constructors of knowledge. This portrait is not the last word on the subject, but it does have the merit of being a coherent account which is, moreover, consistent with the best ideas that research has given us to date.

Throughout the lifespan, though especially during the formative learning years of childhood, we develop increasingly sophisticated and complex theories. These are organised groups of concepts with a defined domain of application, erected upon metaphysical foundations laid down early in life. The components of the theories are organised by relations of existential dependence (White, 1993), as well as by relations of other kinds: it is the relations of existential dependence that govern the resistance to change of any component of a theory. Components that have little else existentially dependent on them are relatively susceptible to change; components that have a great deal existentially dependent on them are relatively impervious to change.

The basic process of theory development is through hypothesis generation and testing (e.g. Kuhn, 1989). There are many methods of hypothesis generation, which I summarised towards the end of Chapter 4. Perhaps most important among these are the various inductive methods, including generalisation from patterns or single instances, analogical reasoning, and the use of simple heuristics.

The primary criterion for evaluating hypotheses is *function*. A hypothesis is incorporated into a theory if to do so is functional for the person concerned—i.e. if it assists them with their practical concerns (White, 1993)—and not if it is not functional. In effect, people believe what it suits them to believe, taking due account of their situation, concerns, goals, and so on. There are two other subsidiary criteria:

1. Evidential criteria. Often it is functional for a hypothesis to be correct or not obviously incorrect. (This does not mean that it is also functional for a hypothesis to be a complete account, only that it be correct as far as it goes: practical concerns tend to dictate what part of the truth people concentrate on.) When this is the case criteria of evidence are used to evaluate a hypothesis. People may use evidence in many forms from single instances through to abstraction of patterns and regularities from multiple instances. There are two important features of the use of evidential criteria: (1) The gathering of evidence is not passive but active, directed by the hypothesis under test and the reasons (practical concerns) for testing it, although people are opportunists and will respond to salient evidence that presents itself under some circumstances (functional criteria again). (2) Hypotheses are never falsified. Disconfirming instances do not disconfirm a hypothesis, but merely limit inductive generalisations that would otherwise be unlimited or insufficiently limited. That is the function of disconfirming instances. (People also learn rules for limiting inductive generalisations, and these rules relate to category systems.) If a hypothesis ever expires, it does so in virtue of the fact that it is no longer useful, that it does nothing for the person who holds it, that it is simply never employed.

2. By degree of fit with existing theories. For example, a hypothesis that is well grounded in the metaphysical axioms of the system will be more likely to endure, and to be formulated in the first place than one that is not (*ceteris paribus*).

We should not think of hypotheses as being confirmed or falsified; we should think of them as persisting or not persisting, being used (useful) or not, having a function or being temporarily or permanently without function.

This general approach can be applied in every domain of knowledge. After all, there is no reason to suppose that infants and children make the same categorical distinctions between different branches of knowledge that we as adults and scientists do, and any domain in which there are regularities and patterns can in principle be approached through hypothesis generation and testing. Consider some examples:

Causation—causal relations, rules, and laws.
Action.
Characteristics of persons (e.g. personality theory).
Moral rules (Smetana, 1993).
Social-conventional rules (Smetana, 1993) and scripts.
Comprehension of stories (Black, Galambos, & Read, 1984; Hudson, 1993), episode structures, interaction sequences.
Categories, and characteristics of things in categories.
Naïve geography (White, 1993): rules about the organisation of (things in) space, places where things are and their reasons for being there.

The naïve theorist develops an understanding of all these domains through hypothesis generation and testing, building theoretical structures in the process. Although the child's cognitive capacities develop, it seems unlikely that knowledge structures at the most basic levels undergo radical transformation, or that their development proceeds through a series of discrete stages. It seems more likely that the psychological metaphysics of understanding are established early in life, probably during the first two years of life, and persist unaltered thereafter as a foundation for less basic knowledge structures which are acquired, elaborated, and modified as development proceeds.

ORIGINS

In the beginning there is no differentiation between action and causation. Infants' only understanding is the experience of producing their own actions. This is the source for not only the basic concept of action, but also the basic understanding of causation in terms of the production of effects. The course of development through infancy is not well known. At some stage, however, infants develop the following concepts, probably at first in relation to their own actions: *causal power*, meaning the specificity of action–effect relations coupled with the stability of causally relevant properties of things, acquired by stage 5 of the sensorimotor period; *releasing condition*, meaning the requirement of certain conditions for a given action to produce a given effect, possibly originating in the appreciation of spatial relations (around stage 4 of the sensorimotor period), or possibly through perception of transfer of properties relations in the launching effect; and *liability*, meaning the capacity of things to be acted upon in certain ways, again with specificity and stability, and again possibly acquired by stage 5 of the sensorimotor period.

Also at some as yet unknown stage during infancy, infants begin to distinguish between action and causation. This is not merely an appreciation of the fact that other things may also be centres of causal powers and the production of effects. It is, eventually, a conceptual distinction between things that have an "I" that produces their actions, and things that merely produce effects through the operation of their causal powers. Infants may not at first know where to draw the line between the former and the latter, but have in principle mastered the conceptual distinction by the end of the sensorimotor period.

By the age of two years, then, infants are in possession of two theories, of action and causation respectively, having a common origin in the experience of producing action and retaining some degree of similarity, but also conceptually distinct from each other:

1. Theory of action. "I" produce action, where it is understood to be up to the actor what he or she does. Action is limited by the range of causal powers at the actor's disposal; these do not cause action themselves, but are understood as instruments used by the actor. For actions upon other things, the actor produces a given effect by a specific kind of action upon a specific kind of thing under specific conditions, that is, actions upon things involve reference to the causal powers of the actor, the liabilities of the thing acted upon, and the releasing conditions which allow the action to have its effect.

2. Theory of causation. Causation involves some causal power of a thing operating to produce a given effect under a given condition, that is, the concepts of causal power, liability, and releasing condition apply as they do to action, but it is the causal power and not the actor that produces the effect, and the property of necessitation applies: If appropriate conditions are set up, the power must operate to produce its effect, and cannot choose otherwise. The causal relation is understood as generative, which is essentially the concept of efficacy without the actor.

These theories, coupled with the psychological metaphysics of the being–happening distinction (White, 1993), constitute the metaphysics of action and causation: They form a conceptual foundation for all subsequent developments, and never change once established. Children may learn different rules for applying the various concepts to different things, but the concepts themselves are fixed.

DEVELOPMENT: ACTION

Taking action first, subsequent developments here mainly concern the kinds of mental state that are usually antecedent to action. The pivotal stage in development is mastery of a simple version of the intentional theory of action, as investigated by Bartsch and Wellman (1989). In the terms I prefer, action is understood as underlain by two functional concepts, a pro-attitude, which is in effect the motivational component of action, and the action belief, which is a component with the informational function of telling the actor how to achieved the desired end. There is no causal necessitation in this model. In the intentional theory of action, the pro-attitude–belief combination is a cause of action, but in children's understanding of action, as in Taylor's (1966) theory, the only cause of action is the actor. The actor can always choose to act or not to act on the basis of a given combination of pro-attitude and action belief. Moreover, not all actions need have any pro-attitude or action belief as their antecedent: Only the actor's performance of action is necessary.

The main development in later childhood is the growing appreciation of sources of consistency in behaviour across instances. At first, children may understand object properties as a source of consistency in responses to them. Later, understanding of the role of personality develops, from traits as underlying consistency in behaviour across similar situations, through traits as underlying cross-situational consistencies in behaviour, to traits as a theory of individuating consistency. This is probably the primary role of traits in the understanding of action throughout life; evidence suggests that they are rarely called upon to explain individual actions, but may be more important as accounts of multiple actions, or consistent tendencies in action.

For adults, as for children, action is understood as performed or produced by the actor. It is up to the actor what he or she does, and in this sense the actor is the only cause of action. The range of actions possible for an actor is delimited by the actor's causal powers. These powers constitute a resource on which the actor draws in the performance of an action. The actor cannot perform actions which the actor does not have the power to perform. This limitation is absolute: Behaviours of the actor brought about in other ways, e.g. by powers external to the actor operating upon liabilities of the actor, are not actions. Every action involves the actor drawing upon the resource of powers.

Powers may be of various kinds. This is the area least well explored by research so far, but some speculative remarks can be made, drawing mainly upon the work of Harré (1983) and Kenny (1989). The most important characteristic of a power in relation to action is the extent to which it urges a person towards one action rather than another. If one can loosely define a disposition as an inclination towards one specific action rather than another, then some powers incline the actor more strongly than others. Some powers do not incline at all, but are merely part of a repertoire, a capacity. Abilities, such as the ability to speak French, are generally of this sort. Others may incline the actor in a weak but general way. Such powers may include traits, for example, which I analysed as a theory of individuating consistency in behaviour: A trait of generosity may incline the actor towards generous behaviour in any situation where there is an opportunity for behaviour of that kind. Other powers may be both more specific and stronger in their force: An attitude of concern for the environment, for example, may incline the actor quite strongly towards a specific kind of generous behaviour (e.g. donation of money to conservation organisations), but not at all towards other kinds of generous behaviour. Other powers may be even stronger, but specific to times as well as to objects: Many desires may be like that. These are not categorical distinctions: Traits, attitudes, abilities, desires, and other types of mental state and characteristic vary in strength, as well as in specificity and stability. The purpose of this paragraph is simply to note that strength of inclination is an important variable in respect of causal powers.

In the theory of action, powers do not compel behaviour. It is always up to the actor what to do. Powers make it easier for a person to do one thing than another; when an inclination to do that thing becomes very strong, as in strong desires, it may be hard for the person to resist, but it is always possible in principle. If there was a case where it was thought literally impossible for the actor to resist the desire, it is doubtful whether people would regard the resultant behaviour as action at all; instead, it would be interpreted under the theory of causation (see White, 1993, pp.246–262, for more on this).

In explaining the origination of action (as opposed to giving meaning to action) people refer to reasons. That is, given a repertoire or range of possible actions, they explain their choice of a particular action by giving their reasons for that action. These reasons most commonly refer to the desire or goal or purpose which the action was intended to fulfil, or to the belief (often identified elliptically by referring to objective facts or states of affairs) that the action chosen was a suitable way of attaining the desire or goal or purpose. They may also, however, refer to any causal power underlying the action that functioned as an inclination, urging the actor this way rather than that: It is therefore in their function as inclinations that such things as abilities, traits, and attitudes enter reasons explanations. Of course, the appropriateness of any particular kind of mental state or characteristic in a reasons explanation depends on the kind of question that has been asked: for example, where the question concerns multiple instances, or consistency over time, reference to characteristics enduring across those instances is required. Traits are therefore usually more relevant in explanations for multiple actions than for single actions.

In the case of action it is appropriate to identify two main kinds of action. One is freely chosen actions, where the actor simply does, or chooses to do, one thing rather than another. For example, I may just choose to raise my arm in the air, and in explaining such an action I refer to nothing other than my own mental states (including beliefs) and powers. The other kind is what I have designated power-resistance relations (White, 1992a; 1993). These are specifically interactions between the actor and some thing, person, state of affairs, etc., acted upon. The effect or outcome is a function of both the powers and actions of the actor and the liabilities or resistances of the thing acted upon. Whether a plate smashes when struck by a hammer depends on the power of the hammer, the fragility of the plate, and the conditions of the interaction, such as the amount of force with which the hammer is applied to the plate. Likewise, whether a person passes an exam depends on the powers of the person, the liability or resistance of the exam (i.e. whether it is easy or difficult) and the conditions of the interaction, which include how the person actually behaves (what they actually do, how hard they try, etc.), and causally relevant external factors and conditions. The only difference between action and causation in such interactions is that in the case of action it is up to the actor what they do—in other words, the set of concepts specific to the understanding of action is used to interpret the actor's contribution to the interaction.

In the case of the actor's contribution to action of any kind, external conditions provide opportunities, not releasing conditions as in causation. That is, when conditions appropriate for a certain action are set up, that action does not follow as a matter of necessity, but only as a matter of the actor's choice. Opportunities relate to both the timing of action (e.g. when exactly to swing the racquet at the ball) and the availability of an opportunity for it (e.g. the presence of a charity box as an opportunity for donation).

For adults, actions are understood as embedded in a complex network of social episodes and rules, extended plans and goals, and multifarious antecedent mental states. Pro-attitudes are understood as having their sources in other mental states such as goals, desires, attitudes, and emotions, though whether these are best conceptualised in terms of their intrinsic qualities as mental states or in terms of their functional significance for the actor remains open to question. Action beliefs are seen as having their source in other beliefs and attitudes and in perception; again, a functional characterisation of these things as providing justification, whether in the form of evidence or in terms of beneficial effects of the belief, may be appropriate. In general, actions are interpreted by adults with the aid of sophisticated acquired social knowledge structures, including syntagmatic and paradigmatic rules, more or less elaborate goal structures, scripts, schemas, and so on. There is still much to learn about how these knowledge structures develop.

DEVELOPMENT: CAUSATION

Development related to the theory of causation can be summarised more simply. The basic theory of causation is at some stage associated with the idea of causal necessitation, or the principle of determinism. Under this, when a causal power operates to produce an effect, it does so as a matter of necessity and is not seen as having the capacity to choose whether to operate or not. There is no causal centre equivalent to the "I" that produces action in the case of causation: Causal powers are simply properties of things which operate when suitable releasing conditions are met.

What follows is mainly a summary of the mature causal powers theory, with some indications of developmental change where appropriate. Causal processing can be either automatic or controlled. Although related in that they share the same basic concept of the causal connection, automatic and controlled processing operate under different circumstances and in different ways. I shall begin with automatic causal processing.

Imagine that someone observes a plate struck by a hammer, upon which the plate breaks. In this case, the observer simply perceives the causal connection. By this I mean not that they literally and accurately see an actual causal connection, but that causal processing in this case is part of the automatic processes of visual (and perhaps auditory) perception. It does not require attentive deliberation, and it is constructive, interpretive, or inferential to no greater or lesser extent than perception in general is. Such automatic causal processing depends on two things:

1.   The basic concept of causation as involving generative mechanisms in which the causal powers of things produce certain effects under certain releasing conditions.

2.   More specific beliefs about the causal powers, releasing conditions, liabilities, and effects that pertain on the occasion in question. People become familiar with or acquire beliefs about the causal powers of a large number of things and types of thing, and it is through this familiarity that causal processing of events involving those things becomes automatic. In the case under consideration, causal perception involves the use of beliefs about the causal powers of hammers (and the liabilities of plates). These beliefs are not required to be correct, although of course they could scarcely be used in processing of stimuli that unambiguously fail to conform to them.

These two types of knowledge are not the subject of attentive delibera-
tion during automatic causal processing. Automatic causal processing occurs when and because beliefs of the sort described can be put to work in perception. Causal processing will be accurate when those beliefs are accurate, and inaccurate when those beliefs are inaccurate. Causal processing is also more likely to be inaccurate when quality and/or quantity of

available relevant information is inadequate. People may also fail to perceive actual causal relations, despite perceiving the things and events involved, if they hold no beliefs about the causal powers of the things involved.

In automatic causal processing the concepts of causal power and releasing condition are implicit, underlying but not attended. In controlled causal processing at least one of these is the subject of attentive processing. By this I do not mean that people think, so to speak, this is the causal power and that is the releasing condition. Rather, in controlled causal processing, some thing or event (or combination of things and/or events) is identified as the cause of some event, and the thing identified as the cause may be either a causal power or a releasing condition (or both or, probably more rarely, a liability). Whatever is not explicitly identified may remain implicit, which means that there can be elements of automatic causal processing even on occasions when controlled causal processing occurs. What people report as the cause is the whole or part of whatever is identified in controlled, not automatic, causal processing, simply because it is that to which attention is given.

Controlled causal processing occurs only for events that cannot be or for some reason are not automatically causally processed, and when the current practical concerns of the individual are such that the individual judges that controlled causal processing will contribute to them in some appropriate way.

An outcome of controlled causal processing that is adequate for the person who generates it has the following characteristics:

1. It is founded on the general concept of a causal connection as a generative relation representing the operation of a causal power of some thing.
2. It involves the identification of a specific causal power or releasing condition or liability (or some combination of these) as the cause of the effect in question.
3. It is directed by and fulfils the aim of contributing to the practical concerns in respect of which controlled causal processing is occurring, specifically by answering the particular causal question posed in respect of those practical concerns.
4. Whatever is identified as the cause will be something already believed by the individual to be a possible cause of the effect in question, and not precluded by the information available to the individual (whether or not such information is correct).

These are the general conditions of controlled causal processing. Every causal inference or attribution can be viewed as an answer to an implicit or explicit question, and the job of the process or method of causal attribution used is to provide something that counts as an answer to the question set. This is an invariable rule because the question set is determined by practical concerns, and it is only something that counts as an answer to the question that has the potential of optimally satisfying those practical concerns. I outlined a rough typology of causal questions in Chapter 7, and I have argued (White, 1993) that the way in which people go about answering a causal question, and the kind of information they prefer to use for that purpose, depend to a large extent on what kind of causal question they have posed.

Under the present view, type of causal question asked is dominant over both information search and causal attribution process. It is therefore important to discover what determines the type of causal question asked. The general answer to this is the practical concerns of the attributer at the time (White, 1984; 1989). That is, causal attribution should be viewed as an activity embedded in and conducted for the sake of some practical concern(s) of the attributer, and the point of engaging in causal attribution is to make the optimal contribution to those concerns. Whether people always or even often succeed in this is an open question. Practical concerns can be of many different kinds, and can be both general, such as gaining mastery of one's life, or specific, such as avoiding being held liable for an accident.

The usual sequence in controlled causal judgement, then, can be summarised as follows: practical concern—posing of causal question—information search—process or method of causal attribution—answer to question posed.

There are several distinct types of conditions relating to action and causation under the causal powers theory. Causal powers are possessed by a thing in virtue of certain enabling conditions (Harré & Madden, 1975). It is important to distinguish conditions which enable powers from conditions which enable the operation of powers. The term I have used for the latter in respect of physical causation is "releasing conditions": These are conditions under which a causal power of a thing operates to produce a certain kind of effect. For example, in the case of a hammer smashing a plate, the releasing conditions include such things as the occurrence of forcible contact between the hammer and the plate. The property of causal necessity applies; when suitable releasing conditions are met, the power must operate. The equivalent to releasing conditions in the case of action is the concept of an opportunity. In a sense all actions depend on opportunities: I cannot even raise my arm if it is tied to my side. Opportunities, however, do not compel, because in the case of action it is always up to the actor what to do, whether to perform a particular action or not.

These are the three most important kinds of conditions under the causal powers theory. Concepts of necessary conditions and sufficient conditions do not apply. The reason for this is that such concepts are mere empirical contingencies: a necessary condition is a condition that is always present when a certain effect occurs; a sufficient condition is a condition that is never present when the effect does not occur. Such empirical notions are meaningless. What matters about a condition is its *function*, not its mere contingency. This is the point that is overlooked in regularity-based theories that attempt to account for conditional relations, such as the probabilistic contrast model (Cheng & Novick, 1990; 1992). People understand conditions in terms of the job they do with regard to action and causation, not in terms of their empirical association with effects.

Causal beliefs may be developed in a number of ways, and again the various inductive methods are likely to be important. A particular problem for children and adults is to learn appropriate extents of generalisation from instances. If one observes the operation of a certain causal power in one thing, producing a certain kind of effect in another thing under a certain set of conditions, how does one know how far to generalise what one has learned? Is the causal power a stable feature of the thing that has it? Is the liability a stable feature of the thing acted on? Do other things of the same kind possess the same causal power or liability? How important are various features of the circumstances under which the power operated? The limits on inductive generalisation from instances are hard to establish, and this represents one of the main problems to be dealt with in the acquisition and development of causal beliefs.

In the case of the theory of action, part of what happens during development is the gradual embedding of individual actions construed under the theory of action in a more elaborate network of concepts and relations. Individual actions are understood as part of an interactive sequence such as a script, and are also understood as resulting from increasingly complex collections of antecedent mental states. A similar kind of development takes place with the theory of causation. In White (1993) I found it convenient to consider this elaboration in terms of a number of distinguishable but interrelated levels.

The lowest level is that of individual causal powers. A causal power is understood as a stable property of a substance, meaning that, when it operates, it always operates in the same way and with the same kind of effect, subject to prevailing conditions and the liabilities of the thing(s) acted on. The next level is a level of categorisation: causal powers may be understood as being of various kinds. For example, any beaker of any kind of acid may be seen as having the same kind of causal power, the power to turn litmus paper pink. There may also be hierarchical levels of categorisation of causal powers, as there are for other things. Since causal powers are properties of things, they are also understood in relation to categories of things, and hierarchical levels of categories of things.

At the next level are what I have called *natural processes*. These are complex causal interpretations of a single event in the physical world, consistent in general structure but different in specific content. An example would be the derailment of a train interpreted as caused by subsidence of the land under the rail, making the rail buckle. Another example would be the smashing of a window, interpreted as caused by the impact of a ball struck by a boy with a bat. Drawing on the psychological metaphysics of the being–happening distinction, we can suppose that everything perceived is either being (non-events), events subject to automatic causal processing, or events subject to controlled causal processing. With this segmentation, a natural process is defined as change in at least one property of at least one thing and in which there are either no events or only events that are entirely automatically causally processed. Essentially, a natural process refers to what connects something we have identifed as a cause with its effect. The boy, for example, might be identified as the cause of the window smashing, and the natural process is the trajectory of the ball from the time it is struck by the bat to the time it contacts the window. Further discussion of natural processes can be found in White (1993, pp.148–157).

At the next level come causal networks and structures. Individual judged causal connections come to be seen increasingly as part of an extended and organised network of events. Questions can be asked about the kind of structures these networks have. For example, I have investigated the common sense construction of causal processes in nature (White, 1992c; 1993). Initial findings suggest two kinds of prevailing causal structure. People tend to see causal connections in nature as organised in unidirectional linear chains. They tend to have consistent ideas about the kinds of things that mark the initiators and terminators of causal chains, but they do not seem to have any ideas about recursiveness or feedback in causal networks in nature. Also, people see categories of things in nature as organised in one-way causal hierarchies; the top level of the hierarchy functions in effect as a source of power that governs the hierarchy as a whole, with causal relations filtering down through the hierarchy but not, to any significant extent, back up through it from the bottom. Both of these findings suggest that people do not understand nature as a mutually interactive system, but rather as a kind of power structure in which some elements are dominant and others are powerless victims. This picture awaits confirmation by further research.

Finally, the highest level of the hierarchy makes up what may be called the world view of common sense. A world view is a coherent set of general beliefs and assumptions about the world and all that is in it, tending to be fundamental and universal in application. The world view of common sense is an equivalent set of beliefs and assumptions widely shared by people within a culture, and tending to act as an organising framework for more specific beliefs, judgements, and inferences about the world and things and events therein. Evidence from one study (White, 1992c, study 3) suggests that certain elements of the world view of common sense resemble the Aristotelian world view, but that there is something of a mix of ingredients resembling elements of various historical world views. The role that a world view plays in shaping beliefs at other levels is not known. Given the generality of scope of a world view, it would seem likely that the world view of common sense has a pervasive influence on causal judgements and beliefs. On the other hand, it is arguable that common sense understanding owes more to enculturation as one ascends the hierarchy of levels. In this case, despite its generality, a world view would be the least basic of the levels of causal understanding, perhaps the most liable to change, and the latest part of the construction of reality to emerge during development. As with so many of the topics addressed in this book, one has to regret the dearth of research.

The causal powers theory stands in need of a great deal of further testing. One feature of the theory that makes it difficult to test is that it does not specify a method or procedure for causal judgement. People are opportunists, using information as it comes to them and as it is useful for whatever they are doing. Although people have preferences for type of information and method of causal judgement, these preferences change from occasion to occasion depending on the prevailing practical concerns of the judge and the type of causal question that has been asked. One can only say that there should be a great variety of methods and procedures of causal judgement. The guiding principle of causal judgement under the causal powers theory is that people generally make causal judgements by applying causal beliefs. Beliefs and judgements may be modified in the light of evidence, but the treatment of evidence is not blindly empirical: People are fundamentally active, imposing constructions on evidence, select-ing evidence as suits them, interpreting in the light of beliefs rather than allowing beliefs to be driven by evidence (Kuhn, 1989; and see Chapter 4).

If the theory is eclectic with regard to methods of causal judgement, how could it be falsified? The answer is that the theory proposes a particular kind of conceptual structure in the head of the judge. The foundation of this structure is the basic theory of causation, incorporating the concepts of the generative relation, causal powers, releasing conditions, and liabil-ities or resistances. Other theories propose different types of conceptual structure. Kelley (1972b; 1973) for example proposed a kind of structure called a causal schema (see Chapter 5). This is essentially an abstract representation of covariation information, a record of experiences of the occurrence and nonoccurrence of an effect in relation to the presence or absence of two or more possible causes. A causal schema contains no causal concepts at all, merely the idea of covariation, or empirical association.

Of course, one cannot see conceptual structures. They do, however, have implications for observable phenomena. One implication of the causal powers theory is that generative relations cues should be preferred over all types of empirical cues, because generative relations cues relate to the basic concepts in the theory. The research by Shultz and colleagues (Shultz, 1982b; Shultz, Fisher et al., 1986) reviewed in Chapter 4 supports the causal powers theory in this respect. The proposition shows that the causal powers theory is falsifiable: The theory would be falsified by evidence that people preferred for causal judgement some cue other than generative relations when generative relations cues were available to them.

There is one final point to make about the causal powers theory. Consider all beliefs held by a person. What is it that marks some of these beliefs out as causal beliefs and distinguishes them from non-causal beliefs? This is the first question that should be addressed by a theory of causal understanding. Until we know what it is that makes a belief a causal belief, we do not have a theory of causal understanding. Clearly, the answer cannot be mere empirical association (as defined under any regularity-based theory) because many beliefs concerning empirical associations are not causal beliefs. What fundamentally makes something a causal belief must be common to all and only causal beliefs. Something common to causal beliefs and also to some non-causal beliefs fails as a candidate. The causal powers theory answers this question by asserting the basic theory of causation as the thing that distinguishes all causal beliefs from all non-causal beliefs. The theory could be falsified if it were shown that there was some belief that people identified as a causal belief that was not understood in terms of the basic theory of causation, or if there was some belief that people identified as a non-causal belief that was understood in terms of the basic theory of causation. At present there do not seem to be any other theories that even address the question of what distinguishes all causal beliefs from all non-causal beliefs. Other theories and models beg this most fundamental question, and instead concentrate on relatively superficial matters such as methods of causal judgement and cues used for causal inference. In this respect, the causal powers theory has no competitors at the moment.

CONCLUSION

Every causal belief, every causal perception, judgement, inference, and attribution, has a place in the organised representation that makes up our understanding of the world. We can only hope to understand causal beliefs and judgements and how they are made by elucidating their place in this understanding of the world. More than anything else, this means elucidating their metaphysical underpinnings, the fundamental assumptions about reality on which they depend. So long as we fail to do this, we will continue to flounder in a morass of disorganised, fragmented ideas and findings.

References

Adelson, E. H. (1983). What is iconic storage good for? *The Behavioural and Brain Sciences, 6,* 11–12.

Alicke, M. D., & Insko, C. A. (1984). Sampling of similar and dissimilar comparison objects as a function of the generality of attribution goal. *Journal of Personality and Social Psychology, 46,* 763–777.

Alloy, L. B., & Abramson, L. Y. (1979). Judgement of contingency in depressed and nondepressed students: Sadder but wiser? *Journal of Experimental Psychology: General, 108,* 441–485.

Anderson, J. (1938). The problem of causality. *Australian Journal of Philosophy, 2,* 127–142.

Anderson, J. R. (1980). *Cognitive psychology and its implications.* San Francisco: Freeman.

Anderson, J. R. (1990). *The adaptive character of thought.* Hillsdale, NJ: Lawrence Erlbaum Associates Inc.

Anscombe, G. E. M. (1957). *Intention.* London: Blackwell.

Armstrong, D. M. (1970). The nature of mind. In C.V. Borst (Ed.), *The mind / brain identity theory* (pp.67–79). London: MacMillan.

Aronson, E. (1969). The theory of cognitive dissonance: a current perspective. In L. Berkowitz (Ed.), *Advances in experimental social psychology* (Vol. 4, pp. 1–34). New York: Academic Press.

Astington, J. W. (1991). Intention in the child's theory of mind. In D. Frye & C. Moore (Eds.), *Children's theories of mind: Mental states and social understanding* (pp. 157–172). Hillsdale, NJ: Lawrence Erlbaum Associates Inc.

Astington, J. W., & Gopnik, A. (1991). Developing understanding of desire and intention. In A. Whiten (Ed.), *Natural theories of mind: Evolution, development, and simulation of everyday mindreading* (pp. 39–50). Oxford: Blackwell.

Astington, J.W., Harris, P.L., & Olson, D.R. (Eds.), (1988). *Developing Theories of Mind*. Cambridge: Cambridge University Press.

Ayer, A. J. (1963a). The concept of a person. In *The concept of a person and other essays* (pp. 82–128). London: MacMillan.

Baillargeon, R. (1987). Object permanence in 3.5- and 4.5-month-old infants. *Developmental Psychology, 23*, 655–664.

Ball, W. A. (1973). *The perception of causality in the infant* (Report No. 37). Ann Arbor: University of Michigan, Department of Psychology, Developmental Programme.

Barenboim, C. (1981). The development of person perception in childhood and adolescence: From behavioural comparisons to psychological comparisons. *Child Development, 52*, 129–144.

Bartsch, K., & Wellman, H. M. (1989). Young children's attribution of action to beliefs and desires. *Child Development, 60*, 946–964.

Bassili, J. N., & Regan, D. T. (1977). Attributional focus as a determinant of information selection. *Journal of Social Psychology, 101*, 113–121.

Baumer, F. L. (1977). *Modern European thought: Continuity and change in ideas 1600–1950*. London: Collier MacMillan.

Beasley, N. E. (1968). The extent of individual differences in the perception of causality. *Canadian Journal of Psychology, 22*, 399–407.

Beauchamp, T. L. (Ed.) (1974). *Philosophical problems of causation*. Encino, CA: Dickenson.

Bennett, M. (1985). Developmental changes in the attribution of dispositional features. *Current Psychological Research and Reviews, 4*, 323–329.

Berndt, T. J., & Berndt, E. G. (1975). Children's use of motives and intentionality in person perception and moral judgement. *Child Development, 46*, 904–912.

Beyth-Marom, R. (1982). Perception of correlation re-examined. *Memory and Cognition, 10*, 511–519.

Bhaskar, R. (1975). *A realist theory of science*. Leeds: Leeds Books Ltd.

Bindra, D., Clarke, K. A., & Shultz, T. R. (1980). Understanding predictive relations of necessity and sufficiency in formally equivalent "causal" and "logical" problems. *Journal of Experimental Psychology: General, 109*, 422–443.

Black, J. B., Galambos, J. A., & Read, S. J. (1984). Comprehending stories and social situations. In R. S. Wyer, Jr., & T. K. Srull (Eds.), *Handbook of social cognition* (Vol. 3, pp. 45–86). Hillsdale, NJ: Lawrence Erlbaum Associates Inc.

Borton, R. W. (1979). *The perception of causality in infants*. Paper presented at the meeting of the Society for Research in Child Development, San Francisco.

Boyle, D. G. (1960). A contribution to the study of phenomenal causality. *Quarterly Journal of Experimental Psychology, 12*, 171–179.

Bretherton, I., & Beeghly, M. (1982). Talking about internal states: The acquisition of an explicit theory of mind. *Developmental Psychology, 18*, 906–921.

Bretherton, I., McNew, S., & Beeghly-Smith, M. (1981). Early person knowledge as expressed in gestural and verbal communication: When do infants acquire a "theory of mind"? In M. E. Lamb & L. R. Sherrod (Eds.), *Infant social cognition* (pp. 333–373). Hillsdale, NJ: Lawrence Erlbaum Associates Inc.

Bridgeman, B., & Mayer, M. (1983). Iconic storage and saccadic eye movements. *The Behavioural and Brain Sciences, 6*, 16–17.

Bronowski, J. (1951). *The common sense of science*. London: Heinemann.

Brown, R. (1973). *A first language: The early stages*. Cambridge, MA: Harvard University Press.

Bullock, M. (1985a). Animism in childhood thinking: A new look at an old question. *Developmental Psychology, 21*, 217–225.

Bullock, M. (1985b). Causal reasoning and developmental change over the preschool years. *Human Development, 28*, 169–191.

Bullock, M., & Gelman, R. (1979). Children's assumptions about cause and effect: Temporal ordering. *Child Development, 50*, 80–96.

Bullock, M., Gelman, R., & Baillargeon, R. (1982). The development of causal reasoning. In W. J. Friedman (Ed.), *The developmental psychology of time* (pp. 209–254). London: Academic Press.

Bullock, M., & Lutkenhaus, P. (1988). The development of volitional behaviour in the toddler years. *Child Development, 59*, 664–674.

Bunge, M. (1963). *Causality: The place of the causal principle in modern science*. Cambridge, MA: Harvard University Press.

Campbell, K. (1976). *Metaphysics: An introduction*. Encino, CA: Dickenson.

Carey, S. (1991). Knowledge acquisition: Enrichment or conceptual change? In S. Carey & R. Gelman (Eds.), *The epigenesis of mind: Essays on biology and cognition* (pp. 257–291). Hillsdale, NJ: Lawrence Erlbaum Associates Inc.

Carey, S., & Gelman, R. (Eds.) (1991). *The epigenesis of mind: Essays on biology and cognition*. Hillsdale, NJ: Lawrence Erlbaum Associates Inc.

Carlson, V. (1980). *Differences between social and mechanical causality in infancy*. Paper presented at the International Conference on Infant Studies, New Haven, CT.

Carr, B. (1987). *Metaphysics: An introduction*. London: MacMillan.

Carruthers, P. (1986). *Introducing persons: Theories and arguments in the philosophy of mind*. London: Croom Helm.

Castaneda, H-N. (1980). Causes, energy, and constant conjunctions. In P. van Inwagen (Ed.), *Time and Cause: Essays presented to Richard Taylor*. London: D. Reidel.

Cha, J. H., & Nam, K. D. (1985). A test of Kelley's cube theory of attribution: a cross-cultural replication of McArthur's study. *Korean Social Science Journal, 12*, 151–180.

Chandler, M., Fritz, A. S., & Hala, S. (1989). Small scale deceit: Deception as a marker of 2-, 3-, and 4-year-olds' early theories of mind. *Child Development, 60*, 1263–1277.

Chatlosh, D. L., Neunaber, D. J., & Wasserman, E. A. (1985). Response–outcome contingency: Behavioural and judgemental effects of appetitive and aversive outcomes with college students. *Learning and Motivation, 16*, 1–34.

Cheng, P. W., & Novick, L. R. (1990). A probabilistic contrast model of causal induction. *Journal of Personality and Social Psychology, 58*, 545–567.

Cheng, P. W., & Novick, L. R. (1991). Causes versus enabling conditions. *Cognition, 40*, 83–120.

Cheng, P. W., & Novick, L. R. (1992). Covariation in natural causal induction. *Psychological Review, 99*, 365–382.

Chi, M. T. H., Hutchinson, J. E., & Robin, A. F. (1989). How inferences about novel domain-related concepts can be constrained by structured knowledge. *Merrill-Palmer Quarterly, 35*, 27–62.

Clarke, D. D. (1983). *Language and action: A structural model of behaviour.* Oxford: Pergamon Press.

Clarke, D. D., & Crossland, J. (1985). *Action systems: An introduction to the analysis of complex behaviour.* London: Methuen.

Cohen, L. B., & Oakes, L. M. (1993). How infants perceive a simple causal event. *Developmental Psychology, 29,* 421–433.

Collingwood, R. G. (1940). *An essay on metaphysics.* Oxford: Clarendon Press.

Collingwood, R. G. (1945). *The idea of nature.* Oxford: Oxford University Press.

Collingwood, R. G. (1974). Three senses of the word "cause". In T. L. Beauchamp (Ed.), *Philosophical problems of causation.* Encino, CA: Dickenson.

Corrigan, R. (1975). A scalogram analysis of the development and comprehension of "because" in children. *Child Development, 46,* 195–201.

Costall, A. (1991). Phenomenal causality. In G. Thines, A. Costall, & G. Butterworth (Eds.), *Michotte's experimental phenomenology of perception* (pp. 51–64). Hove, UK: Lawrence Erlbaum Associates Ltd.

Cowie, B. (1976). The cardiac patient's perception of his heart attack. *Social Science and Medicine, 10,* 87–96.

Das Gupta, P., & Bryant, P. E. (1989). Young children's causal inferences. *Child Development, 60,* 1138–1146.

Dasser, V., Ulbaek, I., & Premack, D. (1989). The perception of intention. *Science, 243,* 365–367.

Davidson, D. (1963). Actions, reasons, and causes. *Journal of Philosophy, 60,* 685–700.

Davidson, D. (1968). Actions, reasons, and causes. In A. R. White (Ed.), *The philosophy of action* (pp. 79–94). Oxford: Oxford University Press.

Debus, A. G. (1978). *Man and nature in the renaissance.* Cambridge: Cambridge University Press.

de Sousa, R. (1987). *The rationality of emotions.* Cambridge, MA: MIT Press.

Dickinson, A., & Shanks, D. R. (1985). Animal conditioning and human causality judgement. In L.-G. Nilsson & T. Archer (Eds.), *Perspectives on learning and memory.* Hillsdale, NJ: Lawrence Erlbaum Associates Inc.

Dickinson, A., Shanks, D. R., & Evenden, J. L. (1984). Judgement of act–outcome contingency: The role of selective attribution. *Quarterly Journal of Experimental Psychology, 36A,* 29–50.

Dijksterhuis, E. J. (1961). *The mechanization of the world-picture* (C. Dijkshoorn, Trans.). Oxford: Clarendon Press.

Ducasse, C. J. (1965). Mind, matter, and bodies. In J. R. Smythies (Ed.), *Brain and mind* (pp. 81–96). London: Routledge & Kegan Paul.

Ducasse, C. J. (1969). *Causation and the types of necessity.* London: Dover.

Ducasse, C. J. (1974a). Analysis of the causal relation. In T. L. Beauchamp (Ed.), *Philosophical problems of causation.* Encino, CA: Dickenson.

Ducasse, C. J. (1974b). Critique of Hume's conception of causality. In T. L. Beauchamp (Ed.), *Philosophical problems of causation.* Encino, CA: Dickenson.

Dunn, J. (1991). Understanding others: Evidence from naturalistic studies of children. In A. Whiten (Ed.), *Natural theories of mind: Evolution, development, and simulation of everyday mindreading* (pp. 51–61). Oxford: Blackwell.

Dunn, J., Bretherton, I., & Munn, P. (1987). Conversations about feeling states between mothers and their young children. *Developmental Psychology, 23,* 132–139.

Eder, R. A. (1989). The emergent personologist: The structure and content of 3½, 5½, and 7½-year-olds' concepts of themselves and other persons. *Child Development, 60*, 1218–1228.

Eells, E. (1992). *Probabilistic causality*. Cambridge: Cambridge University Press.

Einhorn, H. J., & Hogarth, R. M. (1986). Judging probable cause. *Psychological Bulletin, 99*, 3–19.

Emler, N., & Dickinson, J. (1993). The child as sociologist: The childhood development of implicit theories of role categories and social organisation. In M. Bennett (Ed.), *The child as psychologist: An introduction to the development of social cognition* (pp. 168–190). London: Harvester Wheatsheaf.

Emmet, D. (1984). *The effectiveness of causes*. London: MacMillan.

Estes, D., Wellman, H. M., & Woolley, J. D. (1989). Children's understanding of mental phenomena. In H. Reese (Ed.), *Advances in child development and behaviour* (Vol. 22, pp. 41–87). New York: Academic Press.

Evans, J. St. B. T. (1982). *The psychology of deductive reasoning*. London: Routledge & Kegan Paul.

Evans, J. St. B. T. (1983). Selective processes in reasoning. In J. St. B. T. Evans (Ed.), *Thinking and reasoning: Psychological approaches*. London: Routledge & Kegan Paul.

Fabes, R. A., Eisenberg, N., McCormick, S. E., & Wilson, M. S. (1988). Preschoolers' attributions of the situational determinants of others' naturally occurring emotions. *Developmental Psychology, 24*, 376–385.

Farrington, B. (1944). *Greek science: I. Thales to Aristotle*. Harmondsworth, UK: Penguin.

Farrington, B. (1969). *Science in antiquity* (2nd edn.). Oxford: Oxford University Press.

Feinberg, J. (1968). Action and responsibility. In A. R. White (Ed.), *The philosophy of action* (pp. 95–120). Oxford: Oxford University Press.

Feldman, N. S., & Ruble, D. N. (1988). The effect of personal relevance on psychological inference: A developmental analysis. *Child Development, 59*, 1339–1352.

Fenson, L. (1984). Developmental trends for action and speech in pretend play. In I. Bretherton (Ed.), *Symbolic play*. New York: Academic Press.

Ferguson, T. J., & Wells, G. L. (1980). Primacy of mediators in causal attribution. *Journal of Personality and Social Psychology, 38*, 461–470.

Festinger, L. (1957). *A theory of cognitive dissonance*. Evanston, IL: Row, Peterson.

Fiedler, K. (1982). Causal schemata: Review and criticism of research on a popular construct. *Journal of Personality and Social Psychology, 42*, 1001–1013.

Fincham, F. D. (1983). Developmental aspects of attribution theory. In J. Jaspars, F. D. Fincham, & M. Hewstone (Eds.), *Attribution theory and research: Conceptual, developmental, and social dimensions* (pp. 117–164). London: Academic Press.

Fisher, K. W., & Bidell, T. (1991). Constraining nativist inferences about cognitive capacities. In S. Carey & R. Gelman (Eds.), *The epigenesis of mind: Essays on biology and cognition* (pp. 199–235). Hillsdale, NJ: Lawrence Erlbaum Associates Inc.

Fiske, S. T., & Taylor, S. E. (1991). *Social cognition*. New York: McGraw-Hill.

Fitzgerald, P. J. (1968). Voluntary and involuntary acts. In A. R. White (Ed.), *The philosophy of action* (pp. 120–143). Oxford: Oxford University Press.

Fivush, R. (1984). Learning about school: The development of kindergarteners' school scripts. *Child Development, 55*, 1697–1709.

Fivush, R., Kuebli, J., & Clubb, P. (1992). The structure of events and event representations: A developmental analysis. *Child Development, 63*, 188–201.

Flavell, J. H., Flavell, E. R., Green, F. L., & Moses, L. J. (1990). Young children's understanding of fact beliefs versus value beliefs. *Child Development, 61*, 915–928.

Flavell, J. H., Miller, P. H., & Miller, S. A. (1993). *Cognitive development* (3rd edn.). Englewood Cliffs, NJ: Prentice-Hall.

Forsterling, F. (1989). Models of covariation and attribution: How do they relate to the analogy of analysis of variance? *Journal of Personality and Social Psychology, 57*, 615–625.

Frankfurt, H. (1971). Freedom of the will and the concept of a person. *Journal of Philosophy, 68*, 5–20.

Frye, D. (1991). The origins of intention in infancy. In D. Frye & C. Moore (Eds.), *Children's theories of mind: Mental states and social understanding* (pp. 15–38). Hillsdale, NJ: Lawrence Erlbaum Associates Inc.

Frye, D., & Moore, C. (Eds.) (1991). *Children's theories of mind: Mental states and social understanding*. Hillsdale, NJ: Lawrence Erlbaum Associates Inc.

Funder, D. C. (1987). Errors and mistakes: Evaluating the accuracy of social judgement. *Psychological Bulletin, 101*, 75–90.

Furnham, A. F. (1988). *Lay theories: Everyday understanding of problems in the social sciences*. Oxford: Pergamon Press.

Garland, H., Hardy, A., & Stephenson, L. (1975). Information search as affected by attribution type and response category. *Personality and Social Psychology Bulletin, 4*, 612–615.

Gelman, R. (1991). Epigenetic foundations of knowledge structures: Initial and transcendent constructions. In S. Carey & R. Gelman (Eds.), *The epigenesis of mind: Essays on biology and cognition* (pp. 293–322). Hillsdale, NJ: Lawrence Erlbaum Associates Inc.

Gelman, R., Bullock, M., & Meck, E. (1980). Preschoolers' understanding of simple object transformations. *Child Development, 51*, 691–699.

Gelman, R., & Kremer, K. E. (1991). Understanding natural cause: Children's explanations of how objects and their properties originate. *Child Development, 62*, 396–414.

Gemelli, A., & Cappellini, A. (1958). The influence of the subject's attitude in perception. *Acta Psychologica, 14*, 12–23.

Gill, C. (Ed.) (1990). *The person and the human mind: Issues in ancient and modern philosophy*. Oxford: Clarendon Press.

Ginet, C. (1990). *On action*. Cambridge: Cambridge University Press.

Gnepp, J., & Chilamkurti, C. (1988). Children's use of personality attributions to predict other people's emotional and behavioural reactions. *Child Development, 59*, 743–754.

Golinkoff, R. M., & Harding, C. G. (1980). *Infants' expectations of the movement potential of inanimate objects*. Paper presented at the International Conference on Infant Studies, New Haven, CT.

Gopnik, A., & Meltzoff, A. N. (1984). Semantic and cognitive development in 15-to 21-month-old children. *Journal of Child Language, 11*, 495–513.

Gordon, I. E., Day, R. H., & Stecher, E. J. (1990). Perceived causality occurs with stroboscopic movement of one or both stimulus elements. *Perception, 19*, 17–20.

Gorovitz, S. (1965). Causal judgements and causal explanations. *Journal of Philosophy, 62*, 695–711.

Gorovitz, S. (1974). Causal judgements and causal explanations. In T. L. Beauchamp (Ed.), *Philosophical problems of causation*. Encino, CA: Dickenson.

Goswami, U. (1993). *Analogical reasoning in children*. Hove, UK: Lawrence Erlbaum Associates Ltd.

Grice, H. P. (1975). Logic and conversation. In P. Cole & J. L. Morgan (Eds.), *Syntax and semantics 3: Speech acts* (pp. 41–58). New York: Academic Press.

Haber, R. N. (1983a). The icon is finally dead. *The Behavioural and Brain Sciences, 6*, 43–54.

Haber, R. N. (1983b). The impending demise of the icon: A critique of the concept of iconic storage in visual information processing. *The Behavioural and Brain Sciences, 6*, 1–11.

Hadwin, J., & Perner, J. (1991). Pleased and surprised: Children's cognitive theory of emotion. *British Journal of Developmental Psychology, 9*, 215–234.

Hansen, R. D. (1980). Common sense attribution. *Journal of Personality and Social Psychology, 39*, 996–1009.

Harré, R. (1976). The constructive role of models. In L. Collins (Ed.), *The use of models in the social sciences*. London: Tavistock.

Harré, R. (1979). *Social being*. Oxford: Blackwell.

Harré, R. (1983). *Personal being*. Oxford: Blackwell.

Harré, R., & Madden, E. H. (1975). *Causal powers: A theory of natural necessity*. Oxford: Blackwell.

Harré, R., & Secord, P. F. (1972). *The explanation of social behaviour*. Oxford: Blackwell.

Harris, P. L., & Gross, D. (1988). Children's understanding of real and apparent emotion. In J. W. Astington, P. L. Harris, & D. R. Olson (Eds.), *Developing theories of mind* (pp. 295–314). Cambridge: Cambridge University Press.

Hart, H. L. A., & Honoré, A. M. (1959). *Causation in the law*. Oxford: Clarendon Press.

Hart, H. L. A., & Honoré, A. M. (1974). The analysis of causal concepts. In T. L. Beauchamp (Ed.), *Philosophical problems of causation*. Encino, CA: Dickenson.

Hastie, R. (1983). Social inference. *Annual Review of Psychology, 34*, 511–542.

Hazlewood, J. D., & Olson, J. M. (1986). Covariation information, causal questioning, and interpersonal behaviour. *Journal of Experimental Social Psychology, 22*, 276–291.

Heider, F. (1958). *The psychology of interpersonal relations*. New York: Wiley.

Heider, F., & Simmel, M. (1944). An experimental study of apparent behaviour. *American Journal of Psychology, 57*, 243–249.

Heller, K. A., & Berndt, T. J. (1981). Developmental changes in the formation and organisation of personality attributions. *Child Development, 52*, 683–691.

Hesslow, G. (1988). The problem of causal selection. In D. J. Hilton (Ed.), *Contemporary science and natural explanation: Commonsense conceptions of causality* (pp. 11–32). Brighton, UK: Harvester Press.

Hewstone, M. (1989). *Causal attribution: From cognitive processes to collective beliefs*. Oxford: Blackwell.

Hewstone, M., & Jaspars, J. (1983). A re-examination of the roles of consensus, consistency and distinctiveness: Kelley's cube revisited. *British Journal of Social Psychology, 22*, 41–50.

Hewstone, M., & Jaspars, J. (1987). Covariation and causal attribution: A logical model of the intuitive analysis of variance. *Journal of Personality and Social Psychology, 53*, 663–672.

Higgins, E. T., & Bryant, S. L. (1982). Consensus information and the fundamental attribution error: The role of development and in-group versus out-group knowledge. *Journal of Personality and Social Psychology, 43*, 889–900.

Hilton, D. J. (1990). Conversational processes and causal explanation. *Psychological Bulletin, 107*, 65–81.

Hilton, D. J., & Jaspars, J. (1987). The explanation of occurrences and non-occurrences: A test of the inductive logic model of causal attribution. *British Journal of Social Psychology, 26*, 189–201.

Hilton, D. J., & Knibbs, C. S. (1988). The knowledge-structure and inductivist strategies in causal attribution: A direct comparison. *European Journal of Social Psychology, 18*, 79–92.

Hilton, D. J., & Slugoski, B. (1986). Knowledge-based causal attribution: The abnormal conditions focus model. *Psychological Review, 93*, 75–88.

Hobson, R. P. (1991). Against the theory of "theory of mind". *British Journal of Developmental Psychology, 9*, 33–51.

Holland, J. H., Holyoak, K. J., Nisbett, R. E., & Thagard, P. R. (1986). *Induction: Processes of inference, learning, and discovery*. Cambridge, MA: MIT Press.

Holyoak, K. J., & Nisbett, R. E. (1988). Induction. In R. J. Sternberg & E. E. Smith (Eds.), *The psychology of human thought* (pp. 50–91). Cambridge: Cambridge University Press.

Hood, L., & Bloom, L. (1979). What, when, and how about why: A longitudinal study of early expressions of causality. *Monographs of the Society for Research in Child Development, 44* (6, Serial No. 181).

Howe, C., Tolmie, A., & Rodgers, C. (1992). The acquisition of conceptual knowledge in science by primary-school children: Group interaction and the understanding of motion down an inclined plane. *British Journal of Developmental Psycholgy, 10*, 113–130.

Hudson, J. A. (1993). Understanding events: The development of script knowledge. In M. Bennett (Ed.), *The child as psychologist: An introduction to the development of social cognition* (pp. 142–167). London: Harvester Wheatsheaf.

Hudson, J. A., & Nelson, K. (1986). Repeated encounters of a similar kind: Effects of familiarity on children's autobiographic memory. *Cognitive Development, 1*, 253–271.

Hume, D. (1978a). *A treatise of human nature*. Oxford: Oxford University Press. (Original work published 1739).

Hume, D. (1978b). *An Abstract of a treatise of human nature*. Oxford: Oxford University Press. (Original work published 1740).

Huttenlocher, J., Smiley, P., & Charney, R. (1983). Emergence of action categories in the child: Evidence from verb meanings. *Psychological Review, 90*, 72–93.

Iacobucci, D., & McGill, A. L. (1990). Analysis of attribution data: Theory testing and effect estimation. *Journal of Personality and Social Psychology, 59*, 426–441.

Jaspars, J. (1983). The process of causal attribution in common sense. In M. Hewstone (Ed.), *Attribution theory: Social and functional extensions* (pp. 28–44). Oxford: Blackwell.

Jaspars, J., Hewstone, M., & Fincham, F. D. (1983). Attribution theory and research: The state of the art. In J. Jaspars, F. D. Fincham, & M. Hewstone (Eds.), *Attribution theory and research: Conceptual, developmental, and social dimensions* (pp. 3–26). London: Academic Press.

Jenkins, H. M., & Ward, W. C. (1965). Judgement of contingency between responses and outcomes. *Psychological Monographs, 79* (Whole No. 10).

Johnson, C. N. (1988). Theory of mind and the structure of conscious experience. In J. W. Astington, P. L. Harris, & D. R. Olson (Eds.), *Developing theories of mind* (pp. 47–63). Cambridge: Cambridge University Press.

Johnson-Laird, P. N. (1983). *Mental models*. Cambridge, MA: Harvard University Press.

Johnston, L., & Hewstone, M. (1992). Cognitive models of stereotype change: 3. Subtyping and the perceived typicality of disconfirming group members. *Journal of Experimental Social Psychology, 28*, 360–386.

Jones, E. E., & Davis, K. E. (1965). From acts to dispositions: The attribution process in person perception. In L. Berkowitz (Ed.), *Advances in experimental social psychology* (Vol. 2, pp. 219–266). New York: Academic Press.

Jones, E. E., & Harris, V. A. (1967). The attribution of attitudes. *Journal of Experimental Social Psychology, 3*, 1–24.

Josephson, J. (1977). *The child's use of situational and personal information in predicting the behaviour of another*. Unpublished doctoral dissertation, Stanford University, CA.

Joynson, R. B. (1971). Michotte's experimental methods. *British Journal of Psychology, 62*, 293–302.

Kahneman, D., & Tversky, A. (1972). Subjective probability: A judgement of representativeness. *Cognitive Psychology, 3*, 430–454.

Kahneman, D., & Tversky, A. (1973). On the psychology of prediction. *Psychological Review, 80*, 237–251.

Kahneman, D., & Tversky, A. (1982). The simulation heuristic. In D. Kahneman, P. Slovic, & A. Tversky (Eds.), *Judgement under uncertainty: Heuristics and biases* (pp. 201–208). Cambridge: Cambridge University Press.

Kaiser, M. K., & Proffitt, D. R. (1984). The development of sensitivity to causally-relevant dynamic information. *Child Development, 55*, 1614–1624.

Kaiser, M. K., & Proffitt, D. R. (1987). Observers' sensitivity to dynamic anomalies in collisions. *Perception and Psychophysics, 42*, 275–280.

Kant, I. (1929). *Critique of pure reason* (N. K. Smith, Trans.). London: MacMillan. (Original work published 1781.)

Karmiloff-Smith, A. (1984). Children's problem solving. In M. E. Lamb, A. L. Brown, & B. Rogoff (Eds.), *Advances in developmental psychology* (Vol. 3, pp. 39–90). Hillsdale, NJ: Lawrence Erlbaum Associates Inc.

Karmiloff-Smith, A. (1986). From metaprocesses to conscious access: Evidence from children's metalinguistic and repair data. *Cognition, 23*, 95–147.

Karmiloff-Smith, A. (1988). The child is a theoretician, not an inductivist. *Mind and Language, 3*, 183–195.

Karmiloff-Smith, A. (1991). Beyond modularity: Innate constraints and developmental change. In S. Carey & R. Gelman (Eds.), *The epigenesis of mind: Essays on biology and cognition* (pp. 171–197). Hillsdale, NJ: Lawrence Erlbaum Associates Inc.

Karmiloff-Smith, A., & Inhelder, B. (1974). If you want to get ahead, get a theory. *Cognition, 3*, 195–212.

Karniol, R., & Ross, M. (1976). The development of causal attributions in person perception. *Journal of Personality and Social Psychology, 34*, 455–464.

Kassin, S. M., & Baron, R. M. (1985). Basic determinants of attribution and social perception. In J. H. Harvey & G. Weary (Eds.), *Attribution: Basic issues and applications* (pp. 37–64). London: Academic Press.

Kassin, S. M., & Pryor, J. B. (1985). The development of attribution processes. In J. B. Pryor & J. D. Day (Eds.), *The development of social cognition* (pp. 3–34). New York: Springer-Verlag.

Keil, F. (1979). The development of the young child's ability to anticipate the outcomes of simple causal events. *Child Development, 50,* 455–462.

Keil, F. (1991). The emergence of theoretical beliefs as constraints on concepts. In S. Carey & R. Gelman (Eds.), *The epigenesis of mind: Essays on biology and cognition* (pp. 237–256). Hillsdale, NJ: Lawrence Erlbaum Associates Inc.

Kelley, H. H. (1967). Attribution in social psychology. In D. Levine (Ed.), *Nebraska Symposium on Motivation* (Vol. 15, pp. 192–238). Lincoln: University of Nebraska Press.

Kelley, H. H. (1972a). Attribution in social interaction. In E. E. Jones, D. Kanouse, H. H. Kelley, R. E. Nisbett, S. Valins, & B. Weiner (Eds.), *Attribution: Perceiving the causes of behaviour* (pp. 1–26). Morristown, NJ: General Learning Press.

Kelley, H. H. (1972b). Causal schemata and the attribution process. In E. E. Jones, D. Kanouse, H. H. Kelley, R. E. Nisbett, S. Valins, & B. Weiner (Eds.), *Attribution: Perceiving the causes of behaviour* (pp. 151–174). Morristown, NJ: General Learning Press.

Kelley, H. H. (1973). The processes of causal attribution. *American Psychologist, 28*, 107–128.

Kelley, H. H. (1983). Perceived causal structures. In J. Jaspars, F. D. Fincham, & M. Hewstone (Eds.), *Attribution theory and research: Conceptual, developmental, and social dimensions* (pp. 343–369). London: Academic Press.

Kellman, P., Spelke, E., & Short, K. R. (1986). Infant perception of object unity from translating motion in depth and vertical translation. *Child Development, 57,* 72–86.

Kenny, A. (1989). *The metaphysics of mind*. Oxford: Clarendon Press.

Kim, J. (1993). Causes and counterfactuals. In E. Sosa & M. Tooley (Eds.), *Causation* (pp. 205–207). Oxford: Oxford University Press.

Kintsch, W. (1970). *Learning, memory, and conceptual processes*. London: Wiley.

Klahr, D., & Dunbar, K. (1988). Dual space search during scientific reasoning. *Cognitive Science, 12,* 1–48.

Klatzky, R. L. (1983). The icon is dead: Long live the icon. *The Behavioural and Brain Sciences, 6*, 27–28.

Kruglanski, A. W. (1975). The endogenous–exogenous partition in attribution theory. *Psychological Review, 82*, 387–406.

Kruglanski, A. W. (1980). Lay epistemo-logic—process and contents: Another look at attribution theory. *Psychological Review, 87*, 70–87.

Kruglanski, A. W., Baldwin, M. W., & Shelagh, M. J. (1983). The lay-epistemic process in attribution-making. In M. Hewstone (Ed.), *Attribution theory: Social and functional extensions* (pp. 81–95). Oxford: Blackwell.

Kruglanski, A. W., Hamel, I. Z., Maides, S. A., & Schwartz, J. M. (1978). Lay persons' sensitivity to statistical information: The case of high perceived applicability. In J. H. Harvey, W. Ickes, & R. F. Kidd (Eds.), *New directions in attribution research* (Vol. 2, pp. 299–334). Hillsdale, NJ: Lawrence Erlbaum Associates Inc.

Kuhn, D. (1989). Children and adults as intuitive scientists. *Psychological Review, 96*, 674–689.

Kuhn, D., & Phelps, H. (1976). The development of children's comprehension of causal direction. *Child Development, 47*, 248–251.

Kun, A. (1978). Evidence for preschoolers' understanding of causal direction in extended causal sequences. *Child Development, 49*, 218–222.

Kuntz, M.L., & Kuntz, P.G. (Eds.) (1988). *Jacob's ladder and the tree of life: Concepts of hierarchy and the great chain of being* (revised edition). New York: Peter Lang Publishing, Inc.

Kunda, Z., & Nisbett, R. E. (1986). The psychometrics of everyday life. *Cognitive Psychology, 18*, 195–224.

Lalljee, M., & Abelson, R. P. (1983). The organisation of explanations. In M. Hewstone (Ed.), *Attribution theory: Social and functional extensions* (pp. 65–80). Oxford: Blackwell.

Lalljee, M., Lamb, R., Furnham, A., & Jaspars, J. (1984). Explanations and information search: Inductive and hypothesis-testing approaches to arriving at an explanation. *British Journal of Social Psychology, 23*, 201–212.

Lalljee, M., Watson, M., & White, P. A. (1982). Explanations, attributions, and the social context of unexpected behaviour. *European Journal of Social Psychology, 12*, 17–29.

Lalljee, M., Watson, M., & White, P. A. (1983). Some aspects of the explanations of young children. In J. Jaspars, F. D. Fincham, & M. Hewstone (Eds.), *Attribution theory and research: Conceptual, developmental, and social dimensions* (pp. 165–192). London: Academic Press.

Landau, B., & Gleitman, L.R. (1985). *Language and experience: Evidence from the blind child.* Cambridge, MA: Harvard University Press.

Langer, S. K. (1967). *An introduction to symbolic logic.* New York: Dover.

Lemmon, E. J. (1965). *Beginning logic.* Wokingham, UK: Van Nostrand Reinhold.

Lepper, M. R., Sagotsky, G., Dafoe, J., & Greene, D. (1982). Consequences of superfluous social constraints: Effects of nominal contingencies on children's subsequent intrinsic interest. *Journal of Personality and Social Psychology, 42*, 51–65.

Lesgold, A. (1988). Problem solving. In R. J. Sternberg & E. E. Smith (Eds.), *The psychology of human thought* (pp. 188–213). Cambridge: Cambridge University Press.

Leslie, A. M. (1982). The perception of causality in infants. *Perception, 11*, 173–186.

Leslie, A. M. (1984a). Spatiotemporal contiguity and the perception of causality in infants. *Perception, 13,* 287–305.

Leslie, A. M. (1984b). Infant perception of a manual pick-up event. *British Journal of Developmental Psychology, 2,* 19–32.

Leslie, A. M., & Keeble, S. (1987). Do six-month-old infants perceive causality? *Cognition, 25,* 265–288.

Lesser, H. (1977). The growth of perceived causality in children. *Journal of Genetic Psychology, 130,* 145–152.

Lewis, D. (1993). Causation. In E. Sosa & M. Tooley (Eds.), *Causation* (pp. 193–204). Oxford: Oxford University Press.

Lewis, M., Stanger, C., & Sullivan, M. (1989). Deception in 3-year-olds. *Developmental Psychology, 25,* 439–443.

Lipe, M. G. (1991). Counterfactual reasoning as a framework for attribution theories. *Psychological Bulletin, 109,* 456–471.

Livesley, W. J., & Bromley, D. B. (1973). *Person perception in childhood and adolescence.* London: Wiley.

Locke, D., & Pennington, D. (1982). Reasons and other causes: Their role in the attribution process. *Journal of Personality and Social Psychology, 42,* 212–223.

Looft, W. R., & Bartz, W. H. (1969). Animism revived. *Psychological Bulletin, 71,* 1–19.

Mace, W. M., & Turvey, M. T. (1983). The implications of occlusion for perceiving persistence. *The Behavioural and Brain Sciences, 6,* 29–31.

Mackie, J. L. (1965). Causes and conditions. *American Philosophical Quarterly, 2,* 245–264.

Mackie, J. L. (1974). *The cement of the universe: A study of causation.* Oxford: Clarendon Press.

Mackie, J. L. (1975). Causes and conditionals. In E. Sosa (Ed.), *Causation and conditionals.* Oxford: Oxford University Press.

Madden, E. H., & Humber, J. (1974). Nonlogical necessity and C. J. Ducasse. In T. L. Beauchamp (Ed.), *Philosophical problems of causation.* Encino, CA: Dickenson.

Major, B. (1980). Information acquisition and attribution processes. *Journal of Personality and Social Psychology, 39,* 1010–1023.

Marks, D., & Kamman, R. (1980). *The psychology of the psychic.* Buffalo, NY: Prometheus Books.

Marks, G., & Miller, N. (1987). Ten years of research on the false-consensus effect: An empirical and theoretical review. *Psychological Bulletin, 102,* 72–90.

McArthur, L. Z. (1972). The how and what of why: Some determinants and consequences of causal attribution. *Journal of Personality and Social Psychology, 22,* 171–193.

McCall, C. (1990). *Concepts of person: An analysis of concepts of person, self, and human being.* Aldershot, UK: Avebury.

McCloskey, M. (1983). Intuitive physics. *Scientific American, 248,* 395–400.

McGill, A. L. (1989). Context effects in judgements of causation. *Journal of Personality and Social Psychology, 57,* 189–200.

Meltzoff, A. N., & Gopnik, A. (1989). On linking nonverbal imitation, representation, and language learning in the first two years of life. In G. E. Speidel, & K. E. Nelson (Eds.), *The many faces of imitation in language learning* (pp. 23–51). New York: Springer–Verlag.

Meltzoff, A. N., & Moore, K. (1977). Imitation of facial and manual gestures by human neonates. *Science, 198,* 75–78.

Mendelson, R., & Shultz, T. R. (1976). Covariation and temporal contiguity as principles of causal inference in young children. *Journal of Experimental Child Psychology, 22,* 408–412.

Michotte, A. (1963). *The perception of causality.* New York: Basic Books.

Michotte, A. (1991b). The prefiguration in sensory data of our spontaneous conception of the physical world. In G. Thinès, A. Costall, & G. Butterworth (Eds.), *Michotte's experimental phenomenology of perception* (pp. 224–226). Hove, UK: Lawrence Erlbaum Associates Ltd.

Michotte, A., & Thinès, G. (1991). Perceived causality. In G. Thinès, A. Costall, & G. Butterworth (Eds.), *Michotte's experimental phenomenology of perception* (pp. 66–87). Hove, UK: Lawrence Erlbaum Associates Ltd.

Mill, J. S. (1967). *A system of logic ratiocinative and inductive.* London: Longman. (Original work published 1843).

Millar, S. (1984). Reasons for the attribution of intent in 7- and 9-year-old children. *British Journal of Developmental Psychology, 2,* 51–61.

Miller, A. G., Schmidt, D., Meyer, C., & Colella, A. (1984). The perceived value of constrained behaviour: Pressure toward biased inference in the attitude attribution paradigm. *Social Psychology Quarterly, 47,* 160–171.

Miller, F. D., Smith, E. R., & Uleman, J. (1981). Measurement and interpretation of situational and dispositional attributions. *Journal of Experimental Social Psychology, 17,* 80–95.

Miller, J. G. (1984). Culture and the development of everyday social explanation. *Journal of Personality and Social Psychology, 46,* 961–978.

Miller, P. H. (1982). Children's and adults' integration of information about noise and interest levels in their judgements about learning. *Journal of Experimental Child Psychology, 33,* 536–546.

Miller, P. H. (1985). Children's reasoning about the causes of human behaviour. *Journal of Experimental Child Psychology, 39,* 343–362.

Miller, P. H., & Aloise, P. A. (1989). Young children's understanding of the psychological causes of behaviour: A review. *Child Development, 60,* 257–285.

Miller, P. H., & Zalenski, R. (1982). Preschoolers' knowledge about attention. *Developmental Psychology, 18,* 871–875.

Moses, L. J., & Flavell, J. H. (1990). Inferring false beliefs from actions and reactions. *Child Development, 61,* 929–945.

Moya, C. J. (1990). *The philosophy of action: An introduction.* Cambridge, UK: Polity Press.

Mulaik, S. A. (1986). Toward a synthesis of deterministic and probabilistic formulations of causal relations by the functional relation concept. *Philosophy of Science, 53,* 313–332.

Natsoulas, T. (1961). Principles of momentum and kinetic energy in the perception of causality. *American Journal of Psychology, 74,* 394–402.

Nelson-LeGall, S. (1985). Motive–outcome matching and outcome forseeability: Effects on attribution of intentionality and moral judgement. *Developmental Psychology, 21,* 332–337.

Newman, L. S. (1991). Why are traits inferred spontaneously? A developmental approach. *Social Cognition, 9,* 221–253.

Nisbett, R. E., Krantz, D. H., Jepson, D., & Kunda, Z. (1983). The use of statistical heuristics in everyday inductive reasoning. *Psychological Review, 90*, 339–363.

Nisbett, R. E., & Ross, L. (1980). *Human inference: Strategies and shortcomings of social judgment*. Englewood Cliffs, NJ: Prentice-Hall.

Nisbett, R. E., & Wilson, T. D. (1977). Telling more than we can know: Verbal reports on mental processes. *Psychological Review, 84*, 231–259.

Novick, L., Fratianne, A., & Cheng, P. W. (1992). Knowledge-based assumptions in causal attribution. *Social Cognition, 10*, 299–333.

Oakes, L. M., & Cohen, L. B. (1990). Infant perception of a causal event. *Cognitive Development, 5*, 193–207.

Onians, R. B. (1951). *The origins of European thought about the body, the mind, the soul, the world, time, and fate*. Cambridge: Cambridge University Press.

Orvis, B. R., Cunningham, J. D., & Kelley, H. H. (1975). A closer examination of causal inference: The roles of consensus, distinctiveness, and consistency information. *Journal of Personality and Social Psychology, 32*, 605–616.

Peevers, B., & Secord, P. (1973). Developmental changes in attribution of descriptive concepts to persons. *Journal of Personality and Social Psychology, 27*, 120–128.

Perkins, D. N. (1988). Creativity and the quest for mechanism. In R. J. Sternberg & E. E. Smith (Eds.), *The psychology of human thought* (pp. 309–336). Cambridge: Cambridge University Press.

Perner, J. (1988). Higher order beliefs and intentions in children's understanding of social interaction. In J. W. Astington, P. L. Harris, & D. R. Olson (Eds.), *Developing theories of mind* (pp. 271–294). Cambridge: Cambridge University Press.

Perner, J. (1991). *Understanding the representational mind*. London: MIT Press.

Philips, W. A. (1983). Change perception needs sensory storage. *The Behavioural and Brain Sciences, 6*, 35–36.

Piaget, J. (1929). *The child's conception of the world*. New York: Harcourt, Brace.

Piaget, J. (1930). *The child's conception of physical causality*. London: Routledge & Kegan Paul.

Piaget, J. (1954). *The construction of reality in the child*. New York: Basic Books.

Piaget, J. (1974). *Understanding causality*. New York: Norton.

Piaget, J., & Inhelder, B. (1969). *The psychology of the child*. London: Routledge & Kegan Paul.

Pillow, B. H. (1989). Early understanding of perception as a source of knowledge. *Journal of Experimental Child Psychology, 47*, 116–129.

Poulin-Dubois, D., & Shultz, T. R. (1988). The development of the understanding of human behaviour: from agency to intentionality. In J. W. Astington, P. L. Harris, & D. R. Olson (Eds.), *Developing theories of mind* (pp. 109–125). Cambridge: Cambridge University Press.

Powesland, P. F. (1959). The effect of practice upon the perception of causality. *Canadian Journal of Psychology, 13*, 155–168.

Pratt, C., & Bryant, P. (1990). Young children understand that looking leads to knowing (so long as they are looking into a single barrel). *Child Development, 61*, 973–982.

Premack. D. (1990). The infant's theory of self-propelled objects. *Cognition, 36*, 1–16.

Pruitt, D. G., & Insko, C. (1980). Extension of the Kelley attribution model: The role of comparison-object consensus, target-object consensus, distinctiveness, and consistency. *Journal of Personality and Social Psychology, 39*, 39–58.

Quattrone, G. A. (1982). Overattribution and unit formation: When behaviour engulfs the person. *Journal of Personality and Social Psychology, 42*, 593–607.

Read, S. J. (1987). Constructing causal scenarios: A knowledge-structure approach. *Journal of Personality and Social Psychology, 52*, 288–302.

Reid, T. (1863a). Letters to Dr. James Gregory. In W. Hamilton (Ed.), *The works of Thomas Reid, D. D.* (6th edn., Vol. 1, pp. 62–88). Edinburgh: Machlachlan & Stewart.

Reid, T. (1863b). Of the liberty of moral agents. In W. Hamilton (Ed.), *The works of Thomas Reid, D. D.* (6th edn., Vol. 2, pp. 599–636). Edinburgh: Machlachlan & Stewart.

Reid, T. (1872). *The works of Thomas Reid* (Ed. W. Hamilton) (7th edn.). London: Longman.

Rholes, W. S., & Ruble, D. N. (1984). Children's understanding of dispositional characteristics of others. *Child Development, 55*, 550–560.

Rholes, W. S., & Ruble, D. N. (1986). Children's impressions of other people: The effect of temporal separation of behavioural information. *Child Development, 57*, 872–878.

Rips, L. J. (1988). Deduction. In R. J. Sternberg & E. E. Smith (Eds.), *The psycho- logy of human thought* (pp. 116–152). Cambridge: Cambridge University Press.

Rips, L. J., & Conrad, F. G. (1989). Folk psychology of mental activities. *Psychological Review, 96*, 187–207.

Ross, L. (1977). The intuitive psychologist and his shortcomings: Distortions in the attribution process. In L. Berkowitz (Ed.), *Advances in experimental social psychology* (Vol. 10, pp. 174–220). New York: Academic Press.

Ross, L. (1981). The "intuitive scientist" formulation and its developmental implications. In J. H. Flavell & L. Ross (Eds.), *Social cognitive development: Frontiers and possible futures* (pp. 1–42). Cambridge: Cambridge University Press.

Ross, L., Greene, D., & House, P. (1977). The "false consensus effect": An egocentric bias in social perception and attribution processes. *Journal of Experimental Social Psychology, 13*, 279–301.

Rotenberg, K. J. (1980). Children's use of intentionality in judgements of character and disposition. *Child Development, 51*, 282–284.

Rotenberg, K. J. (1982). Development of character constancy of self and others. *Child Development, 53*, 505–515.

Ruble, D. N., & Feldman, N. S. (1976). Order of consensus, distinctiveness, and consistency information and causal attributions. *Journal of Personality and Social Psychology, 34*, 930–937.

Ruble, D. N., Feldman, N. S., Higgins, E. T., & Karlovac, M. (1979). Locus of causality and the use of information in the development of causal attributions. *Journal of Personality, 47*, 595–614.

Ruble, D. N., Newman, L. S., Rholes, W. S., & Altshuler, J. (1988). Children's "naive psychology": The use of behavioural and situational information for the prediction of behaviour. *Cognitive Development, 3*, 89–112.

Ruble, D. N., & Rholes, W. S. (1981). The development of children's perceptions and attributions about their social world. In J. H. Harvey, W. Ickes, and R. F. Kidd (Eds.), *New Directions in Attribution Research* (Vol. 3, pp. 3–36). Hillsdale, NJ: Lawrence Erlbaum Associates Inc.

Runeson, S. (1983). On visual perception of dynamic events. *Acta Universitatis Upsaliensis: Studia Psychologica Upsaliensia*. Uppsala, Sweden.

Russell, R. W., & Dennis, W. (1939). Studies in animism: I. A standardised procedure for the investigation of animism. *Journal of Genetic Psychology, 55,* 389–400.

Rybash, J. M., Roodin, P. A., & Hallion, K. (1979). The role of affect in children's attribution of intentionality and dispensation of punishment. *Child Development, 50,* 1227–1230.

Ryle, G. (1949). *The concept of mind.* London: Hutchinson.

Salmon, W. C. (1984). *Scientific explanation and the causal structure of the world.* Princeton, NJ: Princeton University Press.

Santillana, G. de (1961). *The origins of scientific thought: From anaximander to proclus, 600B.C. to 300A.D.* London: Weidenfeld & Nicolson.

Schank, R. C., & Abelson, R. P. (1977). *Scripts, plans, goals, and understanding.* Hillsdale, NJ: Lawrence Erlbaum Associates Inc.

Schauble, L. (1990). Belief revision in children: The role of prior knowledge and strategies for generating evidence. *Journal of Experimental Child Psychology, 49,* 31–57.

Schlottmann, A., & Shanks, D. R. (1992). Evidence for a distinction between judged and perceived causality. *Quarterly Journal of Experimental Psychology, 44A,* 321–342.

Schustack, M. W., & Sternberg, R. J. (1981). Evaluation of evidence in causal inference. *Journal of Experimental Psychology: General, 110,* 101–120.

Searle, J. R. (1983). *Intentionality: An essay in the philosophy of mind.* Cambridge: Cambridge University Press.

Secord, P. F., & Peevers, B. H. (1974). The development and attribution of person concepts. In T. Mischel (Ed.), *Understanding other persons.* Totowa, NJ: Rowman & Littlefield.

Sedlak, A. J., & Kurtz, S. T. (1981). A review of children's use of causal inference principles. *Child Development, 52,* 759–784.

Sexton, M. (1983). The development of the understanding of causality in infancy. *Infant Behaviour and Development, 6,* 201–210.

Shaklee, H., & Elek, S. (1988). Cause and covariate: Development of two related concepts. *Cognitive Development, 3,* 1–13.

Shaklee, H., & Fischhoff, B. (1982). Strategies of information search in causal analysis. *Memory and Cognition, 10,* 520–530.

Shaklee, H., & Goldston, D. (1989). Development in causal reasoning: Information sampling and judgment rule. *Cognitive Development, 4,* 269–281.

Shaklee, H., & Mims, M. (1981). Development of rule use in judgments of covariation between events. *Child Development, 52,* 317–325.

Shanks, D. R. (1985). Forward and backward blocking in human contingency judgement. *Quarterly Journal of Experimental Psychology, 37B,* 1–21.

Shanks, D. R. (1989). Selectional processes in causality judgement. *Memory and Cognition, 17,* 27–34.

Shanks, D. R. (1993). Human instrumental learning: A critical review of data and theory. *British Journal of Psychology, 84,* 319–354.

Shanks, D. R., & Dickinson, A. (1987). Associative accounts of causality judgement. In G. H. Bower (Ed.), *The psychology of learning and motivation* (Vol. 21, pp. 229–261). New York: Academic Press.

Shoemaker, S. (1979). Identity, properties, and causality. In *Midwest Studies in Philosophy* (Vol. 4). Crookston, MN: University of Minnesota Press.

Shoemaker, S. (1980). Causality and properties. In P. van Inwagen (Ed.), *Time and cause: Essays presented to Richard Taylor.* London: D. Reidel.

Shultz, T. R. (1980). Development of the concept of intention. In W. A. Collins (Ed.), *The Minnesota Symposium on Child Psychology* (Vol. 13). Hillsdale, NJ: Lawrence Erlbaum Associates Inc.

Shultz, T. R. (1982a). Causal reasoning in the social and non-social realms. *Canadian Journal of Behavioural Science, 14,* 307–322.

Shultz, T. R. (1982b). Rules of causal attribution. *Monographs of the Society for Research in Child Development, 47,* 1–51.

Shultz, T. R. (1988). Assessing intention: A computational model. In J. W. Astington, P. L. Harris, & D. R. Olson (Eds.), *Developing Theories of Mind.* Cambridge: Cambridge University Press.

Shultz, T. R. (1991). From agency to intention: A rule-based, computational approach. In A. Whiten (Ed.), *Natural theories of mind: Evolution, development, and simulation of everyday mindreading* (pp. 79–93). Oxford: Blackwell.

Shultz, T. R., Altmann, E., & Asselin, J. (1986). Judging causal priority. *British Journal of Developmental Psychology, 4,* 67–74.

Shultz, T. R., & Butkowsky, I. (1977). Young children's use of the scheme for multiple sufficient causes in the attribution of real and hypothetical behaviour. *Child Development, 48,* 464–469.

Shultz, T. R., & Cloghesy, K. (1981). Development of recursive awareness of intention. *Developmental Psychology, 17,* 465–471.

Shultz, T. R., Fisher, G. W., Pratt, C. C., & Rulf, S. (1986). Selection of causal rules. *Child Development, 57,* 143–152.

Shultz, T. R., & Kestenbaum, N. R. (1985). Causal reasoning in children. In G. Whitehurst (Ed.), *Annals of child development* (Vol. 2, pp. 195–249). Greenwich, CT: JAI Press.

Shultz, T. R., & Mendelson, R. (1975). The use of covariation as a principle of causal inference. *Child Development, 46,* 394–399.

Shultz, T. R., Pardo, S., & Altmann, E. (1982). Young children's use of transitive inference in causal chains. *British Journal of Psychology, 73,* 235–241.

Shultz, T. R., & Ravinsky, R. B. (1977). Similarity as a principle of causal inference. *Child Development, 48,* 1552–1558.

Shultz, T. R., & Shamash, F. (1981). The child's conception of intending act and consequence. *Canadian Journal of Behavioural Science, 13,* 368–372.

Shultz, T. R., & Wells, D. (1985). Judging the intentionality of action-outcomes. *Developmental Psychology, 21,* 83–89.

Shultz, T. R., Wells, D., & Sarda, M. (1980). Development of the ability to distinguish intended actions from mistakes, reflexes, and passive movements. *British Journal of Social and Clinical Psychology, 19,* 301–310.

Siegler, R. S. (1975). Defining the locus of developmental differences in children's causal reasoning. *Journal of Experimental Child Psychology, 20,* 512–525.

Siegler, R. S. (1976). The effects of simple necessity and sufficiency relationships on children's causal inferences. *Child Development, 47*, 1058–1063.

Siegler, R. S., & Liebert, R. M. (1974). Effects of contiguity, regularity, and age on children's causal inferences. *Developmental Psychology, 10*, 574–579.

Siegler, R. S., & Richards, D. D. (1983). The development of two concepts. In C. J. Brainerd (Ed.), *Recent advances in cognitive-developmental theory: Progress in cognitive development* (pp. 51–122). New York: Springer-Verlag.

Simon, H. A. (1979). *Models of thought*. London: Yale University Press.

Smetana, J. G. (1993). Understanding of social rules. In M. Bennett (Ed.), *The child as psychologist: An introduction to the development of social cognition* (pp. 111–141). London: Harvester Wheatsheaf.

Smith, E. R., & Miller, F. D. (1979). Attributional information processing: A response time model of causal attribution. *Journal of Personality and Social Psychology, 37*, 1723–1731.

Smith, E. R., & Miller, F. D. (1983). Mediation among attributional inferences and comprehension processes: Initial findings and a general method. *Journal of Personality and Social Psychology, 44*, 492–505.

Smith, M. C. (1978). Cognizing the behaviour stream: The recognition of intentional action. *Child Development, 49*, 736–743.

Smith, P., & Jones, O. R. (1986). *The philosophy of mind: An introduction*. Cambridge: Cambridge University Press.

Smith, P. B., & Bond, M. H. (1993). *Social psychology across cultures: Analysis and perspectives*. London: Harvester Wheatsheaf.

Sophian, C., & Huber, A. (1984). Early developments in children's causal judgements. *Child Development, 55*, 512–526.

Sosa, E. (Ed.) (1975). *Causation and conditionals*. Oxford: Oxford University Press.

Sosa, E., & Tooley, M. (Eds.) (1993a). *Causation*. Oxford: Oxford University Press.

Sosa, E., & Tooley, M. (1993b). Introduction. In E. Sosa & M. Tooley (Eds.), *Causation* (pp. 1–32). Oxford: Oxford University Press.

Spelke, E. S. (1982). Perceptual knowledge of objects in infancy. In J. Mehler, E. C. F. Walker, & M. Garrett (Eds.), *Perspectives on mental representation*. Hillsdale, NJ: Lawrence Erlbaum Associates Inc.

Spelke, E. S. (1991). Physical knowledge in infancy: Reflections on Piaget's theory. In S. Carey & R. Gelman (Eds.), *The epigenesis of mind: Essays on biology and cognition* (pp. 133–169). Hillsdale, NJ: Lawrence Erlbaum Associates Inc.

Sperling. G. A. (1960). The information available in brief visual presentation. *Psychological Monographs, 74* (Whole No. 498).

Stern, D. N. (1985). *The interpersonal world of the infant*. New York: Basic Books.

Stipek, D. J., & Daniels, D. H. (1990). Children's use of dispositional attributions in predicting the performance and behaviour of classmates. *Journal of Applied Developmental Psychology, 11*, 13–18.

Stipek, D. J., & Decotis, K. M. (1988). Children's understanding of the implications of causal attributions for emotional experiences. *Child Development, 59*, 1601–1610.

Storms, M. D. (1973). Videotape and the attribution process: Reversing actors' and observers' points of view. *Journal of Personality and Social Psychology, 27*, 165–175.

Strawson, G. (1992). *The secret connexion: Causation, realism, and David Hume*. Oxford: Oxford University Press.

Suppes, P. (1970). *A probabilistic theory of causality*. Amsterdam: North Holland Pub. Co.

Suppes, P. (1984). *Probabilistic metaphysics*. Oxford: Basil Blackwell.

Sutherland, N. S. (1959). Motives as explanations. *Mind, 68*, 145–159.

Taylor, R. (1966). *Action and purpose*. Englewood Cliffs, NJ: Prentice-Hall.

Taylor, R. (1974). *Metaphysics* (2nd edn.). Englewood Cliffs, NJ: Prentice-Hall.

Taylor, S. E. (1981). The interface of cognitive and social psychology. In J. H. Harvey (Ed.), *Cognition, social behaviour, and the environment* (pp. 189–211). Hillsdale, NJ: Lawrence Erlbaum Associates Inc.

Taylor, S. E., & Fiske, S. T. (1975). Point of view and perceptions of causality. *Journal of Personality and Social Psychology, 32*, 439–445.

Tetlock, P. E. (1983). Accountability and complexity of thought. *Journal of Personality and Social Psychology, 45*, 74–83.

Tetlock, P. E. (1985). Accountability: A social check on the fundamental attribution error. *Social Psychology Quarterly, 48*, 227–236.

Thinès, G., Costall, A., & Butterworth, G. (Eds.) (1991). *Michotte's experimental phenomenology of perception*. Hove, UK: Lawrence Erlbaum Associates Ltd.

Toulmin, S. (1970). Reasons and causes. In R. Borger, & F. Cioffi (Eds.), *Explanation in the behavioural sciences* (pp. 1–26). Cambridge: Cambridge University Press.

Toulmin, S., & Goodfield, J. (1961). *The fabric of the heavens*. London: Hutchinson.

Toulmin, S., & Goodfield, J. (1962). *The architecture of matter*. London: Hutchinson.

Tversky, A., & Kahneman, D. (1973). Availability: A heuristic for judging frequency and probability. *Cognitive Psychology, 5*, 207–232.

Tversky, A., & Kahneman, D. (1974). Judgement under uncertainty: Heuristics and biases. *Science, 185*, 1124–1131.

Urmson, J. D. (1968). Motives and causes. In A. R. White (Ed.), *The philosophy of action* (pp. 153–165). Oxford: Oxford University Press.

Uzgiris, I. C. (1984). Development in causal understanding. In R. M. Golinkoff (Ed.), The development of causality in infancy: A symposium. *Advances in Infancy Research, 3*, 125–165.

Vallacher, R. R., & Wegner, D. M. (1987). What do people think they're doing? Action identification and human behaviour. *Psychological Review, 94*, 3–15.

von Wright, G. H. (1974a). Causality and causal explanation. In T. L. Beauchamp (Ed.), *Philosophical problems of causation*. Encino, CA: Dickenson.

von Wright, G. H. (1974b). *Causality and determinism*. New York: Columbia University Press.

Wason, P. C. (1960). On the failure to eliminate hypotheses in a conceptual task. *Quarterly Journal of Experimental Psychology, 12*, 129–140.

Wason, P. C. (1968). "On the failure to eliminate hypotheses ..."—a second look. In P. C. Wason & P. N. Johnson-Laird (Eds.), *Thinking and reasoning* (pp. 165–174). Harmondsworth, UK: Penguin.

Wasserman, E. A. (1990a). Attribution of causality to common and distinctive elements of compound stimuli. *Psychological Science, 1*, 298–302.

Wasserman, E. A. (1990b). Detecting response–outcome relations: Toward an understanding of the causal texture of the environment. In G. H. Bower (Ed.), *The psychology of learning and motivation* (Vol. 26, pp. 27–82). New York: Academic Press.

Wasserman, E. A., Chatlosh, D. L., & Neunaber, D. J. (1983). Perception of causal relations in humans: Factors affecting judgements of response–outcome contingencies under free-operant procedures. *Learning and Motivation, 14*, 406–432.

Wasserman, E. A., Elek, S. M., Chatlosh, D. L., & Baker, A. G. (1993). Rating causal relations: The role of probability in judgements of response–outcome contingency. *Journal of Experimental Psychology: Learning, Memory, and Cognition, 19*, 174–188.

Watson, J. S. (1984). Bases of causal inference in infancy: Time, space, and sensory relations. In R. M. Golinkoff (Ed.), The development of causality in infancy: A symposium. *Advances in Infancy Research, 3*, 125–165.

Weiner, B. (1979). A theory of motivation for some classroom experiences. *Journal of Educational Psychology, 71*, 3–25.

Weiner, B. (1985). An attributional theory of achievement motivation and emotion. *Psychological Review, 92*, 548–573.

Weiner, B. (1986). *An attributional theory of motivation and emotion*. New York: Springer-Verlag.

Weiner, B., Frieze, I. H., Kukla, A., Reed, S., Rest, S., & Rosenbaum, R. M. (1972). Perceiving the causes of success and failure. In E. E. Jones, D. Kanouse, H. H. Kelley, R. E. Nisbett, S. Valins, & B. Weiner (Eds.), *Attribution: Perceiving the causes of behaviour* (pp. 95–120). Morristown, NJ: General Learning Press.

Weir, S. (1978). The perception of motion: Michotte revisited. *Perception, 7*, 247–260.

Wellman, H. M. (1977). Preschoolers' understanding of memory-relevant variables. *Child Development, 48*, 1720–1723.

Wellman, H. M. (1978). Knowledge of the interaction of memory variables: A developmental study of metamemory. *Developmental Psychology, 14*, 24–29.

Wellman, H. M. (1988). First steps in the child's theorising about the mind. In J. W. Astington, P. L. Harris, & D. R. Olson (Eds.), *Developing theories of mind* (pp. 64–92). Cambridge: Cambridge University Press.

Wellman, H. M. (1990). *The child's theory of mind*. London: Bradford Books/ MIT Press.

Wellman, H. M. (1991). From desires to beliefs: Acquisition of a theory of mind. In A. Whiten (Ed.), *Natural theories of mind: Evolution, development, and simulation of everyday mindreading* (pp. 19–38). Oxford: Blackwell.

Wellman, H. M., & Bannerjee, M. (1991). Mind and emotion: Children's understanding of the emotional consequences of beliefs and desires. *British Journal of Developmental Psychology, 9*, 191–214.

Wellman, H. M., & Bartsch, K. (1988). Young children's reasoning about beliefs. *Cognition, 30*, 239–277.

Wellman, H. M., & Estes, D. (1986). Early understanding of mental entities: A reexamination of childhood realism. *Child Development, 57*, 910–923.

Wellman, H. M., & Woolley, J. D. (1990). From simple desires to ordinary beliefs: The early development of everyday psychology. *Cognition, 35*, 245–275.

Wells, D., & Shultz, T. R. (1980). Developmental distinctions between behaviour and judgement in the operation of the discounting principle. *Child Development, 51,* 1307–1310.

Wells, G. L., & Gavanski, I. (1989). Mental simulation of causality. *Journal of Personality and Social Psychology, 56,* 161–169.

White, A. R. (1968). Introduction. In A. R. White (Ed.), *The philosophy of action* (pp. 1–18). Oxford: Oxford University Press.

White, P. A. (1984). A model of the layperson as pragmatist. *Personality and Social Psychology Bulletin, 10,* 333–348.

White, P. A. (1986). On consciousness and beliefs about consciousness: Consequences of the physicalist assumption for models of consciousness. *Journal of Social Behaviour and Personality, 1,* 505–524.

White, P. A. (1988). Causal processing: origins and development. *Psychological Bulletin, 104,* 36–52.

White, P. A. (1989). A theory of causal processing. *British Journal of Psychology, 80,* 431–454.

White, P. A. (1990). Ideas about causation in philosophy and in psychology. *Psychological Bulletin, 108,* 3–18.

White, P. A. (1991). Ambiguity in the internal/external distinction in causal attribution. *Journal of Experimental Social Psychology, 27,* 259–270.

White, P. A. (1992a). Causal powers, causal questions, and the place of regularity information in causal attribution. *British Journal of Psychology, 83,* 161–188.

White, P. A. (1992b). *Is there a dispositional bias in attribution?* Unpublished manuscript, Department of Psychology, University of Wales College of Cardiff.

White, P. A. (1992c). The anthropomorphic machine: Causal order in nature and the world view of common sense. *British Journal of Psychology, 83,* 61–96.

White, P. A. (1993). *Psychological metaphysics.* London: Routledge.

White, P. A. (1994). *The naïve analysis of freely chosen actions.* Manuscript submitted for publication.

White, P. A. (1994). Causal and non-causal interpretations of regularity information. *British Journal of Social Psychology, 33,* 345–354.

White, P. A. (in press). Use of prior beliefs in the assignment of causal roles: Causal powers versus regularity-based accounts. *Memory and Cognition.*

White, P. A. & Milne, A. (1994). *Phenomenal causality and the perception of energy transmission in multiple-object collisions.* Unpublished manuscript, Department of Psychology, University of Wales College of Cardiff.

White, P. A., Milne, A., & Hatziyiannis, E. (1993). *Causal perception and associative accounts of causal judgement.* Unpublished manuscript, School of Psychology, University of Wales College of Cardiff.

Whiten, A. (Ed.) (1991). *Natural theories of mind: Evolution, development, and simulation of everyday mindreading.* Oxford: Blackwell.

Wilensky, R. (1983). *Planning and understanding: A computational approach.* Reading, MA: Addison-Wesley.

Wilson, J. T. L. (1983). A function for iconic storage: Perception of rapid change. *The Behavioural and Brain Sciences, 6,* 42–43.

Wimmer, H., Hogrefe, J., & Perner, J. (1988). Children's understanding of informational access as a source of knowledge. *Child Development, 59,* 386–396.

Wimmer, H., Hogrefe, J., & Sodian, B. (1988). A second stage in children's conception of mental life: Understanding informational accesses as origins of knowledge and belief. In J. W. Astington, P. L. Harris, & D. R. Olson (Eds.), *Developing theories of mind* (pp. 173–192). Cambridge: Cambridge University Press.

Wolf, D., Rygh, J., & Altshuler, J. (1984). Agency and experience: Actions and states in play narratives. In I. Bretherton (Ed.), *Symbolic play* (pp. 297–328). New York: Academic Press.

Wright, E. F., & Wells, G. L. (1988). Is the attitude–attribution paradigm suitable for investigating the dispositional bias? *Personality and Social Psychology Bulletin, 14*, 183–190.

Yuill, N. (1984). Young children's co-ordination of motive and outcome in judgements of satisfaction and morality. *British Journal of Developmental Psychology, 2*, 73–81.

Yuill, N. (1992). Children's production and comprehension of trait terms. *British Journal of Developmental Psychology, 10*, 131–142.

Yuill, N. (1993). Understanding of personality and dispositions. In M. Bennett (Ed.), *The child as psychologist: An introduction to the development of social cognition* (pp. 87–110). London: Harvester Wheatsheaf.

Zelazo, P. D., & Shultz, T. R. (1989). Concepts of potency and resistance in causal prediction. *Child Development, 60*, 1307–1315.

Zuckerman, M. (1978). Actions and occurrences in Kelley's cube. *Journal of Personality and Social Psychology, 36*, 647–656.

Zuckerman, M., & Evans, S. (1984). Schematic approach to the attributional processing of actions and occurrences. *Journal of Personality and Social Psychology, 47*, 469–478.

Author Index

Subject Index

Titles in the Series
Essays in Developmental Psychology
Series Editors: Peter Bryant, George Butterworth, Harry McGurk

Cox: Children's Drawings of the Human Figure
0-86377-268-4 1993 168pp $37.50 £19.95 HB

Forrester: The Development of Young Children's Social-Cognitive Skills
0-86377-232-3 1992 232pp $37.50 £19.95 HB
0-86377-371-0 1995 232pp $15.95 £9.95 PB

Garton: Social Interaction and the Development of Language and Cognition
0-86377-227-7 1992 160pp $37.50 £19.95 HB
0-86377-370-2 1995 160pp. $14.95 £8.95 PB

Goodnow/Collins: Development According to Parents: The Nature, Sources and Consequences of Parents' Ideas
0-86377-161-0 1990 200pp. $15.95 £8.95 PB

Goswami: Analogical Reasoning in Children
0-86377-324-9 1993 176pp. $17.95 £9.95 PB

Goswami/Bryant: Phonological Skills and Learning to Read
0-86377-151-3 1990 174pp. $16.95 £8.95 PB

Harris: Language Experience and Early Language Development: From Input to Uptake
0-86377-231-5 1992 160pp $35.95 £19.95 HB
0-86377-238-2 1992 160pp. $16.50 £8.95 PB

Hobson: Autism and the Development of Mind
0-86377-229-3 1993 256pp $46.95 £24.95 HB
0-86377-239-0 1995 256pp. $15.95 £9.95 PB

Langford: Approaches to the Developmental of Moral Reasoning
0-86377-368-0 1995 240pp $34.95 £19.95 HB

Siegal: Knowing Children: Experiments in Conversation and Cognition
0-86377-158-0 1991 128pp $31.95 £19.95 HB
0-86377-159-9 1991 128pp. $14.50 £7.95 PB

Smith: Necessary Knowledge: Piagetian Perspectives on Constructivism
0-86377-270-6 1993 256pp $46.50 £24.95 HB

Sonuga-Barke/Webley: Children's Saving: A Study in the Development of Economic Behaviour
0-86377-233-1 1993 168pp $28.50 £14.95 HB

White: The Understanding of Causation and the Production of Action: From Infancy to Adulthood
0-86377-341-9 1995 320pp $37.50 £24.95 HB

*For UK/Europe, please send orders to: Lawrence Erlbaum Associates Ltd., Mail Order Department, 27 Church Road, Hove, East Sussex, BN3 2FA, England. Note, prices shown here are correct at time of going to press, but may change. Prices outside Europe may differ from those shown. **Please send USA & Canadian orders to:** Lawrence Erlbaum Associates Inc., 365 Broadway, Hillsdale, New Jersey, NJ07642, USA.*

Titles in the Series
Essays in Cognitive Psychology
Series Editors: Alan Baddeley, Max Coltheart, Leslie Henderson & Phil Johnson-Laird

The series *Essays in Cognitive Psychology* publishes brief volumes, each of which deals with a circumscribed aspect of cognitive psychology. Taking the subject in its broadest sense, the series undertakes to encompass all topics either informed by or informing the study of mental processes and covers a wide range of subjects such as human-computer interaction, social cognition, linguistics and cognitive development as well as those subjects more normally defined as "cognitive psychology".

Berry/Dienes: Implicit Learning
0-86377-223-4 1993 208pp $37.50 £19.95 HB

Conway: Flashbulb Memories
0-86377-353-2 1995 144pp $31.95 £19.95 HB

Evans: Bias in Human Reasoning: Causes and Consequences
0-86377-156-4 1990 $13.95 £8.95 PB

Eysenck: Anxiety: The Cognitive Perspective
0-86377-071-1 1992 198pp $29.95 £19.95 HB

Frith: The Cognitive Neuropsychology of Schizophrenia
0-86377-224-2 1992 176pp $34.50 £19.95 HB
0-86377-334-6 1995 176pp. $14.50 £8.95

Gathercole/Baddeley: Working Memory and Language
0-86377-289-7 1993 280pp. $22.50 £11.95 PB

Hulme/MacKenzie: Working Memory and Severe Learning Disorders
0-86377-075-4 1992 160pp $37.50 £19.95 HB

Johnson-Laird/Byrne: Deduction
0-86377-148-3 1991 256pp $26.95 £14.95 HB
0-86377-149-1 1992 $256pp 16.95 £8.95 PB

Logie: Visuo-spatial Working Memory
0-86377-107-6 1994 176pp $31.95 £19.95 HB

Moxey/Sanford: Communicating Quantities
0-86377-225-0 1993 144pp $37.50 £19.95 HB

Plaut/Schallice: Connectionist Modelling in Cognitive Neuropsychology: A Case Study
0-86377-336-2 1994 168pp $29.95 £19.95 HB

Taft: Reading & The Mental Lexicon
0-86377-335-4 1993 168pp $18.95 £9.95 PB

Teasdale/Barnard: Affect, Cognition and Change
0-86377-079-7 1993 254pp $46.95 £24.95 HB
0-86377-372-9 1995 254pp. $15.95 £9.95 PB

Watt: Visual Processing: Computational Psychophysical and Coginitive Research
0-86377-081-9 1987 168pp $33.95 £19.95 HB
0-86377-172-6 1990 168pp. $13.95 £8.95 PB

For UK/Europe, please send orders to: *Lawrence Erlbaum Associates Ltd., Mail Order Department, 27 Church Road, Hove, East Sussex, BN3 2FA, England. Note, prices shown here are correct at time of going to press, but may change. Prices outside Europe may differ from those shown. **Please send USA & Canadian orders to:** Lawrence Erlbaum Associates Inc., 365 Broadway, Hillsdale, New Jersey, NJ07642, USA.*

Titles in the Series
Essays in Developmental Psychology
Series Editors: Peter Bryant, George Butterworth, Harry McGurk

NECESSARY KNOWLEDGE
Piagetian Perspectives on Constructivism
LESLIE SMITH
(Lancaster University)

This monograph addresses a central problem in Piaget's work, which is the temporal construction of necessary knowledge. The main argument is that both normative and empirical issues are relevant to a minimally adequate account of the development of modal understanding. This central argument embodies three main claims.

One claim is philosophical. Although the concepts of knowledge and necessity are problematic, there is sufficient agreement about their core elements due to the fundamental difference between truth-value and modality. Any account of human rationality has to respect this distinction.

The second claim is that this normative distinction is not always respected in psychological research on the origins of knowledge where emphasis is placed on the procedures and methods used to gain good empirical evidence. An account of the initial acquisition of knowledge is not thereby an account of its legitimation in the human mind.

The third claim relates to epistemology. Intellectual development is a process in which available knowledge is used in the construction of better knowledge. The monograph identifies features of a modal model of intellectual construction, whereby some form of necessary knowledge is always used. Intellectual development occurs as the reduction of modal errors through the differentiation and coordination of available forms of modal understanding.

Piaget's work continues to provide distinctive and intelligible answers to a substantive and outstanding problem.

Contents: Preface - Or Hill Climbing with Jean Piaget. Toward an Epistemology of Necessary Knowledge. Piaget's Empirical Epistemology. Methods. Procedures. Tasks. Alternative to Constructivism. Epistemic Construction. Conclusion - Necessary Knowledge and Piagetian Research.

ISBN 0-86377-270-6 1993 256pp. $46.95 £19.95 hbk

For UK/Europe, please send orders to: *Lawrence Erlbaum Associates Ltd., Mail Order Department, 27 Church Road, Hove, East Sussex, BN3 2FA, England. Note, prices shown here are correct at time of going to press, but may change. Prices outside Europe may differ from those shown.* **Please send USA & Canadian orders to:** *Lawrence Erlbaum Associates Inc., 365 Broadway, Hillsdale, New Jersey, NJ07642, USA.*

Titles in the Series
Essays in Developmental Psychology
Series Editors: Peter Bryant, George Butterworth, Harry McGurk

NEW IN PAPERBACK...

AUTISM AND THE DEVELOPMENT OF MIND

R. PETER HOBSON
(University of London)

"...the author presents a new and intriguing theory of human development...This book requires attention from all those interested in the theoretical basis of normal child development and especially those who also have an interest in autism...this is a valuable and thought provoking account. It challenges contemporary theories of child psychology and is sure to stimulate further discussion in the literature." **Journal of Child Psychology and Psychiatry,** Reviewed by John Swettenham

"This is a very important book. Researchers who study the social perception and cognition of typical children often make reference to children with autism, and researchers who study children with autism often make reference to typical children. But this is the first major attempt to address these very important issues across the two populations systematically. It is now the definitive work in the area.... a wonderful book. It is one of the more insightful analyses in the newly emerging area of study concerned with how children understand their social worlds and the many ramifications that this understanding has for their cognitive and social lives. And the author's first hand knowledge of autistic children gives it a unique flavor. It will be the jumping off point for all future analyses."
Michael Tomasello (Emory University, Atlanta)

Contents: Preface. Prolegomena. The Picture of Autism. Interpersonal Relatedness I: The Normal Infant. Interpersonal Relatedness II: The Case of Autism. The Growth of Interpersonal Understanding. Conceptual Issues I: On Understanding Minds. Conceptual Issues II: On Thought and Language. Thought and Language: The Case of Autism. The Development of Mind and the Case of Autism.

ISBN 0-86377-229-3 1993 256pp. $46.95 £24.95 hbk
ISBN 0-86377-239-0 1995 256pp. $15.95 £9.95 pbk

For UK/Europe, please send orders to: Lawrence Erlbaum Associates Ltd., Mail Order Department, 27 Church Road, Hove, East Sussex, BN3 2FA, England. Note, prices shown here are correct at time of going to press, but may change. Prices outside Europe may differ from those shown. Please send USA & Canadian orders to: Lawrence Erlbaum Associates Inc., 365 Broadway, Hillsdale, New Jersey, NJ07642, USA.